The
Indian
Craze

◆ ◆ ◆ OBJECTS/HISTORIES

Critical Perspectives on Art,
Material Culture, and Representation

A series edited by Nicholas Thomas

Published with the assistance
of the Getty Foundation.

The Indian Craze

• • •

PRIMITIVISM,
MODERNISM, AND
TRANSCULTURATION IN
AMERICAN ART,
1890–1915

Elizabeth Hutchinson

Duke University Press   Durham and London   2009

© 2009 Duke University Press

Designed by Heather Hensley

Typeset in Whitman by Tseng
Information Systems, Inc.

Library of Congress Cataloging-in-
Publication Data appear on the last
printed page of this book.

· · · For Jane Ames Hutchinson (1938–1990) · · ·

Contents

Illustrations

◇ ◇ ◇   *Acknowledgments*

No book can be written without a great deal of intellectual and personal support, and I have accrued more debts than I can acknowledge here. Several institutions supported my research and writing, including the National Endowment for the Humanities, the Georgia O'Keeffe Museum and Research Center, the Sterling and Francine Clark Art Institute, and the Winterthur Museum and Country Estate. Mary Lou Hultgren of the Hampton University Archives and Michelle Delaney at the National Museum of American History have my unending appreciation for opening their wonderful collections to me early on. And I am grateful to Barbara Buhler-Lynes, Heather Hole, and Eumie Imm-Stroukoff at the O'Keeffe; Michael Ann Holly, Mark Ledbury, and Gail Parker at the Clark; and Anne Verplanck of Winterthur for their careful nurturing of the scholarly communities gathered there. The schools for which I have worked have offered both financial and material support as well. I am particularly grateful to the University of New Mexico for a Research Allocations Committee Grant and a College of Fine Arts Career Enhancement Grant that spurred my research, to Barnard College for a Special Assistant Professor Leave that got the final chapters under way, and to the Columbia University Seminars, which awarded money from the Leonard Hastings Schoff Fund to underwrite my indexing. Barnard College and Columbia University have also supported my ability to hire excellent research assistants, including Terri Weissman, Gillian Osborne, Minou Arjomand, Samantha Friedman, Mark Watson, and Xsusha Flandro. For help obtaining illustrations, I would like to thank Catherine Johnson and Kristin Blanford of the National Arts Club, Stephanie Gaskins of the Ipswich Historical Society, and Stephanie Ogeneski of the National Museum of the American Indian.

This book began as a dissertation at Stanford University, and built on the insights of the advisors of that project: Wanda Corn, Alex Nemerov, and Robert Warrior, all of whom have remained important mentors and role models. My debts to them will never be repaid, and I only hope I can offer the same high expectations and thoughtful feedback to my own students. This project would not have developed the way it has if I hadn't been allowed to participate in the vibrant intellectual communities at the Stanford Humanities Center and the Smithsonian American Art Museum. My doctoral research was also supported by a Henry Luce Foundation/ACLS Predoctoral Fellowship and a Dissertation Research Grant from the Schlesinger Library of Radcliffe College.

Many of these chapters have been presented as talks at regular meetings of the College Art Association, the American Studies Association, the Native American Art Studies Association, and the American Anthropological Association and I am grateful to fellow panelists and audience members for their thoughtful questions and responses. I would also like to thank The Museum of Native American Art and Culture, the Georgia O'Keeffe Museum, Stanford University, the Center for Advanced Study of the Visual Arts, the British Museum, Rutgers University, Bryn Mawr College, and the University of New Mexico for allowing me to speak about this work and receive vital feedback.

Aspects of the argument in chapter 4 were previously published in "'When the Sioux Chief's Party Calls': Käsebier's Indian Portraits and the Gendering of the Artist's Studio," *American Art* 16.2 (July 2002): 40–65; and a section of chapter 5 appeared in "Angel DeCora and the Transcultural Aesthetics of Modern Native American Art," *Art Bulletin* 84.4 (December 2001): 740–756. The argument at the end of chapter 5 was worked out in two essays that also incorporate the writings of Charles Eastman: "Native American Art and Modern Indian Identity," in *Seeing High and Low: Representing Cultural Conflict in American Visual Culture*, ed. Patricia Johnston, 194–209 (Berkeley: University of California Press, 2006); and "Indigeneity and Sovereignty: The Work of Two Early Twentieth-Century Native American Art Critics," *Third Text: Critical Perspectives on Contemporary Art and Culture* 52 (Autumn 2000): 21–29. I am grateful to the editors and readers of these publications for their thoughtful feedback and to the publications themselves for permitting me to reprint this material here. I would also like to express my appreciation to the wonderful staff at Duke University Press—especially Ken Wissoker, Mandy Earley, and Molly Balikov—for making the production of this book go so smoothly.

Most importantly, I want to thank my colleagues in art history, American studies, and Native American studies for the lively and challenging discussion. Wanda Corn and Janet Berlo are the most generous scholars and teachers I know, and I strive to live up to the standards they set. My students at the University of New Mexico and at Barnard and Columbia deserve special mention for inspiring and challenging me. Those who straddle the line between colleague and friend are too numerous to name, but I will single out Rachel Adams, Bill Anthes, Kathleen Ash-Milby, Elissa Auther, Leigh Culver, Rosalyn Deutsche, Rob Frankel, Adam Lerner, Monica Miller, Liz Phillips, Kristin Schwain, and Joyce Szabo, all of whom have contributed materially to the book you hold in your hands. Rebecca Bahr, Geoff Batchen, Marcella Hackbardt, David Hutchinson, Geoff Hutchinson, Elizabeth Rambeau, Kishwar Rizvi, Gus Stadler, and Ellen Todd have been particularly stalwart supporters through thick and thin. Finally and always there is my son Jacob Ames Frankel, who teaches me about the relationship between art and life every day.

I am not the new Indian,

I am the old Indian adjusted to new conditions.

Laura Cornelius

◇ ◇ ◇   *Introduction*

On Columbus Day in 1911, a Native American artist named
Angel DeCora stepped up to a podium to tell an audience of
other progressive, educated Indian people about the importance of art to their struggle for political and cultural recognition. As she told her listeners, "[The Indian's] art like himself is indigenous to the soil of his country, where, with the
survival of his latent abilities, he bravely offers the best pro-
ductions of his mind and hand which shall be a permanent
record of the race." In her works and her writings, DeCora
saw Native art made in both "traditional" and "nontraditional" genres as a means for Indian people to negotiate their
relationship to their changing historical circumstances. Borrowing from the socially oriented aesthetics that dominated
the American art world of the time, she also described art
as a potentially rich site for transcultural exchange and national cultural development. As she said, "The Indian in his
native dress is a thing of the past, but his art that is inborn
shall endure. He may shed his outer skin, but his markings
lie below that and should show up only the brighter."[1]

Americans have tended to see Native American culture
as separate from mainstream culture, drawing its legiti-
macy from a commitment to timeless traditions that pre-
date interaction with European Americans. This attitude

not only contradicts the rich histories of intercultural exchange that preceded European colonialism in many parts of the Americas; it also has resulted in a canon that rejects large bodies of art that were made for circulation outside Indian communities. DeCora grew up on the Winnebago reservation in Nebraska, and was later given a rigorous grounding in Euro-American culture at Smith College and other East Coast schools. Early in her career she lived a bohemian life in a New York City garret, where she played music and ate chop suey with other struggling artists. DeCora's attempts to retain a connection to traditional values while embracing the opportunities presented by modern society were not isolated. They echo those of countless Indian people who have responded to changing conditions through the exchange of goods and ideas with outsiders.

Despite her immersion in mainstream culture, however, DeCora's professional opportunities were limited by her ethnic identity. Indians and non-Indians alike expected the artist to use her talents to help her people, and she rarely turned down an opportunity to do so. DeCora's burgeoning career coincided with a time of tremendous stress in Native communities as Indians were subjected to unprecedented political and popular pressure to assimilate into mainstream American society. Reservations were blighted by poverty and corruption, and both supporters and critics of indigenous culture felt that traditional lifeways were destined to be lost. Like other educated Indian people of her generation, DeCora worked to ameliorate the situation of other, less-privileged Natives. Over the course of her career, she focused on illustrations of Native life in her own art work, collaborated with other Native artists on exhibition pieces, and nurtured a generation of students by designing and teaching in the Native Indian art program at the United States Indian Industrial School at Carlisle, Pennsylvania. DeCora brought to this work a desire to demonstrate the modernity of Indian people and their potential to contribute to American culture. She shared this ambition with many educated Indian people of her generation.

This book returns to that period to help understand DeCora's goals, particularly the idea that art could be a means by which both Indians and non-Indians could contribute to American modernity. DeCora's values built on the aesthetic ideas of the day, which promoted art as a solution to many of society's ills. Her belief that mainstream culture would take an interest in the work of Native artists was the result of what I am calling "the Indian craze." The term comes from articles on the widespread passion for collecting Native American art, often in dense, dazzling domestic displays called "Indian corners." This collecting trend stemmed from the increased availability of Native American art at the time. At the beginning of the twentieth century, Native American art could be purchased from department stores, "Indian stores," and other commercial venues from New York to Chicago, from Boston to Los Angeles, that stocked Indian baskets, blankets, and bowls by prominent collectors and members of the general public. This was possible because of a dramatic increase in the production of art for sale, both on reservations and, surprisingly, in venues dedicated to the eradication of Native culture such as government boarding schools.

In 1904, *American Homes* ran a piece describing "the craze for using Indian ornaments."[2] The article called the phenomenon a "fad" and a "fancy," suggesting a taste for Native American home decorations was a passing fashion. This book proposes that, to the contrary, the Indian craze was a significant artistic phenomenon with lasting effects on both American art history and U.S. Indian policy. My argument is based in part on taking the private collecting of Native American art seriously. In doing this, I link collecting to other activities, including the inclusion of handmade Native American artifacts in exhibitions sponsored by museums, arts and crafts societies, and international expositions and the use of indigenous handicrafts as models for artists and craftspeople exploring new, formalist, aesthetic practices.

The standard history of the mainstream interest in Native American material culture as "art" focuses on the role of New York painters in the Southwest in the 1920s and 1930s. I show that this cross-cultural conversation occurred earlier and in fact spread across the nation, from west to east and from reservation to metropolis. My discovery that Native art was displayed and collected in urban contexts in the earliest years of the twentieth century allows me to show that indigenous handicrafts played a significant role in American explorations of modernity in art, legitimizing an interest in formal abstraction and contributing to emerging notions of artistic creativity. As I show, artists, teachers, and critics associated with the development of American modernism, including Arthur Wesley Dow, Charles Binns, and Gertrude Käsebier, were inspired by Native art, included Indian handicrafts in their own exhibitions, and used them as models in courses in fine art and design. In limited ways, Native artists were also able to achieve recognition as modern artists.

As I explain in the following chapters, non-Native artists, critics, and collectors involved in the Indian craze comfortably mixed ideas about aesthetics and politics, private and public, and primitive and modern, confusions that typified the revolutionary social ambitions of the modernist movements then emerging. Supporters of the Indian craze shared their enthusiasm through exhibitions, lectures, books, and hundreds of articles in popular magazines; they praised both the formal qualities and the intellectual sensibilities they saw reflected in Native American art. Discussions of Native American art were used to help accommodate cultural changes in mainstream America, including increased immigration, rapid industrialization, and evolving concepts of subjectivity. Promoters of Native American art were supporters of what Jackson Lears has described as "antimodernism"—a cultural retreat from "overcivilized" urban industrial American and a turn to seemingly preindustrial cultures perceived as more physical, authentic, and direct.[3] Among other things, antimodernists responded to the disjunctures of modernity by arguing for an integration of art and life, which allowed for a new understanding of the value of well-crafted, useful handicrafts, including those from indigenous traditions. At the same time, the institutions promoting Native American art are those we consider to be extremely modern: department stores, settlement houses, world's fairs, and avant-garde artists' organizations. This forces a reexamination of the notion of primitivism, which is frequently understood as situating indigenous cultures *outside of* and *in opposition to* modern culture.[4] During the Indian craze, however, audiences assessed Native handicrafts alongside modern commodities and modernist works of art, enhancing the modernity of these supposedly primitive objects.

The Native presence in department stores, world's fairs, and settlement houses was not limited to mute objects. Native people of this generation moved through such spaces in the conduct of trade and the pursuit of employment, in the course of receiving a government-mandated education and in following their own desires to engage the modern world. The Indian craze influenced the curriculum of the Indian schools, which became important sites for the production and distribution of handicrafts. Reservation officials and social reformers seeking to build economic, religious, and cultural ties between Indian people and mainstream Americans also developed projects designed to capitalize on the popularity of Native American art. Significantly, these activities offered Native actors in each of these spheres an education in mainstream aesthetics. While few of these efforts were well documented by indigenous participants, I recover something of their experiences by analyzing photographs and written documents and by looking closely at the works themselves. I pay particular attention to the words of Native intellectuals of the time who used their education to seek a platform from which to comment on and ameliorate indigenous conditions. Like DeCora, several chose to fight these battles in the realm of culture, pointing to the accomplishments of Indian people in the arts as a sign of their value to mainstream America.

Flawed though they were, the social ambitions of early modernism appealed to Native intellectuals.[5] Modernist principles were attractive to members of many marginalized groups within the United States and beyond, who saw its principles as compatible with their goals of sexual equality, racial tolerance, and an end to colonial rule.[6] Aspects of the Native experience are comparable to those of other Americans, including blacks and urban immigrants, who faced, and sometimes spearheaded, similar attempts to use culture to define their place in society. The Indian craze was a transcultural phenomenon that brought Indians and non-Indians together. The concept of transculturation was developed by the anthropologist Fernando Ortiz early in his 1940 book *Cuban Counterpoint* to examine the cultural mixing—or hybridity—that characterized the indigenous and Afro-Cuban experience of colonialism.[7] As Ortiz explains, this involves more than the simple replacement of traditional beliefs with European ones; instead it led to the creation of new cultural forms that reflect marginalized peoples' diverse relationships to mainstream culture. Ortiz's emphasis on the variety and complexity of transcultural phenomena makes his theory particularly valuable for the investigation of Native American art, as it allows for individuality in artists' interactions with the values and institutions of tribal and mainstream cultures.[8] Transculturation also allows for the transformation of mainstream ideas through cultural contact, and this book traces the complexity of both sides of the artistic exchanges that made up the Indian craze.

Just as early twentieth-century viewers saw Indian and non-Indian objects side by side, in this book I look at Indian and non-Indian art worlds together. In so doing, I challenge the artificial division between mainstream and Native American art history. Today Native American art is conventionally exhibited in its own section of a museum, if not in a museum dedicated exclusively to indigenous materials. Contemporary artists exhibit in galleries and annual juried exhibitions that admit only enrolled tribal members. Scholars attend special conferences and teach distinctive courses that segregate Native art history from that of the United States and the rest of the world. The use of a special category for Native American art history can have its uses, but it must be understood as the product of a colonial culture that subordinated marginalized cultures by defining them as incompatible with modernity.[9] The economic value and aesthetic acceptance of Native American handicrafts for mainstream audiences encouraged policy makers to look upon art as an aspect of so-called traditional culture that might be perpetuated despite the official policy of assimilation. Telling this story not only illuminates the contradictions of federal Indian policy; it also puts Indian people back into history, situating their actions alongside those of others who experienced marginalization at the time.

It is not enough to identify the negative effects of racialist beliefs; we must also come up with new paradigms of analysis that permit new kind of questions about ethnicity and culture.[10] This book moves beyond identifying the racism of turn-of-the-century culture to ask how discussions about ethnicity and art illuminate a key debate within mainstream art history, that of the relationship between art and craft. The Indian craze was used by artists and critics interested in promoting the decorative arts as a means of bridging the gap between art and life. While the dominant history of modernism, advanced by Clement Greenberg and his followers in the mid-twentieth century, emphasized modernist art's self-referentiality and privileged painting and sculpture over mediums associated with utility and commerce, contemporary scholars have revealed the influence of decorative objects on the development and dissemination of modernist ideas.[11] Native American art was a component of the aesthetic worlds in which this history unfolded.

While several scholars have noted the arts and crafts movement's interest in select tribal arts, such as Navajo weaving or Washoe baskets, this book is the first project to comprehensively relate the Indian craze to the emergence of modernist aesthetic ideas. I believe that the absence of any previous study of this interaction is due in part to the fact that Native American art history has unwittingly reinforced the distinction between art and craft advanced by mid-twentieth-century theorists. For much of the twentieth century Native American art has been separated into studies of mediums associated with Western academic traditions (often referred to as "modern" Native American art) and handicrafts (or "traditional" arts). Books exploring the relationship between Native American art and mainstream aesthetic trends have primarily addressed Indian painting.[12] They have also focused on art from the interwar years or later. Looking at an earlier period, when the hierarchy between art and craft in the mainstream art world was less stable, allows us to recognize the modernity of a wider variety of Native objects, including those made for pure aesthetic contemplation, those made for use, and those made for circulation outside indigenous communities.

To achieve these goals, the present volume maps the major sites of the interaction of Native American art and mainstream American aesthetic debates. Chapter 1, "Unpacking the Indian Corner," traces the increasing visibility of Native American art in the early twentieth century in Indian corners, the dense and vibrant installations of collections that typically appeared in dens, porches, or living rooms of the period. Using the collection of the New Yorker Joseph "Udo" Keppler as a centerpiece, I analyze the contents and display techniques used in such spaces in relationship to what Tony Bennett has identified as the "exhibitionary complex"—a visual aesthetic affecting commercial, artistic, and private spaces that reflects the increasing materialist orientation of commodity culture. Shifting to an analysis of the sale of Native art at Wanamaker's department store, I demonstrate the degree to which the commercialization of Native American art was accomplished by the use of aesthetic language, paving the way for indigenous material culture to be seen as art. Revealing that Wanamaker's employees included Native Americans, I explore the impact of the Indian corner on Native artists, paying particular attention to contemporary changes for Navajo weavers.

The next chapter, titled "The White Man's Indian Art: Teaching Aesthetics at the Indian Schools," analyzes how the United States government appropriated the mainstream aestheticization of Native art to serve its own goals through the Native Indian arts program. Introduced in 1901 by Estelle Reel, the superintendent of Indian schools, the program sought to add work in traditional handicrafts to the other vocational curricula at both reservation-based and off-reservation schools. This curriculum departed from the Indian schools' earlier emphasis on "kill[ing] the Indian . . . [to] save the man," but it was no less assimilationist.[13] Through discussions of course materials, school exhibitions, and individual works of art, I show how the Indian craze contributed to the "modernization" of Native art, turning native students into workers producing for a mainstream market. My argument links the role of art in Indian education with its use by urban social reformers at settlement houses and manual training schools, strengthening the connection between my narrative and more familiar episodes in American cultural history. Analysis of photographs and student writing allows some insight into the student experience, which I present as very diverse. Using the notion of "survivance," as defined by the Anishinaabe literary theorist Gerald Vizenor, I explore how individual nations, particularly the Wisconsin Oneida, have come to see the art forms taught at the schools as part of their own constantly evolving tribal traditions.

My third chapter, "Playing Indian: Native American Art and Modern Aesthetics," traces the place of indigenous handicrafts in the American art world. Analyzing articles in art journals such as *Brush and Pencil* and *International Studio*, exhibitions at arts and crafts societies and the National Arts Club, and art schools from Boston to New York, I demonstrate how Native American art was seen as a model that could teach modern artists lessons about form and technique. The heart of this chapter is an exploration of the pedagogy of Arthur Wesley Dow, an early advocate of "pure design" who is remembered as the teacher of several members of the Stieglitz circle, including Georgia O'Keeffe and Max Weber. Alongside these familiar figures I look at some of the first Native artists to achieve name recognition, particularly the Pomo basket makers William and Mary Benson, and show how racism undermined their ability to be recognized as modern artists.

The book ends with close studies of two artists who applied a modern notion of "Native" aesthetics to their work: one Anglo and one Native. "The Indians in Käsebier's Studio," my fourth chapter, focuses on Gertrude Käsebier, a European American student of Dow. She became a leading member of Alfred Stieglitz's Photo-Secession, who embraced the principles of an emerging American modernism. The chapter examines a series of portraits of Native American performers from *Buffalo Bill's Wild West* show who posed for the photographer between 1898 and 1901. Several of these sitters are shown in the act of drawing, and I relate the formal qualities of their work to the darkroom manipulations of pictorialist photographers. The chapter argues that Käsebier's models provided an ideal of primitive creativity that Käsebier used to resolve the contradictions of being a modern artist and a modern woman at the same time.

The final chapter, "Angel DeCora's Cultural Politics," explores the work of Angel DeCora, a Winnebago painter and teacher who was the most prominent Native artist of her generation and a vocal supporter of Indian civil rights. I trace DeCora's unusually rich artistic education, which began when she was still a child on the reservation and later included courses with the Anglo-American painters Dwight Tryon, Frank Benson, Edmund Tarbell, and Howard Pyle. DeCora worked as an illustrator for several years, but her career took a turn in 1905, when she was hired to establish a Native Indian art program at the Carlisle Indian Industrial School. While Reel's Native Indian art program was primarily vocational, DeCora's had ambitious aesthetic and political goals. The chapter traces the influence of her diverse experiences in her art work and her teaching. It ends with an analysis of a series of lectures given toward the end of her life, in which DeCora argued that Indian artists were natural modernists positioned to contribute actively to the progress of mainstream American art.

World War I brought an increasing European focus to the mainstream art world while focusing Native intellectuals' energies toward other cultural battles, and with these changes, the Indian craze came to an end. I conclude the book with a discussion that relates the ideas and accomplishments of this period to the resurgence of interest in Native American art in the interwar years and examines the legacy of this period's mixture of aesthetics and cultural politics in our own time.

I hope this book begins a series of dialogues—between interconnected artistic communities, between the too frequently divided fields of Native American and "American" art history, between "art" and "craft," and between scholarly disciplines—that can contribute to a decolonization of American art history. This concept of give and take offers a useful step out of some of the problems that confront scholars of marginalized traditions.

While much of the feminist and postcolonial scholarship that has come out in recent years focuses on the relationship between isolated disempowered groups and a dominant center, it is also vital to engage in studies that investigate the complex relationships *among* diverse communities and between these groups and the aesthetic challenges of the modern world, revealing a more nuanced understanding of modern visual culture as a field in which multiple participants have a stake as makers, critics, and consumers.

CHAPTER ONE

An Indian Corner in your home adds to the artistic effect.
Advertisement for the Hyde Exploring Expedition, 1902

Unpacking the Indian Corner

In 1903, the magazine *The Papoose* published seven photographs of the "Indian corner" installed by the cartoonist and publisher Joseph "Udo" Keppler in his Manhattan home (figure 1). The photographs reveal three connected spaces: a large "den" that includes a desk and seating area, a small alcove with a day bed, and a connecting hall dominated by a glass case (figure 2). Each space teems with Native American artifacts accented by simple furnishings. Keppler's collection was not unique. The Indian corner was a widespread home decoration fad that was promoted by illustrated magazines, Indian traders, and urban marketers, including department stores. Owners of Indian corners ranged from people of modest means who kept a few items on a shelf to large-scale collectors such as Keppler, many of whom accumulated valuable and important pieces that later became the core of museum collections across the country.

While many photographs of Indian corners were published at the turn of the century, the *Papoose* photographs of Keppler's display offer an unusually rich document of such a space. They show objects drawn from a wide variety of Native American nations. On one wall of the study, the rounded forms of southwestern basket plaques mingle with dangling beaded bags gathered from Plains tribes.

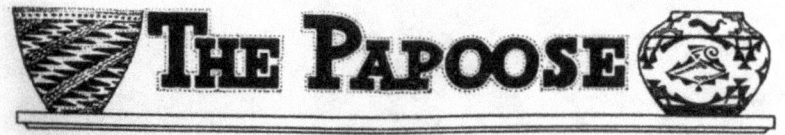

MARCH, 1903

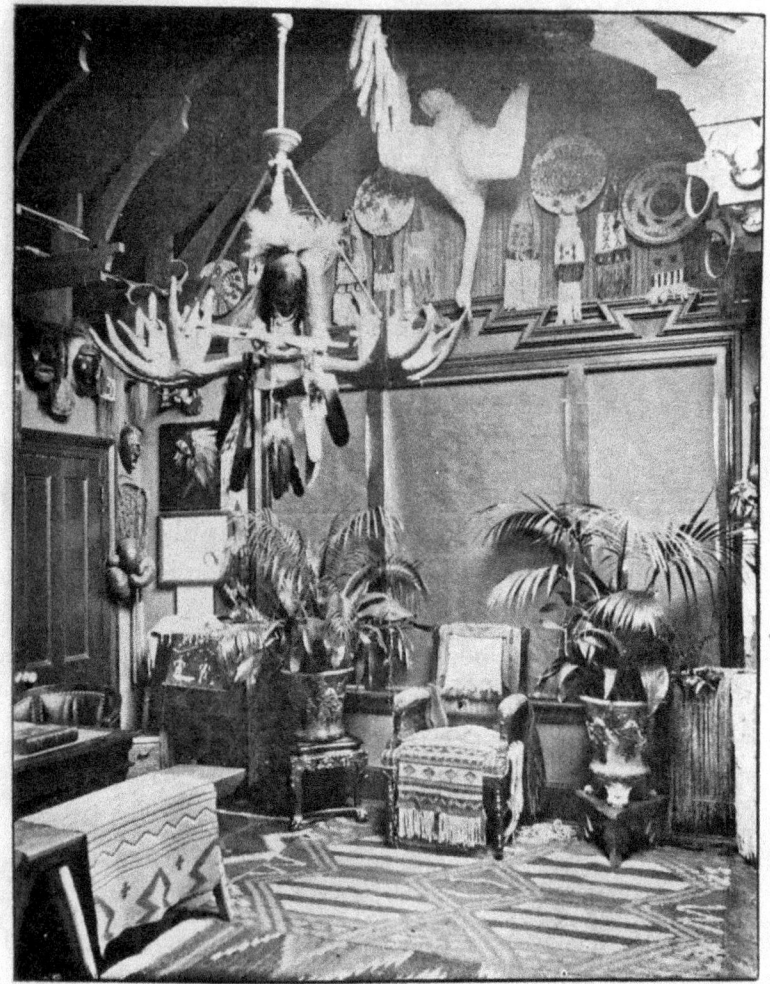

A UNIQUE CHANDELIER COMPOSED OF MOOSE ANTLERS DESIGNED
BY MR. JOSEPH KEPPLER FOR HIS INDIAN ROOM

FIGURE 1 Joseph "Udo" Keppler's study, from *The Papoose*, March 1903, 1.

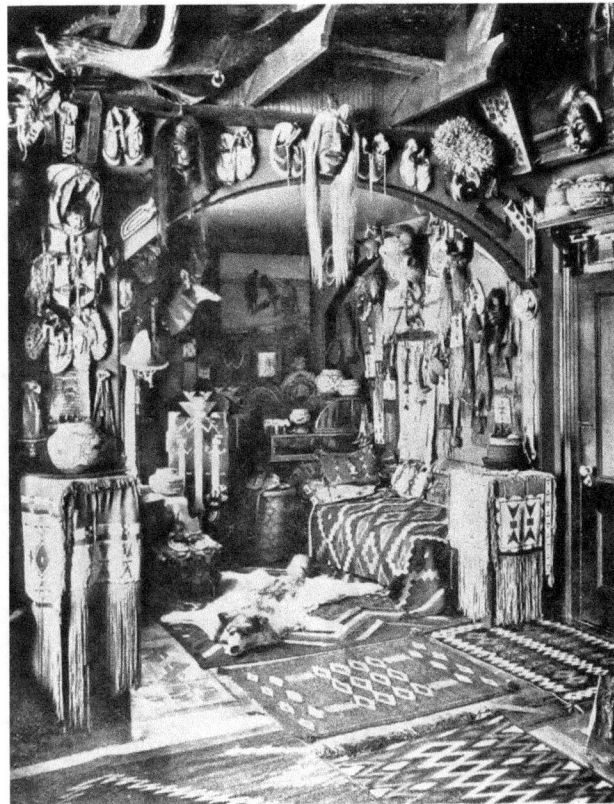

FIGURE 2 Alcove in Joseph "Udo" Keppler's home, from *The Papoose*, March 1903, 6.

The other wall bears a collection of Iroquois false-face masks. Navajo blankets cover the floor and several pieces of furniture, their contrasting geometric patterns providing a dazzling display. A print portraying a Sioux warrior is wedged into the corner. In other photographs, we can see a hearth surrounded by clubs, arrows, masks, and Hopi trays; a standing case filled with more plains beadwork; and an alcove appointed in a similar fashion to the main room.

Photographs of other Indian corners from contemporary publications reveal Keppler's collection as elaborate but typical (see figure 3). Indian corners routinely included handicrafts of diverse materials and cultural origins. Such diversity is reflected in a 1904 article on this decorating "fad," which described a room thus: "a Winnebago curtain drapes an ample doorway, an Iroquois blanket stains the wall with brilliant color, and one of Navajo weave conceals a couch."[1] As in Keppler's home, collectors clustered objects made of the same materials together, sometimes in a special case or set of

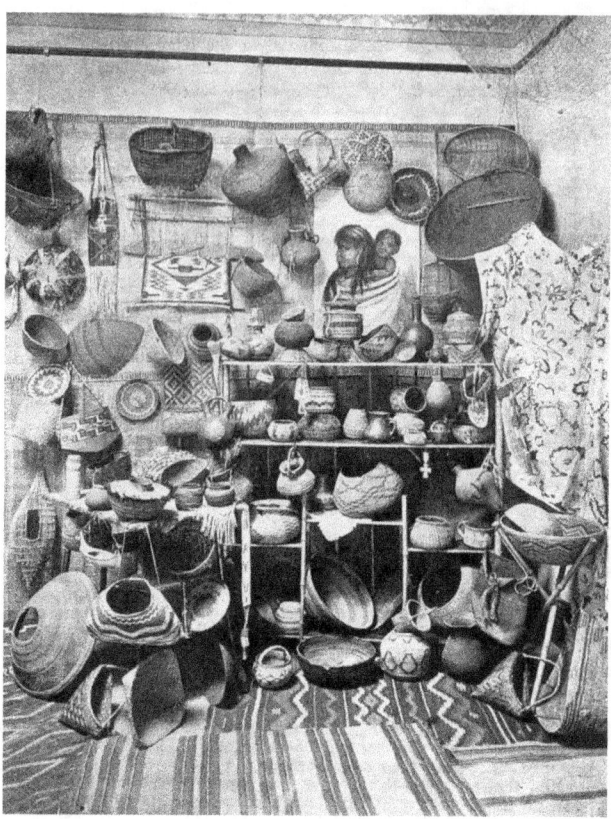

FIGURE 3 "Part of One of the Earliest California Collections," from *The Basket* 2.1 (1904), 20.

shelves. Even if the collector focused on a single kind of object, such as baskets or weavings, the display generally juxtaposed examples of the medium from different tribes and areas resulting in an array of diverse shapes, patterns, and ornaments. A graphic representation of an Indian—a calendar or a photograph or, perhaps, a framed print—usually accompanied the handicrafts.

Such pictures were known as "Indian portraits." They came in a variety of mediums and sizes. They could also conform to different styles. The Sioux man on Keppler's wall resembles the straightforward, almost ethnographic, busts of nationally known Indian painter Elbridge Ayer Burbank (figure 4). In 1898, the Chicago-based magazine *Brush and Pencil* published an article on Burbank that included copies of his portraits that could be cut out and framed.[2] The magazine published other Burbanks in subsequent issues and also offered copies via mail order.[3] Prints weren't the only form of Indian portraiture—photographers such as Frank A. Rinehart vended their wares

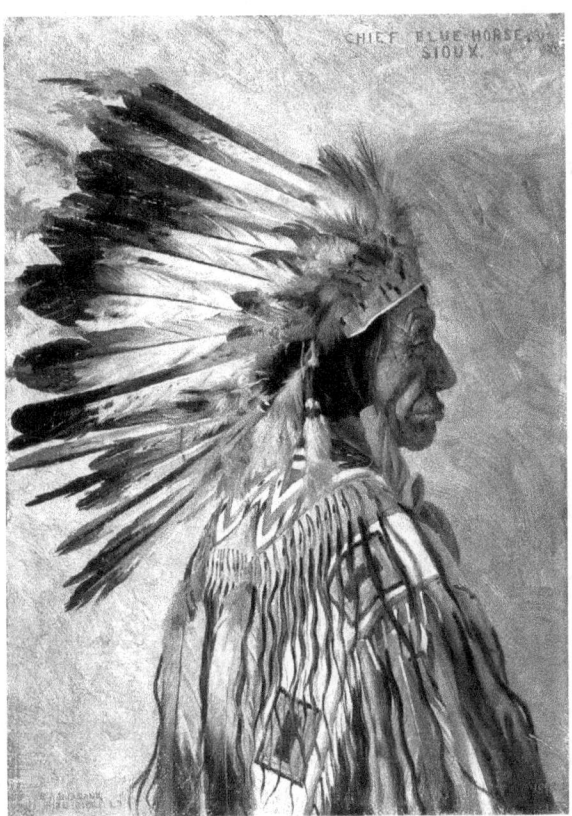

FIGURE 4 Elbridge Ayer Burbank, *Chief Blue Horse, Sioux*, 1899. Oil on canvas. Edward E. Ayer Collection, The Newberry Library, Chicago.

through advertisements, and art dealers and *Brush and Pencil* also promoted so-called Indian calendars, proclaiming one "The Sensation of the Year."[4] In keeping with their title, Indian portraits were usually annotated with the name of the sitter. But they tend to position the sitter as passive. Chief Blue Eagle, for example, doesn't attempt to engage the viewer's gaze, but instead looks away, as do the subjects of the portraits on Keppler's walls. These isolated figures are usually depicted in traditional dress and engaged in a "timeless" activity, such as caring for children, or doing nothing at all.

In many ways, the Indian portraits are the key to the Indian corner, for this simulated presence of the original makers and users of the objects on display highlights their assumed absence from modern domestic space. Indian corners define their owners as *not* Native and thus also as having none of the qualities associated with indigenous people. Not dependent on preindustrial tools, collectors are able to appreciate them for their aesthetic value alone. The ability to collect such objects is a hallmark of a modernity presumed available only to European Americans. A poem by Alvida Kelton Lee published in 1899 highlights this impression:

Down from my study walls they gaze,
    These grave, grim men of alien race;
They make me dream of some dim forest maze
    Or wild trail leading on to wilder place.

. . . From that dark frame a brave old warrior looks
    His calm disdain upon my pampered ease,
Till I could trade my easy-chair, my books,
    For mat of rushes by the brown tepees

. . . They give me strength, each pictured face,
    They teach me scorn of petty ills,
And courage to press onward in the race,
    Up to the summit of life's highest ills.[5]

Lee's poem repeats the Indian corner's pattern of juxtaposing two antithetical worlds, the wild forest and the comfortable study. But though the writer describes the natural world as having greater appeal than her own, she presents it as one impossible to reach. Similarly, the portraits in Keppler's corners do not offer windows onto actual Indian lives but situate their models in blank expanses of space into which the viewers can project their own interpretation. Rather than document individuals' and tribal nations' complex negotiations with their changing circumstances, these portraits and the collections of which they are a part are designed to stimulate the collector's imagination.

Discussions of the Indian corner frequently link it to "antimodernism," a term coined by T. J. Jackson Lears to describe the "recoil from 'overcivilized modern existence to more intense forms of physical or spiritual experience," identified with preindustrial culture.[6] The fact that many collections were installed in Adirondack cabins, hunting lodges, and suburban dens — places associated with male retreat from bureaucratic labor and urban commercialism — reinforces this interpretation. These associations are not incorrect, but they are incomplete, most obviously as they fail to account for the ways in which collecting Native American art was also a means of embracing modern culture. As I will show, the acquisition of Indian handicrafts at the turn of the century must be understood as an aspect of, as well as an antidote to, the spread of commodity culture. The accumulation and display of these goods demonstrated a sensitivity to the material object and a capacity for taste that were distinctly modern pleasures.

The craftspeople who supplied the work displayed in these collections also negotiated modernity's promises and challenges. While Euro-American collectors may not have known it, many of the designs, techniques, and forms of the objects they owned were innovations developed by craftspeople aware of non-Native markets. It is thus useful to understand the Indian corner as a "contact zone," a term defined by anthropologist Mary Louise Pratt as a space of intercultural negotiation in which European Americans and Natives encounter each other's practices and values, albeit under conditions of radical inequality.[7]

In this chapter I explore the modernity of the Indian corner by reading it in relationship to the spread of the culture of consumption. In doing so, I look closely at both the contents and the display of collections of Native American art. Key to my argument is the fact that indigenous handicrafts were both purchased and displayed in urban contexts. Departing from studies that emphasize Indian traders based on or near reservations, I look at marketers and collectors located in major cities, particularly New York. The cosmopolitan nature of the city allows me to explore the participation of Indian people, including Native artists, in the culture of consumption. During this period, Indian people regularly flowed through the cities of the United States on diplomatic missions, as members of performing groups, en route to government boarding schools, and increasingly as individuals in search of the employment and social opportunities offered by a modern city.

This work bears a debt to earlier work on the marketing of Native American art. Early studies of Indian traders have been joined by examinations of curio dealers in western cities.[8] To this date, however, few have paid attention to the sale of Native handicrafts in eastern cities. The lack of scholarship here is a shame, because ignoring the urban component of this history can unintentionally reinforce the very primitivism that studies of so-called tourist arts seek to challenge, by associating Native American art with western reservations and tourist depots perceived as removed from cosmopolitan modernity. Phil Deloria has noted the persistence of the cultural trope of the primitive Indian to this day, despite the fact that we all know better. "According to most American narratives," he writes, "Indian people, corralled on isolated and impoverished reservations, missed out on modernity. . . . [However,] a significant cohort of Native people engaged the same forces of modernization that were making non-Indians reevaluate their own expectations of themselves and their society."[9] By acknowledging the role of Native art in the metropolitan phenomenon of the Indian corner, we can reinsert Native Americans and their art into the modern history of which they were a part.

THE ORIGINS OF THE INDIAN CORNER

Personal collections of Native American objects date to the earliest years of European settlement of the American frontier. Thomas Jefferson installed some of the materials brought back by Lewis and Clark at Monticello, and a fair number of military officers picked up souvenirs on western postings.[10] But the spread of this taste beyond individuals with regular contact with Indian people is a Victorian development, facilitated by advances in both domestic decoration and the distribution of Native American handicrafts.

The Indian corner is an example of the "cozy corner," a type of domestic space developed in the mid-nineteenth century. The first cozy corners were outfitted with pillows and textiles from the Middle East, reflecting an Orientalist association of the region with comfort and luxury, but Japanese themes were also common. Cozy corners reflect the shifting association of middle-class homes in the second half of the nineteenth century from sites of work to retreats from the workaday world.[11] This change defined a new role for domestic decoration: to provide cheer and nurture individuality. Because of the increasing array of manufactured and imported furnishings available in the Gilded Age, the selection of household decorations was influenced not only by their comfort and convenience but also by the emerging notion that taste was an expression of personal identity. Cozy corners provided casual spaces for familial interaction that were filled with objects with stimulating forms and textures from exotic locations that epitomized the association of home with escape from modern urban culture.

This phenomenon was influenced by the ideas of the British critics John Ruskin and William Morris, which spurred an international arts and crafts movement. The term "arts and crafts" has been associated with an unrealistic desire to return to a premodern utopian age; Eileen Boris suggests the term "aesthetic reform" as a more appropriate description of the efforts that followers of Ruskin and Morris undertook to influence the culture of the Progressive Era.[12] The movement placed particular emphasis on the value of household furnishings, suggesting that exposure to simple, well-designed, often handmade wares in the home could help assuage what Ruskin called "the anxieties of the outer life" and develop character and taste.[13] Aesthetic reformers praised cultures perceived as untainted by modern industrialism, celebrating the craftsmen of the Middle Ages and Renaissance and looking in modern vernacular traditions for examples of honesty and simplicity in materials and design. Aesthetic reformers celebrated the material culture of rural areas such as Ireland as survivals of premodern traditions. They also looked to non-European culture as a source, especially cultures falling under the political and economic influence of European superpowers.[14] Handcrafted exotic objects from Asia, including Indian paisley shawls, Arabian carpets, and Japanese screens, were brought into the bourgeois home as more "authentic" and healthful than the machine-made bibelots of Western culture. This rhetoric also facilitated the market for Native American objects. While all types of cozy corner were grounded in notions of the exotic, each had particular associations. As I will discuss below, for American audiences, Indian corners were understood to address a variety of cultural needs arising at the turn of the century, particularly the desire for an individual and national sense of mastery in the face of the increasing alienation brought on by industrialized work, urban life, and international trade.

The origins of the Indian corner reveal it to be an artifact of the very modernization it was thought to ameliorate. Specifically, this collecting practice is intimately linked with western expansion. The Indian corner idea was probably inspired by the collections of two prominent New Englanders intimately linked with the investigation of Native life: the writer Helen Hunt Jackson and the ethnographer Frank Hamilton Cushing. Both traveled extensively in the West in the 1880s, the period when the reservation system was becoming codified. Jackson was a travel writer whose exposure to the condition of Native Americans led her to pen the best-selling Indian reform–oriented novel *Ramona*.[15] Cushing conducted ethnographic expeditions to the Southwest, first under the auspices of the Smithsonian and later for the Boston philanthropist Mary Tileston Hemenway. Each was the subject of admiring profiles in the periodical press, some of which mentioned their collections of Native American art.[16]

These early models notwithstanding, the Native version of the cozy corner was dependent on the development of off-reservation distribution of Native American handicrafts. Native Americans had traded baskets, blankets, apparel, and tools with their non-Indian neighbors since the beginning of European settlement. In some areas, such as Niagara Falls, craftspeople also produced curios to sell as souvenirs to tourists.[17] The marketing of Native American art exploded at the end of the nineteenth century, when traders began addressing urban consumers directly through advertisements, special sales, and mail-order catalogues, enabling them to purchase goods from a wide array of areas without leaving the city. One well-informed writer claimed in 1901 that $18,000 of Indian goods was being sold in New York annually.[18]

Who was buying this material? Otis Mason's *Aboriginal American Basketry*, first published as an annual report of the National Museum (now the Smithsonian Institution) but republished in 1904 by Doubleday, includes an eight-page appendix listing the collections of prominent Americans such as John Wanamaker, Phoebe Apperson Hearst, and Mrs. Leland Stanford, as well as those of other, less well-known individuals spread across the country.[19] A closer examination of one such collection, that of Udo Keppler, will reveal some of the reasons for this popularity.

Following in the footsteps of his father, Joseph Keppler Sr., Udo worked as a political cartoonist for *Puck*, the magazine founded by the elder Keppler in 1876. He took over direction of the magazine upon his father's death in 1894. By the late 1880s, however, he was devoting time to his interest in Native American culture, particularly to his work with the Seneca of upstate New York. Keppler corresponded actively about matters related to culture and politics with several prominent Seneca "culture brokers" (Native people who work as intercessors between Indian and non-Indian worlds), including the chief, Edward Cornplanter; his son Jesse, a writer and artist; and the ethnologist Arthur C. Parker.[20] Along with his friend Harriet Converse, an amateur ethnologist who had been adopted into the Seneca nation, Keppler conducted research on ceremonials that resulted in a lengthy paper on false-face masks published by the Heye Foundation in 1941.[21]

When Converse died in 1903, Keppler was given her place in the tribe. He worked against the allotment of New York reservations and was involved in other issues pertaining to Seneca sovereignty. Keppler was also involved in the welfare of numerous individuals; his correspondence describes visits he made to a number of families and gifts and favors that he shared with them. Keppler socialized with other European Americans interested in Native American culture. He numbered among his friends Theodore Roosevelt and George Gustav Heye, the megalomaniac collector of American Indian art, whose collection became the core of the current National Museum of the American Indian.[22] Much of Keppler's own collection became part of the Heye Foundation's Museum of the American Indian, where he served as vice president for a time. He also made generous gifts to his friend Charles Lummis's Southwest Museum in Pasadena, where he spent winters.

Keppler's collection reflects these scientific and personal connections to Indian people. The false-face masks that dominate his study relate to his scientific research. But at times, Keppler would set up the sale of a valuable object, such as a mask, to a non-Indian collector, which he explains as motivated by a desire to provide the original sellers with income, and there is no indication that he made a profit on these sales. He also writes of purchasing, and often reselling, corn husk dolls, slippers, moccasins, baskets, and other inexpensive items for Native artists. Other objects have no connection to his scientific activities. These include decorative objects from the West and Southwest, such as the Navajo weavings that line the floors and embellish chairs in every room of his Inwood home. Some pieces are clearly well-made treasures that have been handed down through generations, but others appear to be items produced during Keppler's time explicitly for intercultural trade. While his papers don't record his source of non-Iroquoian objects, they were undoubtedly purchased through middlemen — western dealers, urban retailers, or even Indian reform organizations. Keppler had connections to each of these. For example, *The Papoose*, which published the photographs of his collection, was owned by the Hyde Exploring Expedition, a trading company based in Arizona that reached urban audiences through mail order and through outposts in New York, Boston, Philadelphia, Newport, and Los Angeles.

The range in quality and value of Keppler's objects poses a challenge to those who would try to fix him within a certain category of ethnographic collector. Was he primarily an ethnographer, interested in making scientific study of the false-face societies? Was he an aesthete interested primarily in the formal qualities of objects? Or was he a sentimental consumer who used his purchasing power to solidify personal relationships and aid the needy? Could his taste resemble the superficial interest of the tourist? Since the beginning of the twentieth century, critics have divided collections of non-Western objects according to the writers' support of different disciplines, particularly anthropology and art. These categories reinforced the professionalization that both the art world and the social sciences experienced at the end of the nineteenth century, something reflected in the creation of public museums with collections organized along scientific and aesthetic lines before these disciplines were fully integrated into the academy. These museums distinguished themselves from the eclectic dime museums of an earlier generation, whose collections invoked a variety of associations from the historical to the sensational.[23]

Turn-of-the-century commentators used these categories to distinguish between "serious" collectors and dilettantes. For example, a 1904 article accused "popular" collectors of "promiscuous and unintelligent buying," while the "true lover" had a "far more genuine" interest in Native American culture.[24] More recently, Molly Lee has written of the need to look closely at the diverse engagement of collectors. She has distinguished different strains of collecting of Alaska Native objects, ranging from acquisitions by tourists with a brief and superficial relationship to Native culture to those of specialized collectors with an ongoing, often professional, relationship with specific indigenous communities, and to aesthetic reformers who appropriated indigenous art to support their larger social goals.[25]

Lee acknowledges the difficulty of this task, for while academic disciplines were emerging at the turn of the century, they had not finished doing so—if indeed they ever have. Still more challenging is the fact that the same objects and even the same collection could take on a different meaning in a new context. The collecting of Native American art, especially by museums, has become an important scholarly subject in the past two decades.[26] Historians have noted both the means by which indigenous objects left their communities—gift, trade, sale, theft, and so on—and the ways in which these dislocations were attended by changes in the objects' meaning. These changes in meaning refer not only to the shift from an indigenous user to a non-Indian collector, but also the shifts undergone as collected objects change location. Thomas Jefferson's collection of artifacts from the Lewis and Clark expedition later were owned by the showman P. T. Barnum and eventually came into the collection of the Peabody Museum of Archaeology and Ethnology at Harvard. Each venue invited viewers to relate differently to the objects on display. If the significance of individual objects is controlled by context, then it is nevertheless possible to draw conclusions about the significance of a collection as a whole. For the act of assembling collections has its own history.

The effort to evaluate and categorize collectors relates to this history, particularly to the spread of collecting in the late nineteenth century. The widespread creation of domestic collections is related to the spread of a culture of consumption. As T. J. Jackson Lears has argued, the urbanization and industrialization of the nineteenth century dislodged older notions of subjectivity whereby one might develop a sense of self in relationship to work, religion, and community. Capitalist society, which connected producers and consumers across geographic expanses via an invisible market, challenged the perception that identity was something fixed and innate. Consumption became one means to redress this alienation or "feeling of unreality," as Lears put it. Social critics, religious leaders, and marketers alike urged people to reintroduce a sense of authenticity into their lives through "therapeutic" leisure.[27] As Lears wrote: "In the embryonic consumer culture of the late nineteenth century, more and more Americans were being encouraged to 'express themselves' . . . not through independent accomplishment but through the ownership of things."[28] Increasingly, people linked their identities to the objects with which they surrounded themselves and saw the act of consumption as an opportunity to be affected by objects as well as to express some inner taste.

The culture of consumption introduced the notion of taste as a signifier of social class. In the late nineteenth century Thorstein Veblen invented the term "conspicuous consumption," or the "wasteful" consumption of goods not to meet physical needs but as a visible sign to others of one's wealth and power. The standards set by what Veblen calls "the leisure class" then become the standard to which the middle and lower classes hold themselves and upon which their reputation is based.[29] As the sociologist Pierre Bourdieu has explained, the notion of "taste" has served to naturalize the elite status of those with the power to consume more by masking the relationship between wealth and discernment.[30]

Collecting inherently fits Veblen's category of wasteful consumption, as it removes objects from use. This gesture was recognized by early scholars of domestic collecting, such as Walter Benjamin, whose 1931 essay "Unpacking My Library" describes the collector as someone with "a relationship to objects which does not emphasize their functional, utilitarian value—that is, their usefulness—but studies and loves them as the scene, the stage, of their fate. The most profound enchantment for the collector is the locking of individual items within a magic circle in which they are fixed as the final thrill, the thrill of acquisition, passes over them."[31] Jean Baudrillard has similarly commented on how the collector overwrites the historical and cultural meaning of an object by inserting it into a context where it refers only to its new owner.[32]

Michel Foucault has connected collecting and display with a modern Western system of power. Many critics in his wake have seen collections of non-Western materials as an embodiment of Euro-American colonial domination, noting, for example, that the Smithsonian's collecting accelerated in the 1870s, when ethnologists thought more knowledge of the Indians would help the U.S. government subdue them.

Such an interpretation is not inappropriate for the Indian corner. Keppler's records do not include a statement of the meaning of his collection, but the captions to his photographs suggest that it is an index to his character. One is captioned, "Where he studies and works and entertains his friends" (figure 5), suggesting a surrounding associated with "authenticity" and leisure.[33] A more extensive meditation on the meaning of the Indian corner is provided by the Indian "expert" George Wharton James, who traded in, wrote about, and lectured on Native American art extensively in the first decade of the twentieth century.[34] James was a British immigrant who began to meet and photograph Indians and establish business ties with Indian traders while in the Southwest recovering from an illness. He wove together his own ideas with those drawn from ethnographers and aesthetic reformers to extol the superior moral and physical benefits of the "simple" life in the American Southwest. James praised collectors as having "wide sympathies, broad culture, and . . . refined mind[s]."[35] The home decoration expert Alice Kellogg suggested that surrounding boys with Navajo weavings

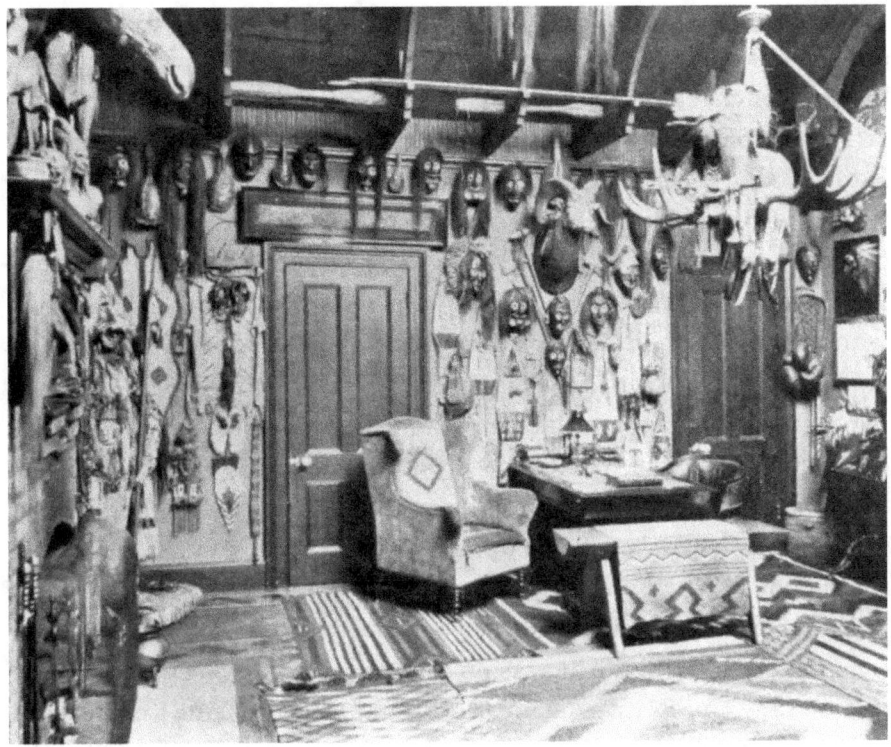

FIGURE 5   Joseph "Udo" Keppler's study, from *The Papoose*, March 1903, 5.

and Plains textiles could stimulate their competitive drive and quest for knowledge.[36]

This rhetoric was tinged with nationalism. The Indian craze was the homegrown successor to the "Japan craze," a similar collecting frenzy that dominated the last quarter of the nineteenth century. Spurred by the Japanese exhibit at the 1876 Centennial Exhibition in Philadelphia and the increasing trans-Pacific trade during the Meiji empire, Gilded Age Americans began decorating their homes with Japanese objects. A wide variety of goods of Japanese manufacture were sold in America, ranging from inexpensive paper fans and lanterns, metal *tsuba* (sword guards), and carved ivories to more expensive enamels, lacquer work, ceramics, and carved and painted screens.[37]

In the 1890s and 1900s, critics used a positive comparison to Japanese art as the basis for the aesthetic qualities of Indian handicrafts. Olive May Percival argued that the quality of Indian art was equaled only by the Japanese and proclaimed, "The collector of Indian baskets knows that a really perfect specimen is quite as rare as a piece of genuinely antique Satsuma."[38] Irene Sargent compared the workmanship of California basketry with Japanese art. As she put it, "The Japanese who glorifies his tea-cup and his screen, is followed in the same path, although with unequal steps, by the Indian woman who realizes in the form, texture and decoration of her food basket conceptions of beauty which no school can justly criticize."[39] Interestingly, such a comparison builds on an earlier trend of comparing Indian people with the Japanese. As Neil Harris and Eunyoung Cho have discussed, the Japanese became America's primary cultural "other" in the 1880s, establishing a standard against which other primitives would be compared.[40] Travelers to the American West frequently described Indian people, especially Indian women, as being physically similar to the Japanese. One Boston woman even saw Dakota Sioux women's buckskin dresses as a variation on the kimono.[41]

Native American art was seen as a distinctly superior form of decoration, in keeping with the increasing nationalism and protectionism of the nation at the time. Native American art allowed people of the United States to combine these nationalist and colonialist interests, by appropriating the material culture of subjugated indigenous people as an expression of national aesthetics. They embraced the fact that Indian art was made out of local materials and described its various forms as a reaction to the national landscape. Most important, critics urged collectors to buy Native products instead of sending money overseas. As one writer put it, "Americans send hundreds of thousands of dollars every year to Germany and Japan for hampers, scrap baskets, clothes baskets, market baskets, work baskets, fruit, flower, lunch and candy baskets, — money which, by every right, should be earned by our needy, capable Indians."[42]

This desire to flex American muscle occurred on a small as well as an international scale. Collectors of Native American art often relate the story of acquisition as a kind of conquest. Consider an anecdote related by journalist Julian Ralph describing his acquisition of a pair of earrings from a Cree girl at a train station: "Among all the Indians there it was the only bit of finery, the only ornament, the only link that connected them with their past. It was all they had. I got it. I put a quarter in the Cree girl's hand, and almost tore the rings out of her ears—for the whistle had blown and the wheels were turning. I have often wondered since whether she cared to part with them."[43] The story's title, "My Indian Plunder," confirms the writer's enjoyment of this triumph.

Keppler clearly had a more congenial relationship with the Natives who provided the objects in his collection. His correspondence reveals this trust. In 1904 Delos Kittle, a Seneca, wrote to say that Keppler was the only one to whom his mother would sell her false-face mask, and that she had rejected earlier offers. While this may only have been rhetoric designed to make the sale, Keppler demonstrated his respect for Kittle by loaning the object back for use in tribal ceremonials at least twice.[44] While Kittle's family seemingly parted with the mask willingly and were compensated for it, it is never-theless possible to read a narrative of power in this transaction. Keppler's collection was assembled during a time of dramatic cultural change for the Seneca, and poverty, leading some to feel they had little choice but to work with the non-Indian "gleaners" who came through searching for traditional objects.[45] Moreover, while Keppler recognized Kittle's desire to use the mask in a ceremonial way, he displayed this powerful object as a domes-tic decoration, leading another Seneca, Edward Cornplanter, to warn him about his careless handling of "dangerous materials."[46]

The *Papoose* article on Keppler's home is titled "A Rare Collection," with a preciousness that typifies this discourse in which Indian objects and the understanding thereof are shown to be hard to come by. Such rhetorical strategies not only add value to the works displayed, but also celebrate the tenacity of the collector. Keppler's collection is ultimately not a sign of the artistry of the craftspeople from whom he got the objects, but of his own skill in assembling the collection, his bravery in making contact with primi-tive craftspeople, and his persistence in finding the definitive explanations of the objects in his possession. Carolyn Kastner has read the collection of the Chicago industrialist Edward Everett Ayer (figure 6) as "a visual meta-phor of his power over the collected cultures." She locates this power in his ability to name the objects and define their meanings. In Ayer's Indian corner, pieces whose uses once relied on their manipulation in space during work or ceremonial are stilled for contemplation by Ayer and his guests. When Ayer donated these objects to the Field Museum, he failed to include

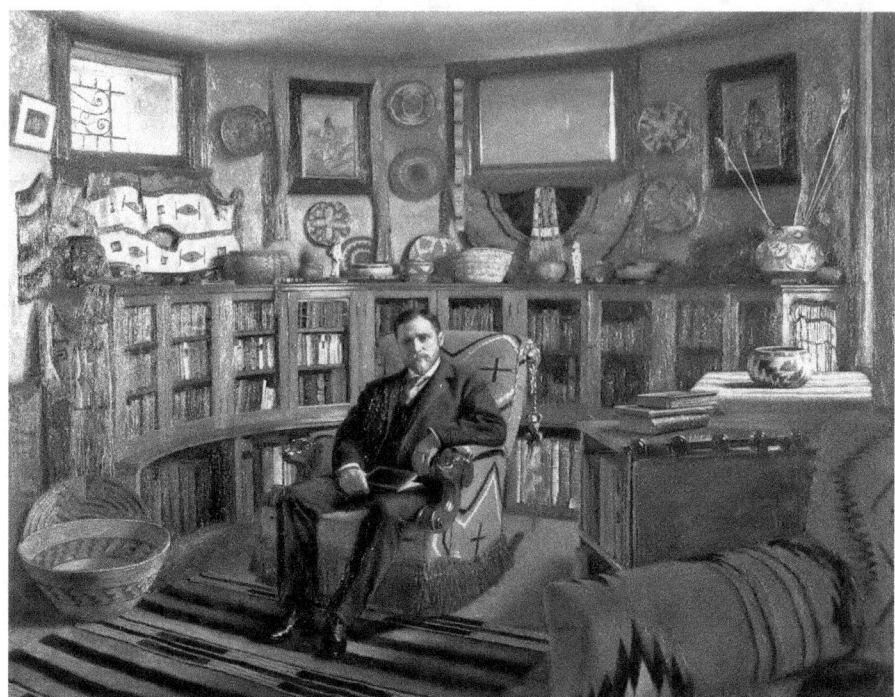

FIGURE 6 Elbridge Ayer Burbank, *Edward Everett Ayer*, 1897. Oil on canvas. Edward E. Ayer Collection, The Newberry Library, Chicago.

information about their origins or makers. Works of diverse artists, periods, and regions became pieces of Ayer's collection, rather than artifacts with individual histories.[47]

Narratives of conquest could also be found in the very placement of Native objects in the European American home. Indian corners frequently appeared in spaces caught between nature and culture such as porches and verandas, providing a metaphoric claim on the wilderness. Such associations were made clear by writers; for example, Gustav Stickley suggested that placing Navajo rugs on porches helped turn them into "peaceful outdoor living rooms."[48] Keppler's interweaving of weapons and hunting trophies with the more peaceful handicrafts in his collection similarly associates the assembly of the collection with conflict and struggle.

Lears finds the desire for a sense of mastery a common response among the American middle classes faced with the challenges of modernity. The arrangement of Indian corners suggests an association with serious study that highlights the power of their owners. George Wharton James surrounded his

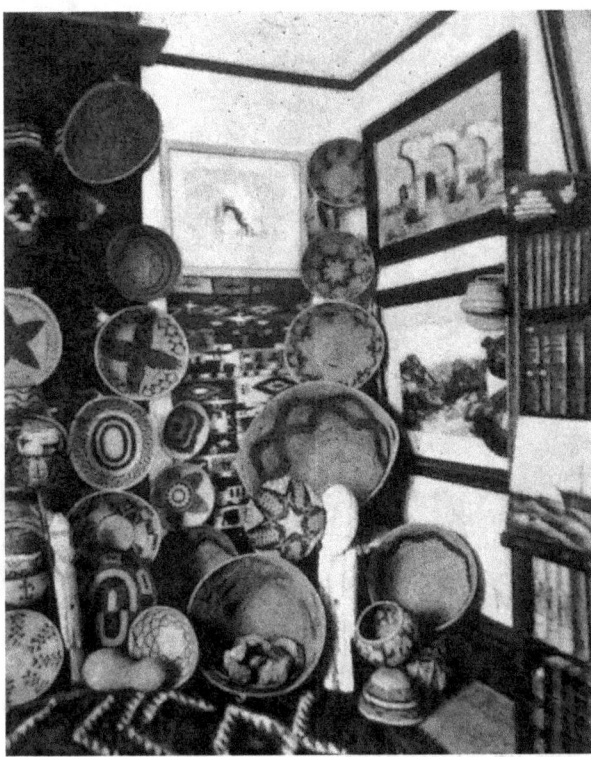

FIGURE 7 George Wharton James's collection, from G. W. James, *Indian Basketry* (Pasadena, Calif.: self-published, 1902), 190.

installations with the attributes of the scholarly life: leather-bound books, old prints, and references to classical antiquity (figure 7). In some corners, such as that of Mrs. Jewett of Lamanda Park, California, objects have taken the place of books, offering their own shapes and decorations as "texts" to be read (figure 8). Informed viewers can see order in the variety included in these displays. For example, Jewett's baskets come from a wide variety of West Coast cultures, from Pomo to Tulare to Tlingit, providing a catalogue-like impression that is enhanced by the ways in which the baskets' different positions highlight the variety of materials (feather, shell, grass, bark) and techniques (twining, plaiting, wicker, coiling) utilized. Articles on collecting recommended such variety; *The Papoose*, for example, suggested that "a basket collection without a Washoe is like the play of Hamlet with Hamlet omitted."[49] The Washoe tribe, whose land spans the California-Nevada border around Lake Tahoe, produced coiled basketry known for its tiny stitches and intricate designs. The author may have been referring specifically to the work of Louisa Keyser, also known as Dat-so-la-lee, whose fine work became

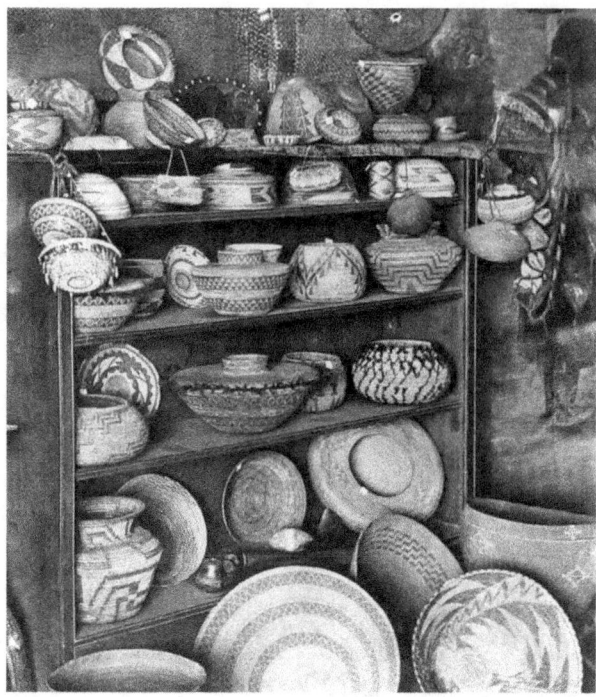

FIGURE 8 "Part of the Jewett Collection," from Olive M. Percival, "Indian Basketry: An Aboriginal Art," *House Beautiful* 2 (1897): 153. Avery Architectural and Fine Arts Library, Columbia University, New York.

well known through her work for a Carson City clothing store, Emporium Company, where she demonstrated and sold her work.[50] Collectors went to great effort to have objects from as many tribes as possible in their displays. Articles focusing on the traditions of a specific tribe or region or medium created categories to be filled. For example, between 1897 and 1905, *House Beautiful* ran articles on Chilkat blankets, Navajo weaving, Pueblo pottery, and diverse basket traditions.[51] The adherence of Indian corners to an ideal of order and classification complemented this scholarly drive for complete representation.[52] Even Keppler's eclectic collection has a certain tidiness, with each object occupying its own space and similar materials assembled together on walls or shelves, or in cases.

Encounters with nature could promote the characteristics needed for such mastery: physical and psychic health, energy, sincerity.[53] As John Higham has explained, "Nature . . . represented that masculine hardiness and power that suddenly seemed an absolutely indispensable remedy for the artificiality and effeteness of late nineteenth-century urban life."[54] Native objects perceived as belonging to nature rather than culture because of their materials and the nonindustrialized mode of their production and exposure to Indian culture was part of the drive to redress the effeteness of civilization. The fine craftsmanship, durable materials, and romantic associations of Native American handicrafts were perceived as therapeutic. For example, one article encouraged the use of Indian motifs as nursery decorations to stimulate a young boy's imagination.[55] The same boy might have joined the Woodcraft Indians, an early rival of the Boy Scouts, or be sent to camp in the Adirondacks as he grew older to continue the healthful influence of the natural world.[56]

The display strategies involved in the Indian corner enhanced this notion of an encounter with "authentic" primitive life. Without letting the eye dwell on one individual object, Indian corners impress the viewer as dynamic, visually and physically stimulating spaces. Leaning against the wall, draping jauntily off furniture, trailing fringe and feathers, stacked on shelves or hanging in clusters, the objects in Keppler's Indian corner spark the desire to enter the space and pick them up, set them into balance or merely run our fingers over their varied surfaces. Articles promoting Indian corners suggest the therapeutic value of making contact with another, more authentic culture. Native qualities such as hard work, spirituality, and commitment to community are described as immanent in beautiful, well-made, "traditional" wares.

Following Lears, several scholars have emphasized the way in which American Indian art is associated with spaces and ideas seemingly antithetical to urban modernity. Elizabeth Cromley, for example, emphasizes the association of Native handicrafts with nature: "In rustic settings close to nature such as lodges and camps . . . Indian objects were allied with natural objects—antlers, boulders—and reinforced the nature theme in these interiors. . . . In these rooms, Indian objects stand for the admired 'simple life,' in which overcivilized bourgeois owners could be revivified by nature."[57]

For Indian corners to work the way many collectors said they did, it is necessary to see Native American art as the product of a premodern world cut off from contemporary life. Writers at the turn of the century worked hard to maintain this cultural and temporal boundary by emphasizing the value of objects made using so-called traditional forms and materials. This celebration of so-called traditional art as pure and unchanging disregarded the actual history of several artistic traditions. Navajo weaving, for example, had always been produced for both community and external use and had changed continuously in response to new materials and markets. When the Navajo migrated to the Southwest in the sixteenth century, they learned to weave cotton on upright looms from the Pueblo people they encountered there. Not long afterward, the Spanish arrived with flocks of churro sheep, and the Navajo began working in wool. The imprisonment of the tribe by U.S. troops in the 1860s disrupted shepherding and weaving, but also exposed the Navajo to European American clothing and textiles. In 1869, with the establishment of the Navajo Reservation and the increasing influx of European American manufactures into New Mexico and Arizona, new materials, new designs, and new uses for Navajo weaving were introduced, including the transformation of wearing blankets into rugs. Many weavers were attracted to the brilliant colors achieved by using synthetic dyes made in Germantown, Pennsylvania, and used them instead of the traditional natural dyes. The expanded palette available with these new materials inspired weavers to create designs that incorporated many colors in one piece, creating a new style of blanket called an eye-dazzler (see plate 1). Weavers also broadened the motifs used in their work. Early Navajo weaving was dominated by stripes, crosses, and lozenges, all forms whose symmetry reflected the Navajo aesthetic of *hozho*, or beauty derived from harmony and balance.[58] During the nineteenth century, weavers introduced motifs derived from Mexican sarapes, and increased their incorporation of pictorial designs representing animals, trains, buildings, letters, and other aspects of their changing surroundings.[59]

Collectors could be critical of these developments. Many rejected the brilliant eye-dazzlers and criticized patterns they found nontraditional. Some dealers developed ways to discourage such practices. John Lorenzo Hubbell hired Elbridge Ayer Burbank to paint copies of "traditional" designs to hang on the walls of his trading post in Ganado Arizona to serve as a model for weavers.[60] Other traders refused to buy textiles with chemical dyes in the wool.

Weavers weren't the only ones to suffer such criticism and control. George Wharton James accused a Native Californian weaver of "vicious imitation" for putting English letters into her design in what he saw as a ploy to attract a customer.[61] Such critics abhorred Native artists who reminded buyers of the commercial strategies of their own culture—pursuit of novel or inexpensive materials, exploration of fashion over tradition, strategies designed to tempt the customer. These biases still wield influence, as many of the major collections in American museums were put together by the collectors who held them. As Ruth Phillips and Christopher Steiner have pointed out, both anthropologists and art historians have ignored the study of indigenous handicrafts made explicitly for trade, seeing them as a poor container for the "pure" cultural or aesthetic values they cherished.[62] Yet these objects provide a privileged venue for the exploration of cultural adaptation and intercultural exchange. With the interruption of traditional lifeways due to U.S. expansion in the nineteenth century, many indigenous groups had expanded handicraft production. Craftspeople used their work to explore ways to be simultaneously modern *and* Indian. Craft production was an aspect of traditional culture that was not viewed as threatening to American assimilationist efforts. It offered a means of physical and cultural subsistence, helped usher in a cash economy, and sometimes spurred artistic innovation.

The primitivist rhetoric of the Indian corner suppressed this history, however. And the association of Indians with the preindustrial past and the interpretation of their goods as "natural" products at the time certainly reinforces the impression that collectors were conservative traditionalists. But there is equally strong evidence that collectors of Native American art embraced the potential of modern culture. This is well illustrated by the fact that the largest group of collectors were women. Mason's book on basketry served as a vital guide and handbook for collectors.[63] Significantly, his appendix listing prominent collectors includes far more women than men. While there is no evidence that women routinely collected different objects than men, women collectors clearly related this activity with female gender roles. The Indian portraits in women's Indian corners are frequently pictures of Native women and children, reminding viewers that much of what is on display is women's work, and women collectors may have taken inspiration from Native American artists in their own needlework and craft projects.[64] The painting accompanying Mrs. Jewett's basket collection (see figure 8) resembles the portraits and genre scenes Grace Carpenter Hudson painted of the Pomo living near her Ukiah, California home (see plate 2). In addition to working as a successful artist, Hudson and her husband assembled an extraordinary collection, much of which was acquired by the National Museum in 1899 for $3,260.[65]

Women began collections as part of a broader exploration of new social roles of the time. Some women used their interest in Native American art as a springboard to public social and professional work. Many of the articles on Indian handicrafts were written by women, who were entering the field of journalism: Olive May Percival and Irene Sargent, whom I mentioned earlier, as well as Neltje Blanchan Doubleday and Claudia Stuart Coles.[66] Many allied their interest in Native American art with their philanthropic work on behalf of Indian people. Women's entrance to the professional world at the turn of the century occurred first in fields that were perceived as compatible with feminine concerns. Teaching, nursing, and social work built on women's familial responsibilities. Women had been an active force in the American Indian reform movement since its founding in the late 1880s, citing a sympathy for the disadvantaged that had also involved them in abolitionism and urban social reform movements.[67] By the end of the century, missionaries and reformers frequently became involved in the marketing and sale of Native American art as a means of raising money for the communities they worked in and drawing attention to their cause. In 1901, Doubleday, who was a member of the Woman's National Indian Association, encouraged fellow members to create Indian corners, saying, "The Pueblo *jardiniere* in the drawing-room naturally turns the conversation of many callers toward Indian pottery and then toward the Indian."[68]

Clearly these women did not reject modernity. Involvement in the Indian reform movement allowed them to circulate in the public sphere, gaining cultural authority and for some, economic independence. Rather than see them as antimodern, it may be more useful to read them as primitivists. Gail Bederman has analyzed the utopian writings of Charlotte Perkins Gilman in this light. As she notes, women participated in the ideology of the strenuous life, capitalizing on its arguments for the advancement of civilization while changing around the terms of the ideal sought to one in which women's role was vital to resolve the problems brought on by modernization.[69] Margaret Jacobs's important study *Engendered Encounters* looks at the complex desires of American women who advanced their own modern agendas through careers emphasizing the preservation of Native American culture.[70] Cultural primitivism, defined as the celebration of a culture perceived to be of a lower order than modern Western society, has often been optimistic about the potential to improve modern life.[71] Collectors of Native American art proposed this reformation could come about through one of the most modern routes of all: consumption.

WANAMAKER'S "WIGWAM OF INDIAN CURIOSITIES"

The modernity at the heart of Indian corners is not a secret, nor does it require knowledge of the biography of their owners. It can be seen in their very appearance; this dynamic display that I noted above borrows heavily from contemporary commercial installations. Photographs of department store counters and show windows reveal a similar aesthetic of abundance, variety, and tactility to great effect, as an illustration of yard goods department in L. Frank Baum's 1900 treatise on dry goods merchandising illustrates (figure 9). The colored walls, glass cases and windows, and dramatic lighting that appear in Keppler's retreat have been described by William Leach as visual strategies developed in the late nineteenth century to stimulate consumer desire.[72]

Leach has traced the origins of shopping to the department stores that emerged in the late nineteenth century. Prior to this, consumers went to the store to fill their needs, and clerks generally retrieved items from behind the counter. With the increased sale of manufactured and luxury goods (or "fancy goods" as they were called), stores changed to inspire people to purchase things they didn't need. Store interiors became more elaborate and elegant to encourage women to prolong shopping trips. Restaurants, lecture halls, and even meeting rooms offered to women's social organizations encouraged women to feel their every need could be met within the stores' walls. The use of new technologies such as electric lighting, elevators, and even plate-glass display cases enhanced the excitement and modernity of the shopping experience. Displays within department stores reinforced this sense of spectacle. Employees arranged goods to give an impression of luxury and abundance—goods were arranged in stacks and piles and sited so that customers could spot them from afar and investigate color and texture up close. Such displays encouraged viewers to seek out experiences that held visual pleasures independent of moral or narrative meanings.[73]

The similarity between Keppler's abundant display and the cases at Marshall Field's demonstrates that this culture of display was widespread. Tony

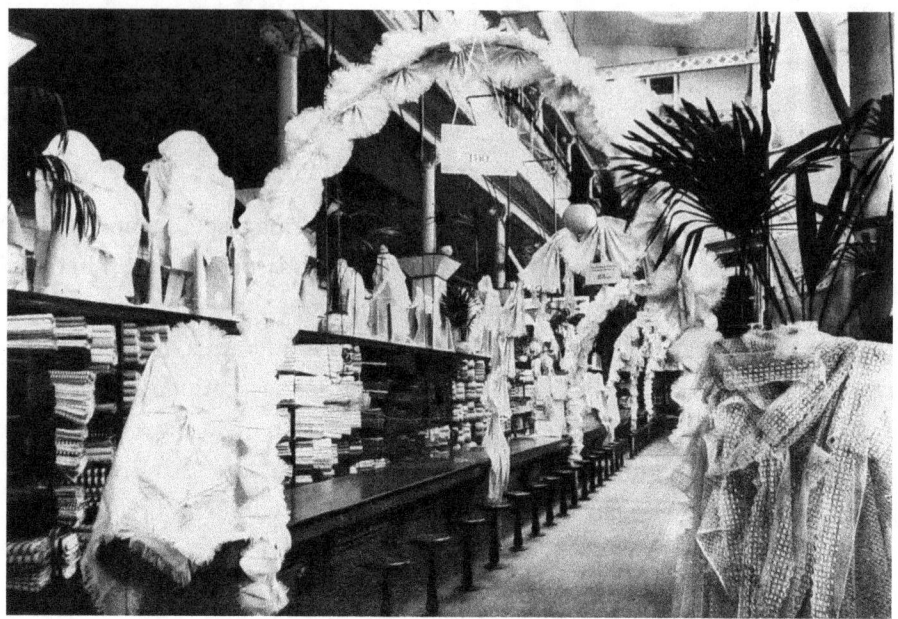

FIGURE 9 "Interior," from L. Frank Baum, *The Art of Decorating Dry Goods Windows and Interiors: A complete manual of window trimming, designed as an educator in all the details of the art, according to the best accepted methods, and treating fully every important subject* (Chicago: Show Window Publishing, 1900), 216. Rare Book and Manuscript Library, Columbia University, New York.

Bennett has argued that the cultural changes of the nineteenth century precipitated a broad "exhibitionary" complex that influenced the design of "history and natural science museums, dioramas and panoramas, national and, later, international exhibitions, arcades and department stores."[74] Exhibitionary culture relies on the nineteenth-century idea of putting the world on display as an expression of the desire to collect and organize knowledge. These institutions were committed to objects' ability to convey information and even influence their viewers, an idea that is essential to both museums and purveyors of commodities.[75] Bennett stresses that these institutional spaces facilitated the examination of other people as well as objects, and links these sites to the rise of a new social order under which individuals increasingly police their own behavior in response to the omnipresence of public surveillance.

Department store display influenced the display of objects in other spaces, such as art museums and anthropological collections. Neil Harris, for example, has argued that turn-of-the-century museums moved away from crowded exhibitions emphasizing education or aesthetics toward more spare and elegant displays because of the increasing power of department stores. He quotes John Wanamaker, who stated, "In museums, most everything looks like junk even when it isn't, because there is no care or thought in the display. If women would wear their fine clothes like galleries wear their pictures, they'd be laughed at."[76] In 1918, M. H. de Young recounted the influence that modern emporia wielded on him when he was planning the Golden Gate Memorial Museum, the San Francisco art museum that later came to bear his name. "In New York I went through the curio shops, second-hand stores and odd corners. There, too, I went to Tiffany's, and there my education in museums went several steps ahead. My training in museums went along step by step like a baby's education in life. When I thought I knew a good deal about them, I found that I didn't. At Tiffany's I learned some more."[77]

While Bennett and Harris do not discuss private collections, the Indian corner makes it clear that individuals shared display strategies with museums and department stores, which were, significantly, the other spaces in which urban Americans most frequently encountered Native American handicrafts. For, while it is romantic to assume that Indian corners demonstrated their owners' actual contact with Indian people, it is likely that most were assembled by collectors with limited experience of this kind. Many would have obtained their collections in one of the spaces described by Bennett, such as a World's Fair or a department store. Even Keppler may have done this. His collection included many items from the West and Southwest. We cannot rule out the possibility that he collected baskets and beadwork during trips across the country, but even in that case it is unlikely he had the same intimate contact with Western artists that he enjoyed among the Seneca. Moreover, within walking distance of the *Puck* offices were several purveyors of Native goods, including curio shops, private dealers, and department stores.

In March of 1898, the *New-York Tribune* announced that a special display of "Indian Curiosities" had opened at Wanamaker's Astor Place emporium.[78] Although he is well known as a social reformer with a particular interest in Native American culture, Wanamaker was not unique in marketing Native American art.[79] His rival Frederick Loeser held a sale of Navajo rugs in June the preceding year.[80] De Young's beloved Tiffany's and Macy's also frequently carried selections of Indian goods, and New York's shopping district boasted at least four stores specializing in Native American merchandise over the course of the first decade of the twentieth century. In point of fact, residents of most major American cities had multiple local sources for Native American art during the Indian craze. According to an advertisement in *House Beautiful*, the Chicago retail giant Marshall Field's was a source for "baskets, weapons, pottery, pipes, bead and porcupine embroidery, and many other interesting and decorative articles, handiwork of the Sioux, Apache, Winnebago, Chippewa, Moki and Maricopa Indians."[81] Field's had competitors in Chicago from the department store Schlesinger and Mayer and an outpost of the Fred Harvey Company, a concessioner affiliated with the Santa Fe Railroad, which set up business in the Auditorium building in 1903. Residents of Washington, D.C., could visit Woodward and Lathrop for their needs, and citizens of Boston, Philadelphia, Seattle, and southern California had sources as well.

Scholars have known that department stores sold Indian handicrafts for decades, since the earliest studies of traders. But studies have ignored the urban market for Native goods, a market fueled not only by department stores, but also by furriers, saddleries, and special "Indian stores" often operated by agents of western curio dealers, all of which vended Native handicrafts in the heart of the commercial districts of America's largest cities. In addition, western dealers often advertised in the newspapers and magazines read in eastern cities, offering potential customers specific goods or catalogues. Recent scholarship on curio shops is beginning to introduce purveyors who were not necessarily acquainted with the artists; but, by focusing on shops that specialized in Native American materials, it misses the way in which the display and marketing of Native American art was not special, but rather was typical of the transformations in commercial culture of the turn of the century.

Exploring the role of department stores in this history reminds us that Native American art was marketed using the most up-to-date strategies of the day and presented alongside diverse objects of high monetary and aesthetic value. This is because the power of indigenous objects at the beginning of the twentieth century was related to the power given to all objects at that time, undermining the argument that Native objects gained meaning from their perceived distance from the world of commodities. The Native

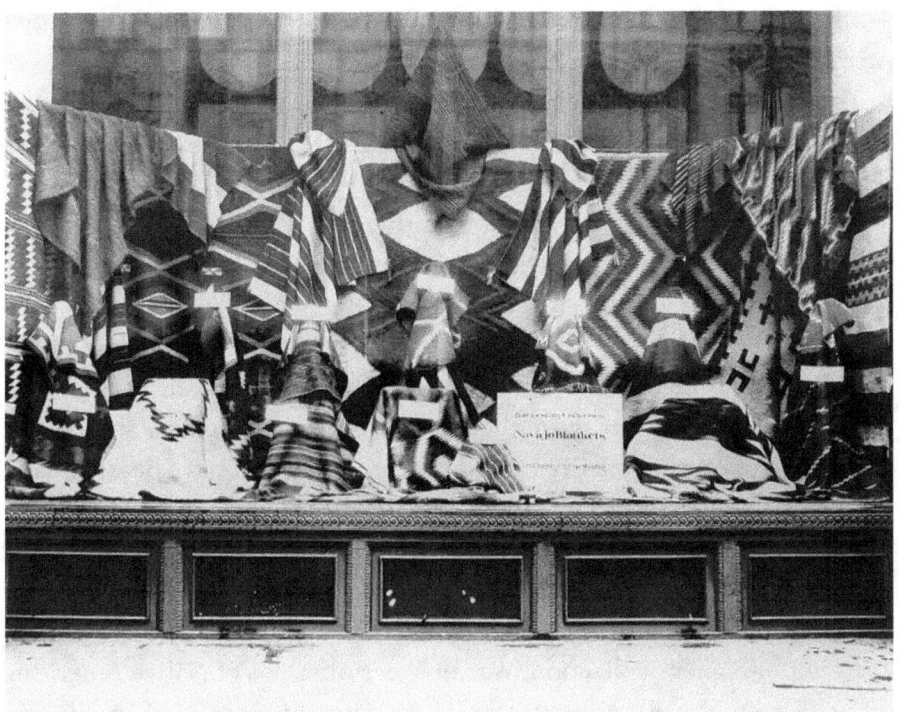

FIGURE 10 Navajo blankets for sale in the window of the Marshall Field's department store, Chicago, 1899. Inv. no. 82–1428, National Anthropological Archives, Smithsonian Institution.

objects for sale in these venues were frequently produced for sale to a geographically remote and anonymous buyer, like many of the "fancy" items available in department stores, such as Japanese fans or Rookwood pottery, reminding us that commodities made for sale to an unknown and anonymous buyer need not be industrially or mass produced.

The meaning of Indian handicrafts during the Indian craze was thus to some degree conditioned by the other objects that surrounded it. At this time, department stores offered a wide array of goods, from clothing and furniture to food, sewing supplies, and plants. Inexpensive wares were presented alongside pricey luxuries, including artistic ceramics and silverware and even oil paintings. Department stores were intercultural marketplaces, weaving together foreign and domestic, rare and quotidian, high and low. A photograph of a collection of Navajo blankets for sale in a Marshall Field's window from 1899 gives a sense of how well suited nineteenth-century serapes and eye-dazzlers were to this form of alluring display (see figure 10).

Advertisements from the period give further insight into the place of Native American art in the turn-of-the-century department store.

The most comprehensive record of department store marketing of Indian art in this period comes from John Wanamaker's New York store, at the time the largest department store in the nation. Wanamaker touted his stock of Native goods immediately after acquiring the store in 1896. One advertisement from 1897 reads: "The quick intelligence of New York, Greater New York and the vicinage is realizing that this store is at the natural center of local travel." Further down it says "In preparation for exhibition: Antique Textiles, some notable pictures, Navajo Blankets and Curios."[82] Wanamaker's store took advantage of the increased links between distant nations of the time to offer wares from a variety of cultures. His store boasted halls dedicated to Egypt, Greece, and the Near and Far East, all of whose stock changed regularly with the arrival of new shipments from distant ports, which were duly noted in newspaper ads.[83] New shipments from Alaska or the Southwest were similarly noted.

As with Keppler's collection, Wanamaker's offerings of Native American art were quite varied. Advertisements describe different kinds of objects from a wide array of places and at varying prices. They list objects that range widely in value, suggesting a need for diversity in display. For example, one notice mentions a Navajo blanket valued at $150, a beaded baby carrier on sale for $75, and a Poma [sic] feather basket offered for $65, alongside other items valued from 25 cents to a dollar.[84] In addition to articles of clothing and house decoration, Wanamaker also stocked feather headdresses, birch bark canoes, and bows and arrows.

In addition to listing items on sale, advertisements demonstrate the rhetoric used to sell Native handicrafts. They often describe potential uses for the objects on sale, recommending Navajo rugs for dens or porches, for example, or suggesting sweet grass baskets for holding Easter eggs, sewing, or calling cards. It is possible that Wanamaker displayed some objects in a simulated domestic setting that encouraged shoppers to envision the use of Native goods at home, something done for the products of other non-European cultures. For example, it is known that Marshall Field and Company's Carpet Hall displayed Near Eastern carpets and tapestries in an Orientalist setting.[85] Baum's illustration of "a Cozy Corner" utilizes a similar strategy (see figure 11).

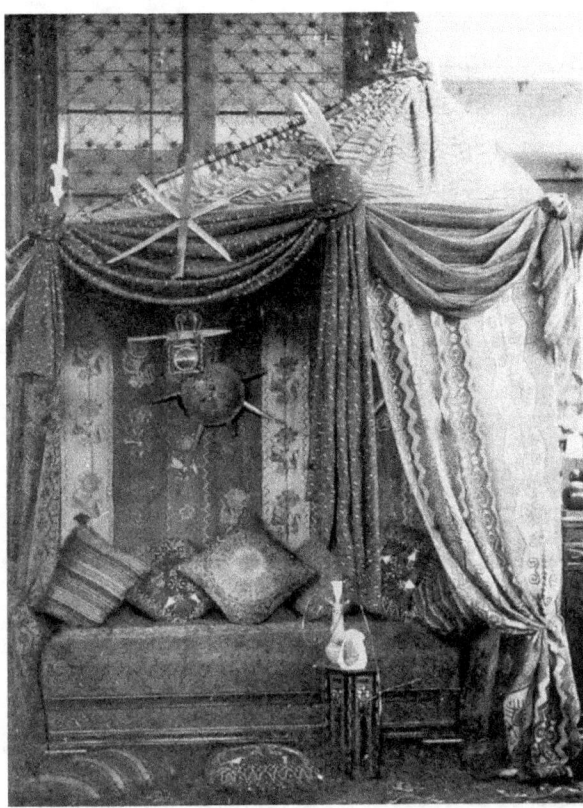

FIGURE 11 "Cozy Corner-Welch," from L. Frank Baum, *The Art of Decorating Dry Goods Windows and Interiors: A complete manual of window trimming, designed as an educator in all the details of the art, according to the best accepted methods, and treating fully every important subject* (Chicago: Show Window Publishing, 1900), 220. Rare Book and Manuscript Library, Columbia University, New York.

Many of the themes struck by department store advertisements rehearse the rhetoric of power discussed above. For example, in 1903 Wanamaker advised readers of the *New York Times* that "a glass case in the Indian Section holds a small, but intensely interesting collection of relics" assembled by a former U.S. marshall.[86] The collection is said to "bring up with vivid distinctness scenes of Indian life and warfare on the Western prairies and mountains." Specific objects are linked to leaders in the Indian wars, including Sitting Bull, Little Wound, and Hard Heart.

As this advertisement indicates, department stores sometimes exhibited and sold the private collections of local citizens and people passing through. In this example, Wanamaker used a glass case to highlight the value of a selection of objects within the larger "Indian department." Objects enclosed in cases were no doubt surrounded by abundant displays of less expensive goods that customers could handle without assistance. In 1901, Wanamaker invited George Wharton James to exhibit part of his collection during the author's lecture tour of the East Coast. An invoice sent by James to Wanamaker shortly thereafter lists a large number of Navajo weavings, some southwestern and California baskets, and a handful of pottery, as well as some tools such as small looms, a spindle, and a seed cleaner. The invoice indicates that some of the treasures, such as James's famous "railroad blanket" (see discussion below) and a "fine Mono rattlesnake basket," were for display only and gives wholesale and retail prices for the others.[87]

James gave three public lectures during the exhibition of his collection.[88] The use of "experts" to authenticate the value of the works on display was a common marketing strategy of the time. James's collection was installed in Wanamaker's Art Gallery, a space more frequently given over to the paintings of Alma-Tadema and Bouguereau, and this gesture added still more to the value of the works on display. James routinely used aesthetic language to describe both the form and the meaning of Native American art. Referring generally to ideas drawn from Ruskin and Whistler, he argued, "The basket to the uncontaminated Indian meant a work of art, in which hope, aspiration, desire, love, religion, poetry, national pride, mythology, were all more or less interwoven. Hence the work was approached in a spirit as far removed from that of mere commercialism, passing whim or fancy, as it was from that of levity, carelessness, or indifference. There was an earnestness of purpose, a conscientiousness of endeavor in the gathering of the materials, their preparation, their harmoniousness, and then in the shape, the design, the weave, the *tout ensemble*, that made basket-making to the old Indian as almost an act of religion."[89]

Reinforcing the bias against Native culture that betrays an interest in modernity, James celebrated the "uncontaminated Indian" and made reference to the Kantian ideal of autonomous art whose value lies outside the parameters of history and daily life. Consumers would not have been surprised to encounter artistic language in a retail establishment. Wanamaker and his peers were some of the most avid supporters of both academic and contemporary artists well into the 1920s, offering dedicated galleries for the display of paintings and including works of art in the more public spaces. While some journals and galleries dedicated to the cultivation of modern art often distanced themselves from the commercial world, it appears that artists embraced the opportunity for exposure that the stores offered. James's tone is another illustration of the overlapping concerns in the artistic, scientific, and commercial worlds and the reliance of all on public display.

As seen in the example of Dat-so-la-lee mentioned above, retailers also invited native craftspeople to demonstrate their work. Wanamaker's hosted an Abenaki weaver and her daughter during a special sale of woodlands baskets.[90] During the woman's "performance," the store also featured a wigwam and a selection of woodlands material culture, including birch bark canoes, dolls, and moccasins, making her seem like a live version of the portrait at the heart of an Indian corner.

Wanamaker's strategies reflect widespread practices in the marketing of Native American art from the time. Like department stores, dealers described practical uses for Native objects. They also sought to enhance the value of their wares by exaggerating their age or rarity. And they certainly capitalized on a romantic nostalgia for the old West. The exhibition of a craftsperson alongside objects for sale was particularly common. Beginning with the World's Columbian Exposition in 1893, World's Fairs had featured live exhibitions of Native people (see figure 12). As the market for Native American handicrafts spread, organizers of both ethnographically oriented exhibitions and commercial displays encouraged Indian people to demonstrate and sell their work. As I explore further in chapter 3, artists accepted such work for the income it offered and sometimes also because of the opportunity to travel, meet other Natives and non-Natives, and perhaps to serve as culture brokers mitigating the damaging aspects of Indian-white interaction of the period. Dealers in Native handicrafts picked up on this idea as well. The Fred Harvey Company provides perhaps the most dramatic example of this phenomenon.

Harvey initially provided refreshments and lodging for passengers on the Santa Fe Railroad, but in 1902 the company capitalized on passengers' interest in Native handicrafts by establishing an "Indian Department." The department opened handicraft stores in Chicago, Albuquerque, and at the Grand Canyon. In addition, it organized exhibitions for international expositions to highlight the products made along the railroad's route. The Harvey company regularly used artist demonstrators to promote their wares in both of these venues. Among these were the celebrated Hopi-Tewa potter Nampeyo. Nampeyo was known for her Sikyatki-revival style vessels, which incorporate forms and decorations from shards found at an abandoned Hopi village near her home on First Mesa. Through her association with the trader Thomas Keam and anthropologists working in the area, she became the best-known Pueblo potter of her generation. In 1904, the Harvey company built "Hopi House," a three-story building modeled on Hopi dwellings, to showcase and sell southwestern Native art and to offer tourists a chance to see artists at work. Nampeyo lived with her family on the top story for parts of 1905 and 1907, and other artist-demonstrators occupied the building when they were absent.

Another important artist who worked for the Harvey company was the Navajo weaver Asdzaa Lichii' (Red Woman), known as "Elle of Ganado," who worked in the Indian Building—Harvey's museum and showroom in Albuquerque—beginning in 1903. (see figure 13).[91] Elle was featured prominently in Harvey marketing materials and was selected to weave blankets to be presented to important people, including President Theodore Roosevelt. San Ildefonso potters Julian and Maria Martinez, who later became famous for their black-on-black ware ceramics, also worked as artist-demonstrators for the Harvey company early in their careers.

While department stores employed strategies used by other promoters of Native American art, it is important to note that their tactics resemble the packaging of other kinds of commodities as well. Glass cases, abundant displays designed to entice the senses, and packaging and educational programming designed to spur the consumer's imagination were all part and parcel of the department store experience. While some contemporary scholars argue that the largest market for Indian art at this time came from tourists seeking souvenirs of a western trip that served to contrast Native and modern life, department stores integrated Native American art into a highly modern experience.

For many turn-of-the-century viewers, looking at Native American art was part of an experience that demanded that it be viewed alongside other kinds of commodities. While it is clear that this was the case in department stores, the ads placed by dealers on the pages of eastern magazines might be said to have had a similar effect. The columnar layout of turn-of-the-century advertising created juxtapositions as stimulating as those on department store floors. For example, an ad placed by Fred Harvey in the *Chicago Daily Tribune* in 1903 appears adjacent to promotions of kid gloves, mantles for

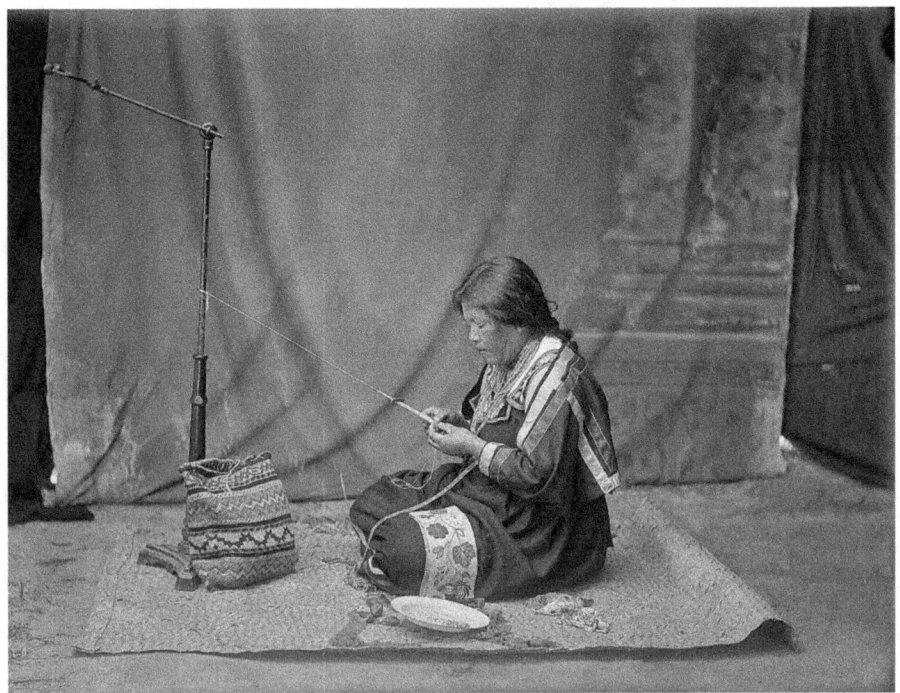

FIGURE 12 Charles H. Carpenter, "Jane Walters, Chippewa, at the Louisiana Purchase Exposition." Gelatin silver print, 1904. Inv. no. CSA14488, © The Field Museum, Chicago.

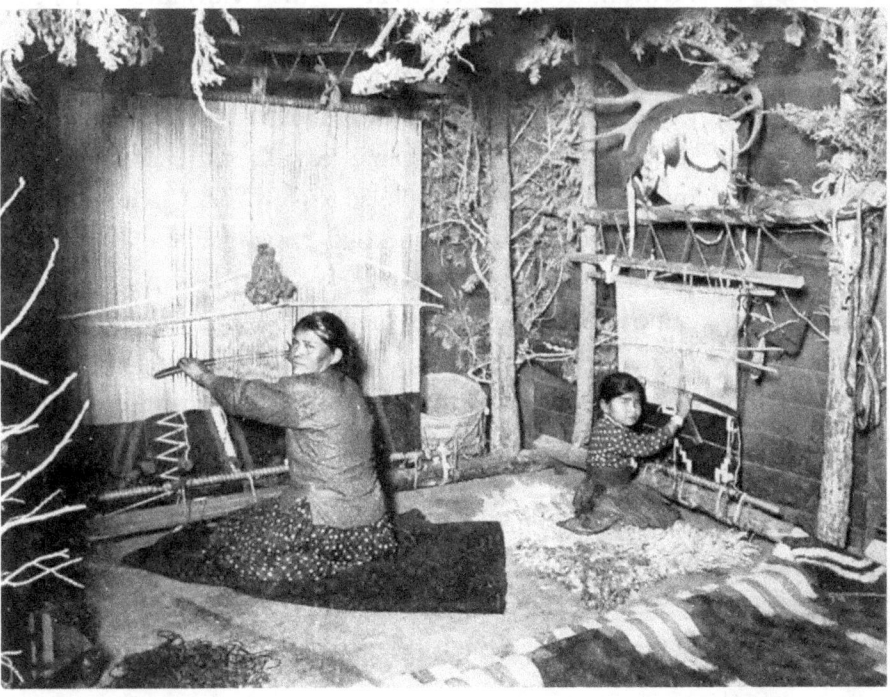

FIGURE 13 "Elle, of Ganado, Ariz., One of the Best Living Weavers," from George Wharton James, *Indian Blankets and Their Makers* (1914; New York: Tudor Publishing, 1937), plate 141.

gas lamps, and champagne.[92] Department stores were committed to the ideals of order and hierarchy. These values are implicit in the separation of goods into different departments and into areas geared toward shoppers with different amounts of money to spend. At the same time the presence of diverse objects in the same space encouraged comparison between them. The juxtapositions provided within department stores allowed Native arts to be valued in a variety of ways from works of art, to children's toys, to utilitarian objects. This is no less true in ads. For example, while some ads listed Native goods alongside exotic wares from the Far East, others compared Indian objects to similar goods made in Germany or England, presenting their value in terms of utility and affordability.

The exoticism of Native American art was another selling point. It is significant, however, that this exoticism played out across the shopfloor. This point is well illustrated by a display of linens assembled into a diorama of Venice reproduced in Baum's manual on dry goods marketing (figure 14). Significantly, the "Indian Section" of Wanamaker's was located adjacent to, and sometimes within, the "Oriental" department, something that reminds us that earlier marketers of Native American art routinely used the successful marketing of Japanese goods as a model and a referent. One ad reads "Orient and Occident alike contribute lavishly to the vividly interesting collection held by our . . . Curio Store." The claim is followed by a list of wares from America, Japan, China, and the Near East.[93]

The weaver in Wanamaker's store in 1901 may have been a craftsperson who had worked at the Buffalo Fair that same year. She may have also been one of the many Indian people who had moved to New York City after studying at a boarding school in the hopes of finding employment and, perhaps, of living in the modern metropolis. The pages of local newspapers of the time frequently featured stories of Indian men and women working as janitors or factory workers who enhanced their income by serving as "professional Indians" when the opportunity presented itself—posing for artists, participating in pageants, or making "Indian" art.[94]

Many of these individuals who made money "playing Indian" had attended U.S. government boarding schools or otherwise been subject to federal efforts to assimilate Indian people into mainstream society. Indian schools and religious and secular reservation reform projects pursued this goal by immersing Native people in the English language, Christian religion, and

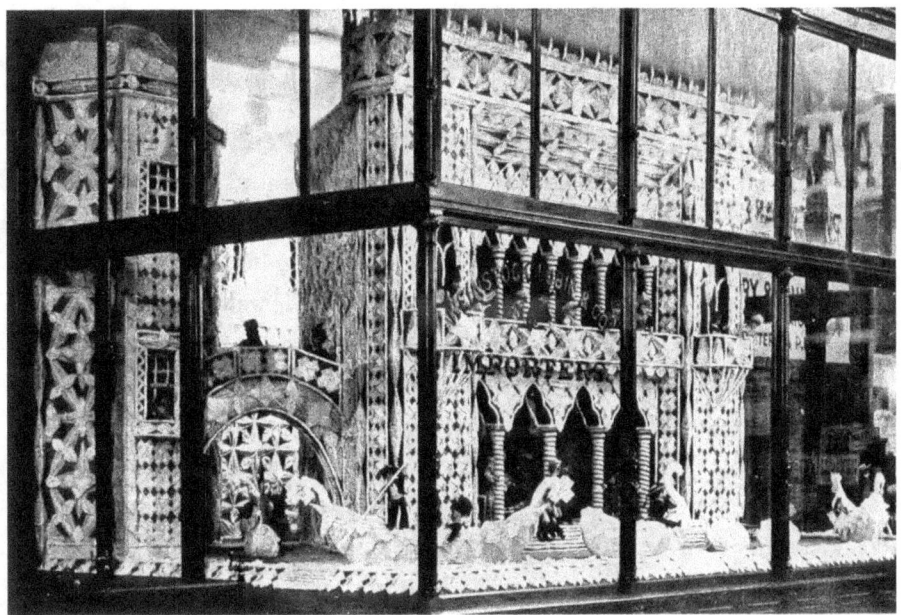

FIGURE 14 "A Scene in Venice," from L. Frank Baum, *The Art of Decorating Dry Goods Windows and Interiors: A complete manual of window trimming, designed as an educator in all the details of the art, according to the best accepted methods, and treating fully every important subject* (Chicago: Show Window Publishing, 1900), 107. Rare Book and Manuscript Library, Columbia University, New York.

Western notions of individuality. As these efforts coincided with the arrival of the "culture of consumption," reformers incorporated wage labor and the concept of therapeutic consumption into Indian education (for more on this, see chapter 2). But Indian people also learned of the mainstream desire to see them engaged in nonindustrialized work and through this became indoctrinated in the exhibitionary complex.

If we want a full understanding of the marketing of Native American art at this time, we must consider the fact that Indian people may also have made up a portion of the department store's urban clientele. Indian shoppers were participants in the culture of consumption, but they also brought their own experiences of discrimination to bear on their understanding of how indigenous art was sold. The complexity of this experience might be extrapolated from the experiences of Luther Standing Bear, an Oglala Sioux leader who was educated at the Carlisle Indian Industrial School. As he recounts in his memoir *My People the Sioux*, Standing Bear became particularly familiar with the culture of consumption when he went to work in Wanamaker's Grand Depot.[95] The origin of the job was philanthropic. John

Wanamaker had visited Carlisle and had been impressed with the ambition of the school head, Richard Henry Pratt, to inculcate a superior moral integrity and work ethic on his students. According to Standing Bear, who had internalized much of Pratt's social Darwinism, Wanamaker invited Pratt to send two boys to work in the store to help demonstrate the capacity of Indian people to be "civilized." Starting out as a clerk, Standing Bear was quickly promoted to a job on the floor, where he worked locked inside a glass vault, unpacking and labeling precious jewelry. Having literally entered the display case, Standing Bear could be seen as having a particularly acute experience of the department store's staging of private character. His hard work, his honesty, and of course his exoticism were all part of the show. Standing Bear later put this familiarity with staging the self to use as a performer with Buffalo Bill Cody's *Wild West* troupe and an actor in western films. During these experiences, Standing Bear worked to improve the conditions of Indian people employed in these exhibitionary positions, negotiating travel itineraries with Cody in the 1890s and helping to organize Indian labor in the film industry in the 1910s.

Natives who hadn't been to boarding schools as Standing Bear had could also respond critically to modern life. This can be seen in developments in indigenous art. Consider the famous "railroad blanket" that was part of George Wharton James's collection[96] (see figure 15; the blanket is also visible in figure 7). The multicolored blanket depicts a crowded scene of trains crossing and recrossing the pictorial space. The trains pull people, cattle, and cargo and, in an ingenious touch, a sleeping car with passengers depicted on stacked berths. In a possibly spurious account, James noted that the weaver traveled to Gallup to examine the trains that had begun invading the fields around her home in the 1880s.[97] Regardless of the weaver's actions, the blanket seems to give visual form to destabilizing experiences of a modern annihilation of time and space. Birds take flight and people crowd together as if disturbed by the intrusion of this powerful machine into their world. The asymmetrical design contradicts the stability and order that are the hallmarks of earlier Navajo weaving, suggesting a surge in creativity inspired by the disruptions of history.

When Indian handicrafts appeared in Indian corners, they *were* cut off from the meanings and uses they had traditionally held in their tribal communities. But this was part of a larger transformation being experienced

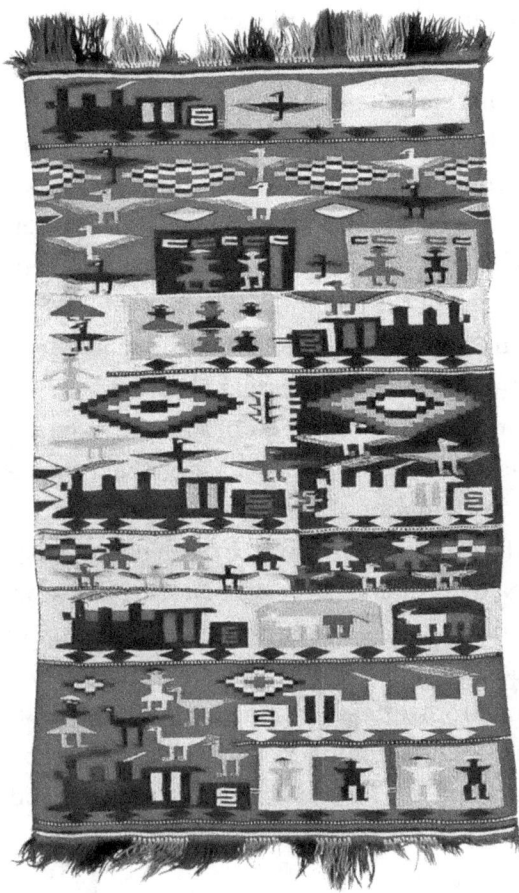

FIGURE 15 Unknown Navajo weaver, Germantown blanket, ca. 1880. Wool with natural and synthetic dyes. San Diego Museum of Man.

and responded to in Native America. While I do not want to downplay the ongoing damage caused to Indian people by this history, it is useful to look more closely at how Native material culture records an intercultural response to the disruptions of modernity, criticizing it while embracing its underlying structures, using it to create points of identification and distinction between cultures. Ruth Phillips has recently argued for a need to study indigenous objects made for intercultural markets as a means of coming to terms with the Native experience of modern history. She writes that such objects, long rejected by the critics informed by the primitivism of the early twentieth century as "inauthentic," simultaneously reinforce cultural divisions between Native and non-Native culture and break them down. She explains that while they led to a fixing of iconographic and generic types, "the exchanges themselves were inherently dynamic, continually destabilizing the stereotypes by stimulating new appropriative acts that threatened, in turn, to blur the outlines of otherness that defined each of the parties involved."[98] Thus we might see handicraft production as part of a complex indigenous reaction to the profound pressures to adopt mainstream cultural, economic and political values during this period.

This chapter has argued that while Native American material art is often thought of as a collectible available only to adventurous tourists, it was in fact widely available in the early years of the twentieth century. Urban consumers encountered Indian handicrafts in the same contexts in which they came in contact with other commodities, and collecting Native American art was part of a broader exploration of commodity culture. Rejecting rhetoric that would describe the taste for Native art as conservative or anti-modern, I propose that both the consumption and the production of Native American art of this time was quintessentially modern. In the chapters that follow, I continue to integrate Native American art and Native American people with a discussion of the cultural and aesthetic developments facing the country as a whole at that time. My purpose is not to erase the difference between the experiences of people from different ethnic backgrounds, but, rather, to see these differences as essential to understanding the landscape of modernization, something Indian people have experienced intensely and responded to in a variety of ways.

The Indians as a people must be led to see the importance of developing the work they are so gifted in doing, and to help supply the market's demands; and thus take a long step in the direction of self-support; which, after all, is the end of all Indian Education.
Estelle Reel

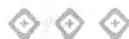

The White Man's Indian Art

TEACHING AESTHETICS AT THE INDIAN SCHOOLS

In 1904, the superintendent of Indian schools, Estelle Reel, visited the government boarding school in Albuquerque and discovered Navajo students so eager to weave that they had used the legs of upturned chairs to frame their looms.[1] Reel's encounter in Albuquerque made a deep impression. Shortly after her return, she recommended the hiring of Navajo women to teach weaving as part of the school's vocational training. Her welcoming attitude toward Native art was not limited to the curriculum at this school. As part of the *Uniform Course of Study* she had issued in 1901, Reel encouraged United States Indian school superintendents to implement courses in Native American artistic traditions at both day and boarding schools, using local Native craftspeople as teachers.[2] Indian service publications came to refer to this as the "Native industries" curriculum.

We can't see what Reel saw, but a photograph from the Phoenix Indian school in 1903 recalls this anecdote (see figure 16). It shows students working side by side on a makeshift loom frame fashioned from what appears to be a bedpost. Posed behind their work with their hands intertwined with the strings of the warp, the weavers seem to be comfortable, literally at one, with their work. The photograph

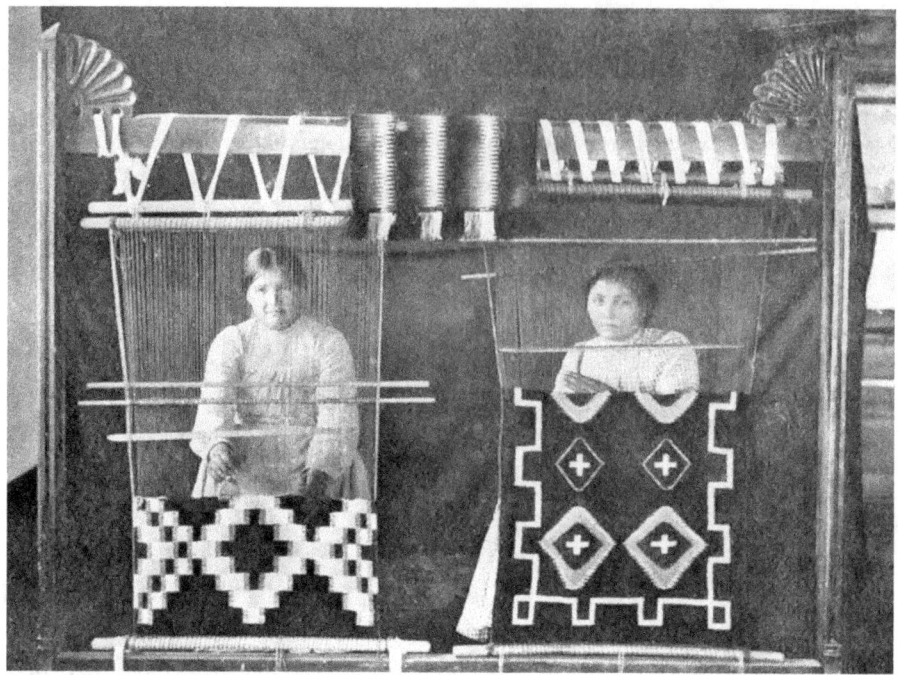

FIGURE 16 "Teaching Blanket Weaving, Phoenix Indian School, Arizona," from *The Report of the Superintendent of Indian Schools to the Secretary of the Interior for the Year 1903* (Washington, D.C.: Government Printing Office, 1904), facing 20.

suggests the aesthetic values ascribed to Native American art by the promoters discussed in chapter 1, for it suggests that art is a natural outflowing of Indian identity. It is hard to imagine a better illustration of William Morris's conception of the joyful artist. The straight, even lines of their blankets demonstrate the careful attention they've shown their craft, while the fact that they are working two very different designs expresses their independence and originality. Despite the fact that they are working in a "traditional" medium, these young women are making handicrafts that live up to modern ideals in both production and final product.

Viewers would have celebrated these young women for perpetuating what they saw as an ancient tradition. As explained in chapter 1, however, Navajo weaving can be better understood as a practice that developed continually, in response to changing historical circumstances. As such, we can best understand the textiles of the turn of the century as "modern" works. The rectilinear border on the textile to the right reinforces this, as this innovation developed to accommodate the European American market for rugs (borders were inconsistent with the aesthetics of wearing blankets).³ If James's "railroad blanket" (see figure 15) responds in part to the encroachment of European Americans and their products into the Navajo world, the textiles made at the government Indian schools reflect an even more radical displacement—the removal of young weavers to the world of the boarding school, where their production and their products would be evaluated primarily by teachers and other government employees.

This chapter examines the Native industries curriculum, which was in place for nearly a decade. Short-lived and never strongly supported by school administrators, these programs were hardly the focus of Indian education during these years. But Reel's reports and her private collection of clippings from 1901 to 1909 trace the spread of Native industries across the country. She records instruction in Indian handicrafts at thirty-five schools, and this number may be incomplete, as her reports often focus on only one part of a school's performance and because Reel was not able to inspect all schools regularly. Nevertheless, over 10 percent of government-funded day schools, on-reservation boarding schools, and off-reservation boarding schools participated in this program. Uneven implementation aside, the Native industries program was the aspect of Native education that received the most public attention in these years, in no small part because Reel held frequent exhibitions of student work.

In its own time, Native industries was praised as turning away from the traditional federal rejection of "traditional" Native culture. More recently, scholars have looked at this and similar programs in an attempt to categorize "good" and "bad" periods of Indian administration.⁴ Such diagnoses are problematic, not only because Reel implemented policies that demanded the eradication of Native culture in other spheres, but also, and more importantly, because such assessments can unwittingly reinforce notions of cultural authenticity that obscure ways in which so-called traditional culture is historically shaped by both Native and non-Native forces.

As I will argue below, the significance of Reel's curriculum reaches beyond the history of Indian education; it is part of an overlap of aesthetic and social concerns that were brought to bear on American educational and reform programs directed at the working classes. As such, it illustrates the contradictory goals of educators and reformers of the time, which simultaneously sought to ameliorate the drudgery of industrial labor by developing the workers' individuality but at the same time was focused on improving industrial labor. At the same time, the Native industries curriculum illustrates a problem peculiar to the Native sector of this workforce, which is the essentialist idea that Native American identity characterized the nature and quality of Indian work. The curriculum simultaneously supports two contradictory notions of ethnic identity: an older model in which racial characteristics might be transcended through the process of "civilization" and a new model emerging at the beginning of the twentieth century in the work of ethnologist Franz Boas and others, valuing cultural difference over cultural hierarchy.[5]

Robert Berkhofer's 1978 book *The White Man's Indian* argues that mainstream American representations of Indian people were always skewed by the intellectual trends affecting Euro-America.[6] This is certainly the case for the Native industries curriculum. Under the guise of preserving "traditional" art, Reel's programs borrowed heavily from mainstream efforts to ameliorate industrial work through handicrafts. As I show below, Reel was particularly indebted to two groups working with immigrants and other members of the urban working class: social reformers and progressive educators.

Reel's investment in indigenous "tradition" is thus deceptive. Close analysis of photographs and written accounts reveals that Native industries courses gave Indian school students a rigorous grounding in mainstream ideas about both art and cultural identity. Rather than seeing this experience as encouraging them to turn away from an authentic Native identity, I see it as part of the long-standing engagement of Indian people with their changing conditions. As for the reservation-based craftspeople supplying the demands of the Indian craze, Native industries' students faced the forces of modernity, often occurred in ways that were beyond their control. Like their counterparts on the reservation, however, they were also able to find ways to make their participation in the Indian craze meaningful.

INDIANS AND INDUSTRIAL EDUCATION

The interest in having Native students perpetuate tribal traditions, and to do so under the leadership of a local Indian teacher, seemed to contradict the historical goal of government-funded Indian education, which was focused on turning tribal people into American citizens. However, Reel's ideas were less at odds with U.S. policy than may first appear. In order to understand her goals, it is useful to rehearse the evolution of that policy.

While non-Indians have run schools for Native Americans for centuries, Reel's career occurred during a period of increased governmental control over Native education. Ulysses S. Grant's "Peace Policy" delegated Indian education to missionaries based on reservations, but an experiment in rehabilitating Plains Indian prisoners through education at the military's Fort Marion in Saint Augustine, Florida, in the mid-1870s led to the establishment of government-funded off-reservation boarding schools. The first such program was established in 1878 at the Hampton Institute in Virginia, a school that had originally been founded for former slaves. In 1879, the Indian Industrial School opened in former army barracks in Carlisle, Pennsylvania, under the leadership of Richard Henry Pratt, the army officer who had been in charge of the Fort Marion prisoners. Both schools attracted substantial attention from the mainstream press, Indian reformers, and government officials as demonstrating the potential role of education in solving the "Indian problem."[7]

The appointment of Thomas J. Morgan as commissioner of Indian affairs a decade later marked the first efforts to create a unified Indian educational policy. Morgan's administration called for increased centralization of the Indian school system. The schools also stepped up efforts for enrollment of all Indian children, often against their own or their families' will. In 1877 there were 48 Indian boarding schools and 102 day schools, with a total average attendance of 3,598 pupils. By 1900, 307 schools had charge of 21,568 pupils.[8] While enrollment numbers were inflated, and students frequently ran away, the 1900 number represented roughly half of the Indian youth living within the boundaries of the United States.

A year into his job, Morgan issued a brief circular titled *Indian Education*, which outlined his goals for the Indian school system. His primary focus was on the transformation of Indian character. Schools should focus on instilling qualities he associated with his own culture, including "the fear of God and respect for the rights of others; love of truth and fidelity to duty; personal purity, philanthropy, and patriotism."[9] He saw this as essential to the eventual integration of Indian people into mainstream society, and he promoted the breakdown of tribal identity by advocating tribally mixed schools in which children were required to speak English, wear Western dress, and answer to new, Anglicized names. He also praised the Dawes Act of 1887, which called for the division and distribution of land held communally by tribes, a process known as allotment.

Morgan defined the chief problem inhibiting Native assimilation as the Indian's inherent aversion to work, a stereotype that had long been used to explain what might also be described as indigenous resistance to colonial control of their labor. He asked teachers to lead their pupils away from "indolence and indifference" into "habits of industry and love of learning."[10] Morgan's circular established an emphasis on industrial education that dominated government policy in the following decades. Morgan was also interested in applying mainstream educational principles in the Indian schools, something that became central to Reel's work.

The vocational training offered by the Carlisle school provided the first model of industrial training used in the Indian school system. Pratt's program split the day into two equal halves, one devoted to classroom work and the other to labor. Students learned trades by providing the domestic and agricultural services needed to keep the school running, and theoretically to prepare students to seek work off the reservation. Despite being made late in Pratt's career, Frances Benjamin Johnston's photograph of the tin shop at Carlisle illustrates his goals (see figure 17). The picture shows young men in Western dress and regimental haircuts in a spacious and well-stocked workshop. They do not look up from their work to address the photographer, but rather concentrate on the various tasks in which they are engaged: cutting, shaping, and assembling tin cups and pitchers. This steady work has obviously been productive: one boy carries two loads of pitchers across the center of the composition, and the walls at the back are filled with shelves more of pitchers and clusters of cups waiting to be taken to other destinations.

Student labor provided for many of the school's needs—producing and preparing food, sewing and laundering, and even making table wares, as Johnston's photograph suggests. Pratt also developed the "outing" system, whereby students were hired out as laborers for non-Indian families, particularly during school holidays. Pratt distinguished this work from pure manual wage labor by emphasizing the idea that living and working among non-Indians would contribute to the students' "Americanization."

K. Tsianina Lomawaima, a historian of Indian education, has suggested

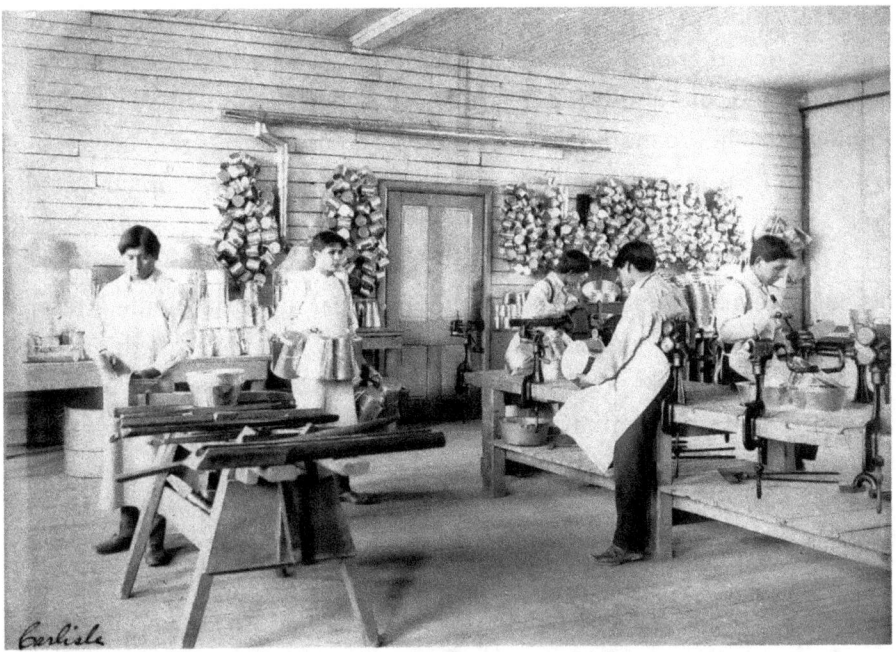

FIGURE 17 Frances Benjamin Johnston, photograph of five boys making tin utensils, Carlisle Indian Industrial School, Carlisle, Pennsylvania, ca. 1900. Inv. no. LC-USZ62–95795, Frances Benjamin Johnston Collection, Library of Congress, Prints and Photographs Division, Washington, D.C.

that manual training in the Indian schools was directed more toward the development of subservience than providing specific vocational goals, especially for women.[11] Luther Standing Bear, who learned tinsmithing at Carlisle, later described this training as a waste, as neither urban manufactures nor reservation life had much need for tinsmiths.[12] We can see these lessons also inculcating students with mainstream ideas about social organization. For example, the skills taught at Carlisle reflected the gendered division of labor of the time: boys were taught agricultural work, carpentry, harness making, and tinsmithing; girls studied cooking, sewing, laundering, and nursing.

Pratt famously argued that the job of the Indian schools was to "kill the Indian and save the Man inside," but many working with Native students had a more nuanced attitude toward the practicality if not the desirability of eradicating Native identity.[13] This situation had both practical and philosophical sources. One problem was the fact that few Indian school graduates actually integrated into mainstream society. Many Native pupils returned to the reservation after their schooling because their mediocre education and the entrenched racism of American society posed barriers to finding employment and community in the city. Those Indian people who succeeded in finding work in urban milieux continuously confronted entrenched stereotypes about "primitive" Indians, which were regularly reinforced by *Wild West* shows, popular literature, and early film. Clearly, many students also felt a longing to rejoin home and family. Lomawaima has argued that Indian boarding schools sometimes strengthened tribal identities while attempting to break them down. Pointing out that they were overfilled with students and frequently understaffed, she suggests boarding schools produced a "culture that was created and sustained by students much more than by teachers or staff."[14] Under these circumstances, pupils found ways to maintain old forms of tribal identity and forge new ones despite the restrictive policies of the time.

Mainstream society continued to expect Native Americans to be Indians despite their education, and Indian people themselves were reluctant to relinquish their tribal heritages. This situation no doubt helped prompt Reel to seek out ways in which the Indian schools could nourish Native cultural expression in a way that didn't threaten the overarching goals of assimilating Native people to U.S. values and governmental control. Significantly, this experiment had already been begun by Reel's predecessor, William N. Hailmann. During Hailmann's administration, teachers began inviting students to write down tribal tales as an exercise in written English. Many of these were reprinted in school newspapers that circulated among bureaucrats and charitable supporters of Indian education. The tales not only demonstrated the students' growing mastery of their new language, they also appealed to the interest in "traditional" culture among readers of non-Indian newspapers. As David Wallace Adams has explained, Hailmann saw this as a way to reinforce the characteristics the schools sought to inculcate in them: if teachers would "seek to better understand the positive attributes of their students' native heritage" it would "'foster . . . these seeds of high character in the children intrusted to his care."[15] In his first year in office, Hailmann even speculated that the schools might benefit from adding courses in "local Indian industries, such as tanning and pottery among the Pueblos, blanket-weaving and silverwork among the Navajoes."[16] Hailmann's reports don't indicate if this directive was followed, but his ideas created a welcoming environment for Reel's reforms.

Reel assumed the position of superintendent of Indian schools in 1898, during the McKinley administration, and she was reappointed by Presidents Roosevelt and Taft, retiring when she got married, to a Washington rancher named Cort Meyer, in 1910. Reel had begun her educational career in Wyoming, serving first as a teacher and later as the state supervisor of public instruction. Her achievement of this prominent public office reflects the powerful role of women in western politics at the time, and some have attributed her appointment to the Indian school service to Republican Party politics.[17] Whether or not this is true, her successful retention of the position of superintendent of Indian schools reflects her ability to link Indian education with mainstream pedagogical trends and her talent for self-promotion.

Reel's position made her one of the highest-paid women in the country (she earned $3,000 a year and had a $1,500 travel allowance), which in turn made her something of a celebrity. Her personal papers include numerous newspaper articles, compiled by a clipping service, that record not only her evolving professional policies, but also discussions of her youth and charm and descriptions of her wild adventures while touring the country to inspect schools. Many clippings heralded the arrival of Reel's *Course of Study*, and several specifically noted the Native industries curriculum. These clippings give further insight into Reel's motivations, for they routinely identify basketmaking and other handicraft traditions as an "industry" with potential to make students "self-supporting."[18]

In focusing on a source of income that might be pursued on the reservation, the superintendent was responding to the changing conception of the Indian school system's goals. By the beginning of the twentieth century, both the Indian service and the mainstream public were questioning the feasibility and, in some cases, the desirability of assimilation. Racism prevented many Indian school graduates from finding work in mainstream communities and many either joined the Indian service or returned to their reservations. During Reel's administration the system gradually shifted emphasis away from the boarding schools in the East to boarding and day schools on the reservation, where education could be more tailored to preparing for occupations suited to their postschool lives in local communities.[19] But Reel's work also brings the Indian schools into broader public debates about art and education. Of particular note is the introduction of art into the public school curriculum by aesthetic reformers dedicated to raising the taste, and thus both the character and the skill of the next generation of industrial workers. Before exploring this aesthetic form of manual training, however, it is necessary to describe Native industries' goals and accomplishments more fully.

THE SCOPE OF NATIVE INDUSTRIES

Discussions of the origins of formal art education in the government Indian school system often begin with Dorothy Dunn's establishment of the studio at the Santa Fe Indian school in 1932, an art program that built on the connections between Pueblo painters and avant-garde artists in the Southwest in the preceding fifteen years.[20] The hostility with which the Bureau of Indian Affairs met the drawing classes offered by Dunn's predecessor Elizabeth DeHuff, wife of the school's superintendent, in 1918, has been seen as evidence that the U.S. Indian administration would not tolerate art education earlier than that. More recently, however, scholars have acknowledged that Esther Hoyt encouraged her students at the San Ildefonso Day School to make watercolors as early as 1900.[21] While Hoyt's interest in Indian art is often thought of as an exception to the Indian service's emphasis on assimilation, her introduction of drawing in the classroom was far from unique. Drawing was part of the curriculum at Hampton and Carlisle, where it was understood as both an essential part of a liberal arts education and a mode of self-expression.[22] Hoyt's interest in art as a means of cultural expression fits Hailmann's interest in this subject and coincides with Reel's national effort to develop handicraft production in the Indian schools.

The introduction of Native industries first appeared in a chapter of Reel's 1901 *Course of Study*. Though this chapter is titled "Basketry and Caning," it quickly becomes clear that Reel's interests extend beyond those topics. The chapter begins with a letter addressed to reservation agents and Indian school superintendents: "It is desired by the Indian Bureau that basketry be taught in the Indian schools. Will you please furnish this office with the names of basket makers on your reservation, sending specimens of the work they can do, and giving all information concerning them that may be of interest and use in the furtherance of this project."[23] Further down the page, Reel also suggests the desirability of hiring weavers, potters, and beadworkers at schools populated by pupils from tribes that excel in those techniques.

Subsequent annual reports from the superintendent's office reflect a variety of artistic traditions being taught. There seems to have been an attempt in many locations to follow local traditions, particularly beadwork in Great Lakes and Plains schools and weaving at southwestern schools with Navajo pupils. Cherokee students studied basketry and pottery, two long-standing local traditions, as well as beadwork. Schools with mixed population taught a variety of mediums.

The Native industries curriculum was not taken up in a systematic manner. Some schools integrated handicraft instruction into classroom work, while others lumped it with vocational training. At many Indian schools, such as the school in Grand Junction, Colorado, Native handicraft traditions were subsumed under "sewing" lessons. In some of these cases, handicrafts were not taught, but students who arrived with artistic training were allowed to continue their work. For example, the annual report of the superintendent of the Red Moon Boarding School on the Cheyenne/Arapaho reservation noted that girls' industrial training focused on sewing, but "when not otherwise employed they have been allowed to make moccasins and other bead work common to their tribe."[24] The matron in charge of the sewing room at the Indian school in Phoenix similarly reported in 1905 that four girls who had arrived with training were allowed to continue weaving.[25] Some of the schools Reel includes on her list of Native industries programs merely encouraged handicraft production during students' leisure time. Joseph C. Hart, superintendent of the Oneida Indian School, reported to Reel that the collection of beadwork he sent her was "filled from work done in spare hours which might otherwise have been spent in idleness or even less profitably."[26]

Basketry dominated the curriculum, even when it was not the best known local product. For example, the Apsáalooke (or Crow) peoples are more known for their beadwork than basketry. Women artists of this nation demonstrated design sensibility and mastery of materials that made their beadwork a coveted trade item across the Great Plains in the nineteenth century.[27] Reel's records indicate that both basketry and beadwork were

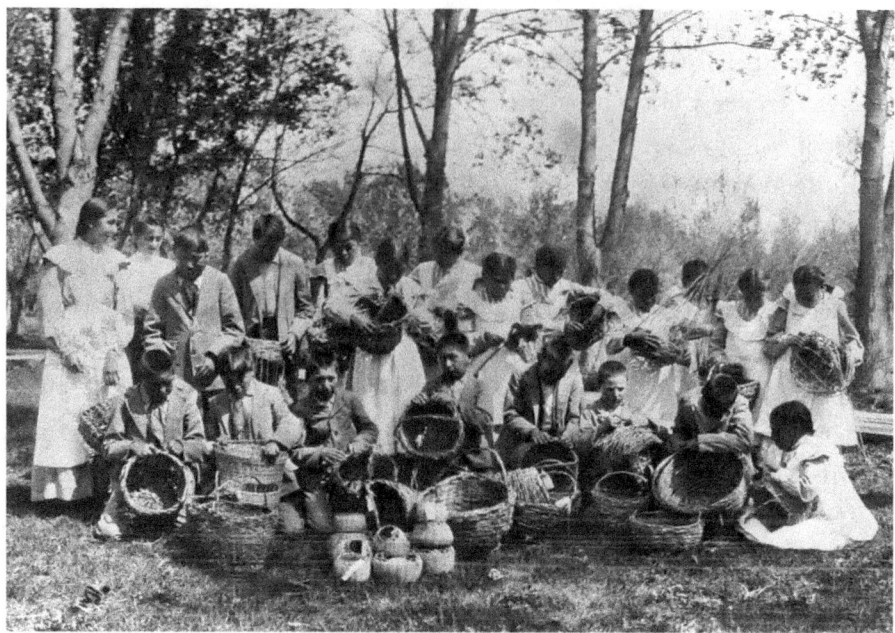

FIGURE 18 Students at the Crow boarding school, Crow Agency, Montana, n.d. (ca. 1903). Estelle Reel Collection, Northwest Museum of Arts and Culture, Spokane, Washington.

taught at the Crow Agency school in Montana. However, a photograph suggests that this school did not use Native industries as a means of perpetuating tribal identity (see figure 18). The children pose in Euro-American ties and pinafores, holding coarsely woven wicker baskets with little "Native" character. Presumably instructors did not know or care that in preparing students to participate in mainstream handicraft production, they were discouraging the continuation of what had once been a thriving trade. But this overlay of older craft traditions with new ones was not an innovation of the Indian schools, nor was this interest in developing handicraft-based industries focused exclusively on Native communities.

THE SOURCES OF NATIVE INDUSTRIES

Reel's *Course of Study* proclaims: "The basketry as woven by Indians for generations past is fast becoming a lost art and must be revived by the children of the present generation." Immediately following, however, Reel identifies the value of Native handicrafts as their potential to compete in a global economy. Students must take up handicraft production, "[so] that they may take their rightful place among the leading basketmakers of the world and supply the demands of the markets for such baskets" (54). Reel also argues that Native industries will stimulate what she calls "race pride," but she reveals that the students' responsibility is less to their own communities than to a national market.

Reel's use of the term "industries" to describe Native artistic traditions fits the Indian school service's historical emphasis on vocational training, but it has more specific sources that link this history to a broader American interrogation of the proper place of industrialism in modern life, and the plight of workers in industrialism. Reel drew on several strains of this inquiry. Her rhetoric draws extensively on that of social reformers who saw art making as noble labor that enhanced the laborer's self-worth while building ties between members of different classes and social groups. At the same time, as an education professional, she borrowed from the manual training movement, which sought to use education to better equip future laborers for their work. Both of these factions built on the ideas of the arts and crafts movement, with its emphasis on maintaining dignity in labor. As I argue below, however, each position was flawed, and the Native industries curriculum as implemented, perpetuated some of the drudgery and alienation of industrial work that it was designed to avoid.

ART AND SOCIAL REFORM

Missionaries and reformers working with Indian women had long used the term "industry" for their efforts to organize Native work along more mainstream lines, something undertaken to increase ties between their communities. An example of this work is Sybil Carter's Indian Lace Association. Carter began this work while serving as an Episcopalian missionary on the White Earth reservation of Anishinaabe in Minnesota in 1887. Her interest in teaching lace drew on her desire to give women an income-producing activity; like many women left without family support, Carter had turned to textile production as a source of money after the Civil War. Carter's "lace industry" quickly spread to other reservations in Minnesota and Wisconsin and eventually to southern California.[28] Her employees taught Indian women lace making, provided materials and patterns, and arranged sales of the finished products through religious and reform organizations on the East Coast. Promoters of their work emphasized the lace makers' ladylike appearance and their fine work (see figure 19).

FIGURE 19 "The Lace Makers of Minnesota, and Specimens of Their Handicraft," from *The Puritan*, April 1899, 32.

A speech made at a prominent meeting of Indian reformers, the annual gathering of the Friends of the Indian at Lake Mohonk, New York, in 1893 inspired other Indian reformers to organize the "Indian Industries League," initially a branch of the Woman's National Indian Association and then a freestanding organization. The league offered financial support to reservation-based handicraft projects organized by missionaries, U.S. government field matrons, and, on occasion, league employees, and marketed their products at meetings of reformers and through commercial venues.[29] League-supported projects include the Mohonk Lodge, a workshop established by Mr. and Mrs. Walter C. Roe, missionaries, where Cheyenne and Arapaho women produced beaded moccasins and other leather items in Colony, Oklahoma; the work of Josephine Foard, a field matron, with potters at the Laguna Pueblo; and Mrs. Mary Eldredge's involvement with Navajo weaving in Jewett, New Mexico.

As the use of French and Italian models by Carter's lace associations indicates, Indian industries were not necessarily dedicated to the perpetuation of Native artistic traditions. However, many reformers chose to build on traditions in which Indian craftspeople were already skilled, attempting to introduce "improvements" in these products to make them more market-able. For example, Carter encouraged Anishinaabe basket makers to pro-duce beaded birchbark napkin rings, Foard introduced chemical glazes and kiln-firing to her Pueblo collaborators, and Eldredge encouraged Navajo women to conduct their work in her specially constructed "industrial room." These alterations were designed to exert an influence over Indian artistic production, "modernizing" and "Americanizing" it. As Frances Sparhawk, secretary of the Indian Industries League, wrote of Eldredge's project in 1893, "The room is not merely for the weaving of their old-time Navajo rugs, so justly famous, but its purpose is expressly to be a place of initiation for these women into work of many kinds, and into our ways of doing work; and to lead them up to modern methods of weaving; also, as far as possible, to teach them to exchange their present desultory methods of work for that regularity necessary to wage-earners."[30]

The Indian Industries League clearly influenced Reel's decision to pro-mote Native industries. Reel had direct connections to the league: her papers include correspondence with the league secretary Doubleday and participation in Indian reform conferences. The curriculum was publicly praised by many supporters of the league's work, including Doubleday and the Californian Charles Lummis, author, editor, and museum founder. Shortly after issuing the *Course of Study*, Reel was invited to serve on the advisory board of Lummis's newly formed Sequoya League, an institution dedicated, in part, to "reviving, encouraging, and providing market for such of the aboriginal industries as can be made profitable."[31]

Sparhawk's words reveal the close ties that the Indian industries program had to industrial projects set up within other communities perceived as needing to learn modern work ethics at the time, including urban immi-grants and the rural poor. The 1890s witnessed the establishment of count-less handicraft projects at settlement houses and other social reform orga-nizations designed to create viable alternatives to factory work among these populations. Both the environments and the focus on craft production were understood to positively influence the participants, facilitating their assimi-lation of mainstream "American" values.[32] Significantly, reformers working with non-Indian communities used the same media as the league members in their work, including pottery (produced by Boston's Saturday Evening Girls) and weaving (the focus of an industrial project set up by Helen Albee in rural Maine), and even lace making (which was taught at settlement houses in New York and Boston)[33] (see plate 3). That urban reformers saw connections between their charges and Native Americans is illustrated at the best-known American settlement, Jane Addams's Hull House. Known for their commitment to arts and crafts principles, Addams and her colleague Ellen Gates Starr included a "Labor Museum" in the settlement, in which members of Chicago's immigrant communities could demonstrate and display traditional handicrafts. The room's displays included Navajo weaving and Pueblo pottery.

Observers of the time noted these similarities between the strategies of Indian reformers and urban activists working in immigrant communities, and tied the efforts of both to the goals of the arts and crafts movement. For example, in 1904 the U.S. Bureau of Labor issued a report by Max West titled "The Revival of Handicrafts in America" that listed handicraft industries around the country, including a majority of those mentioned above.[34] West explicitly linked Carter's, Roe's, and Doubleday's projects with Reel's work, including both in a section titled "Indian Work." More significantly, he referred to the potential of projects in both Indian and non-Indian communities to offer workers "a means of livelihood and a new interest in life" and providing consumers "increased pleasure in the things of daily household use and ornament."[35]

The actual work produced by Native industries students belies the optimism of West's statement. In general, the Indian industries programs encouraged students to produce small-scale, inexpensive items that would offer little help in resolving the economic and cultural challenges facing Indian people. The fate of Native industries was in many ways influenced by the same problems that hindered the success of the arts and crafts movement as a whole. As Eileen Boris has demonstrated, American art firms that strove to reform production through the implementation of the ideas of Morris and Ruskin were rarely successful at producing anything more than a cosmetic change, as the American arts and crafts movement was always indebted to industrial interests.[36] Some industrial teachers seem to have understood this problem. Lucy Hart, a teacher at Oneida Indian School who is discussed further below, acknowledged that the contribution her pupils could make was small, writing defensively that "the argument that such work has no value in itself and therefore should not be taught, has no force, for a real part of the world's people live by making little articles that other people want and are willing to pay for."[37] Hart's comment reveals that, while Indian handicraft projects aspired to give craftswomen the satisfaction of reaping economic rewards for satisfying work, her actual goals were much smaller.

ART AND MANUAL TRAINING

If the Native industries curriculum reveals the overlapping strategies of Indian reformers and those pursuing social reform in non-Indian communities, Reel's curriculum also demonstrates the interconnectedness of Indian schools and public education at this time. This makes sense, as Reel came to the Indian service from a mainstream educational system. Reel demonstrated an interest in educational theory early on. The *Course of Study* she produced for the Wyoming public schools demonstrates Reel's engagement with educational theory. It begins with a list of reference books on pedagogy that incorporates both instruction books and the treatises of educational theorists such as Johann Pestalozzi and Friedrich Froebel. By 1900, Reel was particularly interested in manual training, a pedagogical movement developed to serve the need of outfitting students to work in modern industrial society. She invited leaders in the field to address the Indian department at National Educational Association meetings more than once and in 1903 held a joint meeting with the manual training department.

In its most narrow definition, the American manual training movement had its roots in European vocational education. A Russian display at the 1876 Centennial Exhibition in Philadelphia focusing on workshop-based education for engineers and machinists inspired the creation of similar project-based training at the Massachusetts Institute of Technology and led to the establishment of the Manual Training School (a high school) in Saint Louis in 1879. These early experiments combined exercises dedicated to mastering basic principles of design and construction with their practical application. Other proponents of manual training distanced their work from purely technical or vocational education, stressing instead the idea that training in aesthetics and craftsmanship would develop in pupils a sense of design and a knowledge of production that could be applicable to a wide number of trades. Finally, some educators promoted manual training because of its links to modern theories of individual development and social organization.

They argued that children learn through sensory stimulation and physical activity as much as through memorization and composition, and thus incorporated drawing and craftwork into mainstream curricula in an effort to develop children's mental and physical capacities. Following G. Stanley Hall (who lectured to Indian educators at the National Educational Association annual meeting in 1903), they believed children relived human evolution as they grew, progressing from a kind of "savagery" toward eventual "civilization."[38] This belief made manual training particularly well suited to populations—Native Americans, African Americans, and southern and eastern European laborers—whom many understood as less "evolved" than Americans whose origins were in western and northern Europe.

As Jackson Lears has demonstrated, turn-of-the-century reformers believed in education's ability to resolve social tensions caused by immigration, worker unrest, and "an incipient leisure class" going soft.[39] For example, Nicholas Murray Butler argued that manual training could help future laborers understand the dignity of their work.[40] Meaningful work was an antidote to the most dehumanizing and polarizing aspects of industrialization. In a series of articles on manual training published in *The Craftsman* in 1904, editor Gustav Stickley linked education and social transformation: "to impart manual skill is to multiply the resources of the individual not only as regards his power to accumulate wealth but also permanently to acquire happiness."[41]

Manual training was frequently incorporated into schools dealing with populations who were perceived as unprepared for, or poorly served by, a traditional academic education, particularly those directed at the working classes or communities of color. Societal prejudices generally barred these populations from the social mobility Stickley describes, but turn-of-the-century intellectuals linked manual training with liberation. Booker T. Washington, with whom Reel was sometimes compared, embraced the notion, writing in 1903: "I plead for industrial education and development for the Negro not because I want to cramp him, but because I want to free him. I want to see him enter the all-powerful business and commercial world."[42] Educators sought to create community through a shared respect for labor. In a piece titled "Manual Training and Citizenship," Stickley celebrated the endorsement by the Russian socialist prince Kropotkin of mixing mental work and manual work in a community that brought together people of different nationalities and classes.[43] As another educator put it, "The arts make common ground on which the children of the native born and of the foreign born meet in happy, intelligent, and ceaseless activity."[44]

Reel's efforts make it clear that this common ground could also include American Indian people, who were frequently considered to be outsiders to modernity and civilization as much as the immigrant poor. Closer examination of her curricular goals helps explain how such an education could be geared not only to addressing the specific needs of Indian children but also to the larger project of integrating them into mainstream society. Reel frequently incorporated methods from the manual training in the Indian school curriculum. For example, her 1904 circular titled "Teaching Indian Pupils to Speak English" advocates the use of a sand table and miniature buildings and figurines as a means of engaging young pupils more actively in language acquisition.[45]

It is likely that Reel's decision to incorporate basketry into the Indian school curriculum was also influenced by the manual training movement, which had inspired the establishment of basketry courses in mainstream schools to familiarize students with ideas about materials and construction techniques. Significantly, the basketry curriculum Reel advocates has little Native character. She urges teachers to begin with Madagascar raffia, using lessons drawn from instruction books by Louise Walker, Annie Firth, and Mary White (see figure 20). While the 1901 editions of White's book included an essay on the value of Native basketry, written by Doubleday, these were not books designed to teach Indian traditions. Rather, they were texts in general use for mainstream elementary schools and hobbyists. Following these texts, a general classroom teacher would move from basic mats to small baskets and doll furniture and eventually begin caning the bottoms and backs of chairs. The illustrations of this section of Reel's curriculum are similarly deculturated, as can be seen in diagrams in which neither the maker nor the materials have a distinctive Native identity (see figure 21). The technique for starting a basket that is illustrated is a basic method used by many makers of twined baskets. The lack of distinctiveness is illustrated by the fact that Otis Mason used Mary White's work as the source of his own illustration of the technique.[46]

This association reveals that, as with the reformers' industrial projects, the promotion of "traditional" Native American art in the Indian schools

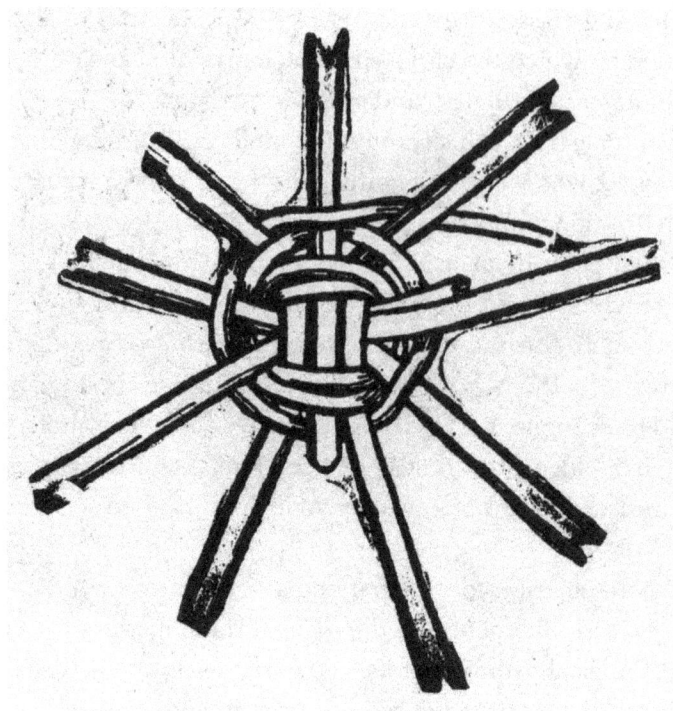

FIGURE 20
Illustration from
Mary White, *How to
Make Baskets* (New
York: Doubleday,
1901), 22, fig. 10.

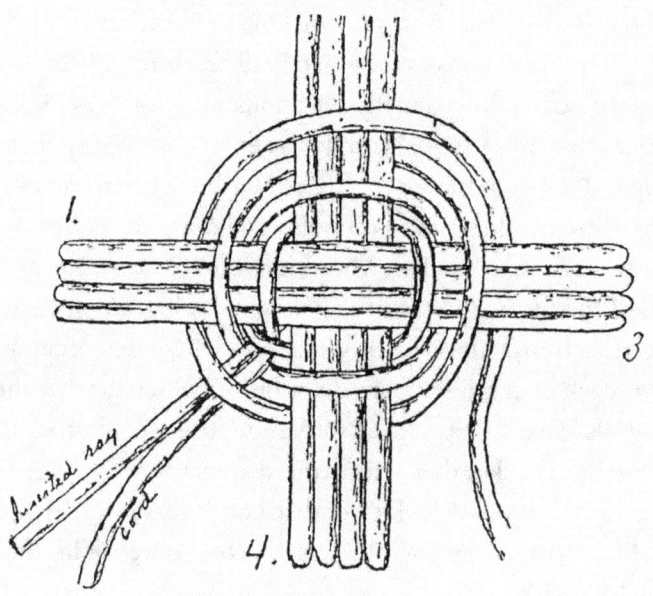

FIGURE 21
Basket-making
lesson, from
Estelle Reel,
*A Course of Study
for Indian Schools*
(Washington, D.C.:
Government
Printing Office,
1901), 212.

was linked with new, mainstream ideas. The early twentieth-century manual training movement was particularly interested in challenging the perceived distinction between applied and fine art. Many of the speakers in the manual training department meetings at the National Educational Association promoted the idea that art was defined by the maker's attitude rather than the form of the finished project.[47] This idea is closely associated with the arts and crafts movement, but as I will explore more fully in my next chapter, it was explored throughout the American art world in the early 1900s, influencing trends in painting and sculpture, art education, and art criticism, as well as the decorative arts community. Through the Native industries curriculum, some of these ideas infiltrated the Indian schools.

Promoters of manual training no doubt welcomed an alliance with the Indian department. Advocates of a destruction of the barrier between fine and applied arts frequently used the celebration of the aesthetic qualities of Native American art to support their goals, and this occurred in talks in the manual training department of the National Educational Association such as Ruby Hodge's "The Relation of Primitive Handicraft to Present-Day Educational Problems."[48] The joint meeting between the manual training and Indian departments in 1903 included a speech by George Wharton James titled "Indian Basketry — Its Poetry and Symbolism," which emphasized the idea that handicrafts are an expression of the makers' character and personality.[49]

Along these lines, Native industries were described as a "natural" application of innate Native talent. The *Course of Study* makes this essentialist notion clear, arguing, among other things, that they have "great finger skill," which makes craft production "particularly agreeable to Indians."[50] Another photograph of a student weaver seemingly supports this stereotype (figure 22). Yet this student of the Fort Lewis School in Colorado is not nearly as comfortable in front of the camera as the girls in the Phoenix photograph, nor is her blanket as flawless as theirs. The photograph, which was also published in one of the superintendent's annual reports (for 1902), highlights the academic nature of the Native industries curriculum. Behind the weaver is a blackboard being used to teach English. Drawings of a cup, a cat, a hat, a flag, and a book are accompanied by their English names written in cursive. The lesson has been copied over twice, suggesting the rote

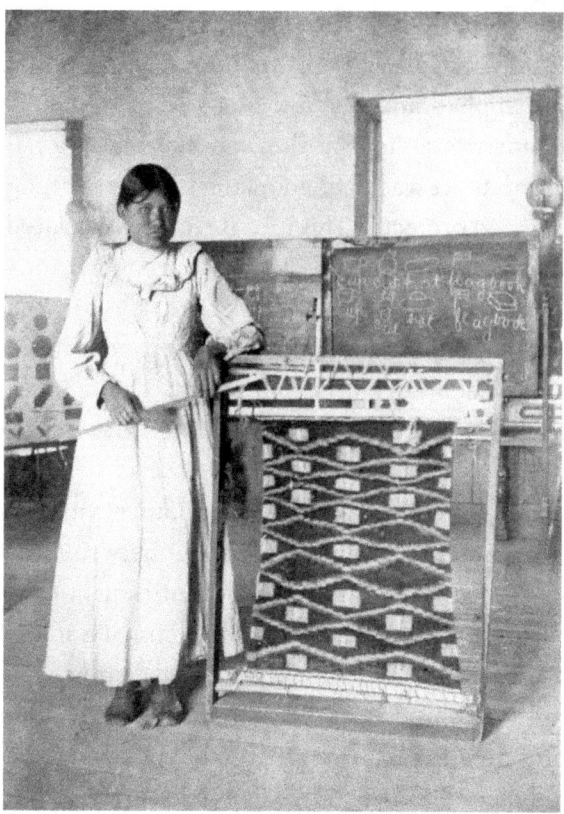

FIGURE 22 "Blanket Weaving in the Class Room as Suggested by the Course of Study, Fort Lewis School, Colorado," from *Report of the Superintendent of Indian Schools to the Commissioner of Indian Affairs for 1902* (Washington, D.C.: Government Printing Office, 1903), facing 20.

learning that was typical of the turn-of-the-century pedagogy. Indian pupils were taught a new language and new values by hard immersion, with little attempt to draw analogies to reservation life. The words chosen for this lesson represent aspects of the European American culture the school wanted its pupils to absorb along with the rudiments of writing: the cup and the cat as attributes of domesticity, the hat standing for Western dress. The flag and the book were probably the most potent symbols of government education—the authority of the federal government over the pupils and its use of the printed word to assert that authority and distance them from their oral traditions.

A chart of geometric shapes behind the student to the left calls to mind Winslow Homer's *Blackboard* of 1877 (figure 23), a sentimental celebration of the virtuous American educator. But while Homer's teacher is one with her hyperdisciplined environment, to the point of mimicking its lines and

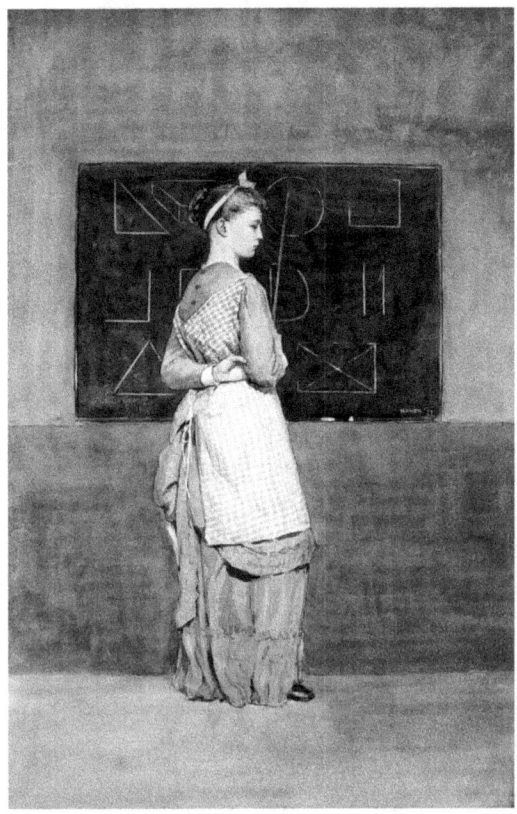

FIGURE 23 Winslow Homer, *Blackboard*, 1877. Watercolor on wove paper, 19 3/4 x 12 3/4 inches. National Gallery of Art, Washington, D.C. Gift (partial and promised) of Jo Ann and Julian Ganz Jr.

angles in the position of her body, the Indian girl chafes against her setting. Holding the pointer-like batten limply in front of her, she balances awkwardly on the outside of her left foot. The object with which the girl is supposed to be naturally comfortable seems to be the most out of place thing in the classroom.

Native industries were regularly praised as reversing the Indian schools' tendency to vilify everything Indian. The *Course of Study* claims, "The importance of preserving the Indian designs and shapes can not be overestimated. The object must be to weave the history and traditions of the tribe in all distinctively Indian work, thus making it historical, typical, and of value. ... Race pride should stimulate them to effort in preserving the work of the past."[51] But as this photograph shows, the appropriation of these traditions to support mainstream educational goals, and even the relocation of these activities to the colonial space of the Indian school, changed these activities, making them at best transcultural practices that partook of both Native and mainstream values and at worst, became another means of mainstream domination.

NATIVE INDUSTRIES AND
ARTS AND CRAFTS AESTHETICS

In their varied locations within the school, Native industries seem to have been taken most seriously in those parts of the country that already had a thriving intercultural handicraft trade, especially the Southwest, but also the Great Lakes, California, and the Pacific Northwest. Indeed, Reel's emphasis on basketry in the curriculum no doubt reflected the primacy of basketry in the commercial market for Native American art. Schools with Navajo children were particularly welcoming to Native industries. This may be related to the fact that schools around the Navajo reservation had a great deal of trouble attracting students, particularly female students, and that their ability to continue practicing a trade of cultural value that could also contribute economically to family welfare may have eased some families' reluctance.[52] The weavers seen in these photographs may have sent their products home to be sold through a local trader; they may also have sold work through the school itself. For sales of student work were an important aspect of the Indian industries curriculum. Some schools had sales rooms and some even advertised for mail-order sales. The Chilocco Indian Agricultural School promoted its shop, The Curio, with an advertisement published regularly in *The Indian School Journal* that read:

> A great injustice has been done true Indian Art by dealers in fake Indian curios. Believing that palming off factory-made imitations is calculated to degrade Indian Art in the eyes of the innocent public, an Indian Curio Store has been established at the Chilocco Indian Agricultural School, Chilocco, Okla. Blankets, Rugs, Moccasins, Baskets, Beaded Work and all manner of Indian hand-work are kept on hand. Indians on the reservation send these goods here to be sold, so you know that you are getting the "real article" when you buy Chilocco goods.[53]

Interestingly, the Indian schools also facilitated the sale of Native handicrafts through traders. Jonathan Batkin has noted that several traders took out advertisements in the schools' newspapers, which circulated widely among supporters of Indian reform; J. B. Moore of Crystal, New Mexico, even used the Indian Print Shop at Chilocco to print his catalogues of Navajo rugs.[54]

Reel's reports do not offer specific information about the money earned through the sale of student handicrafts, but in some places it was significant. The Camp McDowell Day School, located on a Yavapai reservation, reported the sale of seventy baskets for a total of $2550.50 in 1904.[55] After an exhibition of their work in Washington, D.C,. in 1903, during which they presented beaded gifts to President and Mrs. Roosevelt, Oneida students received orders for $50 in beadwork.[56] A 1905 article in Chilocco's *Indian School Journal* also notes the successful marketing of beaded fan chains, lamp shades, purses, and collars by students from the Chilocco (Oklahoma), Bena (Minnesota), Cheyenne (Oklahoma), and Fort Hall (Idaho) schools.[57] None of these records indicate sales prices for individual pieces, nor do they reveal whether students received any of the income. At the beginning of the boarding school era, Fort Marion prisoners had made artwork for sale and had been allowed to keep the proceeds. Teachers felt this would encourage them to see the benefits of wage labor, but drawing may also have had the unintended consequence of providing the Plains warriors with a connection to their own cultural values.[58] The captives drew on the tradition of men's narrative painting, which celebrated the artist's accomplishments in war and hunting. They applied this tradition to drawings made with ink and colored pencil that captured their experiences of mainstream culture. The drawing of uniform-clad prisoners and their European American teachers at the Fort Marion school made by the Cheyenne captive Chief Killer captures the regimented atmosphere that persisted in Indian education under Reel a quarter-century later (see figure 24).

Sales of student work frequently occurred in the context of government exhibitions. The U.S. government had included exhibits on the Indian schools in the government buildings at World's Fairs since the 1893 World's Columbian Exposition in Chicago. Reel continued this tradition but also sought out other venues; for example, she frequently created displays for the annual meetings of the National Educational Association. These exhibitions were responsible for a large number of positive press clippings in Reel's

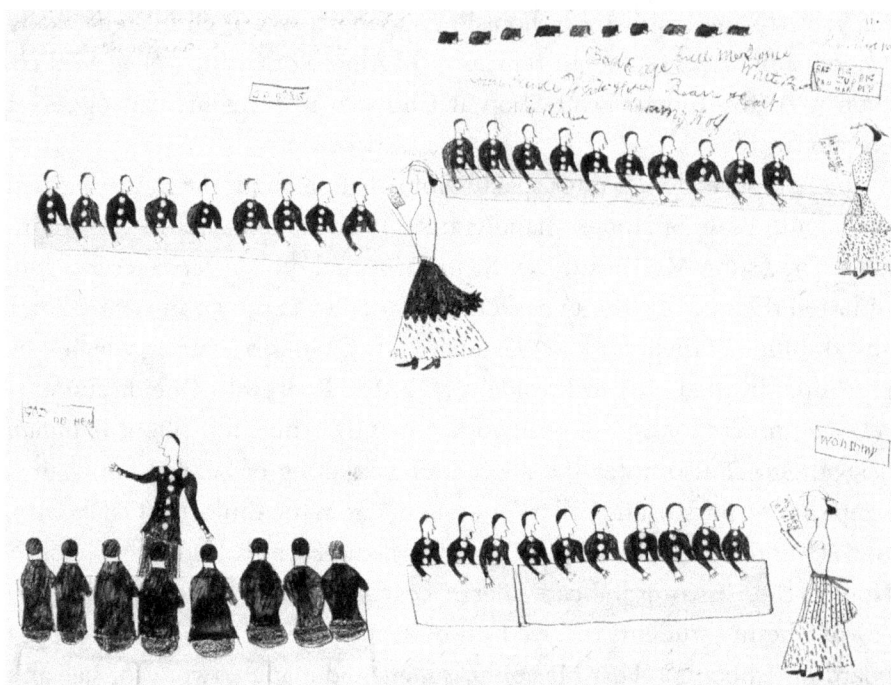

FIGURE 24 Chief Killer (Noh-Hu-Nah-Wih) (Cheyenne), *School at Fort Marion*, 1875–1878. Pen and ink and colored crayon with graphite inscriptions on paper, 8 5/8 × 11 1/4 inches. Hood Museum of Art, Dartmouth College, Hanover, New Hampshire. Purchased through the Robert J. Strasenburgh II 1942 Fund.

papers, demonstrating her familiarity with the nineteenth-century culture of display. As one writer put it, "Such exhibits do more to arouse interest in the Indian question than all the articles that could be written."[59]

Reel's exhibitions include examples of a variety of kinds of student work, including compositions, drawings, and photographs of agricultural projects, but handicrafts dominate in terms of both quantity and visual interest, turning these exhibitions into large-scale Indian corners and endowing them with all of the associations of those private collections. An exhibition of school work held in conjunction with the National Educational Association annual meeting in Boston in 1903, for example, incorporates a variety of objects popular with collectors, such as Pueblo pots, Navajo and Chilkat blankets, Apache baskets, and Navajo jewelry displayed against a backdrop of posters displaying student handicrafts and other work (see figure 25). Like the domestic arrangements discussed in chapter 1, this ensemble is situated in a corner, with objects arrayed so as to invite viewer interaction.

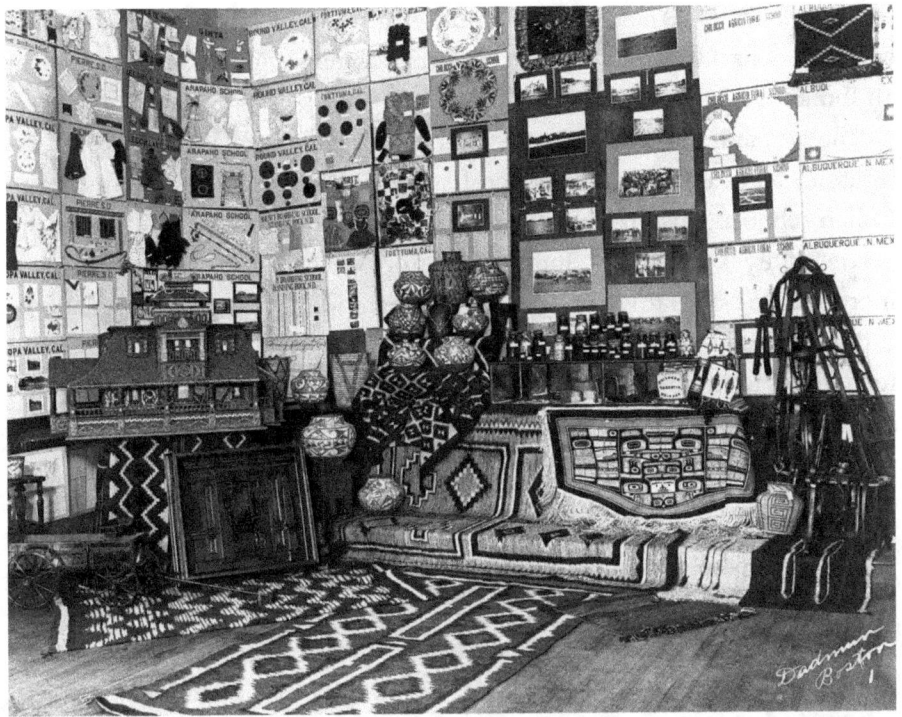

FIGURE 25 Indian schools exhibition, National Education Association annual meeting, Boston, 1903. Estelle Reel Collection, Northwest Museum of Arts and Culture, Spokane, Washington.

Floor rugs reach out at diagonals. The pots and baskets are on receding tiers, drawing the viewer further in. Dangling necklaces and fringes all but demand tactile engagement. The handicrafts serve almost as a barker, attracting viewers close enough so that they can inspect the smaller displays on the posters that hang behind them. There is little doubt that Reel's evocation of the Indian corner was self-conscious. She was herself an early participant in the Indian craze. Her collection of Native American baskets was already publicly known in 1901, and she added to it during her travels and after her retirement to the Pacific Northwest. Upon her death, her large collection was donated to the Mary L. Goodrich Public Library in Toppenish, Washington.[60]

The spirit of the Indian craze was also upheld through comparisons between Native students and participants in the arts and crafts movement. One writer referred to the Chilocco school, which offered classes in lace making as well as beadwork, as the "home of the Indian Roycrofters," linking students with Elbert Hubbard's community of craftspeople in East Aurora, New York.[61] Another article praised the Arizona schools' handicraft curriculum as it was implemented in Arizona and suggested graduates form an Indian arts and crafts guild.[62]

The arts and crafts movement connection helps explain why Reel's exhibitions featured work by older craftspeople who were not students in the Indian schools. This juxtaposition helped to minimize any anxiety over the "authenticity" of the latter. Indian educators were well aware that the commercial value of Native art lay in its associations with preindustrial culture, and despite the innovations introduced in the venues, materials, and techniques used, they promoted student work as "traditional." The commissioner of Indian affairs demonstrated his understanding of the Indian craze when he cautioned:

> The native industry should not be developed so far that there is a destruction of the commercial value of the product when brought into competition with the machine-made articles of deft Yankee construction. There is an unknown value in the basket of the Indian squaw who month after month in a primitive tepee weaves her soul, her religion, her woes, and her joys into every graceful curve and color of her handiwork. Remove these beautiful, sentimental considerations from the basket and place it by the finished product of the white man's factory, and the idea that the native industry of the Indian can be developed into a successful one, by means of which to keep the wolf from the door, does not hold out much hope.[63]

Records show that the inclusion of work by older craftspeople was typical in Indian school exhibitions. For example, a circular asking for submissions of student work for exhibition at the Detroit National Educational Association conference and Buffalo Exposition in 1901, also requested "some of the native work done by the Indians of each tribe under your care."[64] The author of one article on the Boston exhibition attributes the success of the display to this feature and quotes one visitor saying, "Small wonder . . . that these Indian children do such fine work, for if these beautiful articles could be produced from almost nothing by hands taught only by the necessities of life, what results will come by careful instruction under improved surroundings!"[65]

This statement highlights the vexed status of "tradition" in the Indian industries curriculum. On the one hand, the highly valued quality of authenticity depended on a direct connection between modern products and those of the past. At the same time, the schools also needed the public to recognize their accomplishments in integrating Native pupils into modern society if they wanted the public's continued support. Some in the Indian education community accused the exhibitions of pandering to mainstream primitivism. An article published in the Carlisle Indian Industrial School's newspaper *The Red Man and Helper* about an earlier exhibition criticized Reel for using "the flimflam methods of a Wild West show" to "catch the crowd of casual sightseers."

The article notes, "The Indian is a drawing card in any enterprise that thrives by novel methods of advertising, as Buffalo Bill shows, Kickapoo Medicine Guilds and Iroquois Curio Booths attest. The over-sanguine American public is easily pleased, easily deluded for a time into believing that things are just what they seem."[66] The author, who may or may not have been Native, identifies the exhibition as a sales ploy—one, moreover, that plays into mainstream stereotypes of savagery, arguing that the "hodge-podge of bead-work, embroidery, [and] basket-work" do little to illustrate the academic and industrial education offered in the schools. In fact, the exhibitions might actually be understood as an excellent example of the lessons offered by Indian schools at this time, though the lessons I refer to were not those laid out in Reel's curriculum. For the dramatic contrast between the vibrant, textured objects in the foreground and the flat, washed-out, miniature examples of student work on the posters behind seems to argue visually that the "modernization" of Indian students through education strips away the energy and beauty of Native culture.

ART AS INDUSTRIAL LABOR

The relocation of traditional practices to the Indian schools certainly changed them. The Indian schools altered the physical space in which art making occurred, from exterior and interior spaces on tribal lands to the inside of institutional buildings. Native children had frequently learned handicraft techniques by watching elders who practiced them as a regular part of family and community activities; Indian schools isolated the younger generation and broke the learning down into lessons. Similarly, for many Native craftspeople, the process of art making extends through seasonal cycles of gathering and preparing materials and producing the final work; the schools focused only on this last step, providing students with materials ready for assembly.

Something of this can be seen in a photograph of the weaving room at the Navajo Boarding School in Fort Defiance, Arizona, which was repeatedly used to show the success of the Native industries curriculum. The photo, however, also illustrates the ease with which supposedly culturally fulfilling activities could take on the aspects of industrial drudgery (see figure 26).[67] The image at first seems to illustrate a harmonious and communal artistic endeavor. The students are not in a classroom—this space is given over entirely to weaving. Beautiful blankets cover the walls and floors and cushion the seats upon which the weavers sit. The looms are set close together, and girls of different ages work alongside one another. A teacher, perhaps the Navajo Mrs. Nelson German employed at the school as a weaver, bends over to help one of the smallest girls in the back, while the foremost pupil seems to be waiting to ask for assistance in the foreground.

The picture includes all the steps involved in making a blanket. The girls in the foreground are spinning the raw wool into skeins of coarse yarn. The blankets being woven seem to grow from left to right, showing the progress taken en route to producing the finished examples that hang above. The girls focus on their work alone, not on interacting. In the context of the Indian schools' ideology, the room takes on an assembly-line quality, as a comparison with a photograph of child factory labor brings out (see figure 27). Despite its social goals, manual training frequently embodied the very impersonal drudgery it set out to ameliorate. This is consistent with mainstream attempts to integrate arts and crafts ideals and industrial education. As Eileen Boris has noted: "American educators . . . attempted to appropriate art and the artist's joy in labor for the work ethic, but craftsmanship had little place in the new factory system, and in the existing society, child development occurred within capitalist social relations."[68]

Even when pursued during leisure time, Indian industries offered mixed messages. In another picture from the Phoenix Indian school (the same school as in figure 16) indigenous artwork is marginalized (see figure 28). Despite being titled "Teaching Native Industries," there is no teacher in sight. The students are clearly seated on the floor of a hallway, not a classroom or sewing room. This sense of marginalization is reinforced by the fact that Phoenix didn't hire a Native weaving teacher until 1906, even though the school was located close to several Arizona tribes famous for their basketry skill. When Phoenix did hire a woman named Jennie Coartha, to serve as a Native industries teacher, it paid her ten dollars a month, sixty-two dollars less than a regular classroom teacher, indicating that this was a low-wage, part-time job.[69]

In fact, the tenuous nature of the Native industries programs was related to the schools' budget problems. Reel's reports show an ongoing struggle to deal with inadequate funds and substandard facilities. Outbreaks of contagious illnesses or fires in school buildings routinely ground operations to a halt. Often a significant portion of the school year was spent recruiting students, and for many of the reservation-based schools, classroom instruction was primarily devoted to teaching the English language. Many schools did not have the money to hire an extra instructor and delegated the work to a teacher or a matron. Sometimes the work was carried out by a reservation employee who was not on the school staff. At the Puyallup school in Washington, basketry was taught by Lida Quimby, a non-Indian field matron (an agency employee whose job was designed to instruct adult women in domestic affairs) who had support from the Indian Industries League.[70]

Yet the young women in the Phoenix photograph appear to be competent and comfortable with their work. Clearly, students who had studied handicraft traditions at home and understood the cultural and economic value they had for tribal communities would have reacted positively to the invitation to pursue them at school. Even those students who were not already accomplished may have welcomed the break from the otherwise intensely non-Indian curriculum. The benefits would have been particularly high when Native teachers were employed. As Lomawaima has shown, Native teachers served as role models and mentors for Indian school students, helping them negotiate the demands of school culture and reinforcing their tribal identities.[71]

LEARNING THE LESSONS OF "NATIVE INDUSTRIES"

First-hand accounts of the student responses to the Native industries curriculum are hard to find. Most appear in official Indian school sources and must thus be understood as being to some degree tailored to the schools' needs. Reading these documents closely may yield unintended information

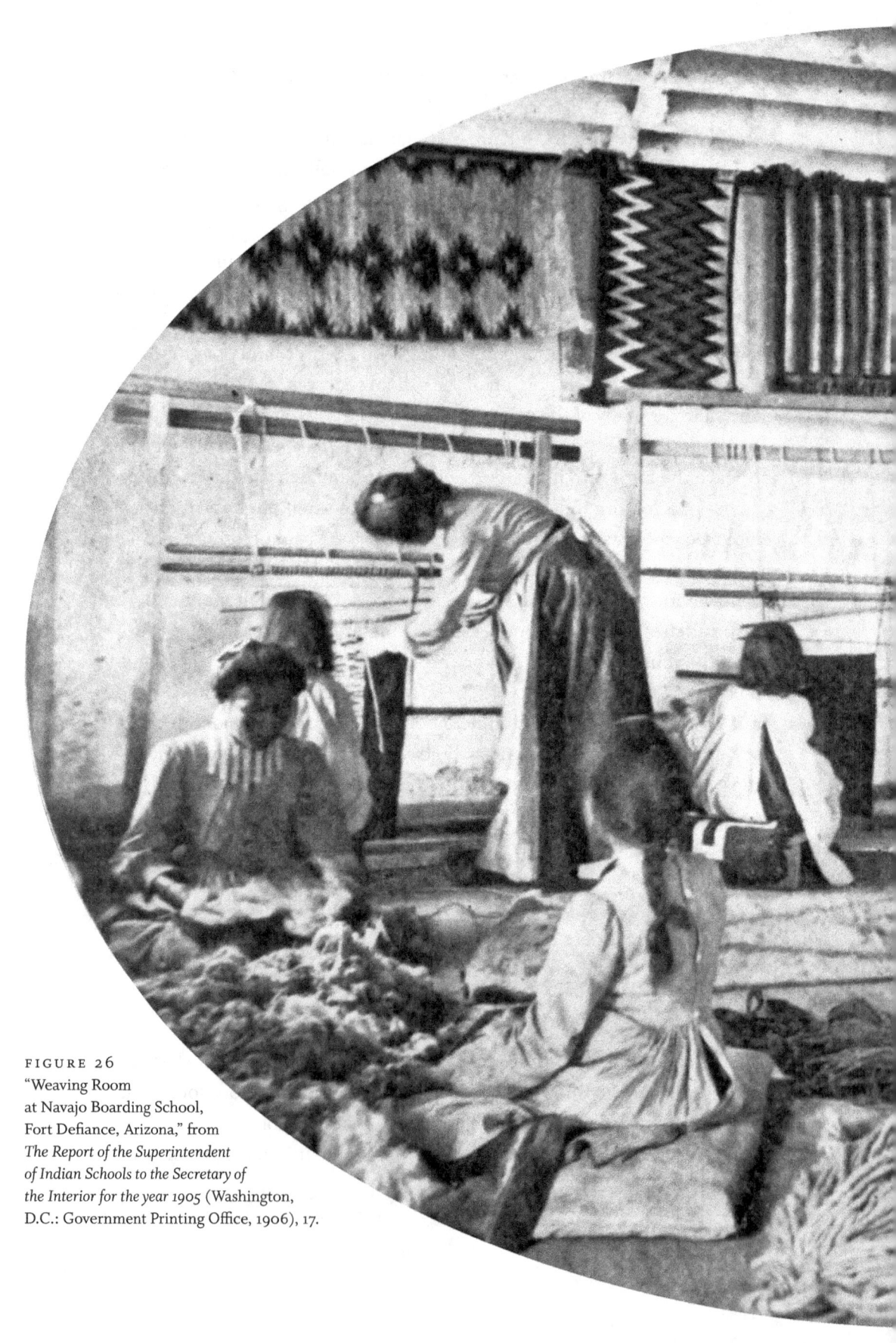

FIGURE 26
"Weaving Room
at Navajo Boarding School,
Fort Defiance, Arizona," from
*The Report of the Superintendent
of Indian Schools to the Secretary of
the Interior for the year 1905* (Washington,
D.C.: Government Printing Office, 1906), 17.

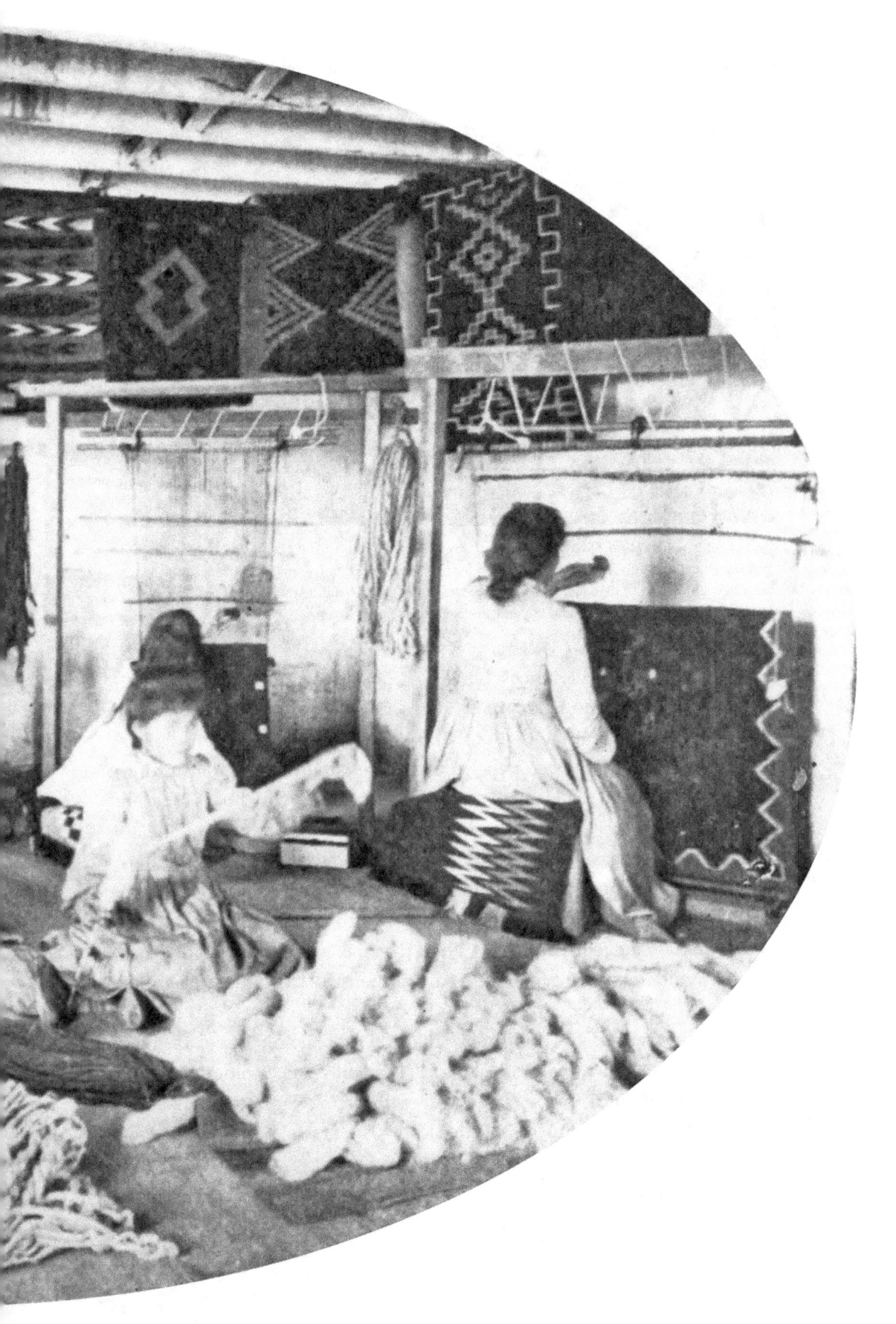

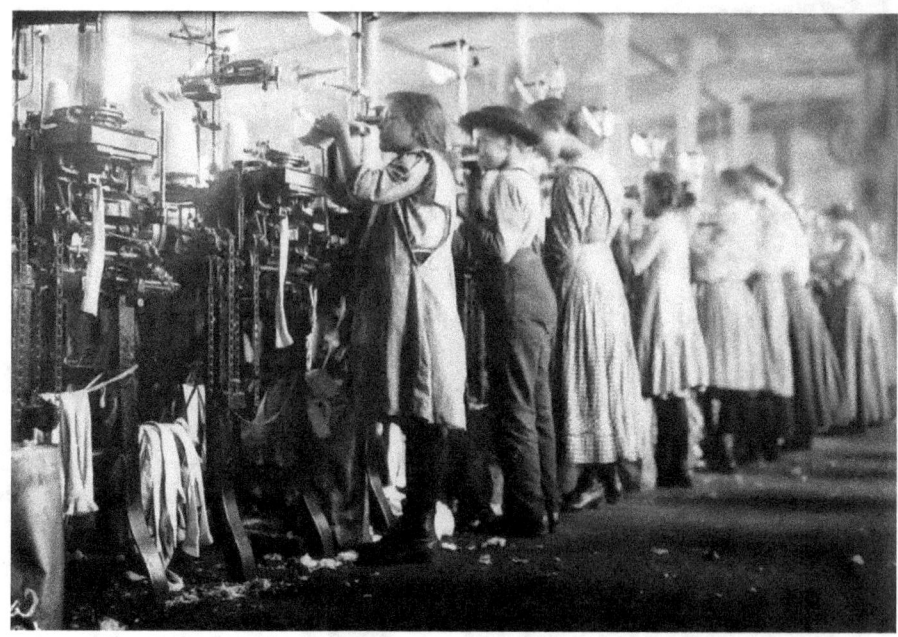

FIGURE 27 Lewis Hine, "Some of the Young Knitters in London Hosiery Mills. Photo During Working Hours. London, Tenn." Photographed for the National Child Labor Committee, 1908–1912. Record group 102 (102-LH-1884), National Archives and Records Administration, Records of the U.S. Department of Commerce and Labor, Children's Bureau, Washington, D.C.

about the students' experiences, however. For example, In 1904, Indian industries students at the school in Chilocco, Oklahoma, pushed themselves to prepare an exhibit of their work for display at the upcoming World's Fair in Saint Louis. The Chilocco paper praised one pupil in particular for her industry. It informed readers that she had "spent all her work hours for *eight months* in making *one piece* of lace. It is exquisite in every way and *an Indian girl made it*" (emphasis in original).[72] The paper declared that she undertook the hard work to "prove her worth" to the fair's visitors. Students were clearly aware that when they submitted objects to Reel's exhibitions, their work would be judged. They understood that the reputation of Indians as a group would impact its reception and that their work could in turn influence how Natives were seen.

Clearly Indian girls invested more than their economic hopes in their ability to succeed at Native industries. This small chance to demonstrate the value of Indian culture was endowed with the power to legitimize the students in the eyes of European Americans. The message that perfect be-

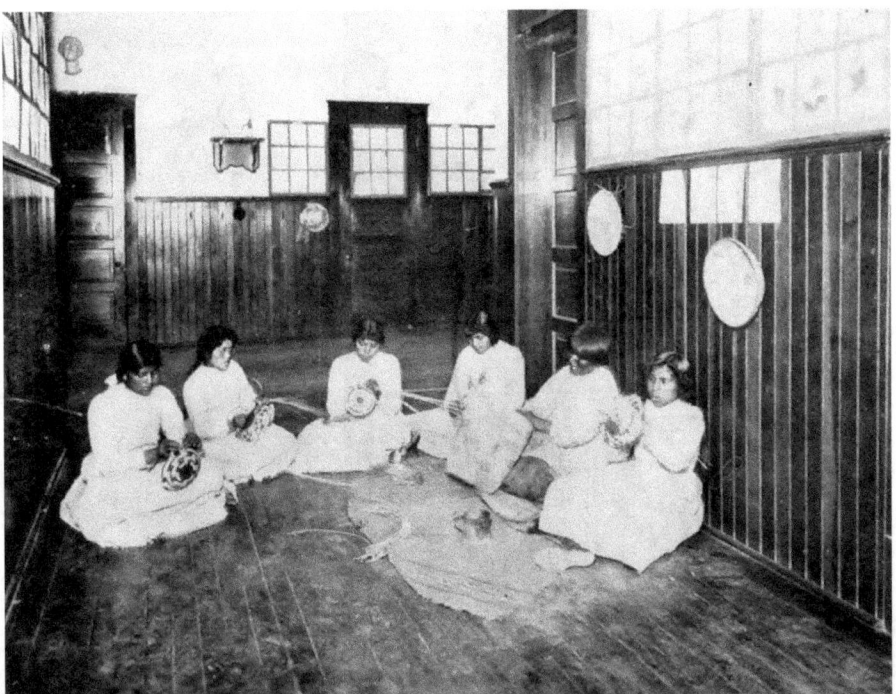

FIGURE 28 "Teaching Native Industries, Phoenix Indian School, Arizona," from *Annual Report of the Superintendent of Indian Schools to the Commissioner of Indian Affairs for the year 1903* (Washington, D.C.: Government Printing Office, 1904), facing 18.

havior, including hard work, was a necessary component of convincing non-Indians that Indian people were worthy of their attention and support was broadcast to pupils through the Indian industries curriculum and reinforced through Reel's public exhibitions.

A poster from one Indian school exhibition illustrates this point (see figure 29). It features work from the Oneida Boarding School in Wisconsin. The beadwork includes small bags, watch fobs, bracelets, and a net collar, above a row of beaded belts. Nestled among these crafts is a photograph of Oneida students producing the work on display (figure 30). The pupils, clad in crisp white dresses with hair in neat chignons, sit demurely at their desks focusing quietly on the rectangular frames in front of them. Three items spill off the foremost desk into view, a small purse decorated with a cross and two beaded strips that may be bookmarks.

Handicraft classes at Oneida were taught by Lucy P. Hart, a teacher and the wife of the school superintendant. In one essay, Hart described

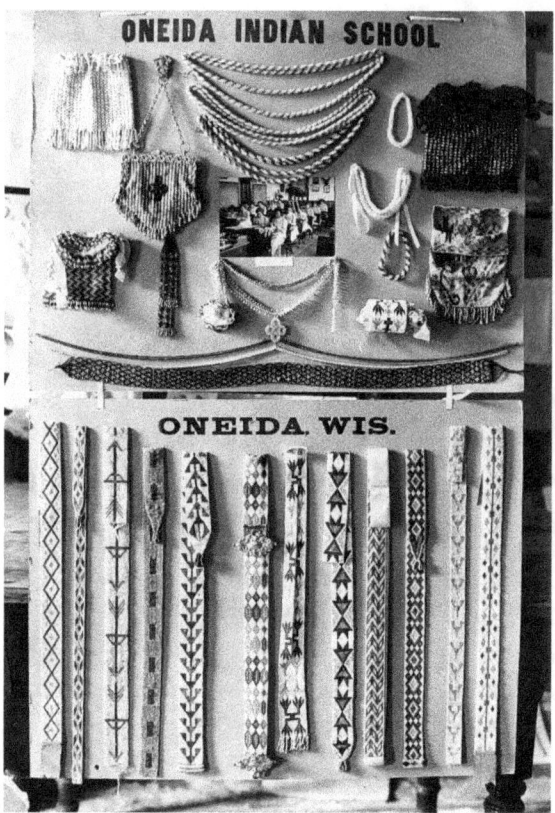

FIGURE 29 Oneida display from the Indian schools exhibition, National Education Association annual meeting, Boston, 1903. Estelle Reel Collection, Northwest Museum of Arts and Culture, Spokane, Washington.

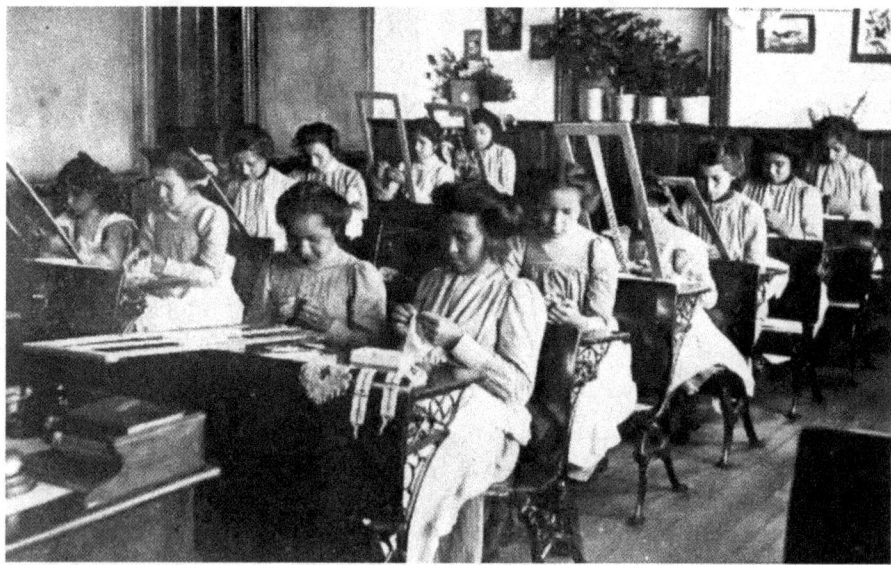

FIGURE 30 "Oneida Students Making Bead Work," from *Chilocco Farmer* 3 (March 1903): 211.

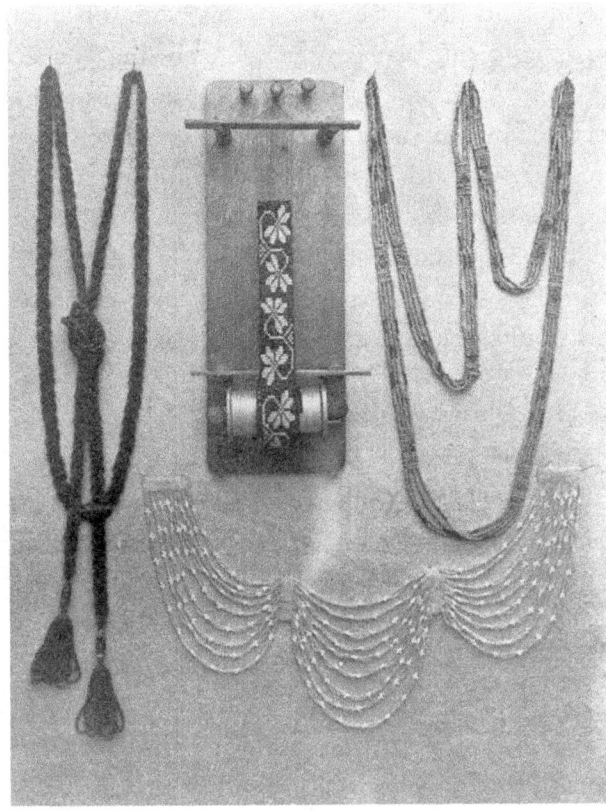

FIGURE 31 Illustration from G. Pomeroy, "Bead Work," *Keramic Studio* 6.9 (January 1905): 207. Courtesy of Winterthur Library, Printed Book and Periodical Collection, Winterthur, Delaware.

her pupils' warm embrace of the addition of beadwork to the curriculum: "They are so often told that everything connected with their ancestors is bad, and should be strictly avoided, that they are glad to find something immediately connected with the home life of the older people that is appreciated by the white people as being really beautiful and, in a way, artistic."[73] But the students' work does not call up a distinctive "Indian" home life. While some of the beaded items on display show geometric designs that could be interpreted as "Indian," others, including the objects decorated with Christian crosses, are less securely culturally located. Indeed, a comparison with a photograph of loomed beadwork made by non-Indian women around the same time suggests a strong exchange of ideas across cultural borders (see figure 31). Contrary to Hart's claims, her pupils' work is less connected to ancestral practice than with that of recent generations who continued and adapted traditional practices in light of increasing mainstream domination.

Hart made it clear that students did not engage in this work solely for pleasure, but as classroom assignments that were evaluated by the teacher. In a 1903 report, she told Reel: "As in other years, basketry and beadwork have received some attention, but in these arts perfection rather than quantity has been the aim, and the work has been a test of neatness and thoroughness rather than a productive industry"[74] Confirming K. Tsianina Lomawaima's assessment of the importance of subservience in the schools, she continued: "All work done is carefully inspected before taken from the frames, and imperfect work pointed out and corrected, thus teaching accuracy and neatness."[75]

CONCLUSION

When Reel retired from her post in 1910 to marry a Washington rancher, the program was not continued and, indeed, it may have been dropped from many schools earlier than this. Only the Carlisle school, which housed a separate art program headed by the Winnebago artist Angel DeCora, the subject of the last chapter of this book, seems to have remained committed to training Native artists. Lomawaima has suggested that the failure to maintain the program may also have been due to a discomfort with the presence of Native teachers in the school system.[76] But the demise of the Indian industries curriculum can also be linked to the inherent problematic educational ideals, whose emphasis on finding joy in labor was profoundly out of sync with contemporary economic reality. Then as now, American consumers who could see the value of well-designed and well-made objects were also unwilling to pay higher prices for them.

But the Native industries program is important despite its failures and shortcomings. Student artwork of this generation can be seen as a document of both assimilationist pressure and native survivance. "Survivance" is a term coined by Gerald Vizenor, the Anishinaabe (Chippewa) Indian scholar and writer, to describe Native endurance and resistance in the face of dominant culture's fictional definitions of authentic Indianness.[77] Key components of survivance are the mastery of dominant codes and an understanding of the fragility of their authority. Like many artists on the reservation, turn-of-the-century Indian students found ways to make these "modern" practices their own.

Oneida beadwork illustrates this point. The use of handicrafts to teach genteel feminine behavior was not Hart's innovation. The Oneida Boarding School curriculum focused on lace making and woven beadwork, two practices that had been introduced in the tribe by female missionaries. In 1894 Sybil Carter sent a teacher to Oneida, and women there began making and selling lace. The use of commercially distributed beadwork looms in Hart's classroom also represents a non-Indian intervention in the course of Oneida art. In 1898 the Episcopalian Sisters of the Holy Nativity had begun promoting the use of looms for beadwork, encouraging Oneida women to produce objects such as small bags, chains, and fobs, that they distributed to non-Indian audiences in a manner similar to Carter. J. K. Bloomfield traces the introduction of woven beadwork to the Oneidas to this project.[78] Much Six Nations beadwork is characterized by appliquéed floral designs on a cloth ground, allowing for fluid lines, and organic shapes that cannot be accomplished with loom weaving. A pair of moccasins made on the Oneida Reservation in Wisconsin in the 1890s demonstrates the vibrant colors and exuberant designs of this tradition (see plate 4).

Though this history is not documented, loomed beadwork may be the result of a more complex intercultural exchange. Woven beadwork was traditional to neighboring tribes with whom the Oneidas had extensive contact, including the Menominee and the Winnebago, and, indeed, it was not unknown to Iroquoians.[79] (For an illustration of Great Lakes beadwork using a loom, see figure 12.)

Regardless of the roots of the technique, the production of beaded articles for sale to non-Indians would have been a familiar idea for Oneida women. Their Iroquoian forebears had sold hand-crafted "curios" to European Americans for well over a century. Morever, they had routinely adopted new forms and techniques in their attempt to attract buyers. As Ruth Phillips has revealed, several types of souvenirs understood as traditional Woodlands work were actually developed in the seventeenth and eighteenth centuries by Ursuline nuns hoping to raise funds from travelers and European patrons.[80] For example, the nuns adapted birchbark containers to produce small lidded boxes with applied designs in moosehair embroidery. Native artisans later took up this practice and added their own innovations.

The intercultural curio market did not offer all participants equal power; Native people and their work were assessed by mainstream ideas about race and gender. But it would be a mistake to see this work as less "Native" than traditions less influenced by Euro-Americans, for to do so robs Indian people of their history. Phillips has argued that participation in intercultural art markets offered craftspeople diverse rewards. These range from the pleasures of pursuing the work—carrying on traditions that were related not only to subsistence but also to the sustaining of culture—to the importance of acquiring funds to support family and community survival and to the satisfaction of participating in modern culture and mastering its ideas about art and character.

As I have discussed above, Indian school officials often got tripped up by a commitment to a fallacious "authenticity." But it is likely that Oneida students were more comfortable mixing indigeneity and modernity. Their tribal history was characterized by an ongoing dialogue with European Americans. The nation descended from two groups who had left upstate New York in the 1820s to settle on land purchased from the Menomenee and Winnebago. Later joined by a small band of so-called pagans, most Wisconsin Oneida were Christians who had adopted many aspects of mainstream culture into their lives and continued to interact with the European Americans who began settling in Wisconsin around the same time as the Oneida migration.

The Oneida did not embrace all aspects of mainstream culture. The community was strongly divided about allotment. And while they initially welcomed the Oneida Boarding School for offering their children a chance to better themselves through education without having to leave the reservation, many pupils came to resent the school's emphasis on labor and discipline.[81] But tribal members understand both of the traditions taught in Hart's classroom as *Oneida* art forms that draw on older skills and on the traditional work of Iroquoian women. They have worked to continue and preserve them. In 1908 an Oneida woman, Josephine Hill Webster, took over the lace-making project, which she continued into the 1940s, long after Carter's organization dissolved.[82] Both traditions are featured today at Nation's Museum near Green Bay.

CHAPTER THREE

The redman would teach us to be ourselves in a still greater degree.
Marsden Hartley

Playing Indian

NATIVE AMERICAN ART AND MODERN AESTHETICS

Among the hundreds of objects on view at the National Museum of the American Indian's exhibition "The Language of Native American Baskets" (fall 2003–spring 2005) were several Pomo baskets made at the beginning of the twentieth century. As the exhibition made clear, there are many ways to interpret these baskets in light of Pomo values and history, but non-Indian visitors to the museum's New York City branch at the George Gustav Heye Center were most acutely aware of their arresting forms and dramatic mixture of materials.

Consider a bowl by an unknown weaver made around 1900 (see plate 5). The weaver has created a pattern on the surface that balances the light and dark colors of the sedge and dyed bulrush root, with the zig-zagging lines growing steadily as the rim of the bowl widens. The small clusters of quail topknot feathers arrayed around the top rim enhance the dynamism of the woven design, while the small round white shell beads offer a stabilizing detail at the very top edge. All of this is executed in impossibly small stitches wrapped tautly around the three willow rods that make up the foundation of this coiled basket.

Such a fine piece does not seem out of place in a plexiglass vitrine in a museum gallery. Indeed, such exhibition enhances our ability to appreciate details such as the simple curvilinear rosette woven into the base of the bowl that contrasts dramatically with the busy geometric patterns on the walls. The stillness of the museum space helps the viewer see how the quail feathers quiver at even the smallest vibration. The display case does deny the viewer a vital aspect of Native basketry, namely the scent of grasses and roots that can still conjure up the sunlight and air of the spaces where these materials were gathered. Otherwise, however, the object seems made for such a display. My emphasis on the formal beauty of a turn-of-the-century basket is not anachronistic. Many of the early collectors of Pomo basketry also stressed their status as art objects. Carl Purdy wrote in 1902 of the weaver's inventive combinations of designs: "These she varies, amplifies and combines in a purely artistic manner. She is not trying to write history of an occurrence, or to embody a religious belief. Her sole aim is to create something beautiful. She is an artist, not a priestess or historian."[1]

Like the Navajo weaving discussed in chapter 1, Pomo basketry is a Native tradition that was profoundly affected by mainstream American expansion. The weavers were the descendants of the aboriginal people who spoke one of the seven distinct Pomoan languages. The Pomo were not organized into a single tribe, but lived in dozens of independent communities spread across the coastal regions north of San Francisco. As for many peoples of the West Coast, weaving was a primary means of producing material necessities, from clothing to containers for gathering and storage to cooking vessels to objects for ceremonial use. The basket reproduced in plate 6, for example, is derived from Pomo cooking bowls. Women prepared acorn mush inside these tight-woven containers by dropping heated stones into the acorn mixture. After a U.S. attempt to confine the Pomo to a single reservation near Mendocino failed, they reorganized several self-owned communities. Weavers began producing work for their non-Indian neighbors early on, but when the railroad reached Ukiah, bringing tourists to northern California, the market expanded. This increase in demand encouraged weavers to experiment with form and design, creating increasingly elaborate feather- and beadwork, integrating new materials, and developing a tradition of purely decorative miniature basketry.[2] Pomo baskets came to general attention through the efforts of early collectors who lived near Pomo communities in northern California, including the painter Grace Carpenter Hudson, who was discussed in chapter 1.

Pomo basketry was appreciated for its aesthetic qualities, as well as its utility, as Purdy's comment suggests. Purdy, a Ukiah-based botanist who was involved in marketing Pomo baskets, was deeply interested in Pomo culture and belief. Nevertheless, he insists that baskets can be understood independent of this, departing from what might be understood as an ethnographic attitude toward the baskets and entering something more aesthetic. Purdy's work illustrates how an aesthetic orientation literature was beginning to diverge from ethnographic scholarship at the beginning of the twentieth century. As Janet Berlo has argued, turn-of-the-century ethnographic writing on Native material culture was largely "classificatory"—defining techniques and distinguishing between regional and historical developments.[3] While Purdy was praising Native artistry, S. A. Barrett and Roland Dixon wrote studies that analyzed Pomo forms and techniques in relationship to other Native Californian groups.[4] To these authors, each basket contributes to the definition of an aggregate "Pomo" type, which in turn could be worked into a larger analysis of the processes of human technological development. The individual weaver's skills and creativity were not only irrelevant to this kind of inquiry, they were distracting.

But Purdy and other dealers, notably the Pasadena-based Grace Nicholson, were very interested in the qualities that made each basket unique and in determining which weavers consistently produced high-quality work. Due to their efforts, collectors began to recognize certain weavers by name and to pay a premium for their work. This was the case, for example, with Mary Benson, the weaver who made the basket featured in plate 6; Benson developed close ties first with Hudson and then with Nicholson, with whom she signed an exclusive contract in 1903. Benson and her husband, William Benson, were members of a small list of "celebrity" Native artists who emerged at this time whose work could command high price and whose close ties to both Hudson and Nicholson led to recognition and travel. In addition to the artists discussed in chapter 1—Louisa Keyser, Nampeyo, and Elle of Ganado—other Native craftspeople known by name at this time include Elizabeth Hickox (Karuk), who also worked closely with Nicholson, and, beginning slightly later, the San Ildefonso potter Maria Martinez.[5]

The existence of an interest in Native American art for its aesthetic qualities and the emergence of artists who were appreciated for their individual
creativity seem to confirm the fact that Native American material culture
was regarded as "art" at the beginning of the twentieth century. This chapter
argues just that, highlighting the presence of Native American material culture in venues we associate with mainstream fine art. I look at discussions
of Native handicrafts in mainstream art journals, art schools, and art exhibitions. This presence is not insignificant. As I show, the presence of Native
American objects in mainstream art institutions supported modern art's
increasingly formalist concerns while providing an example of abstract art's
ability to retain cultural meaning. Moreover, the embrace of an American
"primitive" facilitated the acceptance of new ideas about artistic creation.
However, the classification of Native products as art did not always mean
that they or their creators were accorded the same value as mainstream
artists.

ART AND ARTIFACT

This research challenges the accepted history of the aestheticization of
Native American art. The question of when and how indigenous objects
became "art" has occupied anthropologists and other scholars of culture for
some time.[6] The acceptance of the aesthetic value of Native art has been
understood as a sign of mainstream American openness to seeing Indian
people as equally capable of producing high culture as themselves. By the
1980s, scholars came to understand that all modes of cross-cultural engagement with Native handicrafts—as ethnographic evidence, souvenirs, and
works of art—are based in value systems that are historically constructed
and capable of change and that objects can fall in and out of a classification
over time. James Clifford has usefully argued that the meaning of indigenous objects shifts due to their context, from "souvenir" to "artifact," for
example, or from "artifact" to "art."[7] But we must also pay attention to how
the boundaries of "art" changed historically. Pinpointing the timing of the
embrace of Native American "art" can help us understand how concepts of
ethnicity and aesthetics evolved in tandem.

Conventional wisdom tells us that Americans did not look at Indian art
aesthetically before World War I. Indeed, an exhibition arranged in New
York's Grand Central Galleries in 1931 claims to be the very first exhibi-

tion that treated Native American art from a "purely aesthetic standpoint."[8] Others would date the interest in Native American material culture back to the teens, but not earlier.[9] One of the reasons that the history I'm relating has been forgotten is that this early interest in Native American art did not concern itself with representational Indian art but with pottery, basketry, and weaving. The beginning of this history usually coincides with the introduction of watercolor painting to Pueblo students in government-funded boarding schools in the Southwest, which began to attract the attention of eastern artists and dealers in the 1910s.[10] The inclusion of examples of this work in the exhibitions of the avant-garde exhibitions of the Society of Independent Artists from 1920 to 1922 certainly serves as an important episode of this history.[11] But what of the inclusion of Native basketry and beadwork in the annual exhibition of the National Arts Club twenty years before? In both cases, Native objects were displayed alongside those of non-Indians. Both exhibitions were dedicated to the modern artist's authority over questions of subject, style, and materials, signaled by a rejection of the jury system. And in both exhibitions, decorative panels, textiles, and other examples of so-called decorative art were displayed alongside paintings and sculptures as examples of modern art. This last point offers important insight into why the early history of the aestheticization of Native American art has been lost. For while many early modernists embraced the decorative arts, the reputation of applied art eventually declined, and with it the appreciation of Native material culture.

Most accounts of the aestheticization of Native American art focus on the interpreters' investment in formal beauty independent of cultural meaning. As they rely on an aesthetic ideology that was consolidated in the 1930s in the influential work of Clement Greenberg, it is not surprising that they date the aestheticization of Native American art to the same decade. But the ideas of the thirties emerged from a lengthy negotiation. Prior to the twentieth century, most critics assessed the value of a work of art by analyzing form in relationship to the work's subject. Antiacademic movements in Europe and the United States, fueled by a desire to be "modern" and inspired in part by the objects arriving in Western ports from Asian, Pacific, American, and African colonies and trading partners, increasingly advocated paying attention to the effects of line, pattern, and color. Recent scholarship suggests that the openness toward decorative arts expressed at the turn of the century by adherents to the protomodernism of the arts and crafts movement and its relatives, aestheticism, secessionism, and art nouveau, were partly responsible for the emergence of formalism.[12] It was in this context that writers developed critical language to deal with the abstract qualities of fine and decorative objects.

The American arts and crafts movement's interest in Native American art is well known, but for many years, the arts and crafts movement was understood as a marginal, and largely failed, chapter of mainstream art history. Many define this movement narrowly as the short-lived attempt by craftspeople to have their work accepted as the aesthetic equal of painting and sculpture. Similarly, the failure of the movement's social goals, and to some extent their naiveté, has argued against taking the movement seriously. Most of the workshops, guilds, and companies founded along Morris and Ruskin's precepts had difficulty making a profit through the production of high-quality work, and critics questioned the social impact of producing what were, in reality, luxury items. This reputation led to a dismissal of the widespread artistic interest in Native American art at this time. While several historians of the aestheticization of Native American art have recognized the arts and crafts movement's interest in Native American art, they have not deemed this a "real" aesthetic interest. For example, Jackson Rushing covers this interest in a couple of pages in his 1995 book *Native American Art and the New York Avant-Garde*. Molly Mullin acknowledges this chapter of Native American art history only in a brief footnote.[13]

But the espousal of arts and crafts ideas by successful and influential artists and teachers such as Brush remind us that many of these values were central to painters and sculptors grappling with the challenge to produce modern art. Recent scholarship has demonstrated the broad impact of arts and crafts thinking. Stella Tillyard has argued that the aesthetic emphasis on the decorative arts within the arts and crafts movement was essential for paving the way for modernism, because it made viewers comfortable with nonnarrative art by producing a vocabulary with which to describe the formal attributes of an object and to endow those attributes with meaning. The movement advanced such values as decorative harmony, craftsmanship or technique, and functionality. Moreover, the aesthetic interest in applied and decorative arts offered a new model of the relationship of artists to society, making them less the keepers of universal truths and more the critics of the dehumanizing effects of modern industrial life.

Tillyard argues that early modernists in England learned to dissociate form from content from the celebration of design in the writings of Owen Jones, Morris, and others. The vocabulary they developed to analyze technique and describe pattern and ornament formed a basis for Roger Fry's formalism. Similarly, she traces a link between the movement's commitment to truth to materials and the modernist commitment to medium specificity. She quotes William Morris's interest in working within parameters set by a medium: "It is the pleasure in understanding the capabilities of a special material, and using them for suggesting (not imitating) natural beauty and incident, that gives the raison d'etre of decorative art."[14]

The arts and crafts movement was only one aspect of the international art world that was interested in form and medium at the end of the nineteenth century. Each of the "decorative" art movements explored these issues in diverse ways. And each, in turn, influenced the American art world, which included both artists and critics who had traveled and frequently studied abroad. The interest in finding lessons in form in Native American art goes beyond the arts and crafts movement.

A NEW VOCABULARY

As Tillyard notes, one of the major contributions that the "decorative arts" movements made to modernism was a new interest in formalist language. This vocabulary is abundantly employed in discussions of Native American art in mainstream art magazines. In 1908, Leila Mechlin published an article in *International Studio* urging artists to study the Native American collections in the National Museum. Like Purdy, Mechlin is not interested in penetrating beyond the formal qualities of a work. She writes, "The designs may or may not have symbolic meaning, but they unquestionably possess character and give aesthetic delight." Instead of symbolism, she looks to this work as a model of "decorative effects" and "excellence of design."[15] Articles on indigenous handicrafts could also be found in *Brush and Pencil, Handicraft, Cosmopolitan,* and *The Craftsman,* the largest-circulating American art magazines of the time, suggesting a broad aesthetic interest in Native American art.[16] Numerous essays also appeared in journals dedicated to work in specific media ranging from *Keramic Studio* to *Inland Printer*.[17] In many ways, these essays echo the prose of George Wharton James, who occasionally published in art journals (and served as an editor of *The Craftsman* for a brief period in 1903 and 1904). Like James, art writers described individual objects in detail. But unlike James they celebrate the formal and technical accomplishments of Indian artists over their cultural associations.

An excellent illustration of this genre is provided by an article by the painter Elbridge Ayer Burbank, published in 1900. Burbank's article, "In Indian Teepees," appeared in *Brush and Pencil*, a widely circulating art magazine that devoted attention to American painting, sculpture, and design, as part of a series called "Studies of Art in American Life." In it he ascribed to Native Americans "a high appreciation of the beauty of line and color, and . . . no inconsiderable degree of dexterity in effecting artistic results, especially on purely decorative lines."[18] Throughout the essay Burbank creates an image of the Native craftsperson as an artist. The Apache chief Geronimo, for example, is praised for his "fine eye for line and color" (79). Other artists are praised for taking hours to work out designs "after the manner of more civilized races, and patiently making alterations until they were satisfied" (85). Burbank suggests that Native craftspeople find their inspiration in nature, but he stresses the human decision-making involved in their work. "Nature is viewed through different eyes and different objects recommend themselves as especially suitable for the purposes of design" (81), he writes, adding that in addition to individual choice, artists follow regional and tribal traditions that he likens to "so many different art schools" (81). He puts it succinctly: "In a word, both braves and squaws showed that they were essentially artists, and that they studied for effect as rationally and as carefully as the artists of civilized communities" (87).

"In Indian Teepees" includes a photograph of Burbank's Native art collection. As Burbank regularly painted indigenous subjects, it is tempting to see the collection as an assemblage of props for his work. Since Albert Bierstadt established the tradition after his Western trips of the 1850s and 1860s, it had become common for artists to maintain collections to help them create finished paintings from field sketches and to give studio visitors a sense of the authenticity of their work. In Burbank's time, the best-known studio of this type was Frederic Remington's celebrated atelier in New Rochelle, New

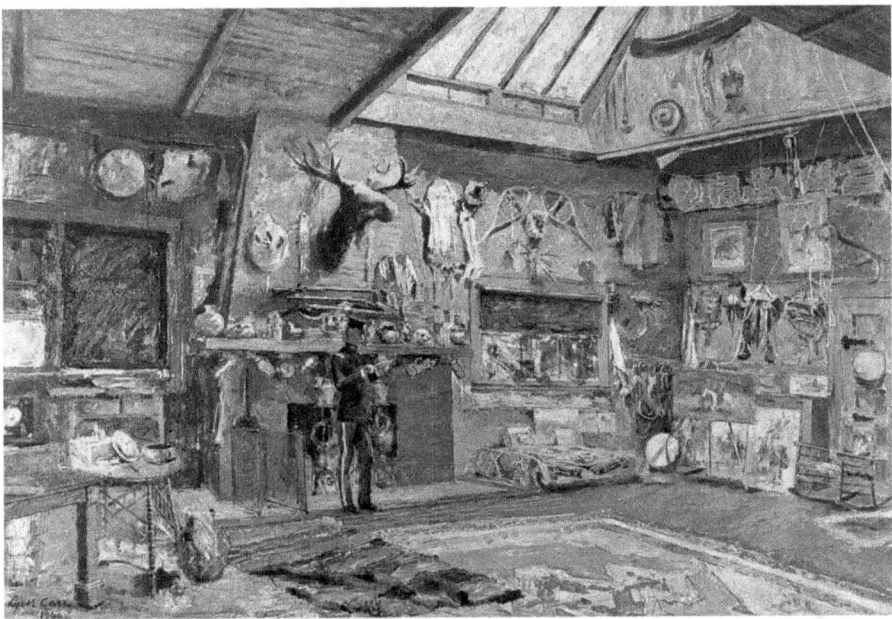

FIGURE 32 Lyell Carr, *Frederic Remington's New Rochelle Studio*, 1900. Oil on canvas. Courtesy Frederic Remington Art Museum, Ogdensburg, New York.

York (see figure 32).[19] But Burbank's language reveals a more than ethnographic interest in Native material culture. He ascribes the same qualities to Native artists that progressive mainstream artists sought themselves, suggesting that he found in their formal qualities an inspiration for his own creative work.

Burbank's use of this formalist language is perhaps surprising, given the realistic nature of his own work. The artist is known primarily for his portrait busts of Native Americans executed in oils or red crayon (see figure 4). Trained in Munich in the 1880s, Burbank turned to Native subjects upon his return to the United States, with the encouragement of his uncle Edward Everett Ayer (see figure 6). Burbank's work met with success. His exhibitions in Chicago sold out, and others encountered his work through reproductions. This commercialism did not put him at odds with the mainstream art world; indeed, art magazines such as *Brush and Pencil* and *The Craftsmen* promoted his work through articles and by offering reproductions as incentives to subscribers.[20]

Both writing and being written about in these magazines put Burbank at the heart of the discussions of modern art, regardless of the seeming conservatism of his own painting. As several scholars have pointed out, the emergence of a specialized art press in the last quarter of the nineteenth century facilitated the conception of art as an autonomous sphere of cultural activity with its own concerns and constituency. Sarah Burns has shown how this development helped solidify the idea of the art world as a self-contained and very modern community. Burns also traces the emergence of art criticism as a profession devoted to documenting and shaping this world. Commentary on individual works of art is quite old, but the development of a professional specialization depended on the expansion of the publishing industry in the nineteenth century. In the United States, the regular review of new work and exhibitions emerged along with mass-produced monthly magazines in the second half of the nineteenth century. In an earlier period, journalists frequently wrote on diverse topics, but by the 1880s magazines such as *Harper's Monthly*, the *Atlantic Monthly*, and *The Century* and several daily newspapers hired writers who focused solely on art. Burns has argued that such publications were essential for the development of professional language addressing small audiences, serving in turn to endorse and justify the emergence of diverse professions and to transform the role of the modern artist.[21] Linda Docherty has demonstrated that American art criticism became increasingly oriented to formal issues during the Gilded Age, valuing technique as an expression of the individuality of the artist.[22] J. M. Mancini reads this formalist language as a means by which critics staked out "professional" territory, in part by emphasizing an aspect of art that separated it from other forms of culture.[23]

Burbank's essay in *Brush and Pencil* utilizes this new language. The term "harmony," which Burbank uses in connection with Native art, constituted high praise, especially in America, where it was associated with James A. M. Whistler's use of musical terms to describe the abstraction in his paintings. Artists from a range of backgrounds celebrated the "decorative" as a means of turning away from public patronage and grand exhibitions to explore the relationship between art and life. Supporters of postimpressionism, the arts and crafts, secessionism, and aestheticism argued that art's "original" role was the embellishment of domestic space, and they created both fine and decorative objects designed to stimulate thought and imagination in private spaces. While many symbolist painters explored the creation of murals for their middle-class patrons' homes, architects, designers, and painters in Vienna were collaborating to create fully designed interiors, such as the "Ver Sacrum" room of the 1898 Secession Exhibition. In England, Roger Fry organized the Omega Workshops, which used modern painters as the designers of affordable housewares and furnishings.[24]

While art history tends to treat these movements individually, their overlapping concerns reveal shared roots. The desire to bridge art and life was inspired in part by the impact of industrialism on daily life. As discussed in chapter 1, as public spaces became dominated by the needs of large-scale manufacturing and distribution, private space was defined as a private retreat from this anonymous world. Many artists who found the academic art world increasingly routinized and oriented toward official public culture sought out alternative ways to produce and distribute work that emphasized private notions of taste and sensibility. One of their inspirations was the result of the global spread of capitalism—the international industrial exhibitions that began with the London's Crystal Palace Exposition of 1851. Designed to advertise and inspire the competitiveness of industrial nations' manufacturing, these exhibitions called public attention to the need to bring aesthetic concerns to bear on modern design. Scholars have traced the vibrancy of the arts and crafts movement in England to a desire to improve both labor and manufactures in the wake of this exhibition.[25]

International exhibitions frequently included displays of the arts and industries of Europe's colonies and non-Western trading partners. The decorative qualities of non-European applied art served as a model for artists in England, France, and central Europe. These exhibitions spurred the commercial market for exotic goods and in turn influenced the marketing of Native American art, as discussed in chapter 1. But they were profoundly influential on artistic debates as well. The products of Japan, newly available in the West after centuries of closed ports, offered a particularly valuable illustration of how utilitarian objects could transcend the barriers between fine and applied arts. Japanese art was featured to great acclaim in international exhibitions in Britain, on the Continent, and in the United States.[26]

Japanese art was an inspiration for Whistler, who began exploring the design of display spaces as a means of controlling the experience of his work.[27] Beginning with his solo exhibitions of the 1870s, Whistler designed wooden frames for his pieces, experimented with new hanging styles, and explored the use of colored walls and decorative textiles to influence the mood of the

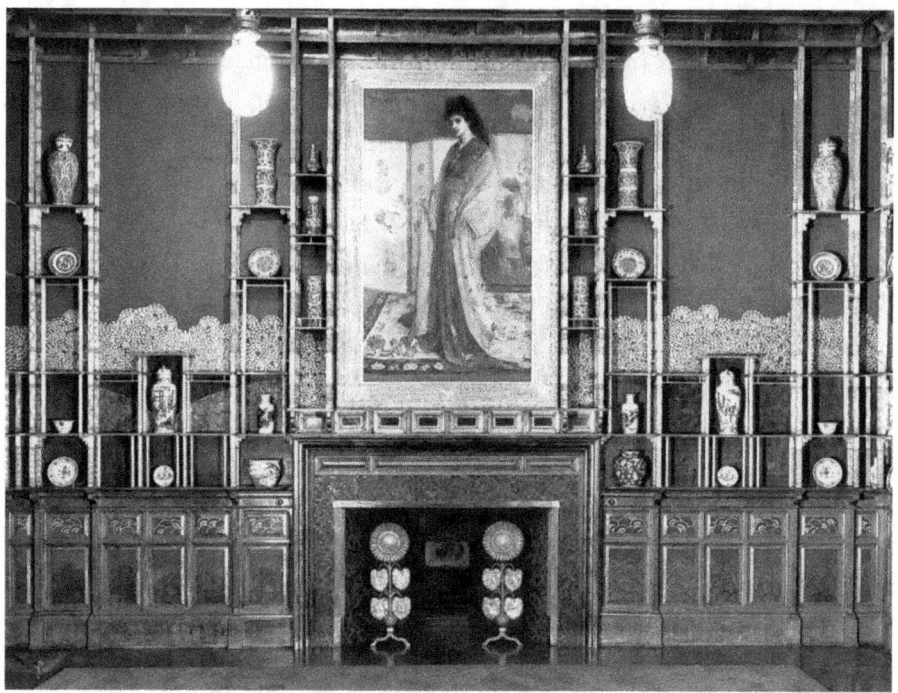

FIGURE 33 James McNeill Whistler, *Harmony in Blue and Gold: The Peacock Room*, 1876–1877, showing his painting *La Princesse du Pays de la Porcelaine*, 1863–1864. Oil and metal leaf on leather, canvas, and wood. Inv. no. F1904.61, Freer Gallery of Art, Smithsonian Institution, Washington, D.C. Gift of Charles Lang Freer.

salon. Whistler's use of Japanese decorative arts as a model for the integration of paintings and decorative arts is evident in the Peacock Room (1876–1867), a dining room created for his patron Frederick Leyland, in which Whistler's painting *The Princess in the Land of Porcelain* (1863–1864) was displayed alongside Leyland's collection of blue-and-white porcelain jars on gilded shelves, against walls and ceiling covered in gilt-stamped, turquoise-painted leather, whose compositions recall folding screens (see figure 33). Whistler's exploration of total design was extremely influential on the development of aestheticism in America. His ideas were also inspirational on the Continent, particularly among the Vienna secessionists, who more than once invited him to join their group and exhibitions.

Americans drew on each of these movements in their efforts to define modern American art. Whistler and the arts and crafts movement were particularly influential. As discussed in chapter 1, supporters of the arts and crafts movement frequently celebrated local traditions as a rejoinder to the homogenization offered by industrial culture. American artists also turned to the folk traditions, developing a vocabulary of regional and historical styles that could contribute a distinctly national character to their work. The Indian craze offers an early chapter of this folk and colonial revival, which gathered force in the interwar years.

MAKING NATIVE ART

The *Brush and Pencil* series to which Burbank contributed his essay "In Indian Teepees" also celebrated Puritan, Dutch, southern, and African American artistic traditions as inspiration and even models for modern artists.[28] My use of the term "models" is intentional. Several writers on Native American art present indigenous handicrafts as a resource for non-Indian artists to engage in preparing their own work. Leila Mechlin, writing in 1908, goes beyond acknowledging the artistic qualities of Native art to suggest that mainstream artists would benefit from the close study of Native work. Mechlin suggests that it is not only the Indian's product but the Indian's process that bears consideration: "In all . . . examples of primitive craftsmanship, the accurate skill of the workman, the patient labor expended upon the execution of the object, and the manner in which it is brought to completion are worthy not only of note but emulation."[29] A large number of articles on Native art in early twentieth-century journals focused on the lessons artists and craftspeople could learn from Native arts. Some focused on specific techniques, such as basketry or beadwork, while others explored how Native art offered a model for design or artistic sensibility. Specialized journals such as *Keramic Studio*, directed at professional, artistic, and amateur potters, included explicit directions for basket stitches and beadwork patterns based on indigenous models in addition to articles simply describing Native traditions.[30] *The Craftsman* published similar "how-to" articles, including patterns for adapting Native designs for embroidery and wall decoration.[31] Some articles explored the adaptation of Native traditions to modern architecture in the Southwest.[32] And other pieces explored the more abstract lessons offered by the study of Native arts, such as the 1903 essay "Building in Clay," by the art potter Charles Binns, which is discussed below.[33]

This generic appropriation of "Indianness" was part of a larger European-American passion for "playing Indian." As Phil Deloria has demonstrated,

Indian masquerade has been a part of mainstream American culture for centuries and was undertaken by those interested in working out an oppositional notion of American identity.[34] Participants in the Boston Tea Party used "Indian" clothing to posit an American identity that was separate from Europe. At the beginning of the twentieth century, "playing Indian" became annexed to antimodernism. Woodcraft Indians and Campfire Girls (early rivals to the Boy and Girl Scouts), hunting and camping enthusiasts, and amateur craftspeople all played Indian to express an alliance with what they saw as traditional "American" values threatened by modern life.

Many such articles were read by hobbyists following a temporary fashion in women's busywork. The copying of Native American art was so rampant in the first years of the century that serious art critics complained about it. Irene Sargent, an editor of *The Craftsman*, wrote in 1904 that, "to imitate the basketry of the North American Indians has recently been the ambition of public school children and the passing fancy of club-women. But while both of these classes have thus satisfied the natural desire to create something; while they have closely copied shape, stitches and design, they have too often failed to seize the meaning of the originals."[35]

The Apache beadwork loom typifies the superficiality that Sargent condemned (see figure 31). A column on beading from *The Papoose* in 1903 highlights the superficial nature of the loom's association with Native craft. It claims that "not an Apache squaw in the West will be gayer with bead work than the summer girl who has gone into bead weaving can be if she chooses this coming season."[36] The folklorist Rayna Green has insisted that playing Indian "depends upon the physical and psychological removal, even the death, of real Indians," and the fact that its heyday coincided with a period of the most extreme pressure upon Indian community to abandon traditional lifeways is no coincidence.[37] "Vanishing race" ideology allowed European Americans to position themselves as the true heirs of Native culture and its appropriate perpetuators.

Sargent distinguished the work of hobbyists from that of true artists. "To study decorative art from the surface: that is, to imitate the designs of authoritative contemporary artists, is not only to remain unenlightened, but it is also to produce poor work; for, in the imitation, the spirit of the original composition will be lost, fitness will, in many cases, cease, and the principles necessary in the first instance, will be useless in the copy."[38] The art world professionals favored by Sargent could also be accused of playing Indian, but they paid closer attention to indigenous artists' handling of materials. One mainstream artist who worked in this vein was George de Forest Brush. Brush made his name as a painter of Plains Indians in the 1880s. He studied in the Paris studio of Jean-Léon Gérôme in the late 1870s. Like many American painters who had studied in the French academies, Brush came home interested in infusing his work with a distinctly American character.[39] He responded to the challenge by producing several genre paintings based on travel among the Plains tribes in the western United States and Canada. Significantly, several of Brush's Indian paintings depict a Native artist in the act of creating or presenting his work, and go beyond a simple idea of savage self-expression. Pictures such as *Aztec Sculptor* (1885), or *The Weaver* (ca. 1889) dignify the artists and their work by giving the men classical bodies and showing them in deep, thoughtful engagement with their creations (see plate 7). While many of the artists celebrated during the Indian craze were women, Brush always used male figures, even when the tradition depicted was primarily associated with women, as is the case in the painting of a man weaving a Navajo textile.[40] The insistence on the masculinity of the Indian artist may be another reflection of his identification with primitive creativity.

Brush's Indian paintings were widely exhibited and received much praise, but they did not sell well, and Brush turned his attention to another national type—the "American girl"—in his modern Madonna paintings of the 1890s. Despite this change in subject matter, Brush had an ongoing interest in Native American art. As his students noted, he kept a collection of Indian handicrafts in his studio and appears to have identified with Native artists. A 1901 talk reveals his primitivist conception of creativity. In it he told his audience "that art has always sprung from the highest, intensest, primitive passions of man."[41] The fact that someone known primarily as a painter, and a rather academic one, was promoting the formal and social lessons offered through the study of Indian handicrafts helps us understand the broad impact of arts and crafts thinking. Brush was clearly affected by the social ideas of Morris and other aesthetic reformers. He was also convinced by the arts and crafts movement's openness to the decorative as well as the fine arts. He demonstrated this more in his teaching at the Art Students League than in his own work. Around 1898 Brush began encouraging students to make Indian handicrafts, particularly hand-built pottery. *International Studio* described the project thus: "Mr. George De Forest Brush . . . has found time to form a class in pottery in which he is teaching the true principles of handicraft." The article notes that this is not a course in design on paper but that students work out their ideas through clay "as did the primitive potter."[42] Brush's class on handicraft was part of an increased emphasis on the applied arts under the leadership of the league's director, John LaFarge, whose own output included both paintings and architectural decoration.[43] According to Brush's friend Frederic Coburn, his goal was to encourage each artist to recapitulate the development of Western art. As Coburn put it, Brush held "that the individual should develop as the race has done, i.e., that he cannot begin by tiptoeing up to the highest type of Greek art, but must begin with the ruder forms of aboriginal art."[44] For anti-modernists such as Coburn, living up to the standards of the past was quite an accomplishment: "Now that we have reached the acme of civilization with our fire-proof skyscrapers and our millions of spindles, it still remains to climb to the height of artistic achievement reached by the Zuni and the South Sea Islander."[45]

Brush's statement implies that the study of indigenous art was a stage through which students could pass. But at some point, handicraft ceased being a tool and became an end for some Brush students similarly devoted to aesthetic reform principles. Calling themselves the Brush Guild, these students began selling their wares and sending work to arts and crafts exhibitions.[46] The guild was made up exclusively of women, who had begun entering art schools in increasing numbers in the last decades of the nineteenth century. As I will discuss further in the next chapter, women artists faced particular challenges at this time, for the public expectations of artistic personality often conflicted with the norms of femininity. Perhaps sensing the challenges facing female painters and sculptors, the guild specialized in pottery, a medium whose appropriateness for women was guaranteed not only by the prominence of indigenous potters but also by European American women's long-standing involvement in ceramics and pottery painting.[47] Their initial sources were Pueblo and Mexican wares, but eventually they added ancient Mediterranean forms and techniques to their repertoire. The group included artists working in other fields, notably the sculptor Lucy Perkins (later Lucy Perkins Ripley), who also studied with Augustus Saint-

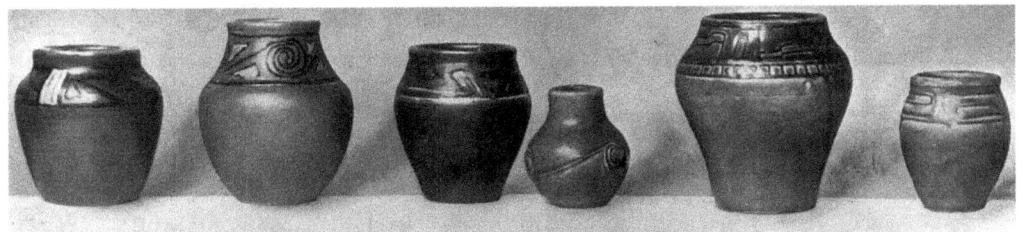

FIGURE 34 "American Indian Ware Design, Matt Glaze," from Charles Binns, "Clay in the Potter's Hand," *Keramic Studio* 3.7 (November 1901): 146. Courtesy of Winterthur Library, Printed Book and Periodical Collection, Winterthur, Delaware.

Gaudens, and art students who left painting and sculpture, such as Elizabeth Burnap Dahlquist, who founded the Shawsheen art pottery company with Edward Dahlquist in 1906. Brush's ideas were disseminated by these artists, through their art potteries and through classes; Perkins taught a course at Chautauqua in 1903, in which students made pots from local clays based on Native American models.[48] Similar projects were rampant in New York and other cities with active art scenes. For example, in 1902 several artists and students organized the Primitive Arts Club in Brooklyn to exchange information on a variety of tribal handicrafts.[49]

Around the same time, pottery students at Alfred University began creating "Indian" pottery (see figure 34). The makers were the protégés of Charles Binns, a ceramist, scholar, and teacher. The British-born Binns had left his position at the Royal Worcester Porcelain works to come to the United States in the 1890s and in 1900 became the founding director of the New York State School of Clay-Working and Ceramics (now the New York State College of Ceramics) at Alfred University.[50] While much of his career was devoted to improving commercial ceramic manufactures, during the latter part of his career he focused his teaching and writing to the exploration of pottery as a craft. From the beginning, Alfred University offered a program in ceramic art as well as one in ceramic technology. In these courses, students were encouraged to oversee the entire pottery process themselves from design through execution. Art students at Alfred were exposed to a variety of methods of forming and decorating pottery and given basic lessons in composition. The work proceeded individually as the students developed their own projects. Because of this, Binns is considered the father of studio ceramics.

Alfred University also offered a summer school, which attracted artists and craftspeople who wanted to enrich their practice without enrolling in a lengthy degree program. The course included instruction in nonceramic arts that were perceived as advancing the craftsperson's skill. An advertisement for the 1903 course lists classes in ceramic design, watercolor and composition, clay building, figure painting, and Indian basketry.[51] While this list doesn't mention it, the summer school also taught Native ceramic technique, including hand building and incised designs. An article of 1903 includes two photographs of "built ware" made in Binns's laboratory classes that clearly have Native inspiration.[52]

The students' interest in Native ceramics went beyond a superficial visual resemblance. Like the artists who played Indian mentioned above, Binns saw Native Americans as artistic role models. He wrote, "For the craftsman nothing is more important than a careful study of early work. This will not lead to copying, but will supply a motive power which cannot be secured in any other way."[53] The work of Binns's colleague Marshall Fry demonstrates this goal. Beginning in 1903 he exhibited hand-built ware to great praise. A reviewer noted, "The influence of the aboriginal Indian is evident in his quaintly modeled bowls and jars, built by hand of a soft buff clay, smeared here and there with a tinge of iron red, which gives the mellowing effect of having been caressed by the fire and the hand of time. The clay is of his own mixing, the ware is un-glazed and fired at a low temperature, but it is truly artistic and American in feeling. The forms are sometimes undecorated, and sometimes have an incised design simple and Indian in character."[54]

Alfred students founded art potteries, including Overbeck and Pewabic, and worked in community ceramics projects in places as diverse as a sanitarium (Marblehead pottery), a women's college (Newcomb), and a settlement house (Hull House). These efforts must be connected to Binns's commitment to the social goals of the arts and crafts movement. His prize-winning article "The Arts and Crafts Movement in America," printed in *The Craftsman* in 1908, exhorts readers to commit to educating the American public to both produce and appreciate handicrafts. He wrote: "Come forth, ye leaders of men! You desire a mission, a vocation. Get up your loom or your wheel in the quiet valley. Gather around you the earnest, simple souls whom the cityward tide has left stranded. Reveal to them the secret chemistry of the woods or the subtle graces of the clay. Bring to bear the arduous training of the schools and the critical atmosphere of the studios. . . . Fear not failure, for honest labor does not fail."[55] Echoing the sentiments of Ruskin and Morris, Binns praised Native ceramics as examples of "honest labor." He told *Craftsmen* readers, "The untutored savage . . . took delight in fashioning vessels of clay. . . . If art be the 'expression of man's joy in his work,' then truly these primitive pots are artistic."[56]

Brush was also a follower of William Morris, and his interest in Native American art reflected his ideas about the social benefits of both producing and consuming art. Brush's aesthetic ideas were integrated into a larger socialist world view that included support of Henry George's single tax, and he frequently shared his ideas on art and politics with his friends in the Art Colony in Cornish, New Hampshire, his students at the Art Students League, and through public lectures.

Art educators of the early twentieth century developed new techniques to teach students to recognize the qualities of different media. The study of indigenous art was one of these techniques. For example, Binns argued that "the work produced in coiling by Indian women is the natural outcome of the clay itself. If forms suitable for clay are to be built, some such line must be followed, not copying, but, with similar material, similar tools and similar limitations, the result would not be true if it were not similar."[57] Similarly, a writer in *Brush and Pencil* emphasized the fact that "the Indian artist works without pattern, model — other than nature — and without rule or compass."[58] The statement betrays the author's ignorance of the rules that dictate many aspects of Native craft production from the gathering and preparing of materials to the construction of the pieces themselves. But this widespread assumption helps explain why Native artists were admired by a generation of artists and art educators attempting to break away from convention-bound academic training. Teachers of studio arts interested in developing their pupils' response to form and technique used Native American art and other non-Western traditions developed exercises designed to ingrain formalist values that could replace the older academic practices emphasizing realistic rendering. Ernest Batchelder's textbook *Design in Theory and Practice*, originally published as a series of articles in *The Craftsman*, illustrates this development.[59] The text, geared toward the artists and designers Batchelder taught at the Throop Polytechnic Institute in Pasadena,

California (now CalArts), and at the Minneapolis Insitute of Arts, builds from simple to more complex exercises. Many of the early tasks use designs drawn from Native American art. For example, chapter 1 uses a large image of a Klikitat imbricated berry basket from Mason's *American Indian Basketry* to illustrate the concepts of space and mass.

ARTHUR WESLEY DOW PLAYS INDIAN

The best known art educator to use Native American art as a model is Arthur Wesley Dow. Dow was an artist and supporter of the arts and crafts movement, but is best known as the teacher of several prominent early American modernists, including Georgia O'Keeffe and Max Weber. Dow began teaching summer classes in his native Ipswich, Massachusetts, in 1891. In 1895 he began spending winters in New York City, where he taught at the Pratt Art Institute and, beginning in 1898, at the Art Students League (alongside Brush). He became the director of fine arts at Teachers College, Columbia University, in 1904. Like Batchelder and Brush, Dow found Native American art a useful pedagogical tool in the training of both fine artists and craftspeople.[60] His students included those full-time students and also professional artists and craftspeople who attended the summer school. The ceramist Marshall Fry was one of his students.

Dow is known for developing what he called the "synthetic method," which deeply influenced American art education at all levels, from primary school and manual training programs through art schools.[61] He spread his ideas not only through classes, but also in lectures and publications. His philosophy is outlined in his 1899 book *Composition*.[62] The book begins with the claim that "art study is the attempt to perceive and to create fine relations of line, mass and color" (21). His method is explained in the following sentence: "That is done by original effort stimulated by the influence of good examples." The subsequent text introduces what Dow considers the three basic components of art: line, *notan* (or balance of light and dark), and color. His exercises use Japanese prints, Gothic architecture, and Persian and Native American textiles as models, among other sources. *Composition* was one of the most influential text books in mainstream art classes in the twentieth century. Interestingly, J. J. Brody suggests that Dow's influence was also felt by Native Americans who were trying to make their work more appealing to non-Indian audiences during this time, noting that a copy was owned by J. B. Moore, the Indian trader known for introducing new design ideas to Navajo weavers near his Crystal, New Mexico Post.[63]

Dow's approach to art began during his academic training in Paris in the mid-1880s. Like so many other Americans, he felt frustrated by the art school curriculum, which he felt focused on mastering illusionistic rendering at the expense of creating beautiful pictures. His academic education would have exposed him to the study of historic ornament such as that illustrated in Owen Jones's *Grammar of Ornament* (1854), and his summers in Brittany put him in the company of innovators, such as Gauguin, who were attempting to insert the decorative qualities of Japanese and local folk art into their work.

Upon his return to the United States in 1889, Dow undertook an intense study of the Pre-Columbian, Ancient Near Eastern, and East Asian art in various Boston collections. He was particularly drawn to Japanese art and served as the assistant to Ernest Fennellosa, curator of Japanese collections at the Museum of Fine Arts, Boston, beginning in 1893. Dow uses numerous concepts and motifs derived from Japanese art in *Composition*, but the book also reveals his nascent interest in indigenous American material. He includes Native objects in a list of global arts praised in his conclusion: "The book will have accomplished its purpose if I have made clear the character and meaning of art structure — if the student can see that out of a harmony of two lines may grow a Parthenon pediment or a Sorbonne hemicycle; out of the rude dish of the Zuni, a Sung tea-bowl, out of the totem-pole a Michelangelo's "Moses": that anything in art is possible when freedom is given to the divine gift of APPRECIATION" (128).

Records from the early 1900s claim that his students at the Ipswich summer school made baskets, pottery, and weavings according to indigenous techniques.[64] A sense of how Dow used Native art can be gained from a 1903 photograph taken at the school (figure 35). The photo illustrates the fact that, like Brush, Dow had many women students. These pupils work at a rustic wooden table set in a bower. In the center of the table is a Pueblo *olla*, and two women work on hand-built pottery nearby. Another woman turns away from the camera to weave on a vertical loom in the manner of the Navajo. The standing woman, whose hands are obscured, may be working or supervising the others. The objects they make do not copy Native American designs, but, rather, seem to be inspired by them.

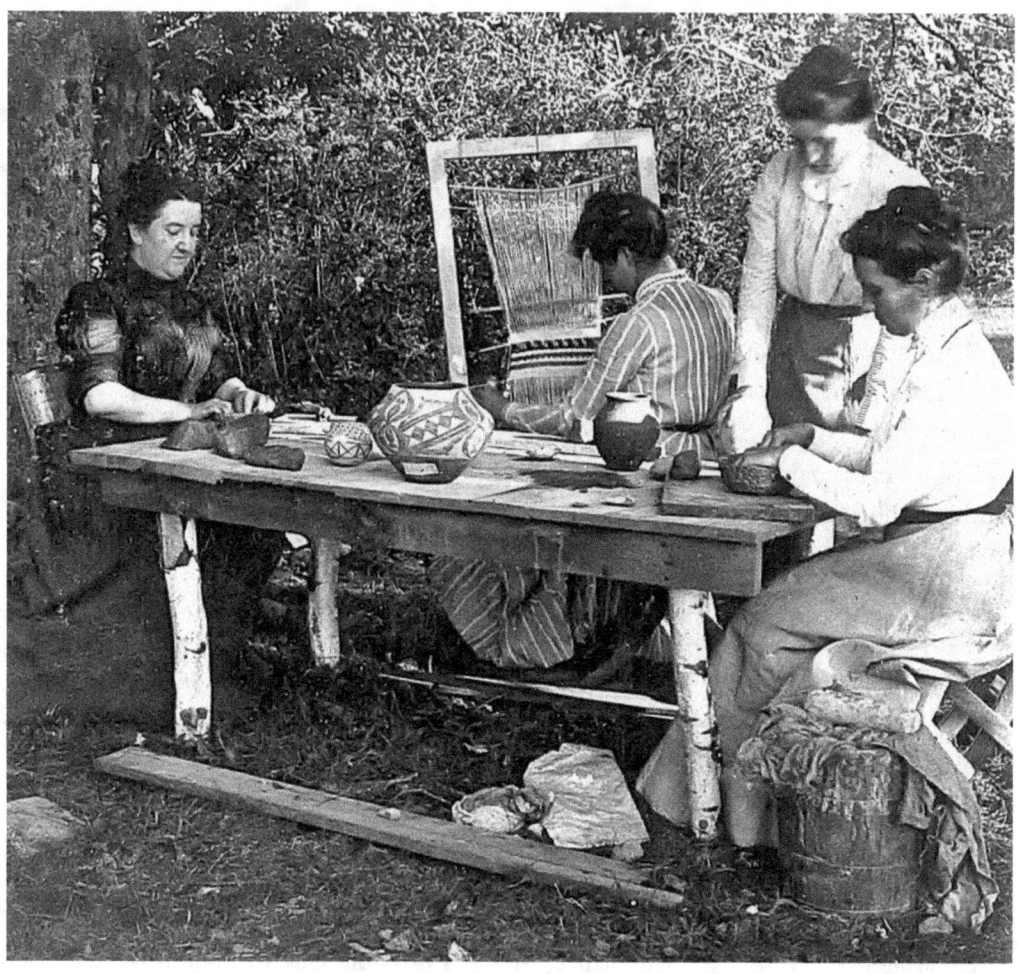

FIGURE 35 Unknown photographer, "Arthur Dow Summer School at Emerson House." Gelatin silver print, n.d. Courtesy of Ipswich Historical Society, Ipswich, Massachusetts.

Dow used Native American art in two ways—from a visual standpoint, it offered examples of line, color, and *notan*. At the same time, he felt that participating in craft traditions was also essential to artistic development. Dow's students were encouraged to use Native techniques to master the relationship between materials and design. Dow felt that working directly with simple materials would awaken a more natural instinctive creativity. His pedagogy was discussed extensively by Sylvester Baxter in the February 1903 issue of *Handicraft*. Baxter was a journalist and strong supporter of urban reform projects in Boston. His article on Dow explains that the artist encouraged his students to go "back to the primitive beginnings of an art, and is shown how to put himself in place of the ancient worker, so far as possible; doing the thing as it was done in the beginning and, by following the primal instincts for art, to develop his work according to natural indications."[65] He encouraged his students to "scrutiniz[e] and study . . . an object of primitive handicraft . . . learning just the processes by which it was made, and then . . . reproduc[e] it just as its makers wrought it" (254).

Part of making things in the "primitive" style involved gathering and preparing local materials. For example, Elizabeth Mason reported that students dug clay for their pottery from a local brook.[66] Baxter explained the significance of this: "The pupils at Ipswich are taught to look to the common things around them for carrying out their work—the barks, the roots, the fibers, the reeds, the rushes, the plants, the sticks, stones, clays and sands. The capabilities of these things in divers directions are studied, and in this way much is learned about the technical and artistic possibilities and the natural limitations of the objects the pupils set out to make."[67]

Dow thus linked his commitment to Native techniques and his passion for the local environment. As a youth, Dow was deeply interested in the colonial history of his native coastal Massachusetts. Like many New England supporters of the colonial revival, he associated Native culture with early American history. Dow would likely have seen Native artifacts exhibited alongside European American ones at local historical societies and venerated both as the products of hearty, moral, preindustrial American culture. Dow was also familiar with the study of Indians in his own time, and he used the work of contemporary anthropologists in his classroom. Baxter attributes his interest in indigenous art to a friendship with the Boston-based ethnologist Frank Hamilton Cushing (figure 36). Cushing, whose controversial career was cut short by illness and an early death, was a pioneer of what would later be called "participant observation." As an employee first of the Bureau of American Ethnology and then of the Boston-based Hemenway Expedition, he had spent most of the 1880s living among the Zuni.[68] Cushing's work involved collecting information on Zuni language and practices, but it emphasized the collection of artifacts. Cushing's first expedition, led by James Stevenson, collected 12,609 objects from Zuni and nearly the same amount from the Hopi between 1879 and 1885.[69] A large number of these were ceramic pieces, a fact that Nancy Parezo attributes to the Pueblo willingness to part with jars and bowls when they would not be

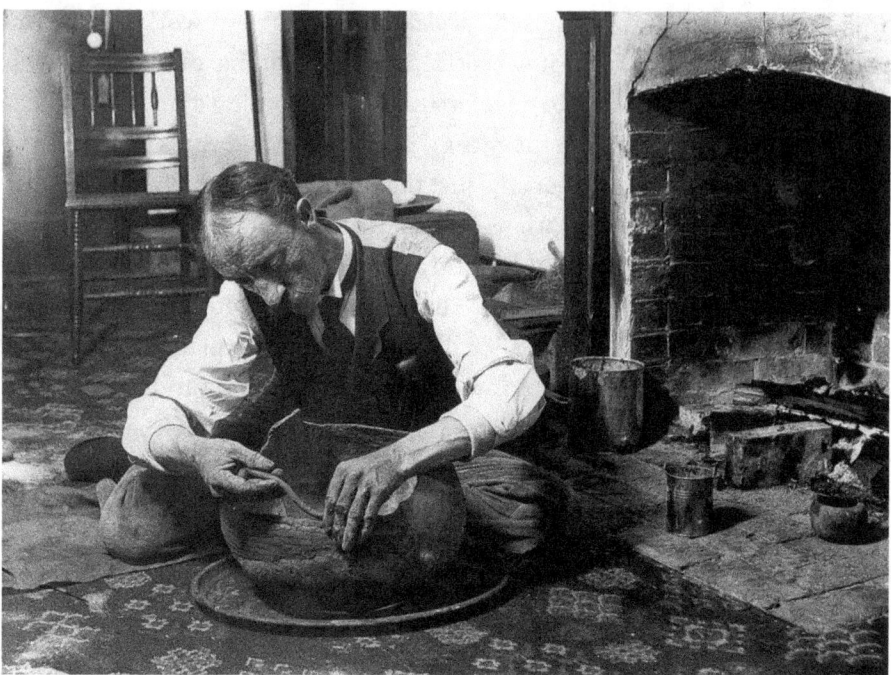

FIGURE 36 Frank Hamilton Cushing demonstrating pottery-making technique, 1890s. Portrait 22-A, National Anthropological Archives, Smithsonian Institution, Washington, D.C.

separated from masks and other ceremonial objects. The Hemenway Expedition collections are also strong in ceramics.

The collecting expeditions of the late nineteenth century became the basis of American natural history museum collections. The Stevenson expedition material went directly to the National Museum, and the Hemenway objects are now housed at the Peabody Museum at Harvard. Thus it was the work of Cushing and his peers that allowed for the aesthetic interpretations of ethnographic collections advocated by Mechlin. But if ethnography laid a groundwork for aesthetics, it is also possible to see aesthetics as an inspiration for ethnography at this time. The interest in collecting Native pottery in the 1880s and 1890s coincided with the aesthetic vogue for pottery, particularly Japanese ware, suggesting that *this* available material might have been more collectible than others, such as discarded clothing or tools.

This connection becomes important when one realizes that Cushing's patrons included people involved in the world of high culture as well as science. For example, the Harvard professor of art history Charles Eliot Norton hosted a reception for Cushing when he brought a delegation of

Zunis to the East Coast in 1882. The group also visited the Paint and Clay Club, a gentlemen's association that included numerous artists among its ranks. The potential overlap between a celebration of Japanese ceramics and Native American pottery is reinforced by the fact that Cushing's supporters included Edward Sylvester Morse, who is best known as a collector of Japanese art.

It is unclear how Cushing and Dow may have met, but the worlds of the two had many points of contact. Mary Hemenway, who supported Cushing's work at Zuni from 1886 to 1889, was a philanthropist who was also dedicated to historic preservation, one of Dow's strong commitments. After giving them part of his collection of Japanese ceramics, Morse held an informal position at Boston's Museum of Fine Arts during the years Dow worked there. Norton was connected to Dow as well as to Cushing: he was the teacher of Dow's mentor Ernest Fennellosa and influenced the establishment of the Society of Arts and Crafts, of which Dow was a member. Baxter himself may have been the link between the two men. He was close to Cushing, having first met him when he traveled to the Southwest as a journalist in search of good stories in the early 1880s, and he remained the ethnographer's friend and supporter thereafter, serving as his colleague on the Hemenway expedition in the rank of secretary-treasurer. Baxter also had ties to the art world. He was married to the sister of the painter Frank Millet, who taught with Dow at Pratt. Moreover, Baxter's wife and Dow were both members of the Society of Arts and Crafts, and the two families' social circles and philanthropic activities overlapped.[70]

Cushing's interest in learning through participation led him to study pottery making and other Zuni craft traditions. He felt the reproduction of Native objects would "recover knowledge of how they had been made and used originally."[71] His writings include detailed descriptions of the processes he learned or recovered in his research. Cushing's sensitivity to form suggests that there was an aesthetic dimension to the scientist's work in this period. This idea is borne out by studies of other pioneering ethnographers interested in tracing the evolution of art. The influential German scholar Ernst Grosse, for example, whose book *The Beginnings of Art* argues for a universal aesthetic impulse, traces the presence of harmony, balance, and rhythm across so-called primitive art.[72] Grosse's use of musical language connects him to the British and continental artistic movements already discussed and their embrace of formalism as a counter to academicism. George Marcus and Fred Myers have described Franz Boas, the German-born "father of American anthropology" famous for introducing a sense of artistic sensibility into the study of primitive art, as having been influenced by modernist art doctrines.[73] It is not unlikely that such ideas could have influenced an artist like Dow, as Grosse's book was widely read in America.

I do not mean to undermine the claim made at the beginning of this chapter that artists and ethnologists looked to Native American art differently. Rather, by stressing Cushing's interest in form, I want to call attention to the fact that both groups emphasized the importance of objects in their investigations. This emphasis highlights how both groups were inspired by the materialism of the age and provides another link to the collectors and marketers discussed in chapter 1. Brad Evans has analyzed Cushing's use of objects in the context of the spread of commodity culture in the Gilded Age.[74] He reads ethnographic collecting as a means of material enrichment that exacerbates the differences between mainstream America (increasingly defining identity through consumption) and its "others" (defined by the act of being consumed).

Objectification is also demonstrated by art teachers' use of Native American art, but in a different way. While ethnographers were dedicated to defining diverse indigenous groups as so many "others" to be consumed, art educators used Native art to aid in the production of new consumables. Frederick Moffat has suggested that one aspect of Cushing's philosophy that would have appealed to Dow was his "belief in the cosmic uniformity of art expression, a uniformity that inexorably bound oriental, occidental, and primitive cultures."[75] Dow's commitment to a universal "primitive instinct" for artistic expression may indeed draw on this idea.[76] But Dow's individualism was tempered by his understanding that personal expression should serve cultural and national needs, and his primitivism incorporated this. As one student put it, the Ipswich classes were not so much about going "back to the primitive way of doing things," as they were devoted to "the wish to inspire in the pupils an appreciation of the possibilities of beauty in the simplest things, and a realization of the *cultural* value of such work executed in a thoughtful and artistic way."[77] As discussed in chapter 1, Native art's cultural value was understood by many Americans of the period to lie in its unquestioned relationship to the American continent. While European American artists had been fighting off criticism that their representational work was derivative of European traditions for nearly a century, Native American art was seen to "belong" to the country. Dow expressed these ideas himself in his 1915 essay "Designs from Primitive Motifs," when he wrote that "we Americans may make an art-use of the naivetés of mound builders, cliff dwellers, pueblo tribes, Alaskans, Aztecs, Mayans, and Peruvians. We shall find in their design a source of fresh impulses for designing in line and in color, for carving and modeling; and these will do their part toward expressing American life through a distinctively American art."[78]

Advancing a universalism that was unable to account for the multiplicity of meanings inherent in Native American art, he essentially encouraged an appropriation of indigenous traditions to support modernism's aesthetic goals. Some educators erased the materiality as well as the cultural meaning of the Native objects being used as models. This is illustrated well by Ernest Batchelder's book *Design in Theory and Practice*. Batchelder's illustrations are taken from well-known examples of Native American art discussed in the *Annual Reports of the Bureau of American Ethnology*, but he does not reproduce the pieces themselves. Instead, he isolates the designs as if they were made to be seen on the flat surface of the page. This reduction of the material impact of the original is accompanied by a reduction in the object's meaning. In his book, the makers of the work are not recognized—the works of diverse tribes all appear under the label "American Indian."

By removing Indian designs from the surface of objects embedded in Indian culture, Batchelder deculturated them, leaving them free for artistic appropriation. The book helped redefine Indian art from a set of objects to a sensibility—an attitude toward the use of tone, shape, and space—that could be used in any medium, applied to any object. As he wrote, "A knowledge of the various historic styles is very important, and should be helpful to us all. But we should bear in mind that such knowledge, no matter how profound, does not necessarily imply an artistic appreciation of good work. There is no merit in any particular type of work; Greek designs are no more worthy than Chinese designs. They must all be brought to the test of fundamental principles, and, lacking an understanding of these principles, we have no criterion other than our personal likes or dislikes by which a judgment may be formed."[79] This radical rejection of the authority of the past marks Batchelder's progressive beliefs. At the same time, by disregarding the cultures from which design sources come, Batchelder suggests that the true artists are his readers, not the providers of his examples.

This is illustrated by his lesson on achieving rhythm through the inter-relation of lines (see figure 37). Much of the work resembles the painted pottery of Nampeyo, the Hopi-Tewa artist. It reproduces the feather and wing forms that characterize her Sityatki-revival ware, as well as the way she uses color and texture of line to enhance the sense of movement around the interiors of her bowls (see figure 38), but it divorces the designs from their original context.

EXHIBITING NATIVE AMERICAN ART

The use of Native American art by critics and art teachers demonstrates that it was being seen aesthetically at the beginning of the twentieth century. But the use of Native objects in these spheres of the art world reinforced the basic premise of modernist primitivism—that the "primitive" is a resource outside the modern that can fuel and improve modern cultural production. While the African masks that inspired Picasso are visible in his early cubist paintings, work made by the students of Brush, Binns, Dow, or Batchelder was not necessarily Native in appearance. Nevertheless, these artists and the members of their audience who read art journals, saw their very han-dling of materials as a primitive process that could revitalize modern artis-tic production. The association between these modern artists and the primi-tive was enhanced by exhibitions that displayed their work alongside that of Native Americans.

As part of the aesthetic celebration of Native American art, art organi-zations began exhibiting Native American objects in the late nineteenth century. In some cases, a museum or gallery hosted a special exhibition of indigenous art. For example, during Dow's tenure there, the Pratt Art Insti-tute Gallery held an exhibition of Native American baskets.[80] The Society of Arts and Crafts, Boston, also arranged for displays of Native art and crafts-people affiliated with the Indian Industries League in their showrooms nu-merous times in the first decade of the twentieth century.[81]

Art museums, particularly those west of the eastern seaboard, added in-digenous material to their collections early on. The Cincinnati Art Museum's collection began before the museum opened in 1886. Five years earlier,

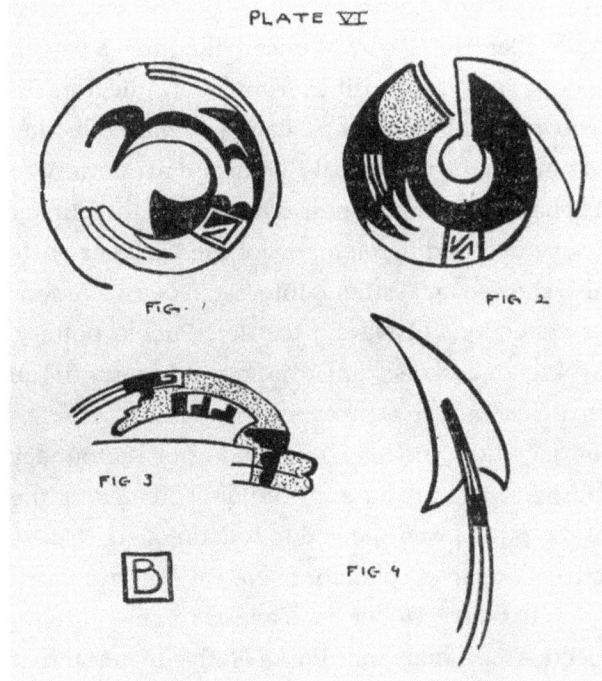

FIGURE 37 Ernest
Batchelder, plate 6 from
The Principles of Design
(Chicago: Inland Printer,
1906), 16. Courtesy of
Winterthur Library, Printed
Book and Periodical
Collection, Winterthur,
Delaware.

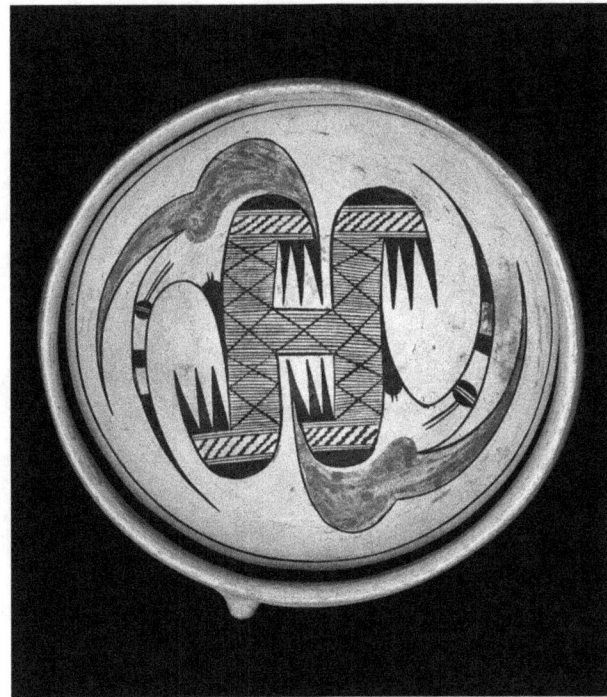

FIGURE 38 Nampeyo
(Hopi-Tewa), bowl in
the Sikyatki revival style,
1900–1907. Terracotta,
white slip, and vegetable
pigments. Hood Museum
of Art, Dartmouth College,
Hanover, New Hampshire.
Bequest of Frank C. and
Clara G. Churchill.

the Women's Art Museum Association began collecting pottery excavated from the remains of a Native village in nearby Madisonville (now a part of Cincinnati) and accepting donations of curiosities from local collectors. In 1885, they expanded the geographical reach of their indigenous collecting by sending ceramic pieces produced by the local Rookwood art pottery to the National Museum in exchange for Pueblo pots collected by the Bureau of American Ethnology.[82] Several founding members of the Denver Artists Club, organized in 1893, also showed an aesthetic interest in Native American art and donated their collections of Navajo textiles, Pueblo pottery, and, later, watercolors, and Indian baskets from around the country to the organization that was later to become the Denver Art Museum.[83] San Francisco's Golden Gate Memorial Museum (later renamed after its founder M. H. de Young) was established when the Fine Art Building erected for the "Midwinter Exposition" of 1893–1894 was allowed to remain open. Its first curator, Charles P. Wilcomb, was an avid collector of Native American artifacts, particularly Californian basketry. Under his leadership, the museum acquired an extensive collection of Indian and Alaska Native material that became its chief attraction. While Wilcomb is sometimes referred to as an ethnologist, his attitude toward the objects in the museum, including works of art, Anglo-colonial artifacts, and Native American material culture, betrays his commitment to the aesthetic ideas discussed above. As he wrote in the museum's 1900 *Annual Report*, "The test applied to each when its admission to the museum was contemplated has been: is it interesting? Does it move thought and appeal to the higher reaches of the imagination?"[84] Wilcomb went on to assemble another fine collection of Native art for the Oakland Museum, where he was founding curator from 1908 until his early death in 1915.

These examples suggest the possibility that Native American art could be appreciated aesthetically without having to be seen as equivalent to the work of mainstream modern artists. However, there are several examples of exhibitions from the turn of the twentieth century in which indigenous art was exhibited alongside that of non-Indians. Many of these were exhibitions of artistic handicrafts. Indian objects were included in several influential arts and crafts exhibitions, including the 1903 exhibition of the Minneapolis Arts and Crafts Society and the "Exhibition of Art Craftsmanship" in Syra-

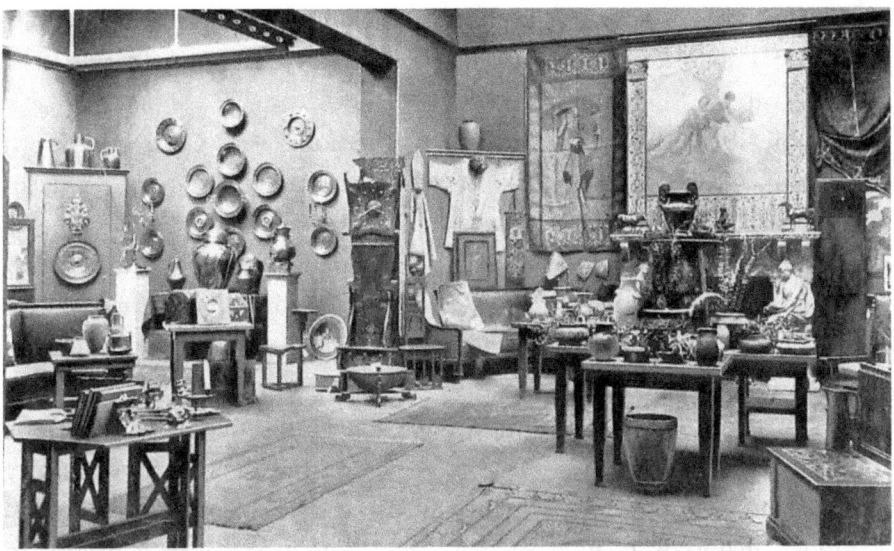

FIGURE 39 "Galleries, National Arts Club: Arts and Crafts Exhibition," from *National Arts Club*, exhibition brochure (New York: National Arts Club, 1901), frontispiece. Private collection.

cuse, New York, and in Boston's Society of Arts and Crafts exhibitions of 1899 and 1907.[85] Supporters of the arts and crafts movement no doubt used the contemporaneous celebration of Native art to support their own claims for the acceptance of the decorative arts.

Native American art was also sometimes displayed in exhibitions that featured not only decorative arts but also painting and sculpture. These installations offer a complex meditation on whether a Native American might be considered a modern artist. One example of this can be found in the 1900 annual exhibition of the National Arts Club in New York City. The display was wide-ranging, incorporating both fine and decorative arts and including a sizable loan of Native baskets, textiles, and beadwork. Although it does not feature the Native American material, a photograph from the Arts Club archives (figure 39) gives a sense of the display. A rather plain room with colored walls provides a simple backdrop for the artworks arrayed within. While there are a large number of objects on display, the works are brought together in clusters at different heights, giving an overall variety to the room that invites examination of each area. Significantly, objects are not separated by medium but are intermingled. The back wall juxtaposes a large painting in an elaborate frame with a tapestry and what appears to be a kimono or robe. Decorative arts are displayed on tables, suggesting their potential for domestic use, and are also hung on the walls, highlighting their aesthetic value.

To understand the significance of the National Arts Club exhibition, it is useful to look briefly at exhibitionary practice of the period. One of the common ways to diagnose the kind of response evoked by an object is through an examination of how it is displayed.[86] Ethnographers and artists come to Native art with different agendas and these agendas are manifest in the way Native objects are installed in natural history museums and art galleries. In natural history museums, emphasis is placed on how the object illustrates a cultural practice, and it is often accompanied by written texts and by other objects that reinforce this association. Art galleries downplay the functionality of objects to bring the viewers' attention to their formal qualities — materials, form, craftsmanship. Labels are frequently limited to a simple identification of the object and tend to emphasize the individuality of the artist or the uniqueness of the work over its representativeness.

As with art criticism and formalist art education, these modes of display were just being developed at the time of the Indian craze. Mary Anne Staniszewski has explored the use of radical display techniques by avant-garde artists in the interwar years. As she argues, "Artists fascinated with the possibility of creating public exhibition spaces saw installation design as one of the many new arenas of mass communication that would transform modern life."[87] The idea that exhibition could be as important to declaring one's aesthetic values as the individual object was actually proclaimed much earlier. Once again following Whistler's cue, modern artists turned away from the crowded salon-style installations of the national academies in the last quarter of the nineteenth century. They developed exhibition techniques designed to solicit a private encounter with the single work of art. These techniques included the isolation of an individual object, the installation of diverse media in the same gallery, and the use of wall color, frames, and lighting to enhance viewers' ability to commune with works on display.

In addition to changing the physical appearance of displays, modern artists also revised the means by which works of art were included in exhibitions. In particular, they challenged the traditional jury system used by art academies, whereby assessments of younger artists' work were carried out by established members of the academy. Such practices served to reproduce traditional standards. In their place, younger artists proposed using individual curators or artists themselves to make selections. In some cases, there was no jury at all—artists simply submitted work to be displayed. The National Arts Club exhibitions were innovative along both of these lines. The illustration of the 1900 exhibition demonstrates the range of materials included in its exhibitions. Ceramics, sculptures, paintings, and textiles are displayed in artful clusters on carved wooden tables and against painted walls. The club supported a number of organizations dedicated to the elevation of the applied arts, such as the National Society of Art Craftsmen and the New York Society of the Keramic Arts. It is notable as the host of the first public exhibition dedicated solely to the promotion of photography as a fine art: Alfred Stieglitz's "Photo-Secession" exhibition of 1902. The Arts Club also supported avant-garde painting, hosting a 1904 exhibition of many of the artists who would later become known as the ashcan school. The support of such a range of artistic projects was a hallmark of the Arts Club's modernity, of its openness to a variety of definitions of art.

The institution was founded in 1898 by Charles de Kay, a writer and, for many years, arts critic for the *New York Times*, who had enthusiastically witnessed the experiments fusing art and life in central and western Europe while serving as a diplomat in Berlin in the early 1890s. An early description of the club's goals reveals this influence: "To promote the acquaintance of art lovers and art workers in the United States one with another; to stimulate and guide toward practical expression the artistic sense of the American people; to maintain in the city of New York a clubhouse with such accommodation and appurtenances as shall fit it for social purposes in connection with art; to provide proper exhibition facilities for such lines of art, especially applied and industrial art, as shall not be otherwise adequately provided for in the same city; and to encourage the publication and circulation of news, suggestions and discussions relating to the fine arts."[88]

Club members were particularly interested in contemporary discussions of art's role in society. The same pamphlet notes that "special fields of the Arts Club are the promotion of the arts and crafts, in order ultimately to improve the quality of our manufactures, and a stimulation of interest in the embellishment of cities and public buildings."[89] In its effort to cultivate national culture, the Arts Club described its galleries as focusing on

American work, although they would feature loans of "European, Oriental and Ancient objects for purposes of comparison and for the stimulus they afford."[90]

The National Arts Club clearly expected its viewers to see the indigenous objects in the same light as the other works on display. This is not surprising, given that several members of the club were major collectors of Native American art, such as Louis Comfort Tiffany and Frederic Pratt, or artists who used Native art as a model for their work, such as Dow and Fry. The works in the 1900 exhibition were loaned by the New York–based dealer Frank M. Covert; they were displayed in the same galleries listed individually in the exhibition catalogue alongside non-Indian works.

The inclusion of Native arts in the 1900 exhibition was not isolated. While the club records are incomplete, we know that it hosted an exhibition of Eskimo art in 1902 and that Indian handicrafts were probably included in later group exhibitions. The National Arts Club also hosted lectures on historical and contemporary Native American art by George Wharton James and Edgar Hewett, the archeologist who became the first head of the Museum of New Mexico, and who later became a promoter of Pueblo Indian watercolors. The National Arts Club is also where, in the winter of 1915–16, Mary Austin and Ina Sizer Cassidy initially formulated their plan to organize the Indian Arts Fund, to purchase and preserve Native American handicrafts and to support contemporary Native artists.[91]

But while the organizers of programming at the National Arts Club and other venues can be understood as seeing Native American artists as sharing their aesthetic values, exhibitions of Native American art reveal the problems that make this identification an appropriation. In each case discussed above, Native artists were not the ones who decided to exhibit their work, nor were they the ones interpreting it. This situation was exacerbated in venues where exhibitions of Native American art were located in close proximity to exhibitions that focused on the sensational exoticism of Native culture. The same tendency occurred in many urban venues, as art museums and galleries were rarely far from theaters hosting *Wild West* shows or nickelodeons showing westerns. A particularly dramatic illustration of this trend occurred at the Louisiana Purchase Exposition, held in Saint Louis in 1904.

In many ways, this exhibition offered the most radical display of Native American art in the early twentieth century. The Louisiana Purchase Exposition was the first American international exposition to include the decorative arts in the Fine Arts Palace—previously, individual artists and artistic firms such as Tiffany and Company had to display their work in buildings dedicated to industrial production. The exposition's art director Halsey C. Ives hoped that the Fine Art Palace would demonstrate that "all art work, whether on canvas, in marble, plaster, wood, metal, glass, porcelain, textile or other material—when the artist-producer has worked with conviction and knowledge—is recognized as equally deserving of respect in proportion as it is worthy from the standpoints of inspiration and technique." The inclusion of Native objects in the art building was the result of a letter written to Ives by the chief of the Applied Art Division, Frederic Allen Whiting, secretary-treasurer of Boston's Society of Arts and Crafts. A month before the show opened, Whiting told Ives that he thought that "some of the best crafts work done in the country is done among the Indians. I cannot see why the Indian should not be considered as an artist craftsman as well as any other worker." Ives responded enthusiastically that there was "ample room for all acceptances on high standard." Whiting had some difficulty assembling works, however. While he demanded that his assistant assemble a collection "considered from a standard of design and workmanship, as in the case of any other work," his lack of connections to Native artists or even to dealers and a tight deadline compromised his ability to assemble a large collection. Fortunately, George Wharton James came through with a sizable loan that included exceptionally good pieces of Californian and southwestern baskets and seven pots by Nampeyo.

Ernest Batchelder assembled a second loan exhibition from a dealer in Pasadena called The Wigwam, which included additional baskets as well as Navajo textiles and silverwork. As at the National Arts Club, these items are all listed individually in the handbook to the exhibition, although the lenders were frequently unable to identify the artist by name. Photographs that exist of the galleries make it difficult to identify individual pieces. However, the style of the installation tells us a great deal about how viewers were encouraged to see the works. The organizers were self-consciously mimicking Whistler's display aesthetics. The building even included a spe-

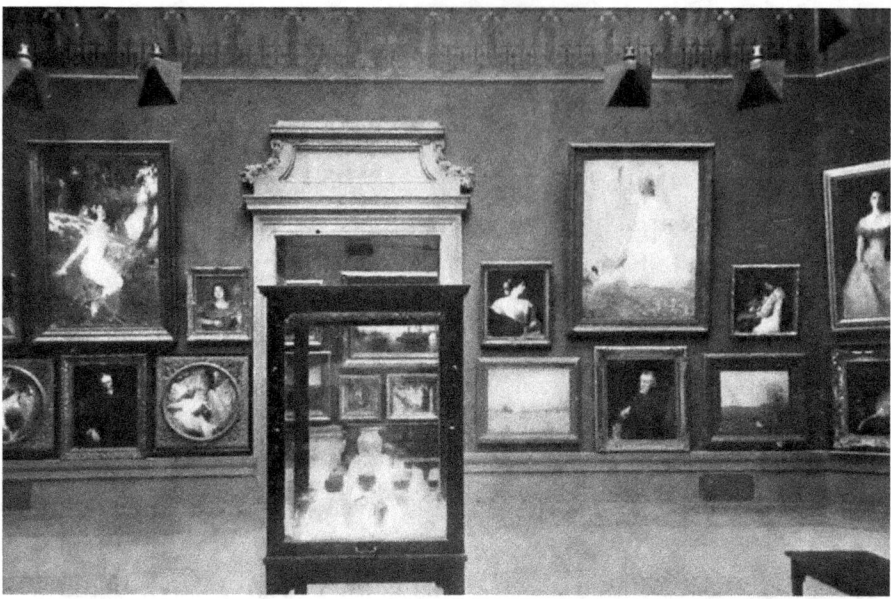

FIGURE 40 "Gallery 2, north wall," from "Division of Exhibits Department B, Art," in *Official Catalogue of Exhibitors: Universal Exposition, St. Louis, U.S.A. 1904*, rev. ed. (St. Louis: Official Catalogue Company, 1904), xlv.

cial gallery dedicated to Whistler's work, which explicitly followed his precepts. Photographs of other galleries show vitrines of decorative objects in rooms that also featured painting and sculpture, demonstrating an aestheticist disregard for high/low distinctions. Records show that great attention was given to ensuring that works exhibited in the same galleries harmonized with one another and that spacing, lighting, and other aspects of display supported an aesthetic effect.[92] Photographs from the art department's *Handbook* illustrate this, such as the one that shows a gallery in which fine and decorative arts are displayed together in a spacious room with colored walls and muted light (figure 40). The simple lines of the wooden moldings, display cases, and furniture work give the room further unity.

Few of the reviews paid much attention to the indigenous art. However, the "Indianesque" works by European American artists were frequently noticed. The display included a number of such works. Emma A. Silvester, a member of the Boston Society of Arts and Crafts, showed some "Indian design" beadwork, craftswomen from rural Maine exhibited woven "Sabatos" rugs with an "Indian design," and several well-known ceramists, including

Charles Binns, Marshall Fry, and Lucy Perkins, shared pots whose hand-built construction and geometric decoration were also associated with Native traditions.[93] Nearby at the Applied Industries Building, the Rookwood Company was praised for work that "illustrated the application to modern art of the forms and decorative motives derived from the fictile art of the North American Indians."[94]

Perhaps the Native art on display was so consistent with mainstream aesthetics that it blended in seamlessly with its surroundings. More likely, viewers were less interested in Native handicrafts presented as "art" than those presented as the curious production of members of a primitive race. They had ample opportunity to encounter Native American art in this way elsewhere at the fair. In response to the national popularity of Native American art, the exposition's anthropology display featured Indian craftspeople from the tribal nations associated with high-quality work, who lived in makeshift Indian villages and spent their days demonstrating their skills and selling work to viewers. Souvenirs and photographs emphasized the purchase of Native American art as an encounter with the representative of an exotic culture (see figure 41).

But if the Native craftspeople at the anthropology display were not able to control viewer's expectations, they *were* in charge of deciding what to display, something not granted to the producers of the work at the Fine Arts Palace. In most cases, we must assume that these decisions were based on what was selling. For the craftspeople at the fair received no wages from the Anthropology Department, and relied on sales for their income. Presumably many artists felt that this opportunity to broaden their audience was worth the long trip to Saint Louis and the uncomfortable accommodations offered them once they got there. Moreover, Indian artists were also given the power to decide *not* to exhibit and sell their work. As John Toutman has recounted, the well-known and well-compensated Pomo basketmakers Mary and William Benson traveled to the fair but stayed only briefly. When they found that they were expected to work uncompensated for the anthropological exhibit in addition to selling their wares, they returned to California.[95] The Bensons provide a good illustration of how Indian artists worked within the severe limitations of the time to exercise the choices they could over the production and distribution of their work.

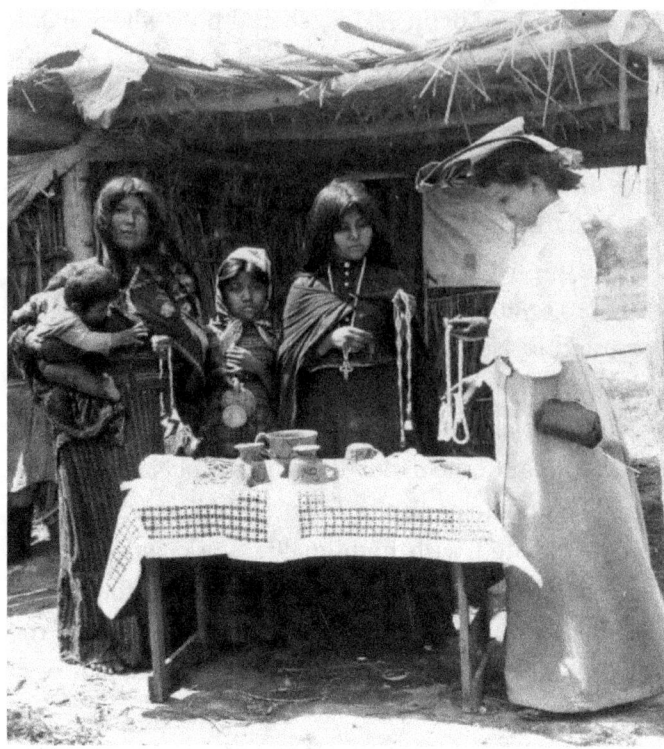

FIGURE 41
William H. Rau,
"23234. Pueblo
Indian Pottery Sellers,
Indian Reservation,
World's Fair, St.
Louis, 1904." Inv. no.
LC-USZ62–108512,
Library of Congress,
Prints and Photo-
graphs Division,
Washington, D.C.

This episode of primitivism's links with modernism differs from some of the better known examples, such as Picasso's interest in African carving, in that American artists of this generation did not mimic Native subjects or motifs. But as writers, teachers, and curators, this generation exerted influence well into the next generation. Their work played a key role in facilitating the transition from the narrative traditions of the nineteenth century to the more abstract art forms of the twentieth, in large part because it offered a way to promote formal concerns without sacrificing art's social value. Artists working with indigenous art forms were able to focus on formal concerns because they were inherently culturally meaningful. Native American art was understood as unimpeachably authentic and inherently American.

At the same time, this history highlights the different aspirations of European American and Native artists at the time. While both aspired to make high-quality works of art, they had different understandings of the significance of that work. Each sought to maximize power in their own sphere. Non-Indian artists, critics, and curators celebrated indigenous art as a means of shifting the focus of the art world to the formalist concerns they found inherently modern. Native artists pursued financial stability, leadership in their own communities, and, if the opportunity presented itself, the chance to explore a broader intercultural world through exchange and travel. This was a modern experience indeed, one that was as strongly conditioned by the economic and cultural changes of the turn of the twentieth century as that of the mainstream artists, as the next chapter will explore.

CHAPTER FOUR

To become an artist at the turn of the century was not only a social matter of training and opportunity, it was also a question of aspiration, of imagining oneself an artist.

Lisa Tickner

The Indians in Käsebier's Studio

As the Indian craze spread, the celebratory image of the Indian artist began to be promoted by artists as well as reformers. This interest can be seen in two photographs of Indian men drawing made in the late 1890s by Gertrude Käsebier, a pictorialist, or artistic, photographer. Käsebier's photographs depict Indian artists as artistic peers. The portraits of Indians in the act of drawing conform to an emerging model of creativity and craftsmanship. The photograph of four Indian artists working together, for example, embodies the values of fellowship, spontaneity, and individuality that were the backbone of the philosophy of William Morris, a founder of the arts and crafts movement (see figure 42).[1] While they draw at the same board, each artist takes a different position: Sam Lone Bear is completely absorbed in his work, while the man across from him considers his next line, and Joe Black Fox looks up as if seeking inspiration.

Käsebier's portrait of Sam Lone Bear, which appeared in an article titled "Some Indian Portraits" in the January 1901 issue of *Everybody's Magazine*, provides further evidence for the suggestion that these portraits are designed to show the Indian models as artists (see figure 43).[2] Lone Bear is not

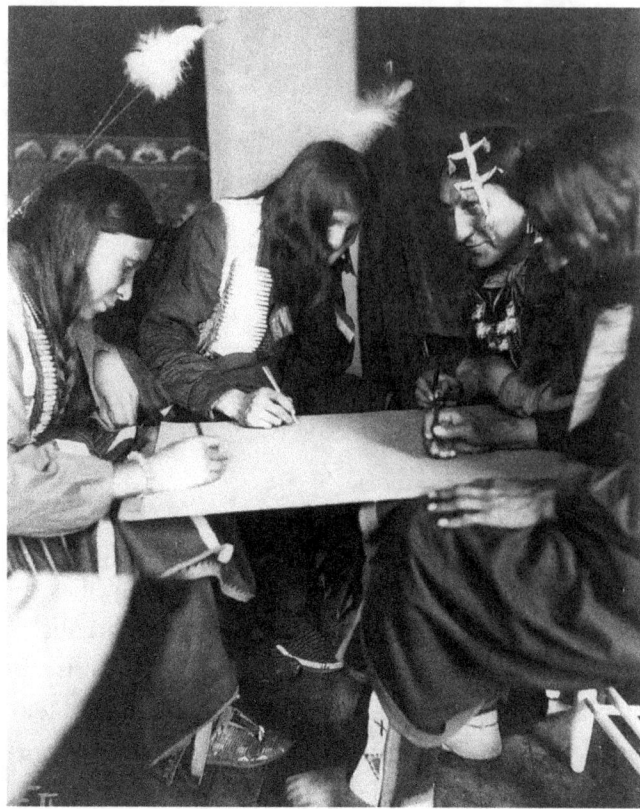

FIGURE 42 Gertrude Käsebier, untitled (Samuel Lone Bear, Joe Black Fox, and two unidentified sitters), ca. 1898. Platinum print, 7 7/8 × 5 7/8 inches. Photographic History Collection, National Museum of American History, Smithsonian Institution, Washington, D.C. Gift of Mason Turner.

depicted in the act of drawing, but is instead shown in a manner conventional for the representation of European artists: he is posed in front of his work. The space behind the artist's head is filled with imagery that matches drawings signed by him that are reproduced elsewhere in the article. The placement of these designs behind Lone Bear's head gives the viewer the impression that they are the product of intellectual, as well as manual, work, and the fact that the hands that produced these sketches are barely visible in the photograph reinforces this. The reference to conventional representations of artists in their studios associates Käsebier's workspace with the Indians' creativity. This chapter looks at Käsebier's representations of Indian artists and their drawings as a means of advancing her own professional and artistic development, and shows how the appropriation of Indian creativity helped her resolve the contradictions of being a modern artist and a modern woman at the same time.

Central to this discussion are the text and illustrations of "Some Indian

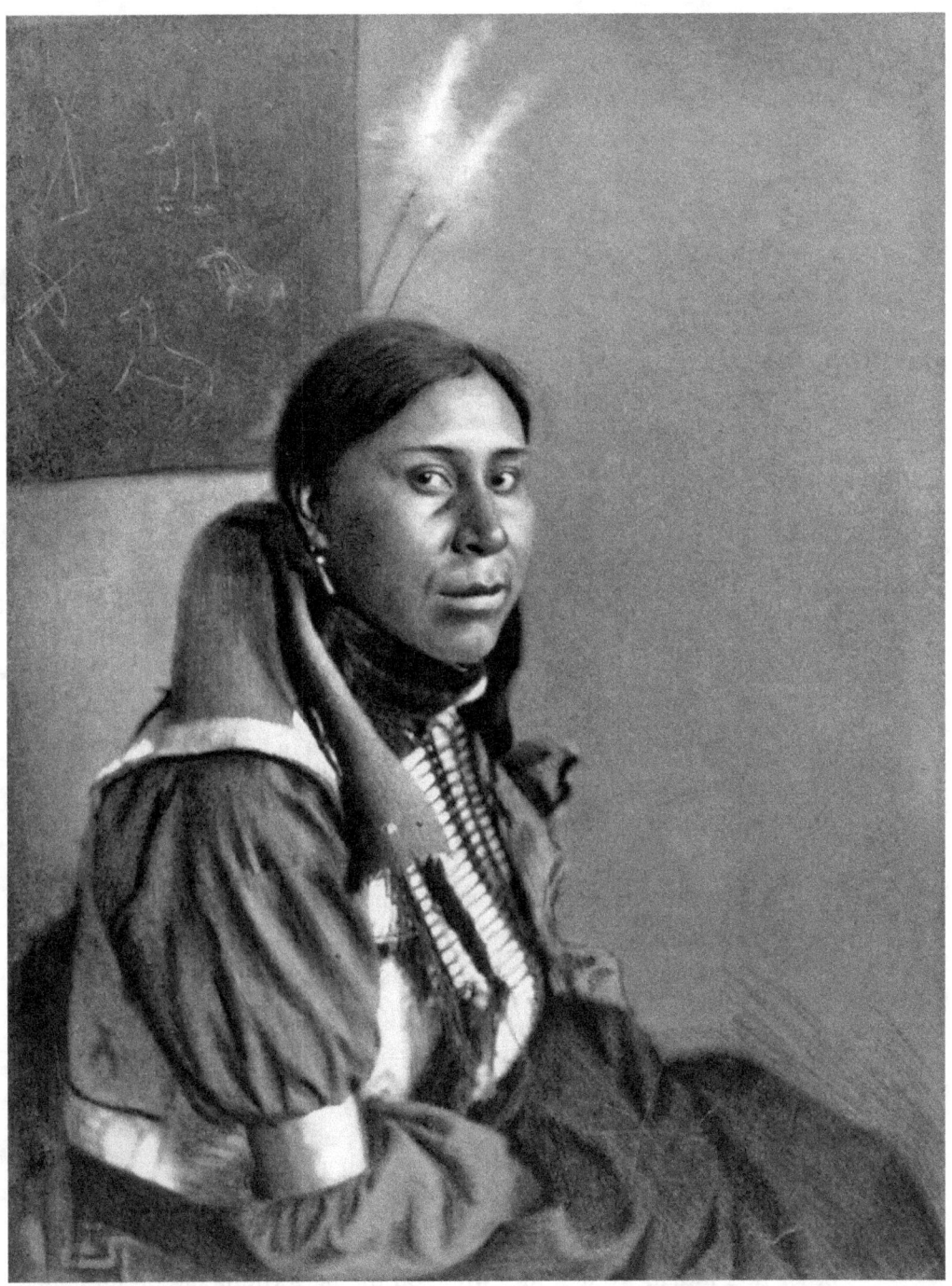

FIGURE 43 Gertrude Käsebier, "Sam Lone Bear," ca. 1898, from "Some Indian Portraits," *Everybody's Magazine* 4.17 (January 1901): 20.

Portraits." Rather than emphasizing the role of Indian art as a tool in the progress of Indian people toward civilization, the article suggests that adopting Indian aesthetics could help non-Indian artists advance their skills and their careers. "Some Indian Portraits" was illustrated with eleven Indian drawings and eighteen Käsebier photographs of *Wild West* show performers. The unsigned text was also likely written by Käsebier. She undoubtedly felt that an article in a high-circulating magazine linking her with a tremendously popular form of entertainment, then at its height, would add to her own reputation.[3]

There is a tension in the article between the subtlety of the photographs and the broad primitivism of the article's text. "Some Indian Portraits" tells the story of a European American woman photographer who invites Indian performers from the *Wild West* show to come to her Fifth Avenue studio for a sitting. The first sentences put the photographer at the center of the story: "The 'Wild West' parade was passing along the avenue. A woman looked down upon it from a studio window and saw Indians, real live Indians, tricked out in gaily colored finery, and astride wiry little horses. The mere sight of their painted dignity was enough to revive for her the fascination of the Plains. She longed for a breath of the prairies, for a far horizon, a dome of blue sky above, the majesty of the storm in the open" (1). When the parade passes out of view behind a skyscraper, the photographer determines not to miss an opportunity to fuel her nostalgia for her western childhood. She writes to the show's impresario and invites the performers to pay her a call. When she arrives at her studio the next morning, the Indians are already there. "She opened the door, and with difficulty suppressed an exclamation of mingled surprise and pleasure. Her request for Indians had been generously complied with. Seated in a large circle around the 'model-throne'—which was occupied by the chaperon as chief—were nine of the most gorgeous braves she had ever beheld" (2).

The article goes on to discuss the visitors' "gorgeous" appearance, their acceptance of a snack of frankfurters, and their use of time between poses to draw and smoke cigarettes. It ends by reproducing letters later sent to the photographer by several of the models that recount their experiences with other non-Indian women met while on the performing circuit and document the difficult transition back to reservation life when the *Wild West* season ends. The inclusion of the letters and drawings is explained by the author's observation that they "amusingly" demonstrate "a certain naïveté and cunning simplicity . . . which seems inherent in Indian nature" (12).

The text idealizes the visitors in antimodernist, primitivizing language, playing their unfamiliarity with the mores of New York artistic society against their honesty, virility, and naive charm. With its patronizing language, the article repeats many of the messages of other contemporary descriptions of Indian culture: Native Americans are "children" whose verbal and visual self-expression is best understood as a means of revitalizing non-Indian culture. While the drawings conform to the style and iconography of the Plains heraldic tradition, their importance as a means of cultural persistence is not explored. Instead, they are seen as the spontaneous products of individual imaginations. Yet the reader is invited to find in the drawings and photographs individuality and strength that are missing in more refined cultural documents. As in other expressions of the Indian craze, they are used to critique the direction that modern American "civilization" has taken. The simplicity of Indian culture is held up as an admirable quality at a time of urban hustle and bustle. The author mourns the loss of the "bands of roving red men, still free to come and go at will, with never a thought of 'reservations,'" and suggests that contact with European Americans has harmed, rather than improved, Native Americans. The poor education and aimlessness that characterize contemporary Indian life "suggest some interesting considerations as to the effects of our civilization upon our Indian wards" (1, 24).

Outside of this article and a few brief lines in personal letters, Käsebier did not discuss these pictures. However, the visuality of the photographs and the text that accompanies them associates them with the primitivism of the early modernist culture in which Käsebier participated. In their struggle for the acceptance of photography as a fine art, pictorialists like Käsebier used the formalist language that dominated contemporary art criticism to celebrate their work. At the same time, they, like contemporary artists working in other media, suggested that art could contribute to national social and cultural progress. "Some Indian Portraits" unites these goals, suggesting a relationship between an interest in Indian art and an interest in Indian welfare and holding out Indian culture as a model for the rejuvenation of non-Indian culture.

The association between her own artworks and Indian creativity was desirable for a photographer who was working to advance the idea of photography as a modern artform. Käsebier was a member of the Photo-Secession, a movement promoting technical and creative experimentation in the medium, operating in New York under the intellectual and organizational leadership of early modernist photographer and impresario Alfred Stieglitz.[4] In advocating a subjective approach to photography, the Photo-Secession and the larger pictorialist, or art photography, movement of which it was a part annexed the language of the arts and crafts movement to bring attention to issues of craftsmanship, composition, tonality, and subjectivity in photography.[5] As in other wings of the arts and crafts movement, some pictorialist photographers capitalized on the discourse of Indian art's celebration of Native American creativity as a means of promoting their own originality. No one did this more than Gertrude Käsebier who, as a former student of Arthur Dow as well as a member of the Photo-Secession, had two strong links to primitivism.

At the same time, Käsebier allied herself politically with progressive women reformers of the day. Like Nellie Doubleday, Estelle Reel, and other middle-class European American women who championed Indian culture during this time, Käsebier celebrated the primitive as a means to explore a modern public sphere. Being a commercial and artistic photographer enabled her to pursue economic independence and self-expression. The wife of a German-born importer, she enrolled in art courses at the newly established Pratt Institute in 1889, when her youngest child was nine. Her artistic education inspired her imagination, but also gave her the idea of supplementing the family income through her work, especially after her husband faced business setbacks in the late 1890s.[6] After seeking some additional artistic training in Europe, Käsebier decided to pursue photography instead of painting, seeing it as a more lucrative, and equally expressive, form of art. She opened her first commercial studio in New York in 1898, and had an active, though not always smooth, career there for over a decade. Like other promoters of Native American art, she embraced the arts and crafts movement's suggestion that artistic and economic success could be linked, and that the promotion of art could effect social change.

Käsebier's studio can be thought of as a kind of Indian corner with one important difference: instead of decorating with Indian *art*, she decorated with Indian *artists*. Though these decorations were less permanent than the textiles and ceramics with which other supporters of Indian aesthetics filled their homes, the photographs offered a permanent record of the visits of Native Americans. The shift changes the associations of such a space away from the nostalgic collection of obsolete works of art to the production of new works made in the spirit of Indian creativity. In Käsebier's photographs, the Indians are presented not only as markers for decorative primitivism, but also as artistic role models whose lack of "civilization" endows their work with an individuality, energy, and honesty to which non-Indian artists should aspire.

The significance of Käsebier's contribution to the Indian craze is two-fold: it locates pictorialist photography at the center of a discussion about the aesthetic lessons offered by Native American art, and it illustrates how non-Indian women used Indian "otherness" as a means of exploring and enhancing their authority within the changing gender roles of the turn of the century. Käsebier's identification with Native draftsmen is not limited to their shared creative talents. She and they are also linked in their marginalization within contemporary debates about the nature of modern American culture. I will suggest that the photographs invite a challenge to the very primitivism they seem to celebrate by highlighting the fact that both the photographer's and her models' careers were impacted by very modern expectations of race and gender behavior.

KÄSEBIER'S PROGRESSIVE PRIMITIVISM

The idea to publish "Some Indian Portraits" likely grew out of several notices on the "Woman's Page" of the *New York Times* in April 1898 and 1899 that Käsebier had photographed *Buffalo Bill* performers in her studio. The very first account suggested the excitement caused by the event: "There was a studio tea up town . . . last week which probably exceeded in originality anything in the nature of an entertainment of that kind ever given. In the first place, the men outnumbered the women three to one, and their attire was more gorgeous than anything that was ever seen in the most startling ball gown. . . . The tea was given in the morning, which was also unique, but quite in keeping with the other features of the affair. . . . The studio was that of Mrs. Gertrude Käsebier and the gentlemen present were . . . nine Sioux Indians."[7] Studio gossip was a staple of turn-of-the-century journalism, and such articles contributed to the contemporary impression of the artist as a bohemian, and stimulated a public desire to make contact with this exotic world. As such, the notices provided free advertising for the artists discussed.[8]

The publicity couldn't have been better timed for the photographer, who had only opened this, her first studio, a few months earlier. While she had received some public acclaim for exhibitions at her alma mater, the Pratt Institute in 1897, she was seeking ways to announce her new professional status. This interest is demonstrated by the location of the studio in the heart of the shopping district called the Ladies Mile, near other photography studios and the New York Camera Club.[9] Käsebier likely welcomed the *Times'* attention. She wanted to dissociate her work from common commercial photography, and thus avoided using print advertising. Instead, she relied on the celebrity of her models to attract attention to her studio. She photographed society beauties and included their portraits in her exhibitions and in the display case set on the street outside her studio.[10]

Photographs like the Indian portraits immediately signaled to the viewer that Käsebier's work was better than the conventional photographs churned out by portraitists and magazine photographers. Despite losing subtlety due to the halftone printing of *Everybody's* pages, these photographs of Indian artists are immediately recognizable as more self-consciously and subtly made than those circulating in popular magazines or government publications. As can be seen in the image of Kills-Close-to-the-Lodge (figure 44), the closely cropped portraits are generally taken full- or three-quarter-face, rather than in profile, providing the impression of an exchange of gazes between equals. The use of soft lighting and plain backdrops enhances the opportunity to appreciate the individual details of the models' faces and clothing. The inclusion of the models' names beneath the pictures further suggests that the images were meant to be appreciated individually.

One of the ways that Käsebier sought to differentiate her work from commercial photography was through her sophisticated participation in the contemporary interest in how artists' workspaces as manifestations of their creativity. Käsebier's portraits of other artists frequently show them to be in her studio. Often these pictures show the sitter posed in front of another Käsebier photograph. For example, a portrait of illustrator Rose O'Neill includes a crisp reproduction of the photographer's 1900 image "Real Motherhood." Such pictures suggest the suitability of Käsebier's work as wall decorations,

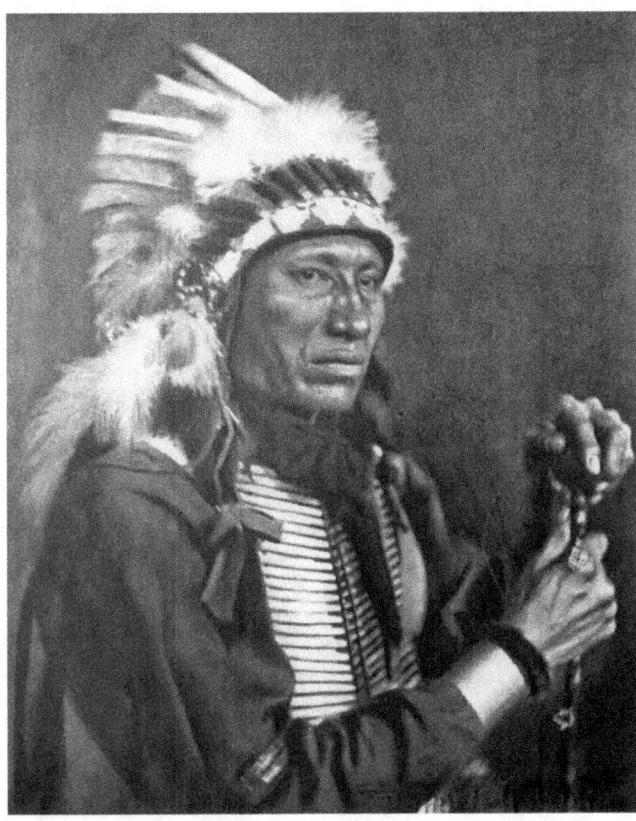

FIGURE 44 Gertrude Käsebier, "Kills-Close-to-the Lodge," from "Some Indian Portraits," *Everybody's Magazine* 14.17 (January 1901): 10.

but they are also a form of self-assertion, a desire to share the stage with the artist depicted. Käsebier includes her portrait of Rodin at the margin of her picture of Everett Shinn from 1907. Barbara Michaels has described this gesture as a kind of "symbolic Käsebier signature," and, indeed, the two pictures she examines are lacking in the literal signature with which Käsebier often embellished her work. But it is worth noting that these symbolic signatures show up predominantly in portraits of other artists. In general, Käsebier portraits use solid backdrops or close-cropping to strip away any sense that the sitter is in a specific locality. The special treatment offered artist-sitters suggests that Käsebier was seeking to offer an association between her own creativity and theirs. This can be seen explicitly in her portrait of Eulabee Dix (figure 45), in which the miniaturist leans over a framed mirror that reflects a large but blurry image of the photographer. The clear reference to the photographer's artistry with soft-focus photography turns the picture into a double portrait.

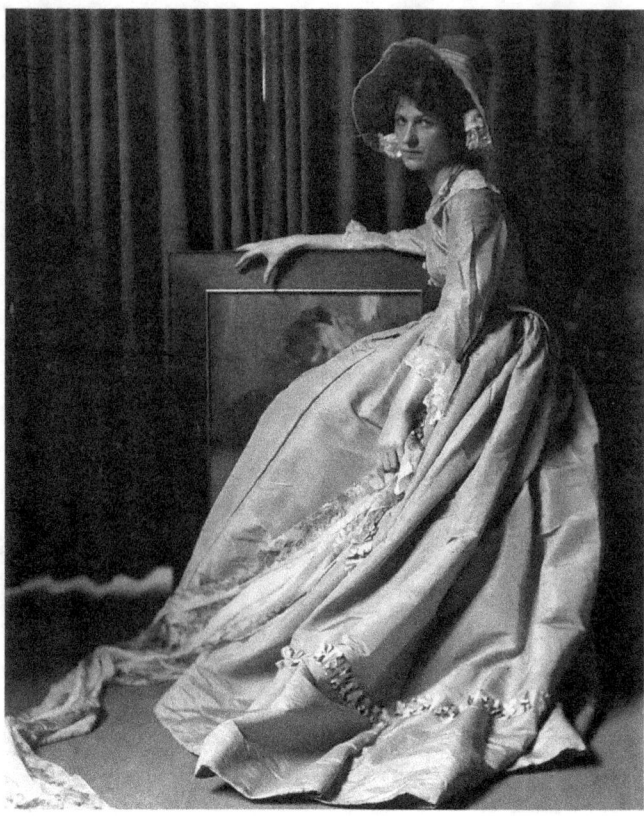

FIGURE 45 Gertrude
Käsebier, "Portrait of
Eulabee Dix," ca. 1907.
Platinum print, 7 3/4 ×
6 1/4 inches. National
Museum of Women in
the Arts, Washington,
D.C. Gift of Joan B.
Gaines.

The Native American models make this connection between artists clearly. The portrait of four draftsmen at the board (figure 42) seems not only to illustrate their work, but to thematize creativity itself. It does this not only in its inclusion of the different facial expressions of the sitters, but also in the way it is posed against a wall where two backdrops almost meet. Instead of showing a finished product—a portrait staged against a backdrop—this picture gives the viewer a glimpse into Käsebier's tools of the trade—her studio as a staging ground, the backdrops as props—even as it shows Indian artists with works in progress. Such a juxtaposition suggests an affinity between their creative processes and her own.

The appearance of Käsebier's studio reinforces the idea that she supported a modern concept of the artist. She filled her first studio with furnishings that would demonstrate her commitment to progressive aesthetic positions. Interestingly, the Indian portraits provide the best documentation of the decoration of this space. Through them, we see the hardwood

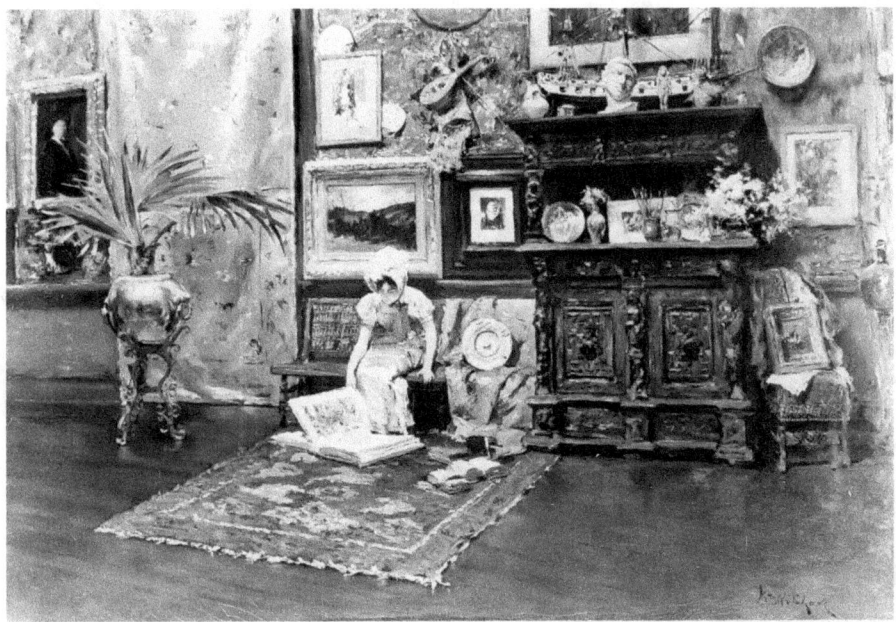

FIGURE 46 William Merritt Chase, *Studio Interior*, ca. 1882. Oil on canvas, 28 1/8 × 40 1/16 inches. The Brooklyn Museum, New York. Gift of Mrs. Carll H. de Silver in memory of her husband.

floor, heavy carved-wood furniture, and plain, painted walls that created the setting for her work. The room has a spare, clean look that distinguishes it from the opulence of Victorian artists' studios, which mirrored the Gilded Age domestic taste for crowded, eclectic interiors, as can be seen in the paintings William Merritt Chase made of his workspace in the 1880s (e.g., figure 46). Like the owners of Indian corners, early modernists adopted an arts and crafts style to embody their aesthetic distance from the generation of artists who preceded them.[11] While Chase and his Gilded Age peers used their studios as places to market their own social connections and cultural sophistication as much as their work, turn-of-the-century artists wanting to demonstrate their commitment to the more austere and personal values of early modernism surrounded themselves with coarse, simple furnishings.

Visitors to Käsebier's studio associated it with the honest craftsmanship embodied by her work. Arthur Dow wrote of her in 1899, the year after the studio was opened: "She is not dependent upon an elaborate outfit, but gets her effects with a common tripod camera, in a plain room with ordinary light and quiet furnishings. Art always shows itself in doing much with few and simple things."[12] The pictorialist photographer and critic Joseph T.

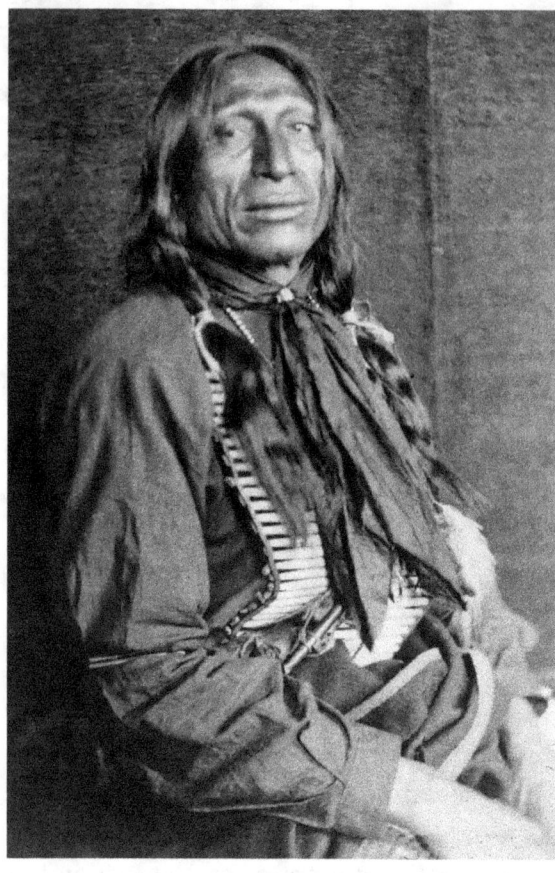

FIGURE 47 Gertrude Käsebier, "Iron Tail," from "Some Indian Portraits," *Everybody's Magazine* 4.17 (January 1901): frontispiece.

Keiley noted the absence of "stage settings" and fancy furniture in his 1899 profile. "The true artist," he wrote, "depends not on these things for a good picture, but upon the individuality of the sitter, the ability fully to understand, appreciate and get in touch with that individuality, and the power to express it most characteristically and harmoniously."[13]

The simple, primitive look of Käsebier's studio is matched by a certain primitiveness in the appearance of her prints. Several of the photographs printed in "Some Indian Portraits" include signs of retouching, such as the exaggerated hatch marks around Sam Lone Bear's lap, on the blanket in Iron Tail's lap (figure 47), and Whirling Hawk's throat and arm. These lines traced in the negative do not serve to minimize a flaw in the composition or bring out a form; they seem instead to endow the prints with a heightened emotional immediacy. Other uses of retouching seem more specifically designed to imitate the Indian models' artistic expression. The photographer has crafted a ghostlike headdress behind Whirling Hawk's head; she is also the person responsible for the copies of Sam Lone Bear's drawings in his portrait.

Unexplainable except as demonstrations of the photographer's whim, these retouchings ask the viewer to acknowledge the role her subjectivity played in making the photographs. As a pictorialist photographer, Käsebier was committed to the idea that photography could be a form of creative self-expression on a par with painting and sculpture. Members of the Photo-Secession asserted their individuality as artists by experimenting with diverse printing processes in pursuit of a distinctive "look." These processes helped bring the photographer's individual sensibility to bear on the prints. As Stieglitz explained, "The modern photographer, through the introduction of a great number of improved printing methods, has in his power to direct and mold as he will virtually every stage of making his picture."[14] Many pictorialists developed elaborate signatures to facilitate the viewer's recognition that their work was comparable to other forms of fine art.[15] (Käsebier's geometric monogram is visible in the lower left of the Sam Lone Bear portrait.) Endowing her prints with a "primitive," subjective, immediate appearance further associated Käsebier with the aesthetic trends of the period.

Pictorialists were particularly interested in aligning their work with the contemporary celebration of handicraft. Their commitment to artistic photography was explicitly designed to provide alternatives to cheap, mechanical commercial photographs. Articles in journals dedicated to cultivating pictorialist photography described composition and printing as requiring intelligence and craftsmanship. Platinum and gum bichromate, processes that brought out the materiality of the paper surface on which the image was printed, recalled the movement's interest in truth to materials. The traces of the photographer's hand in the application and manipulation of emulsion identified the photographer with the artistic individuality Dow and his peers celebrated.

Käsebier's bona fides as a modern craftswoman drew on her personal experience of the simple life during a childhood spent outside of Denver during the 1850s. Her western childhood was routinely presented as an inspiration for the values of independence and originality in her work. As Joseph Keiley explained, "The Wild-nature environments of her early childhood, with the semi-savage and altogether picturesque element of Indian life, its dangers and its poetry, have left indelible markings upon Mrs. Käsebier's character. . . . She sees . . . through [the eyes] of a child, who found companionship in the trees and flowers of the forest, and who came to look upon the Indian as part of that wild nature whose beauty she knew."[16] Käsebier herself connected her rugged childhood with the contemporary ideal of simplicity. She claimed to have learned not only her honest moral outlook but also her aesthetic ideas from "simple people." As she told an interviewer, "My grandmother was of the splendid, strong, pioneer type of women. She was an artist with her loom. She made her own designs, and weaved the most beautiful fancies into her fabrics. She knew life from living, and was great through her knowledge. She was a model to me in many ways, and the beginning of what I have accomplished in art came to me through her."[17]

Käsebier demonstrated her early commitment to preindustrial values in a pair of articles she published in *The Monthly Illustrator* after a summer spent with Frank DuMond's summer art class at Crécy-en-Brie, France, 1893. These articles reveal a primitivist tendency in the making.[18] They are illustrated with her own photographs and heavily laced with reformist nostalgia for preindustrial life. She describes village life as a vanishing culture, noting that young people have abandoned the town for the city. "Old France" is described as "ancient, primitive, soaked with historical associations, breathing of knightly adventure, abounding in picturesque features both of country and people."[19] Käsebier expresses regret that this "ancient, primitive" past of the Old World offered Americans "something the New World could not" in terms of a vision of unalienated, preindustrial culture.[20] For example, she describes Crécy-en-Brie as "a small, restful place, without a railroad, or gas, or electricity, or waterworks, or any of the thousand and one 'modern improvements' upon which Americans love to expatiate, and without which any village twenty-five miles from New York or Philadelphia, not to say of Chicago, would regard itself as only fit for social suicide."[21]

These articles also ally Käsebier with early feminism. She celebrates women's elevated role in French peasant culture as an alternative to the restrictions they experience in her own society. For example, she points out the beauty of the local women's muscular bodies that were "never hampered by the pressure of whale-bone and steel; their lungs are not enfeebled by breathing the vitiated air of close rooms; their strength has not been spent

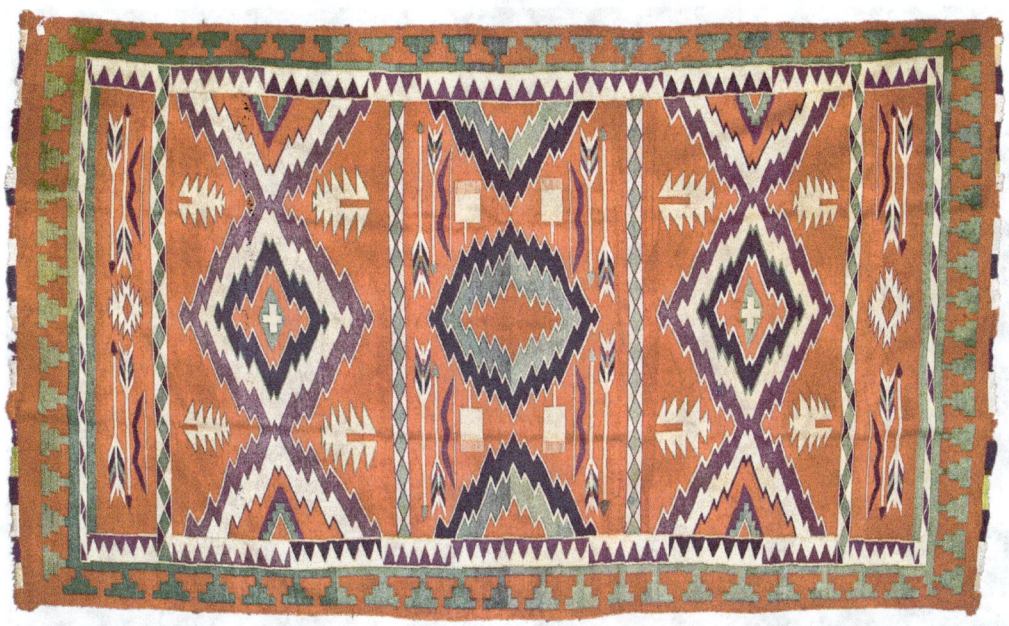

PLATE 1 Unknown Navajo weaver, eye-dazzler rug, collected 1879. Wool with natural and synthetic dyes. Inv. no. 247200.000. Courtesy of National Museum of the American Indian, Smithsonian Institution, Washington, D.C. Photo by NMAI Photo Services Staff.

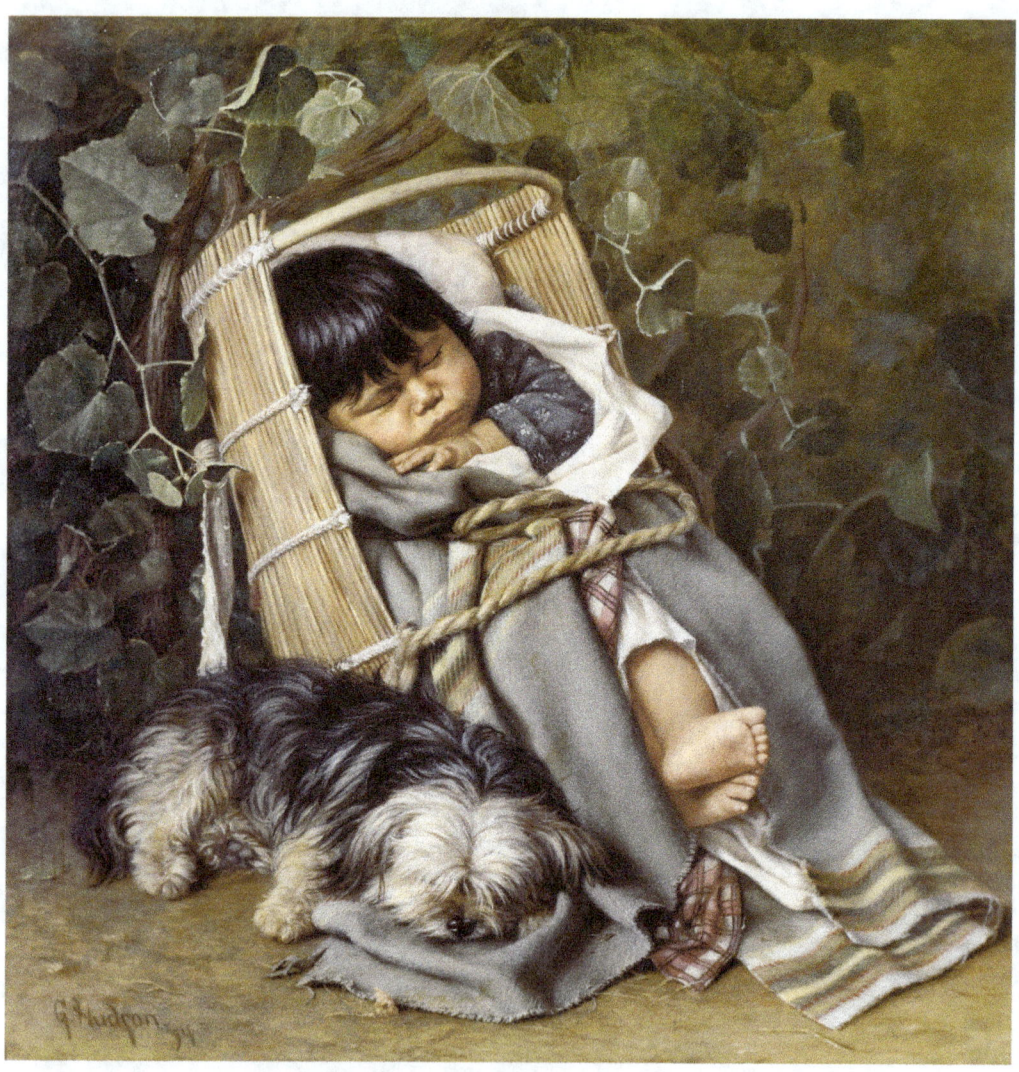

PLATE 2 Grace Carpenter Hudson, *Baby Bunting*, 1894. Oil on canvas, 30 × 31 inches. Grace Hudson Museum, Ukiah, California. Gift of Dorothy and Jean Beatty in memory of Gertrude and Frederick Van Sicklin.

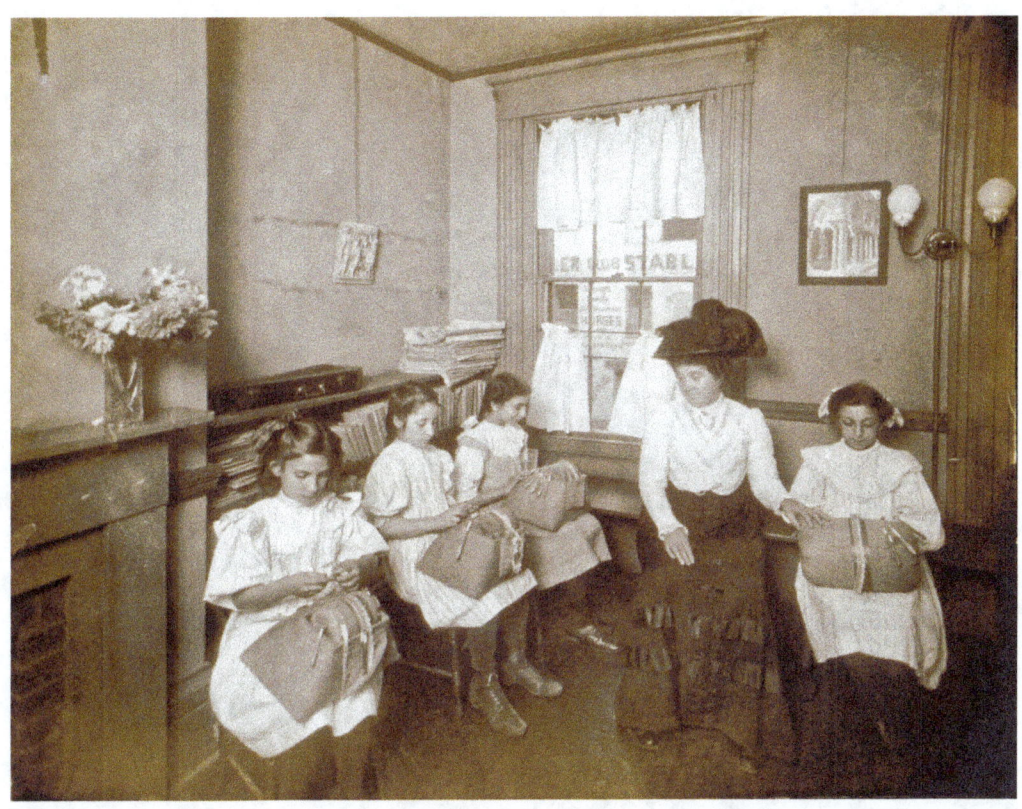

PLATE 3 Lacemaking class at Denison House, Boston, 1909. The Schlesinger Library, Radcliffe Institute, Harvard University, Cambridge, Massachusetts.

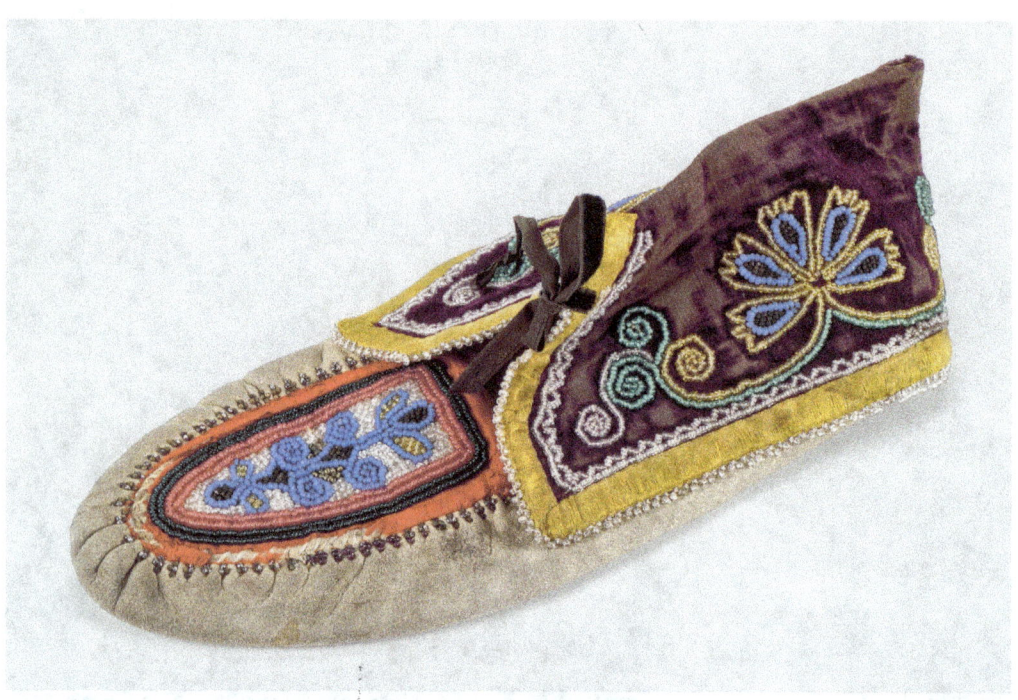

PLATE 4 Moccasin (one of a pair), made in 1893 on the Oneida Reservation, Green Bay, Wisconsin. Inv. no. 198649. From the Charles Edwin Kelsey Collection. Courtesy of National Museum of the American Indian, Smithsonian Institution, Washington, D.C. Photo by NMAI Photo Services Staff.

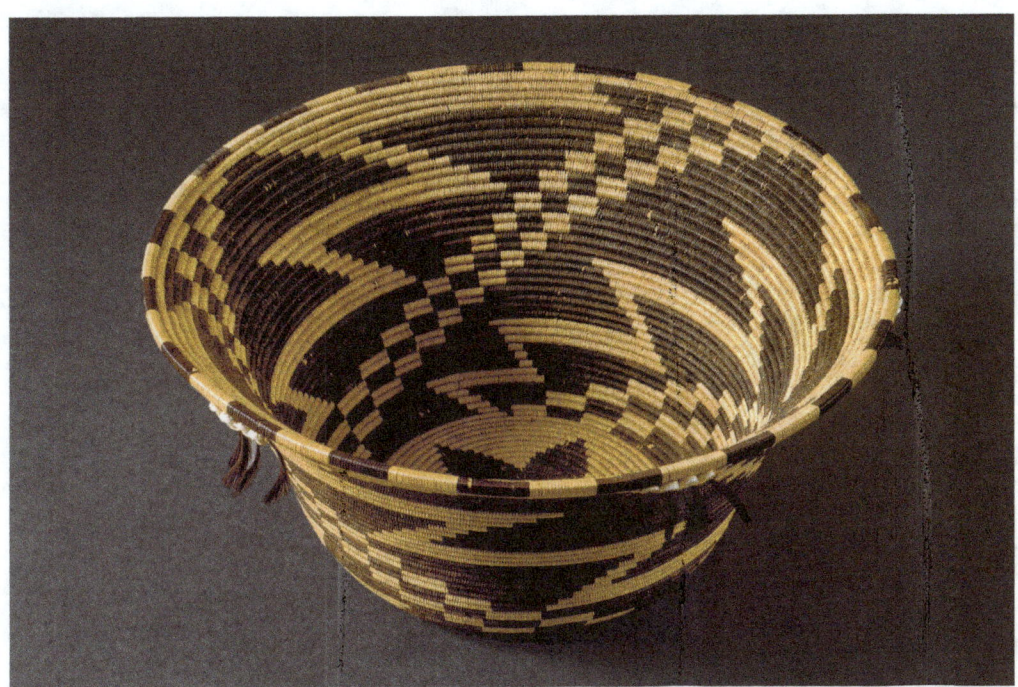

PLATE 5 Unknown Pomo weaver, bowl, ca. 1900. Three-rod coiled willow with sedge root and bulrush root stitches, applied shell beads, and quail topknot feathers. Inv. no. 4/8786. Courtesy of National Museum of the American Indian, Smithsonian Institution, Washington, D.C. Photo by NMAI Photo Services Staff.

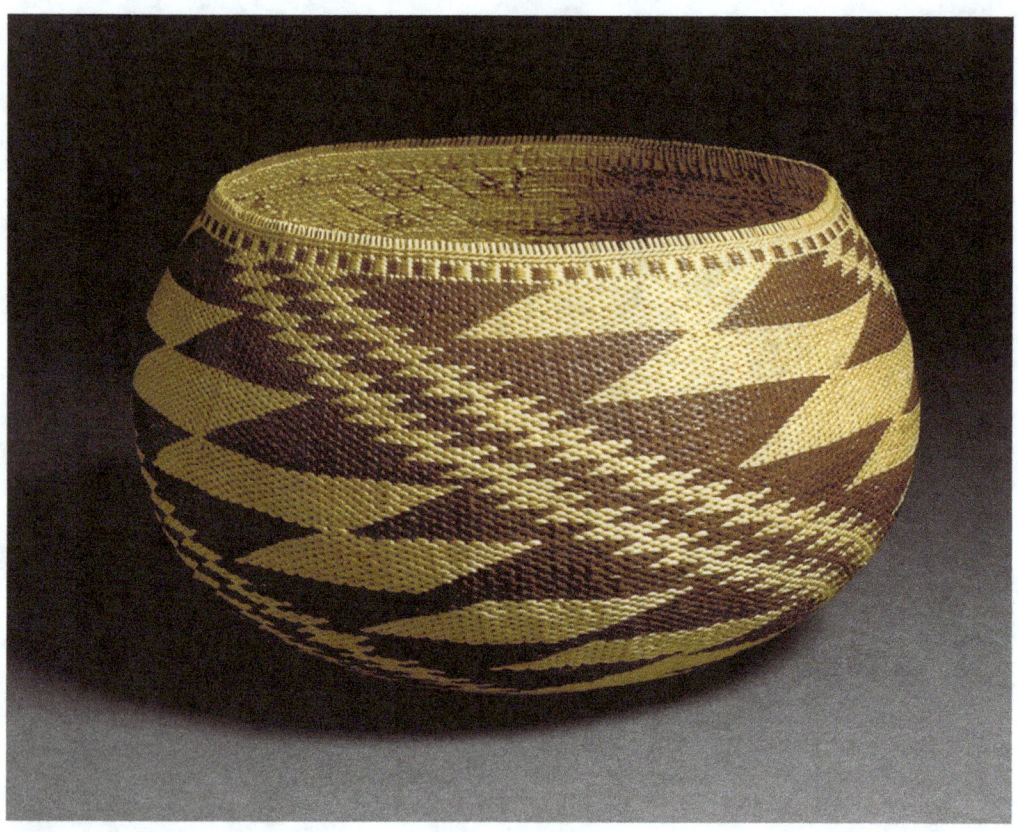

PLATE 6 Mary Benson (Central Pomo), twined model cooking bowl, ca. 1905. Diagonal-twined of redbud and sedge. Inv. no. 24/2139. Courtesy of National Museum of the American Indian, Smithsonian Institution, Washington, D.C. Photo by NMAI Photo Services Staff.

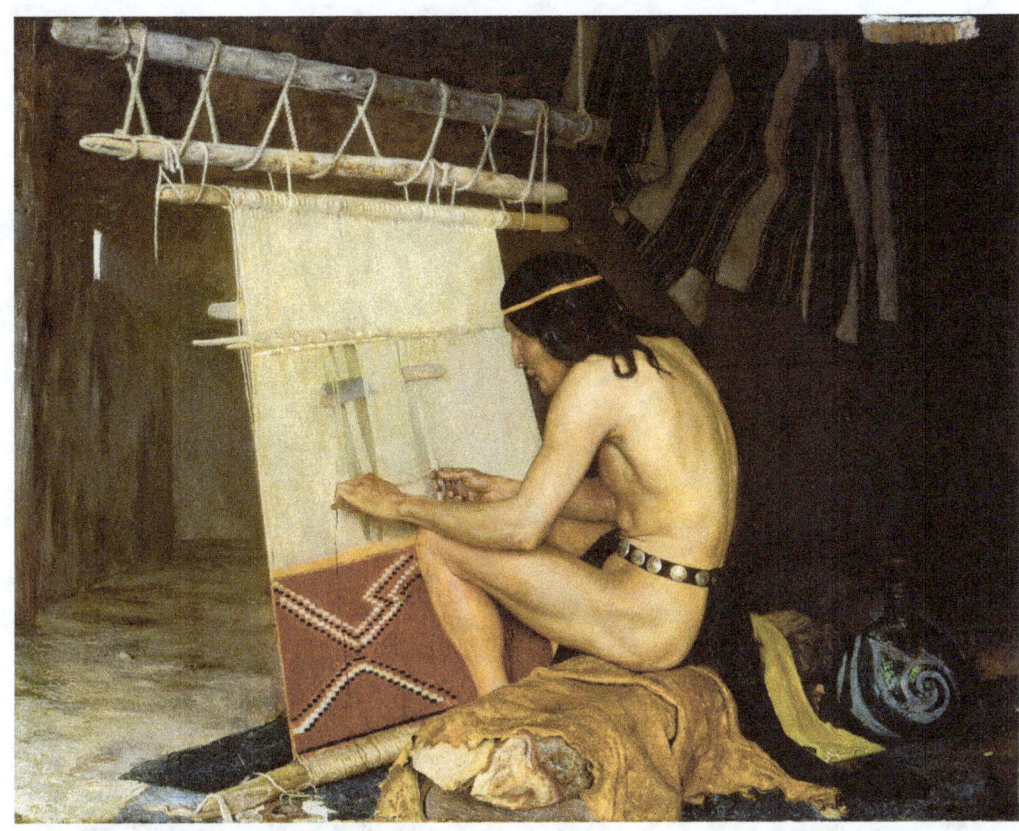

PLATE 7 George de Forest Brush, *The Weaver*, 1889. Oil on canvas, 12 × 15 inches. Terra Foundation for American Art, Chicago. Photo from Art Resource, New York.

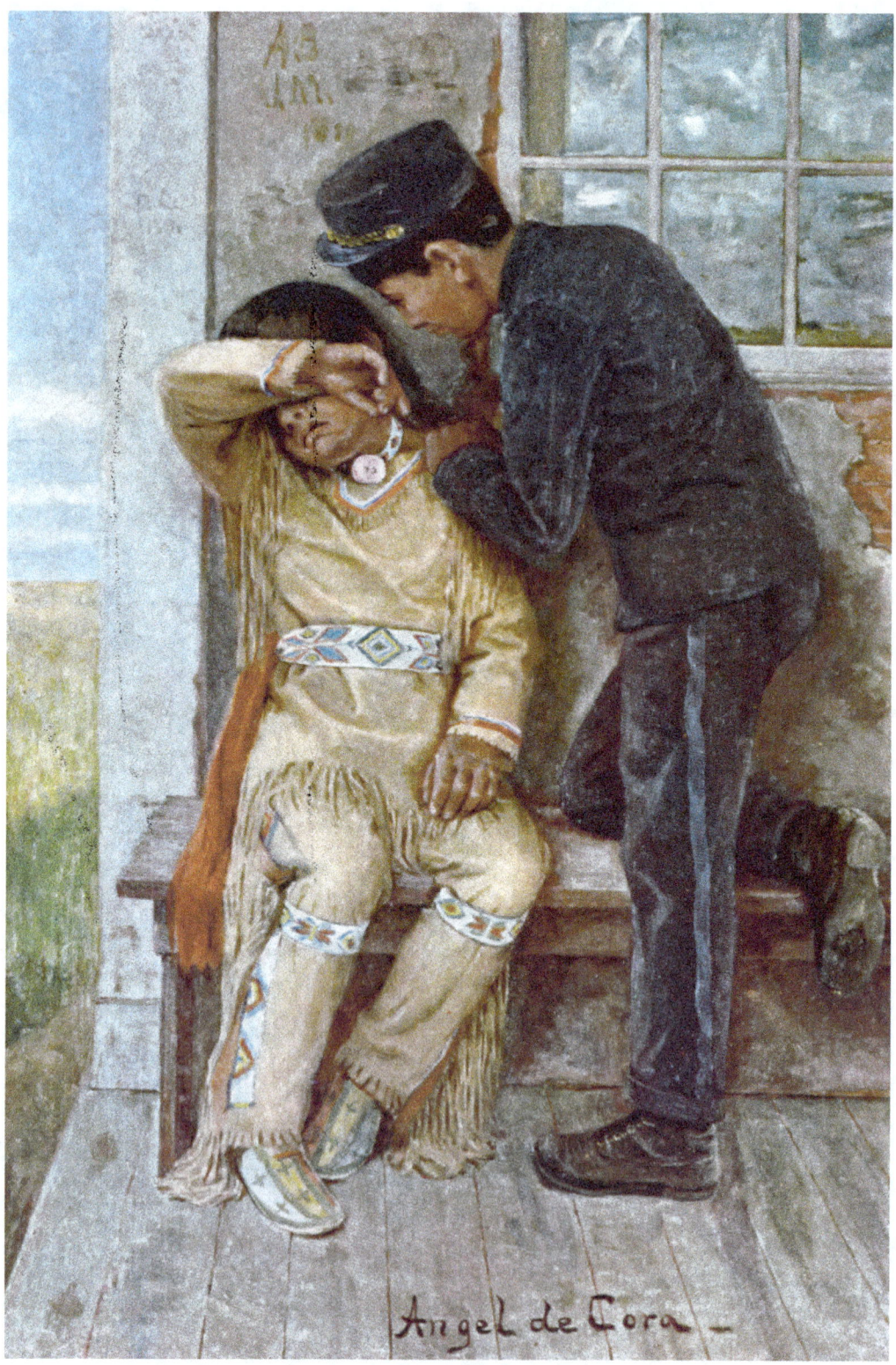

PLATE 8 Angel DeCora, frontispiece for Francis LaFlesche, *The Middle Five: Indian Boys at School* (Boston: Small, Maynard, 1900).

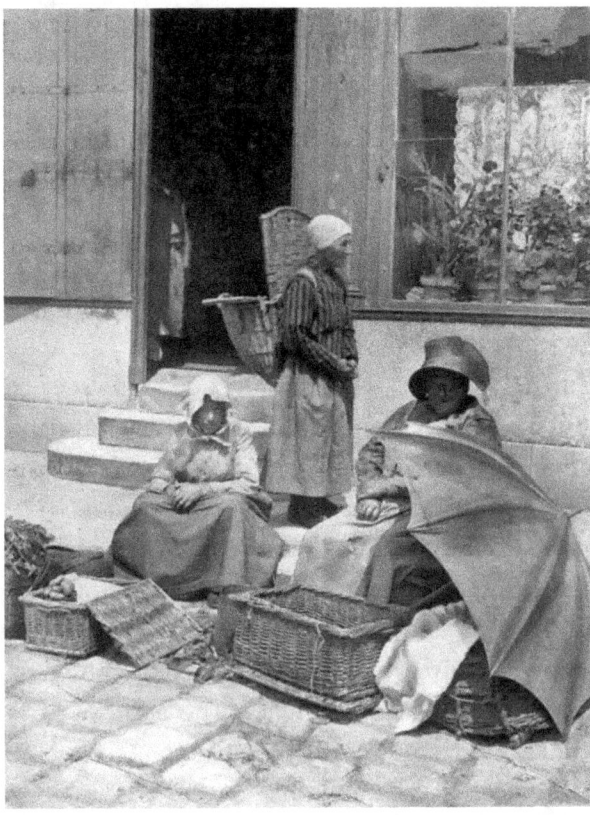

FIGURE 48 Gertrude Käsebier, "The Old Market Women," from "An Art Village," *Monthly Illustrator* 4 (April 1895), 11.

upon the treadle of a sewing-machine; nor do they work with that feverish consuming energy that marks our western race. . . . They are not possessed of a desire to appear what they are not, nor to excel their neighbors."[22]

The photographs that accompany the articles on Crécy are among the first that Käsebier published. Though some have the soft focus that characterizes pictorialist photography, they are more like tourist snapshots than carefully crafted artistic prints. Most are portraits of the village's inhabitants at work. Posed stiffly at the center of the frame in their typical clothing, they sometimes smile, but more often look warily at the camera (see figure 48). These photos *document* Käsebier's primitivism; the Indian portraits *embody* it.

KÄSEBIER AS PRIMITIVE ARTIST

Käsebier's introduction of her own primitive gestures in her prints suggests that she finds Native American life an artistic, as well as a social model.

While Käsebier's presentation of drawings by untrained Indian artists alongside her own work in "Some Indian Portraits" might be seen as a suggestion of contrasts, a chance to demonstrate the difference between "civilized" and "primitive" representation, it is likely that she wanted viewers to see similarities as well as differences in the two kinds of visual expression. Käsebier's training and artistic affiliations would have exposed her to the ideas about primitive creativity advocated by the art educators discussed in chapter 3, especially in her classes with Arthur Wesley Dow.

Käsebier's interactions with the surfaces of the prints—her elaborate printing processes, retouchings, spottings, and signatures—can be seen as signs of her irrational, instinctive engagement with her art. Giles Edgerton described Käsebier as "an emotional artist" whose work was as much the product of her temperament and imagination as her technical skill.[23] She was also an avid student of the occult, given to falling into trances and following mysterious impulses. The interest in connecting the psychological with her artistic production may explain her interest in Native American art. Like Dow's summer students at Ipswich, Käsebier seems to be interested in Indian art as an attitudinal, not a formal, model. The artists at work in her pictures display the sincerity, devotion to simplicity in materials, and individuality of results that mark the arts and crafts community's interest in Native American art. Like other artists interested in Indian art in this period, Käsebier deculturizes the drawings, looking to them for universal lessons about art as opposed to their meanings for the Sioux men who made them.

Nancy Green has provocatively connected Käsebier's exploration of Native American subject matter in her photographs with Dow's interest in "primitive" art traditions as models of "the arts and crafts aesthetic of self-sufficiency in all media."[24] But Käsebier's interest in primitive creativity did not draw on Dow alone. The command to tap into a primal, instinctive source of creativity characterized a shifting concept of the artist at the turn of the century. On both sides of the Atlantic, groups of painters, sculptors, and designers were developing styles to demonstrate their unique modernist subjectivity or psychology.[25] This interest drew artists away from their commitment to illusionistic rendering to a greater involvement in decorative strategies designed to affect the mood, rather than the intellect, of the viewer. Such ideas strongly influenced contemporary artistic photographers, who staked their claim on the affinity of the photographic and painting processes through the use of such words as "temperament," and "individuality." Sandra Underwood has specifically related such terms to the ideology of the arts and crafts movement. Writing about the influential early twentieth-century American art critic Charles Caffin, himself a strong advocate of photography in general and Käsebier in particular, she explains that "Arts and Crafts defined a theory of artistic production which proclaims the work of the individual to be original and unique. The planning and the making of art were believed to engage artistic intuition and judgment."[26]

This interest in intuition fueled pictorialist primitivism, especially for photographers in the circle of Alfred Stieglitz. Stieglitz used exhibitions at his gallery, 291, and his curatorial and editorial work for the New York Camera Club and the Photo-Secession as sites for promoting the creativity of "outsider" artists. The most obvious manifestations of Stieglitz's fascination with "uncivilized" art were the exhibitions of children's drawings and African sculpture that were installed in 291 in 1912 and 1914, respectively. Stieglitz's interest in non-Western art and artistic subjects had, however, manifested itself fifteen years earlier, in his work as a photographic curator and editor, when he published F. Holland Day's "Nubian" portraits in the journal he was editing, *Camera Notes* (see figure 49).

The celebration of non-European artistic traditions as a source of imagery and method for American art might seem to suggest a recognition of the equal status of native and non-Native artists. Käsebier's representation of Indian artists in her studio supports this idea. But even if Käsebier intended to characterize her studio visitors as so many more modern artists at work, the culture within which she worked could not see them this way. Day's and Käsebier's photographs were not seen as signs of respect for another culture. At best, they were demonstrations of the artists' talents that were enhanced emotionally by a touch of exoticism. With their subtle lighting and velvety backgrounds, Day's photographs of Bostonian African Americans and Käsebier's pictures of Indian entertainers were singled out by critics as models of the careful printing and exquisite tonal range to which pictorialists should aspire. When Day's "Ethiopian Chief," for example, was reproduced in the second issue of *Camera Notes*, the editor's comments were limited to an observation of its "delicate qualities."[27] Joseph Keiley similarly uses the appearance of exotic models as a means of praising Käsebier's artistic skill. He

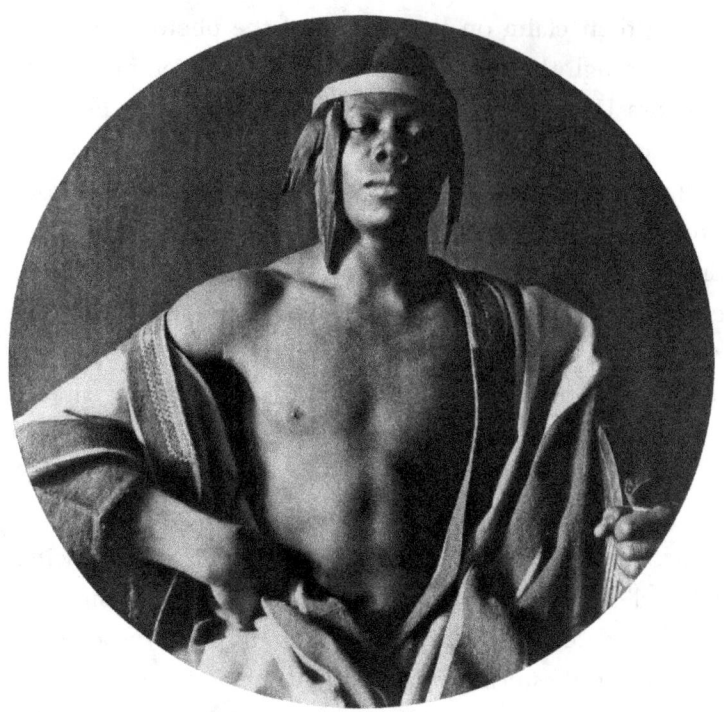

FIGURE 49
F. Holland Day,
"An Ethiopian
Chief," ca. 1897,
from *Camera
Notes* 1.2
(October 1897):
plate 35.

chose her photograph of Kills-Close-to-the-Lodge to illustrate an article on tonality, which he saw as the ultimate test of a photographer's artistic skill, the "medium through which is stamped the artist's individual interpretation of and sympathy with his subject."[28]

Despite his reference to sympathy, Keiley strips the model of his cultural identity; the individuality he is interested in is the photographer's. Indeed, he seems to almost deny the existence of different pigmentation, claiming that it is the photographer who is in "control of the lights and shades of a picture" (145). The information the photograph gives him about Kills-Close-to-the-Lodge is not a sympathetic glimpse into the character or experiences of a *Wild West* performer sitting in a New York artist's studio, but a generic rehearsal of the stereotype of the savage Indian: "There he sits, arrayed in the habiliments of his people, one of the last of a rapidly disappearing race, looking out in proud silence upon that onrolling tide of humanity that is greedily devouring all that was his, and fast crowding his people from the face of the world. Too proud to protest, too thoroughly a warrior to complain, or to bow to the new order of things, he watches stoicly [*sic*]; and unbendingly awaits the inevitable end."[29] This familiar image of the stoic, vanishing Indian is not used to reflect on Kills-Close-to-the-Lodge's personal experiences, but instead to enhance the association between the savage model and the photographer's own primitivism in the use of techniques that brought raw directness to the photographic print. Keiley describes tonal harmony itself in primitivizing terms: "Tones of light and shade, like tones of music, have individually no meaning appreciable by the human intellect, but possess rather a certain sense value, which is pleasing, or otherwise, as it is harmonious or discordant; and, therefore, a combination of such tones may be quite foreign to conventional natural effects, and even diametrically opposed to them, and yet, nevertheless, so harmonious in its tone values as to be pleasing to the senses without appealing to the intellect, and, because of its sensuous charm, may possess an esthetic and lasting value."[30] Keiley's comments typify early modernist primitivism, which used non-European art as a field in which to cultivate new psychological and formal models of art making. While this development was often dependent on the participation of indigenous artists in Western popular culture, it did not often acknowledge them to be part of the same modern world as the non-Native artists, but continued to idealize them as part of a preindustrial ideal doomed by modernity.

PRIMITIVISM AND FEMININITY

"Some Indian Portraits" contributed to making 1901 the high point of Käsebier's professional career. Over the previous two years, Käsebier had participated in every major American photographic exhibition, had sent pictures to be displayed in London and Paris, and had been the subject of profiles in several photographic journals, including *Camera Notes*, *Philadelphia Photographer*, and *La Revue de la Photographie*. Within a few months of the *Everybody's* photo spread, she was the focus of a chapter of Charles Caffin's influential book *Photography as a Fine Art*.[31] *Everybody's* was pleased enough with her work that they hired her to provide photographic illustrations for a serialized novel titled *The Making of a Country Home*.[32] Her skills were also sought out by a new publication, *The World's Work*, dedicated to describing the issues and leaders of the nation's politically progressive community. In the midst of these accomplishments, Frances Benjamin Johnston proclaimed Käsebier one of "The Foremost Women Photographers in America."[33]

Johnston's accolade points out that Käsebier's gender was always a factor in her career. She was trained in an art school specifically designed to prepare women for careers in art at a time when men and women were understood as having distinct talents and capabilities. Building on the association between femininity and art within the arts and crafts movement, middle-class women of Käsebier's time who wanted to use their increased wealth and leisure to pursue an education often chose artistic fields. Schools like Pratt were specifically designed to train women art teachers, designers, illustrators, and painters.

As many scholars have noted, women were directed to fields that were understood as commensurate with a female sensibility. Women art students were encouraged to use art to cultivate their sympathy for children and their facility with offering moral instruction. The success of textile designers like Candace Wheeler paved the way for women to professionalize work in fields that had been traditionally associated with domestic responsibilities. Female members of arts and crafts societies generally worked at handicrafts that were similarly linked to age-old ideas of women's culture: china painting, needlework, jewelry making. In addition to the strength of tradition, these practices were understood as requiring specifically female skills, including patience, neatness, and fine manual dexterity.[34]

Though less traditional than these other trades, photography required many of the same skills, and it became an important option for women who wanted to pursue artistic careers at the turn of the century. Photography did not require the years of academic training that other careers did, which would require women to neglect their family responsibilities. Moreover, their inherent sympathy for other people was thought to enable women to put sitters at ease. In 1890, Catherine Weed Barnes noted that women's characteristic conscientiousness and neatness also suited them for photographic work. In her own articles and speeches, Käsebier allied herself with Barnes in recommending photography as an artform particularly suited to a woman's sensibility; she told one audience, "I earnestly advise women of artistic tastes to train for the unworked field of modern photography. It seems to be especially adapted to them, and the few who have entered it are meeting with gratifying and profitable success."[35]

In general, women's artistic responsibilities matched their domestic ones: their perceived delicacy and sentimentality were understood as suit-

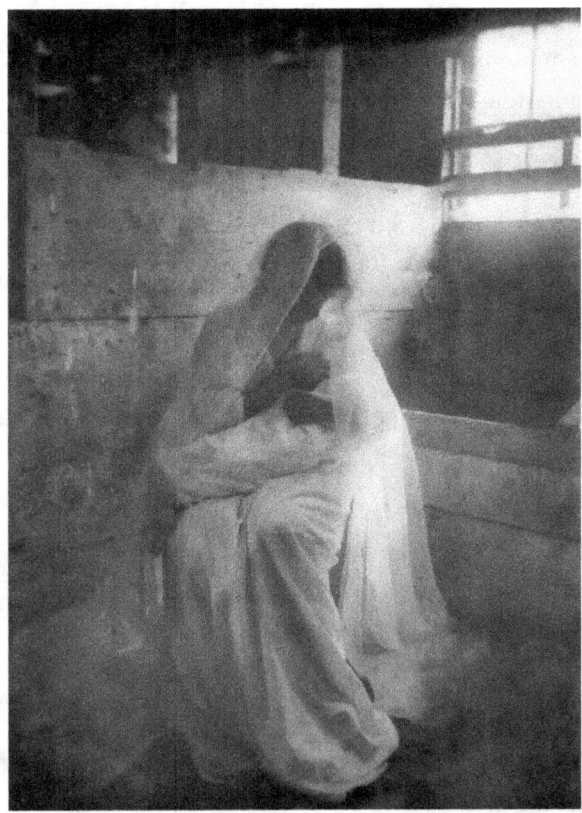

FIGURE 50 Gertrude
Käsebier, "The Manger," 1899.
Platinum print, mounted
on brown paper. Inv. no.
LC-USZC2–5963, Library
of Congress, Prints and
Photographs Division,
Washington, D.C.

ing them particularly well for portraiture, especially pictures of women and
children. In a discussion about a woman who worked almost exclusively
with women and children, Barnes wrote, "The work is infinitely more refined and womanly than much which is eagerly sought after by women."[36]
A significant portion of Käsebier's best known work, including her most
critically acclaimed photographs, "Blessed Art Thou among Women" and
"The Manger" (figure 50), conform to this subject matter.

As I have explained in previous chapters, women embraced a sexual
division of labor within the art world, seeing their ability to contribute *as
women* as a justification for their participation in artistic culture. While the
materials, styles, and subject matter of turn-of-the-century culture drew
on an idea of femininity based on preindustrial domesticity, women artists,
like women reformers, used this idea to cultivate personal satisfaction and
sometimes public acclaim through creative work.

The images in "Some Indian Portraits" identify Käsebier with Progressive

Era women's explorations of new realms of experience that resemble those undertaken by the mainstream women writers and reformers discussed in chapter 1. The article presents female readers with the opportunity to follow the photographer-protagonist through a complex web of commercial, social, and sexual desire. Significantly, these modern experiences are provided by contact with "primitive" others. The visibility of Käsebier's studio in these photographs enhances the impression of the actual presence of the models in a woman's place of work. When the *Delineator* printed a picture of Joe Black Fox, it described Käsebier's studio as the site of a possible exciting encounter: "While Mrs. Käsebier's chief work lies with society people, she has a particular penchant for photographing Indians, especialy [*sic*] those that travel the country with 'Buffalo Bill's' show. These she has made her favorites, and whenever they appear in New York her studio is sure to be full of them."[37] Notices of Käsebier's studio visitors in the *New York Times* also remarked on the social atmosphere of her studio. Significantly, the *Times* highlighted the fact that the Indians were men and the European Americans they met there were women. As one such news item noted, "Callers of this kind might not be so agreeable in a private house, but in a studio it is somewhat different, and Mrs. Käsebier and the young women artists who share the studio with her gaze at their guests with a feeling of deep artistic appreciation."[38] As this statement points out, the studio is not a domestic space. It is an example of the new kinds of locales that middle-class women were exploring at the turn of the century. As much as Käsebier's Indian portraits respond to the changing aesthetic debates of her day, they also respond to changing roles for women. Mixing the "primitive" and the modern, the Indian portraits link Käsebier's professional and social ambitions to those of other Progressive Era women.

One aspect of Käsebier's progressive femininity was her desire to turn her artistic activity into a career. Publishing in *Everybody's Magazine* was a sign of Käsebier's avid pursuit of success outside the circle of art photography. Contrary to some other pictorialists, Käsebier refused to believe in a division between professional and artistic photography. In an 1898 address, she told her audience that "[a photographer] can make a commercial article for the . . . money, and still another to justify himself."[39] For her, art was an expression of individual temperament that found its way into all modes of expression. Moreover, rather than supporting a compartmentalized view of art and commercial work, Käsebier often put the same images to both uses—exhibiting her portraits and selling her noncommissioned work to popular magazines. The Indian portraits are the perfect example of this. Because they were made at the photographer's and not the sitter's or publisher's request, they are not truly commercial portraits. And yet the photographer clearly used them to build up a commercial clientele.

Everybody's was one of the most successful family magazines of the time, reaching an estimated 150,000 homes every month when "Some Indian Portraits" was published, and its readers included many middle-class women who, like Käsebier, were longing to explore their moral and economic power in the public sphere.[40] Owned by Wanamaker's department stores, *Everybody's* appealed to urban readers' interest in a larger world by offering them enticing advertisements and love stories set in historically and geographically remote settings. Through advertisements and articles that more directly addressed questions of taste and consumption, the magazine contributed to the growing idea that the desire to cultivate one's individuality through experience could be accomplished through therapeutic consumption. Käsebier's professional success reflects the fact that she gave magazine readers what they were looking for.

Like other journals of the time, *Everybody's* frequently presented coverage of the West. Stories and artworks by Owen Wister, Charlie Russell, and Carl Rungius set life in the region up as the opposite of the refined industrial culture of the East. "Some Indian Portraits" offers a vision of the primitive West specifically geared toward *Everybody's* female readers by presenting the models as the objects for women's sexual, commercial, and social desire. Within the explicitly commercialized context of *Everybody's Magazine*, Käsebier's photographs depict Indian men like so many more objects for the reader's contemplation, by focusing closely on their physical features and exotic costumes. Matter-of-factly seated against simple backdrops, tightly framed, almost invariably gazing out into the viewer's space, the models present themselves for the viewer's visual assessment. These photographs, though they display people instead of objects, draw on the magazine reader's fantasy of cultivating her own desire through an (in this case symbolic) possession of the exotic as in the photographs of Indian corners discussed in chapter 1. Indeed, the photographs seem to heighten the materiality of the men's bodies and clothes. The relatively high quality of

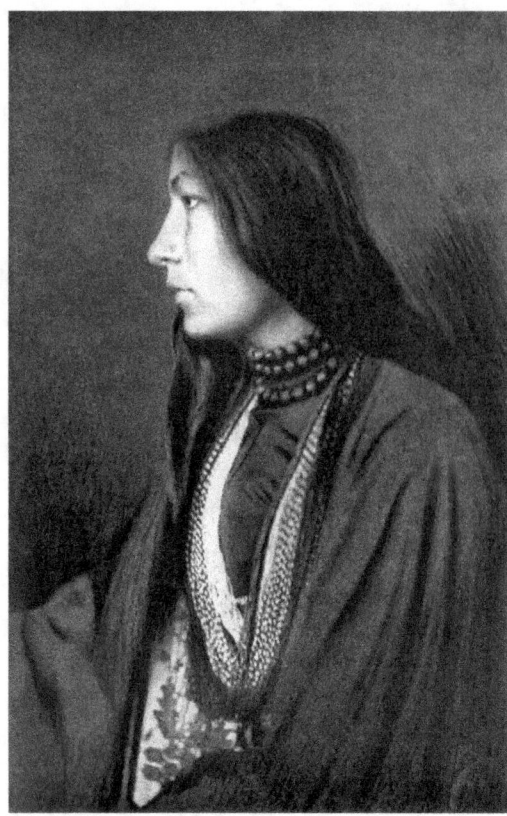

FIGURE 51 Gertrude Käsebier, "Red Bird," from "Some Indian Portraits," *Everybody's Magazine* 4.17 (January 1901): 5.

the halftone prints brings out the creases on the men's faces and captures the reflections of light on their ornaments, the softness of the feathers. The photographer's pictorialist style encourages the viewer to dwell on texture. In the photograph titled "Red Bird" (the Sioux poet and musician Zitkala-Sa), for example, the fact that the model's weighty strands of beads are out of focus in the foreground makes the crisply delineated ones more viscerally appealing (see figure 51). Such attention to detail puts the viewer in the position of a consumer evaluating the appearance of the models in terms of fashion, and indeed, the accompanying text provides lengthy descriptions of the models' attire. "They wore feathered head-dresses that were marvels; short jackets fairly covered with elaborate designs in solid beadwork; flannel shirts of vivid red, blue, and green; . . . brass and silver bands and silver rings stood out against the copper-brown of their arms and fingers" (4).

In addition to contributing to a visceral interest in the exotic aspects of the models' clothing, the article suggests that these pictures offer sexual titillation. The second spread shows a photograph of Amos Two Bulls in profile, which seems to lock gazes with Zitkala-Sa, whose picture appears on the opposing page (figure 52). The author informs us that the feathers in the young man's hair signify that he is looking for a wife (4). The drawings reproduced in the article contribute to the romantic nature of the piece. Page 12 shows two figures, one male and the other female, standing outside a tipi—a young couple outside their home. A few pages later, a similar composition, this time with three male figures and one female, is reproduced with the words "Catch girls" written above them (figure 53). The letters reprinted at the end of the article similarly highlight the theme of courtship. Sammy Lone Bear's missive from October 23, 1898, informs us that there are "Plenty girls over hear [sic]." A letter from 1900 recounts meeting two "nice girls" in Philadelphia, presumably extending the models' interest to European American women like the magazine's readers.

Käsebier was noted for her comfort in admitting her sexuality. Perhaps, as Estelle Freedman and John D'Emilio suggest was the case for other women of this period, marriage provided Käsebier with the chance to assert and explore her identity by exploring her sexual desires.[41] She told more than one acquaintance that she had married her husband because of his looks. (It was a decision she probably regretted. As she put it, "I married legs and I got legs.")[42] Moreover, she publicly connected her photographic practice with her sexual self-possession, in humor if not in plain language. For example, she ended an 1898 lecture on the appeals of photography as a profession for women with the remark: "Besides, consider the advantage of a vocation which necessitates one's being a taking woman"— "taking" having associations not only with attractiveness and deceit but also with sexual intercourse.[43]

The text and images of "Some Indian Portraits" inverts the usual formula of male pursuer and female pursuee, by focusing on the female photographer, and by extension the female visitors to her studio, as the agents in this romance. The article plays with the familiar trope of the sexually charged relationship between artist and model, redrawing the presumed power imbalance based on gender as one based on race. Opening with the photographer's "mingled surprise and pleasure" upon finding these "young educated bucks" and "mighty men of battle" (4) in her studio, the narrative shows her telling them how to pose and even what to wear. At one point,

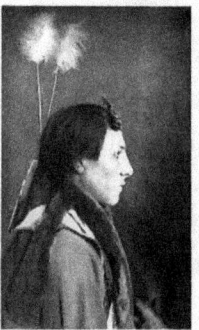
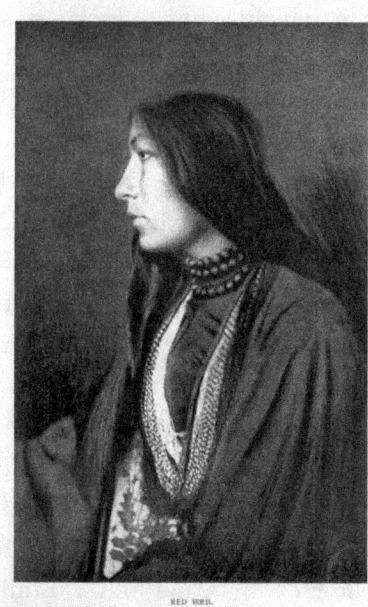

FIGURE 52 "Amos Two Bulls" and "Red Bird," from "Some Indian Portraits," *Everybody's Magazine* 4.17 (January 1901): 4–5.

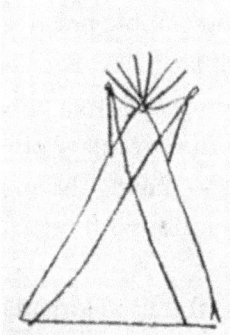
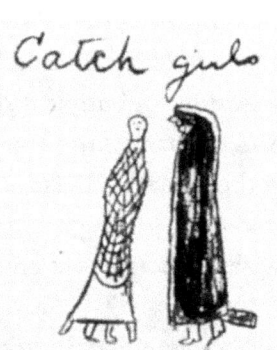
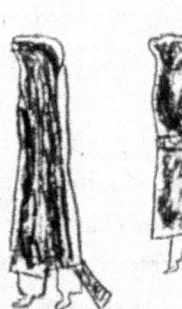

FIGURE 53 Sam Lone Bear, "Catch Girls," from "Some Indian Portraits," *Everybody's Magazine* 4.17 (January 1901): 15.

having "wear[ied] of beadwork and feathers," she even undresses them, as described in this passage: "Quite at random she selected Iron Tail, and proceeded to divest him of his finery. Feathers and trinkets were removed, and amid a dead silence she placed him before the camera and secured the most remarkable portrait of the whole collection" (7). Following the tradition of artists' models, the Indians are presented as passively allowing themselves to be manipulated to fit the mold of the photographer's fantasy. The photographer brings out a quiet, even vulnerable side of these supposedly wild models, suggesting a woman's ability to tame them. Iron Tail is even described as obeying her "like an automaton." The connection between the photographer's control over these bodies and her desire to touch, dress, and manipulate them is reinforced by the fact that although Käsebier made portraits of women and older men, the article reproduces almost exclusively pictures of young male performers. In the picture of White Wolf, the model's casual posture, the slightly open positions of his arms and legs, and his direct look all seem to invite the viewer in (see figure 54). His barely visible wedding band absolves the viewer from the guilt of looking at him as a sexual object, even as it marks his sexual experience. In another portrait, Philip Standing Soldier's hesitant gaze similarly signals a curiosity about the viewer that she is asked to return (see figure 55).

An interesting sign of how the models are fit into the role of becoming the object of the viewer's desire is the fact that the *New York Times* and "Some Indian Portraits" feminize these warriors. The *Times* compared their clothing with dresses and referred to two models as "the belles of the occasion."[44] Throughout these articles there is a suggestion that the disempowerment that the performers suffer by being linguistically and culturally out of place symbolically turns them into women. One notice describes how Joe Black Fox's rosy complexion is set off by a bunch of violets given him by an admirer among Käsebier's friends.

In presenting the models as subjects for female visual delectation, "Some Indian Portraits" is picking up on an idea brought forth by the original accounts of the sittings that resulted in these pictures. The articles repeatedly stress the warm interactions between the models and the women artists in Käsebier's building. The models are described exchanging gifts with these women and posing with them. An April 23, 1899, account mentions "Catch

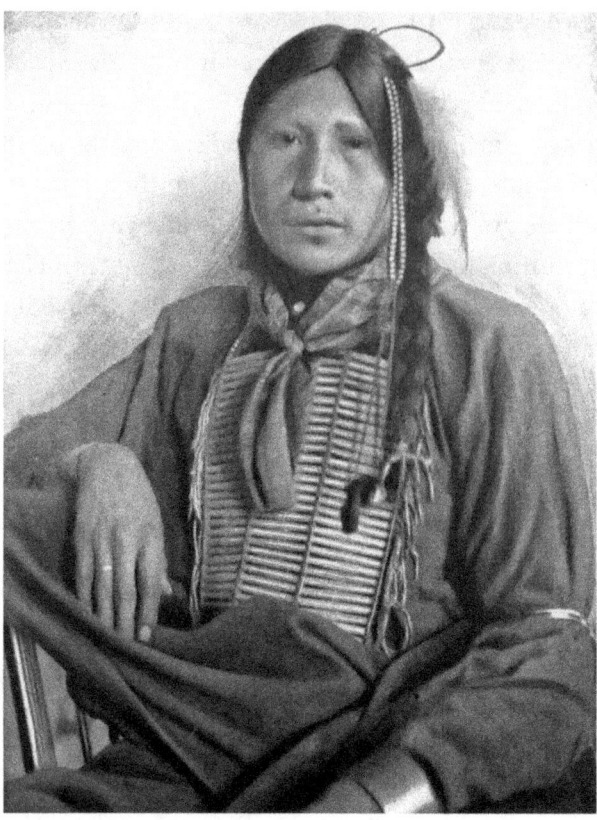

FIGURE 54 Gertrude
Käsebier, "White Wolf," from
"Some Indian Portraits,"
Everybody's Magazine 4.17
(January 1901): 11.

Girls" and suggests Joe Black Fox's interest in "a pretty young matron who
did much to make the stay of the guests pleasant."[45] As with the *Everybody's*
article, the suggestions of the Indian men's desire for European American
women is matched by the women's interest in the Indian men. Articles
sometimes hinted at the possibility of an unconventional alliance, as we saw
in the aforementioned *New York Times* quotation that emphasized the deep
gazes Käsebier and her female associates directed at the Native models.[46]

While attraction to the exotic other is frequently identified as the prov-
ince of European American males, the turn of the century was characterized by white women's increased exploration of non-Western men. While
not specifically identified as sexual objects, Native American men took on
increased prominence as romantic heroes in sentimental fiction of the time
written by women. Helen Hunt Jackson's *Ramona*, in which a half-Indian
girl, raised as white, elopes with an Indian sheepherder, and Emily Pauline
Johnson's magazine sketches of interracial romance presented women

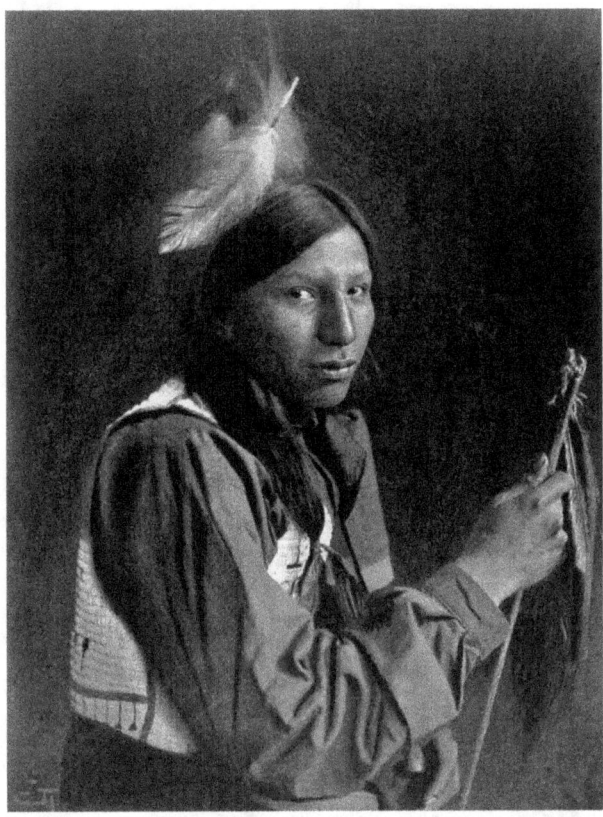

readers with Indian men who combined strong moral principles with hard bodies.[47] *Ramona* went through new printings in 1898 and 1899, and 1900 saw the production of a deluxe illustrated edition.[48]

Interracial sentimental fiction frequently described non-Indian women's interest in Indian men as growing out of their social interest in the "Indian question." Real-life interracial partnerships, like the marriage of Transcendentalist poet Elaine Goodale and Sioux physician/author Charles Eastman, were publicly discussed as alliances between moral crusaders rather than steamy romances.[49] However, the readers of these accounts often added in sexual overtones. Indeed, Valerie Sherer Mathes has suggested that the desirability of Jackson's Indian protagonist Alessandro impeded the political message of *Ramona*.[50] While the novel did not hurt the Indian reform movement that Jackson helped start, most of its readers used it as a tool for fantasy, not for real action.

But to pit women's social reform work against their cultivation of sexual desire would be to miss the interconnected worlds of middle-class female self-development during this period. As Deborah Gordon has pointed out, women with training in social sciences who worked in Indian communities were exploring their own empowerment while pursuing work that was deemed an extension of the nineteenth-century idea of the "woman's sphere." Caring for others did not mean ignoring one's own desires. Gordon writes, "[It] developed from the search for different ways of being white and female. . . . Ironically in these women's search for difference they were constrained by authoritative social relations and thus, literally came to know Native American[s] . . . as the embodiment of their desires. The Other, which they sought in order to change themselves, was eclipsed by their own general understanding of white gender relations."[51] Similarly, Margaret Jacobs has noted that many of the feminists who became interested in Native American culture in the early twentieth century rejected repressive Victorian sexuality and celebrated the Pueblos' relatively open attitude toward sexuality as one of the qualities Western culture should adopt.[52]

The interpolation of reformist ideas in a popular magazine helped women negotiate a balance between their sense of their right to cultivate their own individuality through consumption and their interest in serving others. *Everybody's Magazine* was not an isolated attempt to link these worlds. As William Leach has shown, department stores like Wanamaker's often linked their displays with women's political issues.[53] Several commercial venues in New York more explicitly linked shopping and reform work. One such institution, the New York Exchange for Woman's Work, occupied the rooms directly below Käsebier's. The exchange ran a tearoom and consignment shop founded to help genteel women who had fallen on hard times. It is likely that Käsebier used her display case to appeal to the women who stopped to lunch there. The Exchange itself had played on the consumer appeal of the West, offering at different times dolls shaped like Rough Riders during the Spanish-American War and a year later sold "a large and rare collection of baskets from Alaska."[54]

Like the women anthropologists Gordon studies, Käsebier linked a variety of desires in "Some Indian Portraits," including an appeal to the reformist point of view. The article enumerates several contemporary critiques of the Indian situation. Reservations are described as confining. Government education is exposed as inadequate and corrupting. The author describes "young educated bucks" as corrupted by schooling—turned into dandies "able to write a little, and to speak a comical broken English" (11).

That Käsebier herself promoted the cause of Indian reform is not inconsistent with the other goals of her work. She was a supporter of the Carlisle Indian Industrial School, attending its graduation ceremonies in 1901. Her correspondence with the school's founder, Richard Pratt, and the progressive Yavapai Indian reformer Dr. Carlos Montezuma over the following decade suggests that this interest was ongoing.[55] These social goals, like her artistic ambitions and her exploration of her sexuality, were commensurate with a modern urban woman's activities. Indeed, women justified their exploration of the public sphere in terms of the social need for them to exert their moral influence over a wider field. At the same time, the interest in social uplift did not prohibit women exploring new opportunities outside the home from learning to cultivate their own tastes, and opinions. Such interconnected interests characterize the modern women who consumed the Indian portraits in *Everybody's Magazine* and other popular publications.

THE INDIAN PORTRAITS AND "MODERN" IDENTITY

Like the female promoters of Indian corners, non-Indian women artists promoted interpretations of Native American culture that helped them resolve problems they were facing in their own communities. This is a provocative way to think about Käsebier's Indian portraits. There is reason to believe that Käsebier's artistic community was not comfortable with how her work implied active female desire. As I will show, the critical reception of Käsebier's work avoided some of the most radical implications of her work. Moreover, an understanding of Käsebier's marginalization as a woman within her own artistic community opens up the possibility of reading the Indian portraits as suggesting a richer identification between the woman photographer and the Native American artists than that of other early modernists.

Critics interpreted Käsebier's talent through the lens of femininity. The perception that women's talents lay in their interpersonal skills led critics to focus on Käsebier's studio, rather than her darkroom, as the site of her real work. Giles Edgerton claimed that "her real work is done with the sitter, not in the darkroom."[56] Though he praised others' manipulated photographic prints, Charles Caffin singled out Käsebier's talent as her "keen intuition of character, and a wonderfully swift inventiveness of means to express it."[57] These critics rarely addressed Käsebier's sophisticated darkroom techniques, despite their palpability in her prints. Sometimes this avoidance seems willful. When the photographer's work was reprinted in the first issue of the publication of the Photo-Secession in 1902, the editors identified her as a "straight" photographer, all the while apologizing for the loss of "velvety richness" in the reproduction of a gum print.[58]

The avoidance or outright criticism of Käsebier's printing techniques is related to a contemporary reluctance to see a woman artist's technical proficiency. Kirsten Swinth has observed that the language of art criticism in turn-of-the-century United States tended to identify good technique as a "masculine" quality, associated with capacity to "reason" that was perceived to be challenged by female emotionalism.[59] Käsebier contributed to the understanding of her work as being essentially emotional rather than technical. In an early address, she expressed herself as unversed in what she called "dark-room etiquette": "I confess to staining my hands with pyro, to burning my gowns with acids, sometimes making two exposures on one plate, and sometimes forgetting to make any."[60] Memoirs of her studio assistants confirm her reluctance to admit to technical proficiency, recognizing that "she professes greater ignorance than her results warrant."[61]

As with other aspects of early modernist discourse, the emphasis on technical aspects of artworks frequently masked social concerns. The avoidance of discussing women's activities in the darkroom may stem not only from a low expectation of women's technical ability, but also because the darkroom could be seen as an unseemly place for women. At a time when female virtue was policed by observation of public behavior, the darkroom provided a site in which women's activities were invisible. The New York Camera Club, where Käsebier and other pictorialists worked and exhibited in the late 1890s and early 1900s, understood that the darkroom was a potentially dangerous place. They did not permit women to print on their premises until 1899, when they had constructed darkrooms for men and women on separate floors.[62]

The Camera Club's policy was probably due to the fact that the darkroom was a place where women might be exposed to unwanted physical contact with male photographers. But Käsebier's Indian portraits hint at the possibility that the darkroom also provided the opportunity for physical contact—at least symbolic contact—between women photographers and their models. In her analysis of the photography of Julia Margaret Cameron, Carol Mavor has suggested an association between manipulative printing techniques and caresses. She describes them as "printed with eroticism, as if they have been touched all over."[63] Given the provocative poses and suggestive texts surrounding the pictures included in "Some Indian Portraits," it is possible that critics seeking to advance the cause of art photography wanted to avoid the implication that Käsebier's connection to her sitters would be anything other than a professional, feminine interaction in the light of the studio. In Käsebier's case, the dusky intimacy of the darkroom was not only a potential site for physical bodies to rub up against each other, but also a place where the artist transformed the bodies of her sitters into personal expressions, reflecting her exploration of her sexuality as well as her creativity.

Some critics expressed their anxiety about changing gender roles by criticizing the way Käsebier conducted her career. An example of this can be found in Sadakichi Hartmann's criticism of Käsebier's photographs. Hartmann was a critic and art historian of American painting who contributed photographic criticism to several art journals.[64] He supported the goal of revitalizing American culture through the cultivation of individuality. For instance, he described the value of F. Holland Day's work as its attempt to "render our modern life more harmonious." His celebration of individuality in art builds on a social critique. Day's project is, for Hartmann, "no easy task, truly, in this age of ours, when everything tends towards the effacement of character, when uniformity of dress is almost universal, when the leveling of the classes is every day causing our personality to disappear more and more."[65] Yet Hartmann was unable to appreciate the modernity of Käsebier's mixing of social, economic, and artistic goals in her photographs. He found her work clever but overly picturesque and imitative of old master painting. He recognized the presence of subjectivity in her prints, but reads it as revealing an "apparent, almost obtrusive . . . [and] rather a superficial" individuality.[66] He felt that anyone who made portraits on commission was not capable of being an artist. As he wrote, "In my opinion only men like Messrs. Stieglitz, Day, and Keiley are artistic photographers: like the true artist, they only depict what pleases them, and not everybody who offers them twenty-five dollars in return. This is the line which divides artistic and professional photography, as it does art and pot-boiling."[67]

As I have argued already, the turn-of-the-century art world's retreat from the commercial world was intimately bound up with the methods and materials of the market, but it often downplayed this connection. Thus, instead of seeing Käsebier's very participation in New York's commercial and artistic culture as a sign of her exploration of worlds only newly available to women, Hartmann branded her insufficiently excited about the artistic implications of what was "going on around her in this great city." Käsebier seems to have been aware of how closely artistic photographers scrutinized one another's behavior. She cautioned an audience in 1898 that frequent publication could look "promiscuous."[68] Her language suggests that the criticism of her avid pursuit of clients is linked to a suggestion that this behavior is particularly dangerous for a woman's reputation.

Käsebier's situation illuminates the difficulty in conceptualizing a female modern artist within the critical discourse of the period. Sarah Burns has convincingly argued that the turn of the century brought a watershed of public discussions about what artists were and how they should act.[69] At the same time, this very period brought increased scrutiny of women's behavior as women increasingly entered the public sphere through education, commerce, and work. Despite numerous articles celebrating exemplary women artists, these publications used the idea of an innate female aesthetic to dissociate women from the qualities thought to be required by vanguard artists. Indeed, as Burns has shown, even when women artists deployed the same artistic strategies as men in their work, or the same bravado in their social activities as their male counterparts, it was nonetheless judged in different, and often disparaging, terms. The rejection of Käsebier's configuration of modernist artistic practice contributed to a consolidation of control of aesthetic debates in the hands of men.[70] Both Kirsten Swinth and Sarah Burns see the emergence of gendered language as an attempt to preserve male dominance in an art world with increasing female participation.[71] The solution was to delineate male and female artistic qualities to differentiate and subtly rank men's and women's work.

In borrowing from the arts and crafts movement, early American modernists, such as Stieglitz and his close associates Marsden Hartley and Charles Sheeler, appropriated the movement's fraught negotiation of progressivism and antimodernism. While using their engagement with craftsmanship and individuality as a way to critique the anonymity and powerlessness they perceived to be a product of industrial modernity, at the same time they embraced the notion of artistic progress and invested themselves in the idea that art could lead both practitioners and viewers to higher levels of civilization. Generally this conflict of ideas was not commented upon, nor did it seem to cause difficulty for artists and critics who wanted to play both sides of the argument. Indeed, as Sarah Burns's recent work has demonstrated, no matter how antimodernist, an early twentieth-century artist needed to master the "modern" skills of self-promotion if he or she wanted to succeed in a culture that increasingly asked artists to externalize their creative personas by representing themselves in ways that fit the evolving definition of how an "artist" should behave.[72] Tension nevertheless existed between the "antimodern" or the "primitive" ideals expressed within artistic communities and the demands placed upon them by the public to use "modern" strategies of self-representation.

This tension is visible in the reception of Käsebier's Indian portraits. While the photographer's male artistic peers were comfortable seeing themselves as straddling primitivism and modernity, they downplayed the modernity of Käsebier's and other women's work, praising it in terms of transhistorical female values that linked them to age-old domestic ideals.

Significantly, the use of Indian art as a model for modern art production may have contributed to European American women's unequal status in the turn-of-the-century art world. While they were by no means as clearly identified as working at a distance from modernity as Indian artists, there is some suggestion that primitive art served to control women's participation in artistic culture. A return to the cases discussed in chapter 3 suggests as much. The students that George Brush steered toward making Indian ceramics were all women. Although Dow had male students at his summer school, the people making Indian art in the photograph of his summer school are also women (see figure 35). While all artists were encouraged to learn from Native American designs through the articles and exhibitions of the arts and crafts societies, it appears that the actual imitation of Native American *forms* was often understood as women's work. As I explained in chapter 1, most of the Indian material culture that was characterized as "art" by the arts and crafts movement was made by women, and conformed to contemporary ideas of women's culture. By making hand-built ceramics, baskets with southwestern motifs woven into them, and textiles woven on

Navajo looms, women artists benefited from the understanding that they were participating in noble female traditions. At the same time, this association suggests that it is more appropriate for women to continue these primitive traditions than to explore avant-garde forms of art.

In the face of the sexism of the artistic culture in which she worked, I propose that Käsebier's Indian portraits allow for a critique of the very primitivism they celebrate by suggesting that the photographer and models occupy a similarly marginalized relationship to modern culture. The photographer's use of the discourse of Indian art provides new insights into the roles of gender and race in early modernist aesthetic debates. Käsebier made use of contemporary ideas of "primitive" Indian creativity throughout her career, using her association with it as a way to posit her own modern artistic sensibility. Käsebier deculturated Indian art, in much the same way as her artistic contemporaries who promoted Native American culture in distinctly European American terms. At the same time, in her self-consciousness about her artistic identity, she may have shown a more subtle configuration of Indian aesthetics than her peers. This subtlety draws on her experiences as a woman artist.

While not denying the significance of a difference in economic and cultural power between the photographer and her sitters, I would suggest that these photographs hint at a mutual identification between the photographer and the models. In fact, the photographs seem to suggest that the Indian artists are experiencing the same blending of commercial and "artistic" needs in their own self-expression as the photographer. Reina Lewis has suggested that "women's differential, gendered access to the positionalities of imperial discourse produced a gaze on the . . . 'other' that registered difference less pejoratively and less absolutely than [men's]."[73] Käsebier's Indian portraits can be read as an attempt to reconcile the conflicting needs of a culture with conflicting expectations of the various roles they played, including performers playing to an audience as "authentic" representors of their sex and race. The Indian portraits, therefore, not only reveal the studio to be the site of interconnected desires, they also illuminate how artists negotiated contemporary definitions of creativity and their limitations.

My reading also runs counter to much current scholarship on photographic representations of Native Americans from the end of the nineteenth century, which often concentrates on the question of whether the photog-

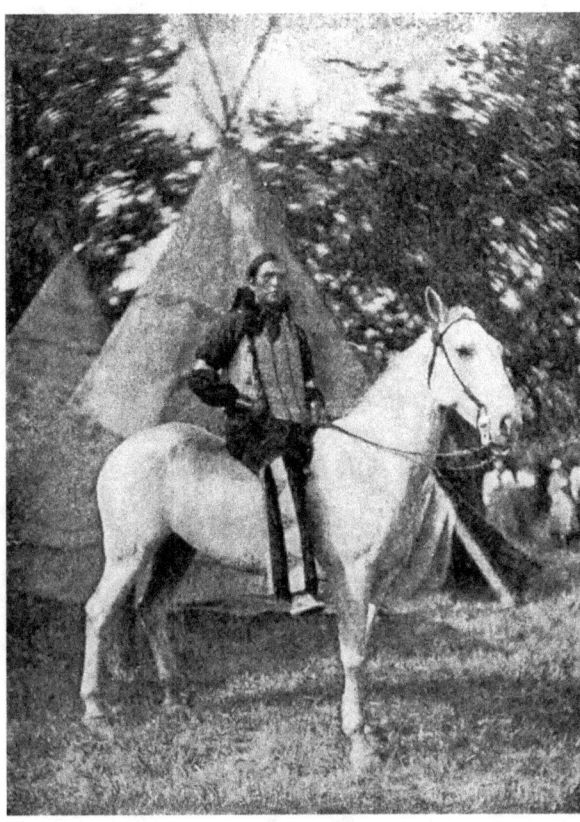

FIGURE 56 Gertrude Käsebier, "High Heron," from "Some Indian Portraits," *Everybody's Magazine* 4.17 (January 1901): 24.

rapher allowed the personality of the sitter to come out in the picture or projected his or her own fantasies of Indianness on the sitter.[74] Criticism of Käsebier's Indian portraits makes use of this approach. For example, in her 1990 book on Käsebier, Barbara Michaels argues that the photographer's pictures of Indians stand out from the stereotypical representations of her time in the individual treatment of the models and the choice to portray them in a contemporary setting (her studio).[75] Jennifer Sheffield Currie disagrees with Michaels, interpreting Käsebier's pictures as timeless images of "Noble Savagery." "Life with the Wild West Show was the reality that Käsebier's subjects experienced," she writes; "however, we receive little, if any, sense of this world when viewing Käsebier's images."[76] While Currie is right that Käsebier did not produce a photo-essay of the daily activities of the performers, the photographer *did* include photographs taken at the troupe's tipi camp in her article, including one featuring High Heron (figure 56).

On initial viewing, this small photograph of the performer in front of a tipi might lead the viewer to think the photographer had been inspired by her encounter with these models to return to the West. But details proving this supposition wrong emerge with the second glance. The lush greenery framing the scene does not does not describe a western landscape, but an eastern one. The background on the photograph includes more than leafy trees; to the right of the tipi the blurry images of European Americans can be made out. They are looking at High Heron, mirroring the viewer's gaze, reinforcing the idea that he is on display. The photograph is not taken during the *Wild West* show, but nevertheless, High Heron is performing. His tipi "home" is just another part of the entertainment. As was typical of the *Wild West* shows, audience members were encouraged to visit the Indian camp and get a glimpse of "authentic" primitive life before and after the stage show.

When touring with the performing company, Käsebier's Indian models were always conspicuous, always on display; and their behavior was always evaluated against a popular stereotype of Indianness.[77] And it is on the Native American models' self-consciousness of their participation in European American fantasies of Indian life that my argument turns. The very question of whether photographs capture the true personality of a sitter links these late twentieth-century critics to an investment in "authenticity" every bit as problematic as the primitivization of Indian models. Rather than trying to find out the "truth" behind the photographs, I find it more productive to look at the images as representations constructed by both the photographer and her models.

Many of these models were professional performers who had been part of Buffalo Bill's troupe for many years before meeting Käsebier, and their appearance in Käsebier's photographs builds on their self-consciousness of non-Indian audience's expectations. Luther Standing Bear, a member of the Wild West Company in the early 1900s, recalled that Indian performers experimented with different roles while on the road, playing Indians of four different tribes and sometimes playing the part of a cowboy for an enjoyable change.[78] Moreover, he suggests that only the most talented and experienced performers were chosen for the troupe. While performing work was underpaid and many aspects of it were experienced as degrading, Standing Bear's memoirs suggest that the performers enjoyed the opportunity to meet people and win them over. The letters sent to Käsebier and reprinted in "Some Indian Portraits" reinforce this impression. Whether or not they truly saw Käsebier and the other women they met on the road as "friends," the correspondents clearly saw something to be gained by writing to Käsebier and by visiting with her when they were in New York. I would argue that these performers had a sophisticated, and playful, approach to the roles they were asked to play, whether it was "artist," "dandy," or "savage," an interpretation that makes reading the expressions of White Wolf and Philip Standing Soldier more complicated (see figures 54 and 55).

While Käsebier clearly had more economic and social power than her models, she also needed to negotiate her own aspirations within society's standards of appropriate female behavior. Käsebier performs the female artist even as her models perform "Indianness." Her work and her lifestyle demonstrated her originality at a time when it was a leading determinant of an artist's merit. She sought out ways to achieve her professional and artistic ambitions, stretching but not compromising her reputation as a woman.

For both the artist and her models, identity limited their professional and personal opportunities. They belonged to groups whose behavior was deemed "authentic" only when it was disengaged from modernity. They responded to this situation by playing these roles with a self-consciousness that betrays a modern understanding of how to maximize their options. In their understanding of the fact that their identity was more of a performance than an expression of some "authentic" core, both Käsebier and her sitters demonstrated themselves to be "modern" artists. As Sarah Burns writes, "This dialectic—artists as actors who are acted upon, representing themselves and being represented—constituted the phenomenon of 'modernization': that process through which artists responded, reacted to, and were remodeled by new conditions of producing and marketing their work, and themselves, in a rapidly urbanizing and incorporating society in which mass culture, spectacle, commercialism, and consumerism were fast becoming common denominators of modern experience."[79] Moreover, in the playfulness with which they appear to have approached this fact, the maker and the subjects of "Some Indian Portraits" push the Indian craze in new directions, revealing its inability to banish marginalized artists from participating in modern life.

The article suggests the possibility of transculturation on several different levels. Käsebier borrows from patriarchal primitivism in order to negotiate a role for herself as a modern artist. At the same time, her own experience of marginalization allowed her to avoid a total commitment to the myth of the authentic primitive Indian and present her models as performers playing roles. The models, in turn, demonstrate a familiarity with non-Indian expectations of their behavior and attempt to turn those expectations to their own advantage. As I will explore in the next chapter, the self-conscious appropriation of primitivism was a strategy Indian people adopted for political, as well as personal, ends.

CHAPTER FIVE

The Indian in his native dress is a thing of the past, but his art that is inborn shall endure. He may shed his outer skin, but his markings lie below that and should show up only the brighter.

Angel DeCora

Angel DeCora's Cultural Politics

In the fall of 1911, the Indian craze was publicly appropriated by Indian people when the Winnebago artist Angel DeCora addressed the first conference of the Society of American Indians.[1] DeCora and her audience, composed primarily of Indians who been immersed in non-Indian values at boarding schools, were familiar with the contemporary celebration of Indian art. Like the promoters of Indian corners and the art critics who celebrated Indian aesthetics, they felt Native American art could contribute to the revitalization and progress of American culture. They also wanted to use the popularity of Indian art to help Indian communities survive economically and culturally. However, they were conflicted about the form this survival should take.

The Society of American Indians was the first Indian-led Indian rights organization in the United States. The group directed its energies to agitating for government policies and social reform projects that would facilitate individual Native American autonomy and citizenship. DeCora was a professional llustrator and designer and the founder of a curriculum in Indian art for the Carlisle Indian Industrial School. Her comment came from a talk entitled "Native Indian Art," which argued for the centrality of artistic production to the economic and cultural survival of Native Americans in the twentieth century. The society took for granted that Indians would be assimilated into European American society; as DeCora's talk demonstrates, however, they did not feel this required abandoning all tribal practices and beliefs.

DeCora's progressivism is typical of the membership of the Society of American Indians. Like other organizations of the day, the society was critical of the social problems that had arisen as a result of industrialization. Moreover, they felt themselves uniquely qualified to offer a critique, as these problems were identified with European, not Indian, racial development. Turning primitivism to their own advantage, members of the society proposed that Native Americans could pursue a model of development that avoided pollution, overcrowding, and child labor. The secret would be to preserve core values that were already part of Indian culture. Most of those present had been born and partially raised on reservations but had come to share the "universal" values of Christianity, education, science, and art during periods of off-reservation schooling. Most had received support from government and reform organizations. During these experiences, they had come to see themselves as belonging to a "race" that was in need of "advancement." At the same time, they were unable and unwilling to condemn all of the traditions they had learned in childhood, joining antimodernist European Americans in thinking that Indian culture was sometimes more healthy and sincere than urban American life.

DeCora was uniquely qualified to make the claim that Indian art could contribute to an integrated American cultural landscape. Native American artists of her generation, such as the Pomo basketmakers Mary and William Benson and the Hopi-Tewa potter Nampeyo, had achieved national name recognition. Other Indian people participated in the arts and crafts movement as craftspeople and even occasionally as critics.[2] But DeCora alone had the combination of training and desire to produce a systematic articulation of Indian aesthetics.[3] In numerous lectures and articles and in her curriculum at Carlisle, she defined the distinctive quality of Indian art as an abstract, geometric sense of design that could be applied to both traditional and nontraditional materials. She utilized the terms of the mainsteam art world in her creative work, pedagogy, and political activism. DeCora and her peers in the Society of American Indians shared many of the values of non-Indians of the time, including a belief in education, hard work, and the power of art. At the same time, her experiences as an Indian woman artist working at the margins of turn-of-the-century European American culture made her aware that the incorporation of Indian people into an American economy and culture was not a simple matter.

Like most European Americans and an increasing number of Native Americans of her generation, DeCora accepted that Indian people belonged to a distinct *race*. Her politicized aesthetics were designed to simultaneously define and unify this race without locking the definition of Indian art into any specific unchanging tradition. She developed an understanding of Native art that would not only provide the opportunity to take pride in the Native American past but also allow Indian people to participate in the economic and artistic culture of the present. At the same time, she challenged the tendency of the discourse of Indian art to deculturize the objects it celebrated, always arguing that Indian art is defined as art made by Indian people.

As this chapter will show, DeCora's career was compromised by her own vulnerability to the romanticizing nostalgia that made mainstream critics continually define Indian art as a thing of the past. At the same time, she, more than any other participant in the discourse of Indian aesthetics, embraced the social-oriented aesthetic ideas of the time. DeCora's belief in the power of design to promote racial understanding resonates throughout her work. At the beginning of her career, DeCora tried to bridge Indian and non-Indian cultures through painting, putting her training at the hands of some of the best known European American art teachers of the day to use. Later, she moved away from illusionistic renderings of figures in space to abstract designs conceived of as constituting a pan-Indian iconography. It was only when she began to focus on the attitudes and objects of the arts and crafts movement that she found a definition of art that enabled her and other Indians to participate in the growing market for "Indian" creations without compromising their aesthetic ideals. In addition, it provided justification for Indian artists to build on their own artistic traditions without locking themselves out of participation in contemporary culture.

An assessment of DeCora's accomplishments is difficult to make because of the limited number of works by her that we have to study. Scholars are restricted to discussing works that are extant, which consist of two illustrated stories in *Harper's Weekly* from 1899, illustrations and cover designs for five books, and a handful of illustrations for the *Indian Craftsman*, a publication of the Carlisle Indian Industrial School, and the Society of American Indians' *American Indian Magazine*. Only a small number of her presumably many paintings have been located.[4] All of these have Indian subject matter, though it is unclear whether she would have always focused on overtly Native American themes if given commercial opportunities to do otherwise; for example, her letters describe making landscape paintings for her own pleasure. In addition to visual evidence for her aesthetic ideas, DeCora has left behind numerous writings, including lectures on Indian art, an autobiographical sketch, and a thick file of letters to Cora Mae Folsom, her former teacher.[5] To assess DeCora's artistic vision we need to consider everything she produced; her illustrations and writings in particular provide a rich resource for the investigation of her politicized aesthetics.

Previous studies of DeCora's work have analyzed her work in relationship to other contemporary artistic representations of Indians.[6] These analyses suggest that the fact that she spent her first nine years living with her Winnebago family in Nebraska enabled her to avoid perpetuating inaccurate popular stereotypes. I agree with these scholars that the grounding in Winnebago values and the strong sense of identity that DeCora received in her early childhood nourished and inspired her throughout her career. However, it is also important to understand the influence of her subsequent education on her aesthetic views. At nine, DeCora left home to attend school at the Hampton Institute in Virginia. Including a one-year hiatus spent with her family, she studied at Hampton for seven years, graduating in 1891. For the following decade, DeCora studied in European American institutions. After a brief stint at a girls academy in western Massachusetts, she enrolled in the art certificate program at Smith College, where she studied with Dwight Tryon. The four years at Smith were followed by two years at the Drexel Academy in Philadelphia and, finally, two years of study in Boston. During these years she began publishing illustrations and graphic designs. In 1905 she was lured away from her commercial career to teach Indian art at the Carlisle Indian school, a position she held until 1915. This position entailed not only teaching, but also theorizing and speaking publicly on Indian art. Although DeCora dreamed of returning to painting when she retired from

Carlisle, this stage of her career was cut short when she died in the influenza epidemic of 1918.

DeCora's work represents the modern Indian condition, characterized by experiences and attitudes that made Native Americans experts in European American as well as tribal cultures. An investigation of the hybrid nature of her art allows us to understand the degree to which DeCora embraced the European American politicized aesthetics of the time. DeCora's outlook was shaped by the sense of purpose she learned at the hands of European American women during seven years in the Indian program at the Hampton Institute in Virginia. DeCora received an education at the hands of the school's reform-oriented staff and on "outings" with the families of female reformers in western Massachusetts. As early as 1895, DeCora showed her commitment to the Indian reform community by addressing the conference of the Friends of the Indian at Lake Mohonk.[7] Such women supported her emotionally and financially, and encouraged her to believe in her artistic ability. The encouragement to exercise her moral authority as a woman and an Indian she got from these women reformers was matched by lessons in the social value of art included in her artistic training. Dwight Tryon taught her to appreciate art's capacity to exert moral and spiritual influence. Her later teachers, Howard Pyle, Joseph DeCamp, Frank Benson and Edmund Tarbell, reinforced his emphasis on art's personal and social rewards.

DeCora's concept of racial aesthetics was inconsistent, sometimes even contradictory. It was the product of both her European American artistic education and her experience as a person whose race and gender continually shaped and delineated her opportunities. Though DeCora claimed she would have loved to have become a landscape painter, she took work where she could get it. Illness and professional biases continually impeded her career, and she frequently found herself resorting to dressmaking, making Christmas "gimcracks," and generally doing what she called "other people's work," in order to make money.[8] The year she left Carlisle she earned extra money by painting Zuni, Navajo, Sioux, and Hopi designs on china pins. As she put it, "Foolish things sell better always."[9] DeCora's interest in negotiating a place for Native American art within turn-of-the-century American culture was not without contradictions, but the fraught politics that inhabit her aesthetic position are an important part of the history of early modernism that we are wont to forget.

DeCora's earliest artworks utilize a strategy typical of educated colonized peoples: the use of Western representational forms to humanize and correct stereotypical imagery.[10] DeCora's professional artistic career began in 1899, when *Harper's Monthly* published two stories that she wrote and illustrated about Indians from unidentified tribes. Their plots locate young Indian women in the kinds of emotional situations typical of European American magazine literature of the day. "The Sick Child" describes a girl's first experience of human powerlessness in the face of death. In "Gray Wolf's Daughter," the heroine decides to pursue her ambition — an education — despite her family's reservations.

The stories put the lessons of sentimental fiction to the work of describing the difficulty of transculturation. Although there is no indication that they are autobiographical, both show young Indian women seeking a balance between their own desires and their tribal traditions, an experience DeCora no doubt faced herself. In "The Sick Child," the heroine wavers in her commitment to the difficult requirements of a healing ritual. Charged with making an offering to the Great Spirit and asking for help, she doubts whether it will help. Though a medicine woman and a medicine man add their healing prayers to hers, the child dies. In the other story, Gray Wolf's daughter gives up her belongings and her role in tribal ceremonials when she leaves home to attend a government boarding school. Though her family is reluctant to let her go, she leaves willingly: "She herself had for a long time desired knowledge of the white man's ways, and now her family had given their consent to her going to school" (860).

DeCora wrote "The Sick Child" and "Gray Wolf's Daughter" while studying at the Drexel Academy in Philadelphia with the premier illustrator of the time, Howard Pyle. Pyle specialized in making romantic and historical pictures of the medieval and colonial eras for magazines and for books of his own original adventure tales. DeCora's opportunity to create and publish these images has been described as the result of Pyle's encouraging her to spend the summer of 1897 with a former schoolmate on the Arikara, Mandan, and Hidatsa reservation at Fort Berthold, North Dakota, where he felt she could cultivate her "distinctly" Indian art by spending more time with "her own people."[11] Pyle's suggestion that she would find "her own people" at Fort Berthold betrays his belief that all Indian cultures were the same. The illustrations for "The Sick Child" were prepared for the teacher's summer illustration course in 1898 in Chadd's Ford, Pennsylvania, to which DeCora had won a scholarship. Pyle admired one of them enough to hang it in the summer school's exhibition at the Drexel Academy that fall.

DeCora's illustrations use European American models of composition and style to bring the reader into an understanding of the characters' situations. The dim light of one illustration for "The Sick Child" (figure 57) illuminates a quiet, touching scene consisting of two women and two girls gathered around a small child who has been taken out of its cradle board. They are surrounded by symbols of their femininity: empty vessels, baskets, and a doll lying in the background. The log-frame lodge in which they sit is lined with soft textiles that enhance the sense of security and comfort of this domestic space. Blankets and bundles hang from the wall beams; the floor is covered in woven mats. Pyle encouraged his students to be close observers of historical detail, and to fully flesh out their compositions so that viewers could imaginatively project themselves into the scene. The deep space of this illustration and the objects that occupy the background are consistent with this approach. As one of Pyle's students later put it, "To be able to live in the scene one was depicting was as essential as being able to draw."[12]

While clearly a Pyle-styled illustration, this one from "The Sick Child" also refers to older traditions of art. The arrangement of figures recalls Renaissance adoration scenes, particularly because of the soft light on the mother's beatific face. The sentimental and religious allusions in this illustration are not accidental—they are consistent with the entire story's attempt to link an Indian story to universal themes. The other illustrations support this connection. The opening image shows the narrator's head, wrapped in a striped scarf, looking up into a darkening sky as if seeking help (figure 58). Though she is clearly dark-skinned, her modest attire and expression fit a long tradition of depictions of pious women. The final image shows the medicine man framed against a dramatic sky. Again, his skin and the band circling his head identify him as Indian, but the pose invokes biblical patriarchs from the Western painting tradition.

DeCora was not the first artist to use classical poses for Indian subjects; her use of this mode to humanize Indian life differs from her predecessors' idealized visions of it. While Brush's pictures of heroically nude Indian men

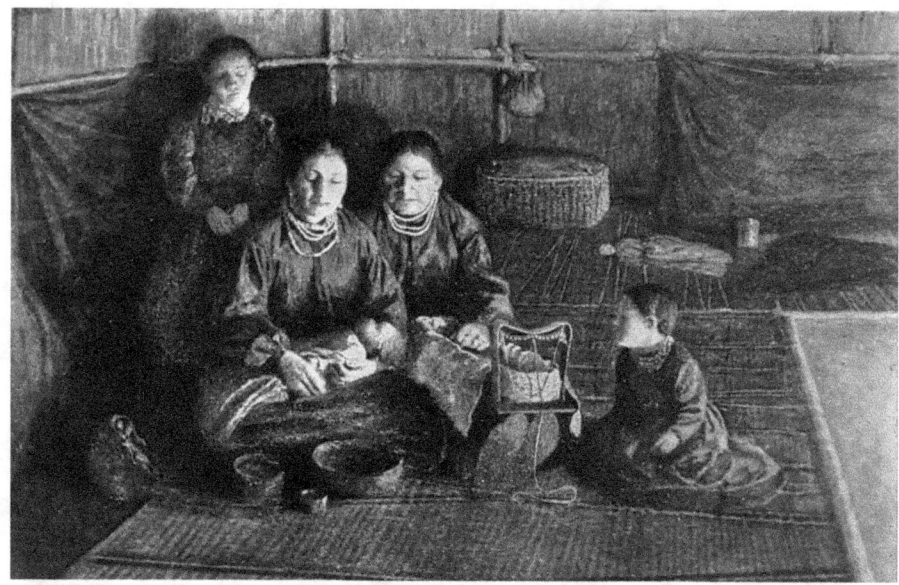

FIGURE 57 Angel DeCora, illustration from "The Sick Child," *Harper's New Monthly Magazine* 98 (February 1899): 447.

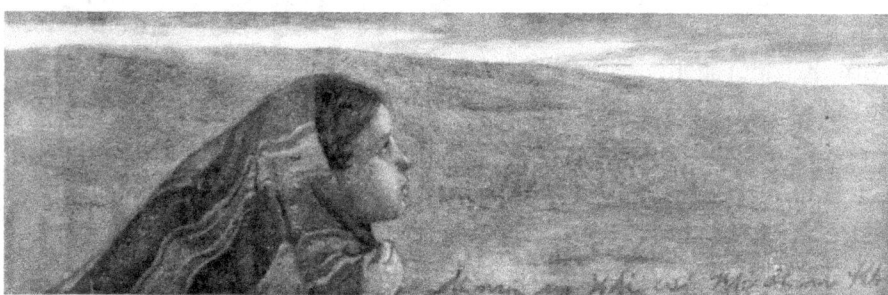

FIGURE 58 Angel DeCora, illustration from "The Sick Child," *Harper's New Monthly Magazine* 98 (February 1899): 446.

encourage viewers to contemplate the nobility of an Indian past, DeCora's pictures are designed to draw attention to the pathos of the Indian present. It is not nudity or drama that attract our attention in "The Sick Child" but the emotion of an event all too common in nineteenth-century America. The women and girls are not dazzling, complicated figures that demonstrate the artist's skill; they are modestly and uniformly dressed, their bodies hidden under loose dark dresses with long sleeves. Even the baby is swaddled in a white gown.

In their ennobling vision of tribal life, these illustrations argue for art's ability to communicate the artist's humanity to her viewers. Such an approach is consistent with the pedagogy of DeCora's first teacher, Dwight Tryon. DeCora studied with Tryon at Smith College from 1891 to 1895. At the time, Smith was one of the few places where women could study art on the college level. Although he followed a typical academic curriculum, moving from cast drawing to life drawing and lecturing on topics like art history and perspective, Tryon's pedagogy was infused with his personal aesthetic ideas. In his critiques, lectures on aesthetics, and the images he acquired or loaned to Smith's Hillyer Art Gallery, where DeCora worked as a custodian, he explained his understanding of art as a universal moral language. His celebration of originality and sincerity on the part of the artist formed the basis of DeCora's later aesthetic theories. He impressed on his students his view that art "'was a humanizer'" and the embodiment of "sincerity and truth" and argued for the importance of art in unifying and advancing American culture.[13] DeCora told her former teachers that she found Tryon's criticism inspiring, and, indeed, she thrived in his classes, earning a departmental prize in her second year and receiving several commendations at her graduation in 1896.[14] Tryon's ideas reinforced the understanding advanced by DeCora's Hampton Institute teachers of art as a civilizer and raiser. Her own experiences backed this lesson up. As she later related, the opportunity to express herself creatively was the only thing that soothed her frustrations and kept her from running away from boarding school.[15]

DeCora used the formal lessons she learned in Tryon's classes to brings the viewer into the scene physically and emotionally, as an illustration for the story "Gray Wolf's Daughter" demonstrates (see figure 59). The low point of view locates the viewer on the grass outside the circle of dancers, in a space set off by the stones and vessels in the foreground; she is a welcome visitor, a complement to the seated women and children behind the dancers. The style of the illustration also brings the viewer in. The soft light and murky background identify the artist with the contemporary style called tonalism, a style in which Tryon excelled.[16] Indeed, the rounded lodge at the right of DeCora's composition could be read as an homage to Tryon's 1889 painting *The Rising Moon: Autumn* (figure 60), one of Tryon's favorites. Like Tryon's French scene, DeCora's picture is designed to capture a mood rather than to illustrate an event. The six figures depicted in her work, visually rhyming the same number of inanimate rocks and baskets in the foreground, don't

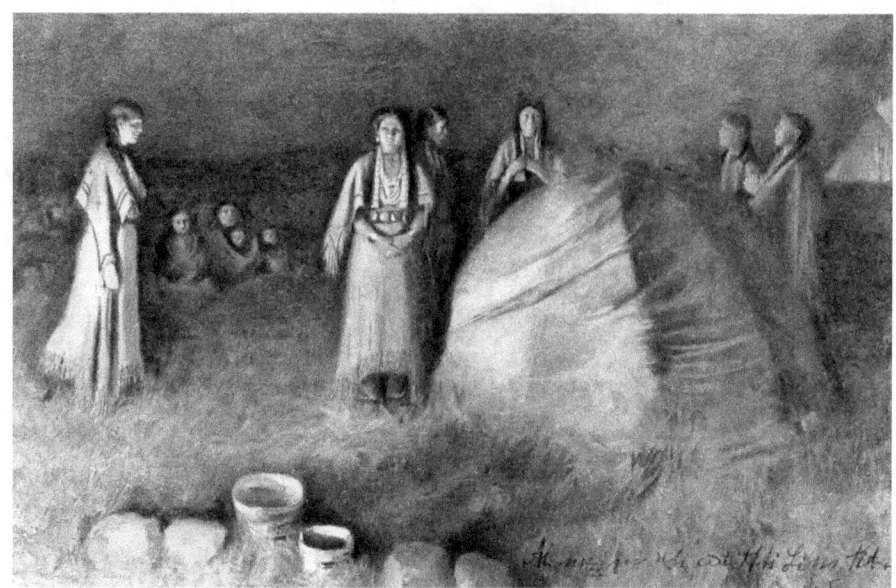

FIGURE 59 Angel DeCora, illustration from "Gray Wolf's Daughter," *Harper's New Monthly Magazine* 99 (November 1899): 861.

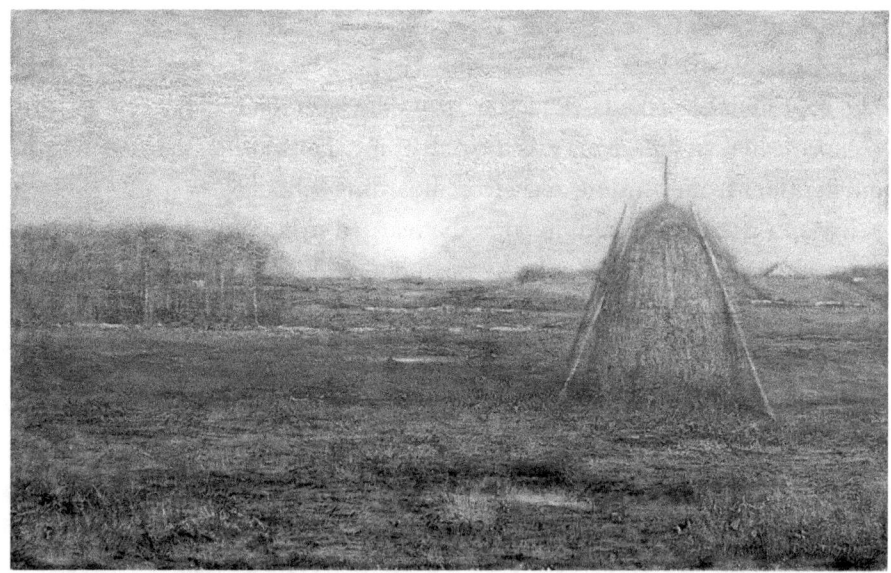

FIGURE 60 Dwight Tryon, *The Rising Moon: Autumn*, 1899. Oil on canvas. Inv. no. F1889.31, Freer Gallery of Art, Smithsonian Institution, Washington, D.C. Gift of Charles Lang Freer.

seem to be dancing, or indeed moving, at all. The active brushwork on the surface of this image does not enhance movement, instead it contributes a hazy quality that casts us at a distance from the scene, as if viewing it through time and space. The dim light makes the figures in the background literally hard to see, as if they were fleeting traces of memory, just beyond our grasp.

DeCora's nocturnes bear not only a formal but also an ideological resemblance to Tryon's work. Tryon encouraged his students to think independently and experiment with their own ways of painting. DeCora's use of his style aspires to both formal innovation and personal expression. Moreover, her early nocturnes display an antimodernist nostalgia for prereservation Indian life that would have appealed to both non-Indian and Indian viewers. Linda Merrill finds in Tryon's New England landscapes both an attempt to create an autonomous aesthetic object and a nostalgia for an idyllic Connecticut childhood that never existed.[17] Tryon's mythic images of old New England fed not only his own personal memory but also a broader cultural longing for a simpler time among the elite whose cultural authority was threatened by industrialization and the social changes that came with it. Aestheticist artists like Tryon were concerned that American culture was becoming decadent in the face of expanding industrialization and commercialism, and they created works of art that would help inspire the nation's cultural ascent. Subtle, harmonious compositions like Tryon's provided the viewer with a chance to escape the dirty, crowded, workaday world of the city and find the repose necessary to dwell on higher things. As Kathleen Pyne has explained, this experience was geared toward the same kind of spiritual regeneration that artists and critics sought. In aestheticist paintings, "beauty is presented for the sake of the viewer; it offers personal delectation and the opportunity for self-culture."[18]

Significantly, Tryon believed that it wasn't every viewer who could appreciate his work. Writing to a patron, he explained: "The 'spirit of art' reveals itself to the ardent lover only."[19] He told Charles Lang Freer that *The Rising Moon* was a picture in which "the average person will see nothing and at first sight will not reveal itself to even more cultured ones."[20] The artistic movement advanced by Tryon and his peers was elitist, but it was not without social goals. Aestheticist painters and critics hoped to provide moral leadership for the entire country, encouraging viewers to cultivate

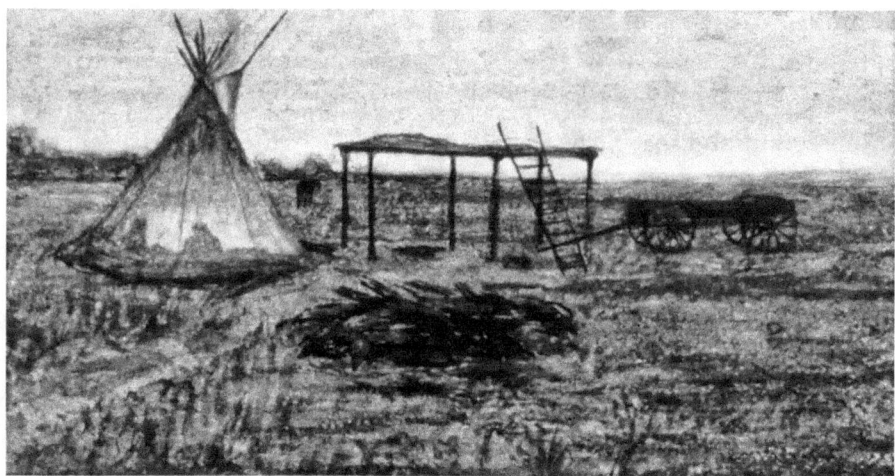

FIGURE 61 Angel DeCora, untitled, n.d. Watercolor on paper. Hampton University's Archival and Museum Collection, Hampton University, Hampton, Virginia.

their own individual powers of aesthetic judgment. As Linda Dowling has explained, aestheticism and the more explicitly socially oriented arts and crafts movement have their roots in the same late eighteenth-century belief that art should provide social cohesion and moral authority in an age when other sources of moral authority (the nobility, the church, etc.) were beginning to break down.[21] Without specifically articulating universal values, supporters of this idea put their faith in art's ability to help individuals transcend their own sense of isolation.

While Tryon and his peers saw their audience as the American cultural elite, DeCora's engagement with aestheticism proposes a different kind of insider audience, a specifically racial one. Though they engage universal themes, DeCora's early images dwell on subjects that she felt had particular meaning for Indians. DeCora's many nocturnes partake of Tryon's nostalgia (e.g., figure 61). The prereservation idyll they present fits a European American taste for imagery that romanticizes the Indian past while identifying Indian culture as inevitably doomed—an attitude Renato Rosaldo has described as "imperialist nostalgia."[22] But rather than emphasize the heroic exploits usually associated with European American images of "the vanishing race," DeCora's nocturnes point to domestic moments of families gathered around the evening fire to reinforce a sense of community, fitting her own childhood memories. "About as early as I can remember," she wrote later, "I was lulled to sleep night after night by my father's or grandparent's recital of laws and customs."[23] The firelit tipi was a touchstone to which she could return to fuel her sense of identity, like Gray Wolf's daughter, who is included in the evening dance even though she is about to leave to pursue nontraditional ambitions.

THE POLITICS OF DRESS

DeCora can be seen as akin to the *Wild West* performers who modeled for Käsebier: to obtain a livelihood, both perpetuated the romantic European American stereotype of Indians. Like other Native American culture brokers of the period, they also hoped to influence the consumers of these images to adopt more sympathetic attitudes toward Indian people. However, as Philip Deloria has pointed out, by "playing Indian," Native Americans could inadvertently perpetuate the idea that Indian culture was a thing of the past and not the present.[24] In other words, by attempting to fight for cultural understanding and respect through idealized representations of the Indian past, DeCora risked reifying an identification of Indian culture with practices that were waning in the face of assimilationist federal policies, and thus suggesting that her culture itself was destined to die out. Already in 1898 DeCora seemed aware of the potential danger in presenting nostalgic images of her race. While some of her illustrations contribute to a nostalgic image of Native life, others confront stereotypes of Indians head-on. This can be seen in the first illustration of "Gray Wolf's Daughter" (figure 62). The image shows a young girl dressed in beaded buckskins posed against a painted hide. The scene illustrates a moment from the story when the girl's mother dresses her for her last dance. The moment of dressing in this regalia is drawn out in the story, giving the reader time to think about the material and symbolic weight of each object: "As she spoke, the mother drew out a basket from under the blankets and took from it a great pile of beads. These she hung around her daughter's neck till they reached half way up to her ears. Then she hung in her ears silver ear-rings that jingled with every movement of her head. Silver rings and silver bracelets on her arms, and then she was ready to join her friends" (862).

A European American viewer of "Gray Wolf's Daughter" might note the model's typical academic pose, and see the picture as an ennobled vision of traditional Indian life, similar to "The Sick Child." Similarly, they might

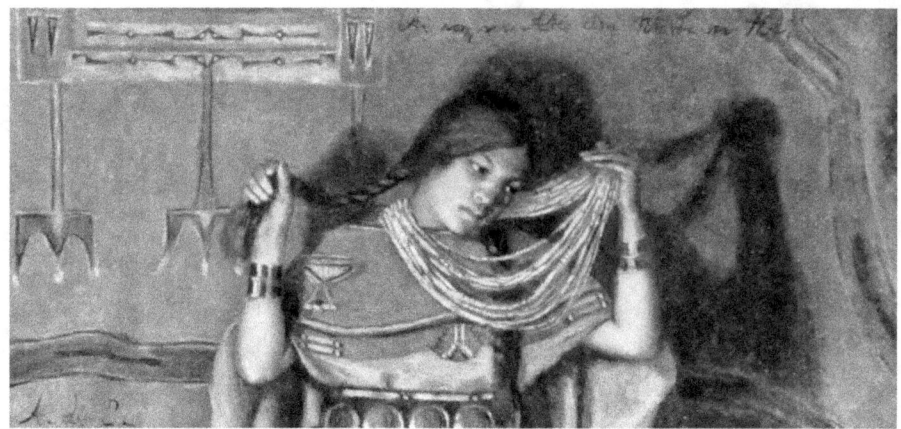

FIGURE 62 Angel DeCora, illustration from "Gray Wolf's Daughter," *Harper's New Monthly Magazine* 99 (November 1899): 860.

recognize the stamp of her teacher in her use of graphic simplicity, dramatic lighting, and use of period costume and props to set the scene. But the image is also in dialogue with stereotypical representation of Indians, especially the image that Rayna Green has identified as the "Indian Princess."[25] Promoted through advertisements, dime novels, and photographs, the Indian princess was young and beautiful, and wore elaborately decorated buckskin clothing and lots of jewelry and was often depicted looking out at the viewer. Modeled on Pocahontas, the Indian princess is young, attractive, and helpful, and serves to suggest Native American openness to, even interest in, European curiosity. Edward Curtis's photograph of a Zuni woman, first published in 1903, exemplifies this type (see figure 63). The sitter looks at the viewer as she holds her necklaces up, seemingly offering her identity up for the viewer's consumption. Despite superficial similarities, DeCora's model reworks this image. Gray Wolf's daughter holds up her beads and braid and examines them, as if questioning her relationship to them. The figure is pinned in place between our close gaze and the geometric patterns behind her which, in their imitation of the angles of her arms and head, threaten to absorb her, to overwhelm her with the material signs of her race.

Gray Wolf's daughter seems to ask wherein Indian identity adheres—in external appearances or somewhere inside. In questioning the relationship of appearance and identity, DeCora was tapping into a significant American discourse of the day. As American culture became increasingly rich

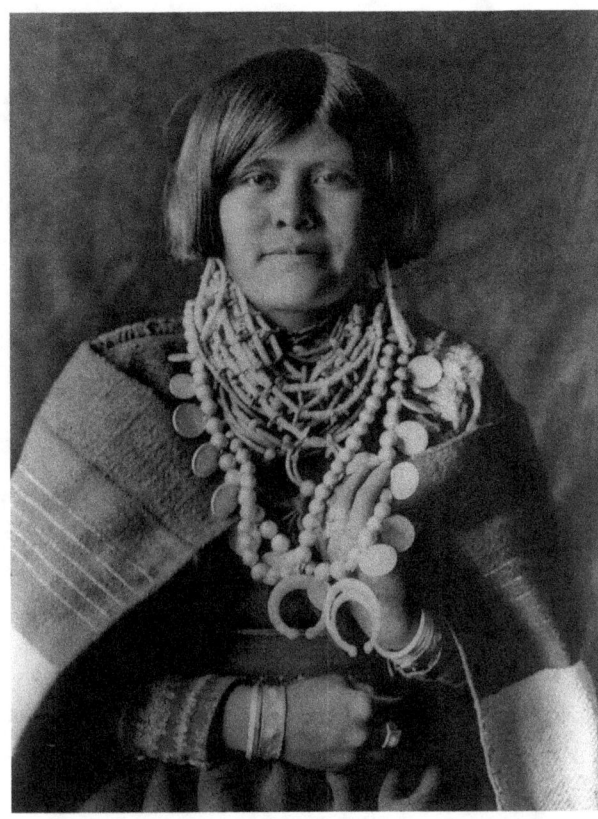

FIGURE 63 Edward S. Curtis, "A Zuñi Girl," from the portfolio *The North American Indian*, 1903. Photogravure. Inv. no. 1988.5.12, States Marshall Service, U.S. Department of Justice, Washington, D.C.

in visual imagery—through photography, illustrations, advertisements—it also became increasingly interested in using the visual as a means of obtaining and circulating knowledge. DeCora's interest in dress was part of a larger cultural obsession with the subject at the time. European Americans used similar criteria in evaluating each other, seeing dress as an index of social rank, as social theorist Thorstein Veblen observed in *The Theory of the Leisure Class*, published the same year that DeCora's story appeared.[26]

The question of the relationship between appearance and identity was particularly relevant to an Indian woman like Gray Wolf's daughter, who was about to leave for a tribally mixed, government-run boarding school. Boarding schools, in their effort to turn Indians into "Americans," forbade the wearing of traditional clothing and cut off their pupils' long hair. DeCora's heroine is aware that these corporeal changes will take place. One of her last acts before leaving home is to give her ceremonial clothing to her sister-in-law. Going to school in her plainest dress gave a physical dimension to the more internal identity transformation she would experience there. The story promotes the female protagonist's decision to follow her desires in a positive light, but it doesn't suggest that this will be easy.

Homi Bhabha has pointed out that racialism is an inherently visual attitude, based on the recognition of otherness.[27] "Gray Wolf's Daughter" suggests that DeCora was aware of this, that Indians already brought a high level of consideration to the impression their appearance would make. The decision whether or not to wear traditional dress was seen as a sign of an Indian's relationship to his or her cultural heritage. For Indian people, the question of making a respectable appearance was bound up with the question of how much to retain their tribal identities in the face of economic and cultural pressures to become "civilized" according to European American terms. Ceremonial clothing could be seen simultaneously as a sign of respect for tribal traditions and an indication of savagery. Confinement to reservations had stripped Indian tribes of most of their traditions, so clothing, which was portable and easily stored, took on increased symbolic importance for families trying to retain their cultural identities. Public celebrations like the Fourth of July became the occasion to cover one's body with heavily beaded clothing as a sign of cultural pride, in what Marsha Clift Bol has recognized as "an endeavor to fill the vacancy left by other lost social institutions."[28]

While the wearing of ceremonial regalia was a way to demonstrate and consolidate status at tribal gatherings, Indian people of this period were learning from the kinds of texts discussed earlier in this study that such displays, in front of European Americans, contributed to their identification as primitive others; Indian people were aware that wearing traditional clothing appealed to European Americans' desire to see them as picturesque vestiges of an exotic and rapidly vanishing culture. Some, like the Wild West performers, chose to turn this non-Indian desire to their own economic advantage, whereas others, such as Sarah Winnemucca Hopkins, worried about contributing to the ideology of the vanishing race.[29]

DeCora's understanding of this situation drew on her own experiences of prejudice and her own vexed relationship to her appearance, which I will illustrate with two photographs made of DeCora by a photographer named Hensel sometime around 1908. The first photograph is a formal portrait of her wearing a beaded dress and long beaded earrings (figure 64). De-

Cora sent this photograph to her Hampton mentor Cora Mae Folsom with a letter explaining that she got a copy of the portrait in exchange for work done for the photographer.[30] We don't know the reason DeCora had her portrait made, but the date coincides with the year she began lecturing publicly on Native American art, and the photograph may have been used for publicity. DeCora presents herself as confident, proud, and comfortable in the beaded dress. She clearly regarded it as a good likeness, or she would not have shared it with a loved one. Another photograph showing DeCora and another Indian woman, likely taken on the same day, makes use of the artist and lecturer as a generic model of Indian womanhood wearing a less distinctive Plains dress (figure 65). DeCora appears on the left wearing a dress and belt similar to those in "Gray Wolf's Daughter." Her companion kneels beside her in the beaded top from the formal portrait. Animal skins covered with painting and quillwork create an "Indian" environment behind them and a beaded cradleboard resting on DeCora's thigh completes the scene.

Perhaps modeling was the "work" DeCora performed in exchange for the print she sent to Folsom. Hensel could have wanted to compete in the booming market for postcard pictures of Indians.[31] This picture, which includes a glimpse of Hensel's studio props above the women's heads, exposes the artificiality of the pose, as does the lack of interest the women show in the cradle and its supposed occupant, but cropped differently, or taken from a different angle, most European American viewers would be willing to believe that the models were "wild Indians" and not college-educated artists. The photograph and another like it now form part of the Richard Henry Pratt Papers at Beinecke Rare Book and Manuscript Library.[32] Though DeCora was a friend of Pratt's, her name does not appear on the photographs, which are in an envelope marked "Indian women."

The references to both Western art and Indian experience in DeCora's *Harper's* illustrations become all the more significant when compared with advertisements showing illustrations of Indians published in the same volume of the magazine (see figure 66). A notice for Burnett's Vanilla Extract, for example, uses pictures of Mexican natives picking and carrying vanilla beans as a sign of the authenticity of their product. The Indians are shown semiclothed. The woman in the lower picture bares a breast and looks somewhat seductively out at the viewer as if to confirm the sexual availability of

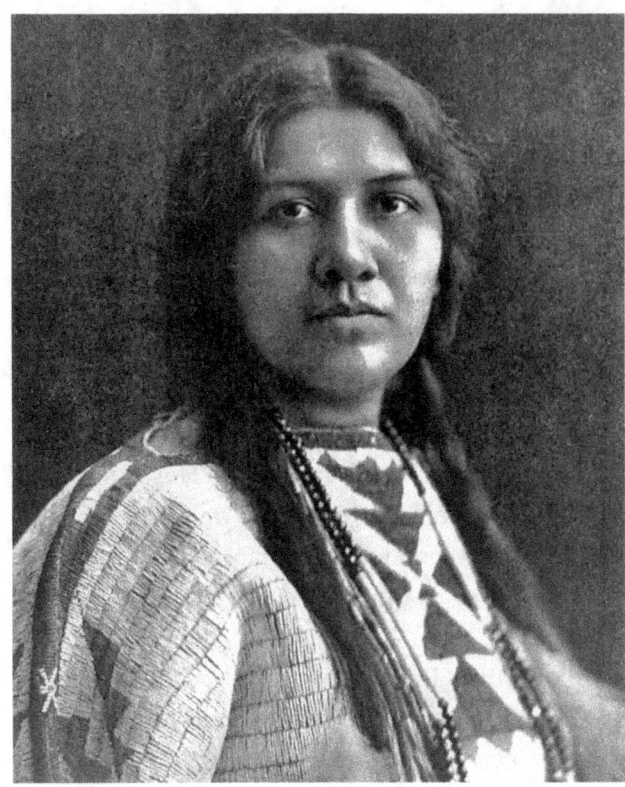

FIGURE 64 Hensel
Studio, "Angel DeCora,"
ca. 1908. Gelatin silver
print. Hampton University's
Archival and Museum
Collection, Hampton
University, Hampton,
Virginia.

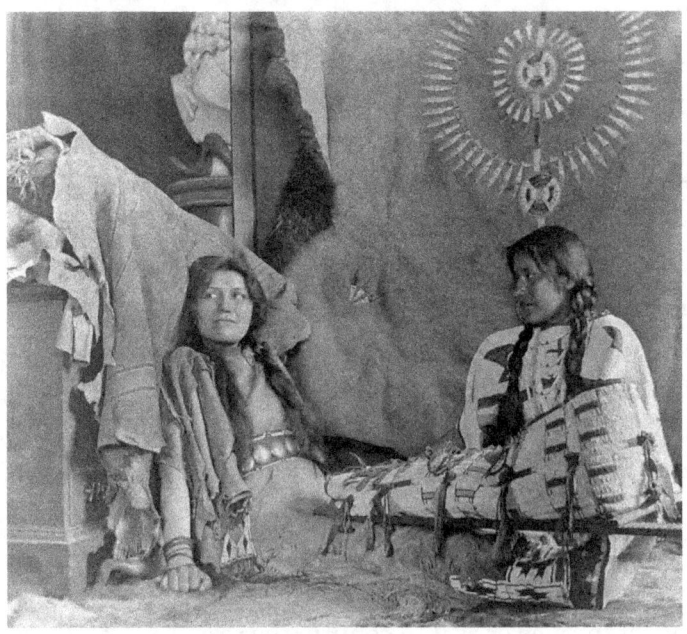

FIGURE 65
Hensel Studio (?),
"Angel DeCora
and an Unknown
Woman," ca. 1908.
Gelatin silver
print. Richard
Henry Pratt Papers,
Yale Collection of
Western Americana,
Beinecke Rare Book
and Manuscript
Library, New Haven,
Connecticut.

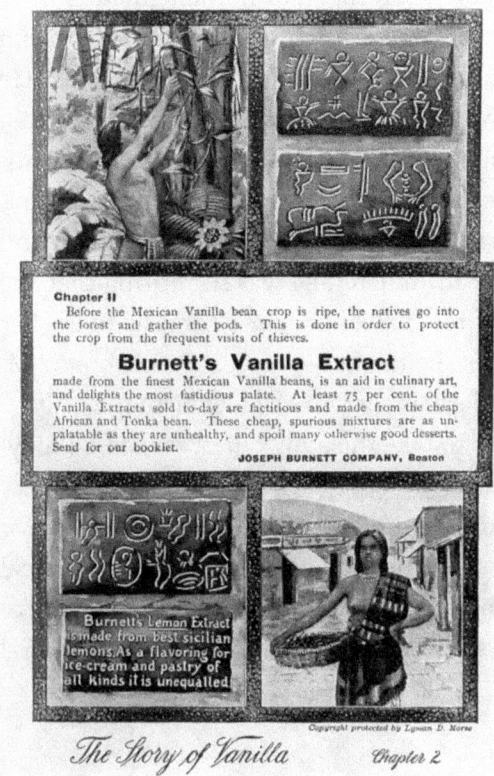

Chapter II

Before the Mexican Vanilla bean crop is ripe, the natives go into the forest and gather the pods. This is done in order to protect the crop from the frequent visits of thieves.

Burnett's Vanilla Extract

made from the finest Mexican Vanilla beans, is an aid in culinary art, and delights the most fastidious palate. At least 75 per cent. of the Vanilla Extracts sold to-day are factitious and made from the cheap African and Tonka bean. These cheap, spurious mixtures are as un-palatable as they are unhealthy, and spoil many otherwise good desserts. Send for our booklet.

JOSEPH BURNETT COMPANY, Boston

Burnett's Lemon Extract is made from best sicilian lemons. As a flavoring for ice-cream and pastry of all kinds it is unequalled

The Story of Vanilla   *Chapter 2*

Copyright protected by Lyman D. Morse

FIGURE 66 Advertisement for Burnett's Vanilla Extract, *Harper's New Monthly Magazine* 98 (February 1899): 93.

"primitive" women. Despite her extraordinary personal history, such stereo-types affected DeCora's personal and professional opportunities. *Harper's* exoticized DeCora just as this advertisemant exoticizes Mexican Indians. Ignoring the college-educated twenty-three-year-old's sophisticated ap-proach to her work, it issued a press release celebrating these stories as those of a "naïve . . . Indian girl."[33]

Popular culture helped determine the way people responded to DeCora, and set up expectations for her to act "wild" while her friends and mentors pressured her to be an example of how Indians could become "civilized." DeCora's correspondence reveals her fear that even her closest friends might treat her as a symbol. Addressing Folsom about an article the latter was writing about her, DeCora wrote, "I hope you [and] . . . the editors won't put me under the heading 'prominent colored women.'"[34]

DeCora's supporters could also be disappointed that she fit the model of civilized femininity too well. Pyle saw DeCora's artistic potential as determined by her race, not her skill, her experiences, or her imagination. Pyle demonstrated his idealized vision of the West when he said, "There is no more picturesque object in the world than the Western cow-puncher."[35] He shared his enthusiasm with several of his male pupils, most notably N. C. Wyeth. DeCora let him down. The West of Pyle and Wyeth was a romanticized place where masculine types could prove themselves physically and emotionally. As he said of DeCora, "Unfortunately she was a woman and still more unfortunately an American Indian. She was so retiring that she always kept in the background of my classes. When I tried to rouse her ambition by telling her how famous she might become, she answered: 'We Indian women are taught that modesty is a woman's chief virtue.'"[36]

Sometimes DeCora used humor to take the sting out of racism. Parodying attitudes that would seem to use science to argue for the inferiority of an Indian intellect, she once asked Folsom, "Do you think it is too much for an Injun to read Darwin?"[37] The sophistication of this comment is typical of the way DeCora demonstrated her familiarity with both Indian and European American cultures, and how she put this familiarity to use as a cultural interlocutor.

FROM ILLUSTRATOR TO DESIGNER

Some time between August 1898 and August 1899 DeCora left Pyle's classes and Drexel Institute. As she later put it in an autobiographical essay, "I used to hear a great deal of discussion among the students, and instructors as well, on the sentiments of 'Commercial' art and 'Art for art's sake.' I was swayed back and forth by the conflicting views, and finally I left Philadelphia and went to Boston" (her decision suggests that she opted for art for art's sake).[38] A letter to her old Hampton mentor Cora Mae Folsom in September of 1899 suggests that the decision was driven more by personal concerns than her aestheticism: "I have made up my mind even as far back as last year that I would not return to Philadelphia even though the only other and only choice left me was killing myself."[39]

Neither DeCora nor Pyle ever discussed her departure from his classes, but Pyle's attitude toward the kind of artistic idealism DeCora held may have also been a factor in this decision. The illustrator publicly disparaged the ideal of art for art's sake that DeCora aspired to. In 1902, he told an audience at the Boston Society of Arts and Crafts that "'Art for Art's sake,' is a high-sounding phrase, and it is imagined (especially in unsuccessful studios) to be rather a fine thing for a painter to paint obscurely, producing great works unrecognized by the vulgar world. From the standpoint of a practical worker, it would seem to be a very plain statement of fact, that, if a cobbler does not sell his shoes, it is because they do not fit the feet of other men, and it would seem an equally natural inference to suppose that the very general failure to sell American pictures is because they do not fit the ideals of American men and women."[40] Given his critique of aestheticism, it is not hard to imagine that Pyle saw DeCora's attempts to change the popular image of Indian life not as a sign of her innovation, but rather proof of her being out of touch with "the ideals of American men and women."

As his regret that DeCora was an Indian woman shows, Pyle also saw DeCora's gender as a detriment to her career. Though he had many women students, there is evidence that Pyle was insecure about the ability of women to succeed in art as well as men. As Michele Bogart has noticed, he offered his female students less encouragement and professional support than his male ones.[41] As he became increasingly able to limit and control the enrollment in his classes, the proportion of male to female students grew dramatically. In the year DeCora left Drexel, Pyle lost 20 percent of his women students. When he broke away from Drexel to found his own school in 1900, he left most of the rest of them behind.

Whatever the reason, or combination of reasons, for DeCora's departure from Philadelphia and a promising career in illustration, by September 1899, she had moved to Boston and enrolled in classes with Joseph DeCamp at Cowles Art School. In the late 1890s Boston was a capital of American high culture, boasting a new Beaux-Arts-style Museum of Fine Art, the nation's leading symphony orchestra and musical conservatory, and the gloriously decorated Public Library, as well as several art schools and clubs.[42] Though the city had a large and important mercantile class, its cultural institutions distanced themselves from the commercial world. In 1897, three of the city's leading painters and painting instructors helped found the Ten American Painters, an exhibition group that seceded from the Society of American Artists because of that organization's increasing commercialism.[43] Over the course of two years, DeCora studied with all three of these men: DeCamp at Cowles, and, later, Edmund Tarbell and Frank Benson at the School of the Museum of Fine Arts. Her understanding of their values is demonstrated in her success: as at her other schools, DeCora excelled as a student, receiving honorable mention in the Concours Scholarships for 1900 and 1901.[44]

Despite her commitment to the aestheticism of her teachers, DeCora continued to do commercial work. Her interest in illustration may have been related to the fact that she felt other Indians would be more likely to see her work if it was mass-produced. In this, she is like the African American civil rights leader W. E. B. Du Bois, who two decades later encouraged Aaron Douglas to devote his talents to making illustrations because that was the only kind of art middle-class African Americans were likely to see.[45] The degree to which her work circulated within progressive Native American circles can be noted in the fact that Indians and Indian reformers provide nearly all of the contemporary criticism of her work.[46]

Significantly, DeCora's commercial work in Boston provided her first opportunities to collaborate artistically with other Indian people, enabling her to see a potential to link personal and professional success with racial uplift. The importance of dress as a site of identity came up again with the commission to provide a frontispiece for an autobiographical book by the Omaha ethnologist Francis LaFlesche, titled *The Middle Five* (see plate 8). At the editor's suggestion, DeCora focused on a moment when the newly arrived LaFlesche (wearing traditional Omaha clothing) is being comforted by a bigger boy wearing a uniform. In DeCora's hands, the picture not only depicts a sympathetic interaction, but also thematizes how the boarding school experience transforms Indian identity. As a student, the young LaFlesche will shed some of his Omaha identity along with his buckskin outfit as he becomes more "Americanized." The school's rigid environment is symbolized by the interconnected lines and rectangles that dominate the right side of the composition. The schoolhouse is a blank, colorless building, with decaying walls and windows that neither reflect nature nor provide a peek into a cozy interior. As contrast, DeCora has included a strip of landscape at the left edge of the picture, a sunny field, and nearly cloudless sky that recede far into the distance. The boy hides his eyes, unable to face his past or his future. But he is comforted by a uniformed boy who, while he may not come from the same tribe, has undergone a similar experience himself. The painting is a reminder that Indian schools were places where Indian children came in contact not only with European American culture but also with other Indians. As Sally McBeth points out, it was in the schools that "an inter-tribal, 'Indian' identity emerged as an important cohesive concept."[47] DeCora had written to LaFlesche that she found his book an apt description of Indian school life.[48] As if to bear witness that she had also shared this experience, DeCora inscribed her initials in pale paint on the wall above the boy's head.

DeCora tried to show her understanding of all that was involved in this transformation by making the boy's Omaha clothing as authentic as possible. In the same letter to LaFlesche, DeCora asked the author for descriptions and photographs that would help her make a more accurate drawing, because she had been unable to find an example of the clothing in Boston. But DeCora's need to work from models sometimes conflicted with her desire to be accurate, and she found herself using the same moccasins, for example, for several different illustrations.[49] Nevertheless, throughout her career she tried to obtain not only accurate clothing but actual members of the tribes she was consigned to depict to use as models for her work.[50] DeCora's interest in tribal specificity might seem surprising in an Indian who was educated away from home as part of a tribally mixed school. But while the administrators of Indian schools were committed to assimilating their pupils into mainstream American culture, this project was impossible to accomplish completely, and students and personnel often reinforced and expanded concepts of tribal identity. Indeed, as K. Tsianina Lomawaima points out, Indians far outnumbered non-Indians at most boarding schools, and groups and gangs frequently formed along tribal lines.[51]

The frontisiece for *The Middle Five* exemplifies DeCora's interest in appealing to the Native Americans in her audience. While most European American children would not notice the difference between an Arapaho and an Omaha shirt, Indian schoolchildren would appreciate her accuracy. DeCora's Indian peers continually complained about the tendency of non-Indian artists to produce generalized representations of Indian culture, mixing and matching imagery from different traditions.[52] DeCora was aware that other educated Indians were part of the audience for her work. Friends from school made up a significant portion of her acquaintance in Philadelphia, Boston, and New York.[53] Her audience also included many Indian people she had never met. Through the efforts of the government and reform organizations, the books and magazines DeCora worked for were regularly purchased for the libraries of Indian schools, and commented on in school and reform publications.[54] Reporting of the appearance of Zitkala-Sa's *Old Indian Stories*, which DeCora also illustrated, the Carlisle school paper claimed, "Thus the Indian is entering into the highest and best places. We are not content to be mediocre."[55] The eventual founders of the Society of American Indians kept tabs on each other through such publications; and one of the society's first acts was to issue its own journal, *The American Indian Magazine*.

In the years following the *Middle Five* commission, DeCora continued to make representational illustrations and began exploring two- and three-dimensional design, a mode of expression that embodied rather than represented her transculturation. Illustration had allowed her to insert Indian characters into a Western artistic tradition, suggesting a need to use the dominant culture's representational forms in order to gain recognition of Indian experience. Design allowed her to suggest the value of the Native American artistic tradition, a value that she explicitly proposed had meaning for both Indian and non-Indian audiences. Significantly, this interest in design, like her interest in illustration, grew out of her involvement in European American artistic communities. While it is likely that DeCora understood that her commercial work had a better chance of reaching a Native American audience than panel paintings, at the same time, the world in which she circulated in Boston enabled her to see applied art as capable of demonstrating the same aesthetic value as fine art. She was able to adjust her commitment to art for art's sake to include a wider range of materials, eventually encompassing traditional Indian handicrafts. Without this shift in her aesthetic outlook at the beginning of the 1900s, DeCora could not have conceived of the racial aesthetic she promoted as a teacher and political activist a decade later.

DeCora's embrace of applied art allies her with the progressive aesthetics of design reformers. The artist's personal and professional connections put her at the center of communities exploring the possibilities of elevating applied art to the level of handicraft. Small, Maynard, the publishers DeCora worked for, were committed to high quality. Following the lead of William Morris's Kelmscott Press, they hoped to make the publication of artistic books profitable. Owners Herbert Small and Laurens Maynard, like many others in the Boston publishing community, had developed a commitment to the principles of handicraft through the mentoring of Charles Eliot Norton, the Harvard fine arts professor and friend of Ruskin. Norton believed that art was defined by good design and technique regardless of medium, and that art could exert a moral force. He demonstrated this through his patronage of Boston's Society of Arts and Crafts, in whose 1899 exhibition DeCora's teachers Howard Pyle and Joseph DeCamp participated. It is unclear whether DeCora herself was in Boston early enough in the year to see the exhibit, which was open the first two weeks in April, but, according to Beverly Brandt, art students from all over New England flocked to it in such numbers that the society set special visiting hours just for them.[56] DeCora may have had the opportunity to study with Norton herself. In 1899 he offered a class in "Imagination in Art" at the School of the Museum of Fine Art.

DeCora's familiarity with these ideas came not only from her teachers, but also from her landlord and patron, Joseph Edgar Chamberlin. Chamberlin was an editor at *Youth's Companion*, a magazine edited by several of Boston's avant-garde book publishers. He was also the author of a regular column in the *Boston Evening Transcript*. DeCora's relationship with Chamberlin and his wife, Ida, became deep and long-lasting. How DeCora found Chamberlin is unknown, though she was probably led to him by Zitkala-Sa, an educated Sioux violinist photographed by Käsebier, who had moved to Boston to study at the conservatory and who was close to Chamberlin's fellow publisher, F. Holland Day.[57] A letter from Ida Chamberlin to Day in September 1899 notes that both Zitkala-Sa and DeCora were staying with them at their house in Wrentham.[58] She remained at their home until 1902, when both she and the Chamberlins moved to New York, where Joseph had accepted a job on the staff of the *Evening Mail*.

It was while living with the Chamberlins that DeCora received the bulk of her illustration commissions, which seem to have come through her Indian contacts rather than Chamberlin's friends. For example, the Boston-based ethnographer Alice Fletcher was responsible for giving DeCora the commission to illustrate *The Middle Five*. However, it would be inaccurate to suggest that these were discrete social circles. Boston intellectuals were connected to one another through the city's publications, universities, and churches. LaFlesche's contract with Small, Maynard was the result of such an interconnection. It came about because of Fletcher's friendship with author and editor Bliss Carman, whose professional activities had nothing to do with ethnography or Indian reform.

Book design was an important point of connection between the fine and applied art circles. This included not only illustrations but book cover design. Book covers had taken on new importance in the appearance-conscious culture of the turn of the century. In 1899, *The Studio*, a leading transatlantic art magazine, had devoted an entire issue to the subject.[59] Two years later an American publisher offered a book about cover designs.[60] While the revival of fine leather stamping and embossing was credited to the British Kelmscott Press, even the British admitted that the American publishing community in Boston produced much of the leading work for trade publishing.[61] Designs by Will Bradley, Bertram Grovesner Goodhue, and Sarah Wyman Whitman for Copeland and Day, John Lane, Houghton Mifflin, and Small, Maynard were featured in Arts and Crafts Society exhibitions and routinely praised in the press (see figure 67). DeCora had the opportunity to join this company when she won a competition to provide the cover design for *The Middle Five* (figure 68). Small and Maynard were so pleased with her composition of two tipis in a field framed by a bow and several conventionalized arrows that they explicitly mentioned "a frontispiece in color and a cover design by Angel DeCora" in advertisements for the book.[62]

DeCora followed the success of *The Middle Five* by designing covers for four more books that she also illustrated: Zitkala-Sa's *Old Indian Legends* (1901), *Wigwam Stories* (1901), *The Indians' Book* (1907), and *Yellow Star: A Story of East and West* (1911). DeCora's designs seem to respond to the increasing interest in simplification and abstraction in book cover design in Boston in the early 1900s.[63] Like the background in "Gray Wolf's Daughter," *The Middle Five* design begins to explore the idea of an "Indian" style. The tipis are covered with abstract designs including a firebird, crescent moons, and large bands of zig-zagging lines. In contrast to the elegant, confident rendering of the bow and arrows that make up the borders of the cover, the tipi decorations are uneven and asymmetrical, perhaps as a way for DeCora to signal that while she appreciated Indian imagery, she was a master of European American methods. With her next two covers, her compositions became flatter and more abstract. In the cover of Mary Judd's *Wigwam Stories* (figure 69), she seems to be more able to recognize the deco-

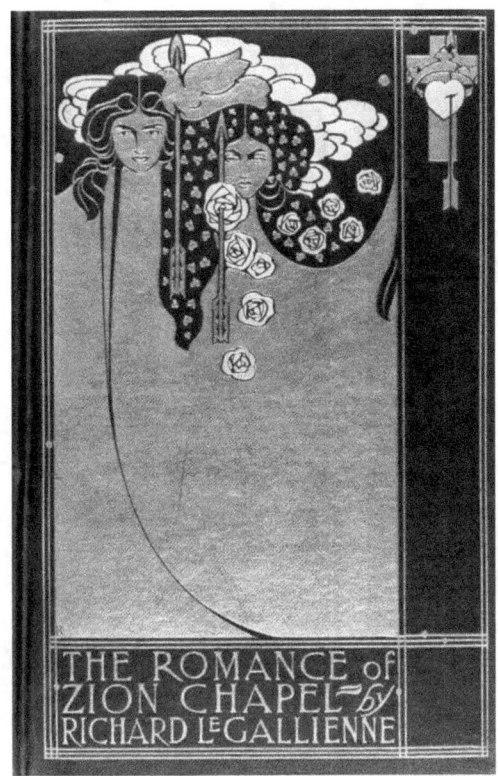

FIGURE 67 Will Bradley, cover design for Richard LeGallienne, *The Romance of Zion Chapel* (New York: John Lane, Bodley Head, 1898). Rare Book and Manuscript Library, Columbia University Libraries, New York.

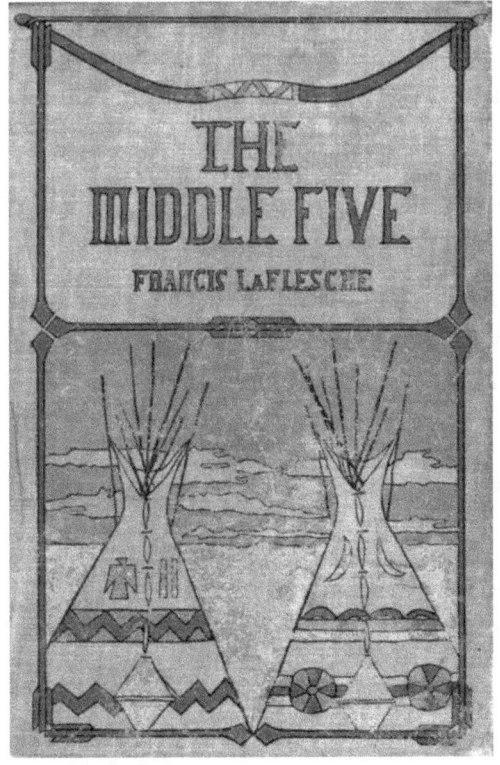

FIGURE 68 Angel DeCora, cover design for Francis LaFlesche, *The Middle Five* (Boston: Small, Maynard, 1900).

rative qualities of Native American design. The simpler, unadorned tipi has itself become decorative. With this project DeCora extended her attempts at "Indian" style into the text field, writing the title in fanciful typography on a stylized stretched skin. The triangular pins that hold the skin in place make up a decorative pattern that spills into the top half of the composition, where a small landscape includes the by-now familiar motif of a tipi illuminated from within. *Old Indian Legends* is DeCora's most "Indian" cover (see figure 70). The attempt to represent space is completely gone. Instead DeCora plays with the materiality of the book, belting it with a beaded garter with tassels that hang down the front.

It appears that DeCora felt more encouraged to explore an "Indian" style in her book covers than in her early illustrations. Book design was clearly located in the realm of applied arts, which was a voracious appropriator of non-European traditions. As one critic put it, "Never in the history of aesthetic expression was the work of past ages and all lands laid so widely under contribution to the work of to-day. From the Greek vase and the Egyptian papyrus to the Indian lotus and the bamboo of Japan, from the symbols of human passion to those of heavenly light and fire, there is hardly a decorative convention that has not been borrowed, adapted, degraded, and restored again in succeeding generations till neither the individual nor the age, if even the nation, can claim them as its own."[64]

DeCora later wrote that she was glad she had never taken advantage of the courses in design that were available at Drexel and the Museum School, which followed "the prescribed methods of European decoration, for then my aboriginal qualities could never have asserted themselves." Nevertheless, she had studied historic ornament at Smith and Drexel.[65] I would suggest that it is not despite but *because* of this approach that her "aboriginal qualities" emerged. At Smith and Drexel she would have attended lectures on the arts of diverse nations, as well as the basic styles and motifs of the classical, medieval, and Moorish ages.[66] And when she moved to Boston, she studied painting with teachers who celebrated the decorative and moral value of Asian and other non-Western artistic traditions. Like the art students discussed in chapter 4, she was trained to think of the art of all cultures as a visual resource for the modern artist.

Transcultural artists like DeCora who saw the products of their own culture being collected and reproduced read in this interest a cultural rela-

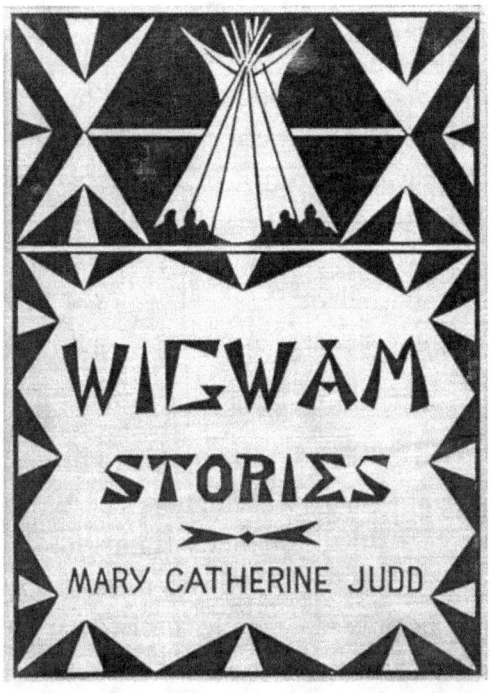

FIGURE 69 Angel DeCora, cover design for Mary Catherine Judd, *Wigwam Stories* (Boston: Ginn, 1902).

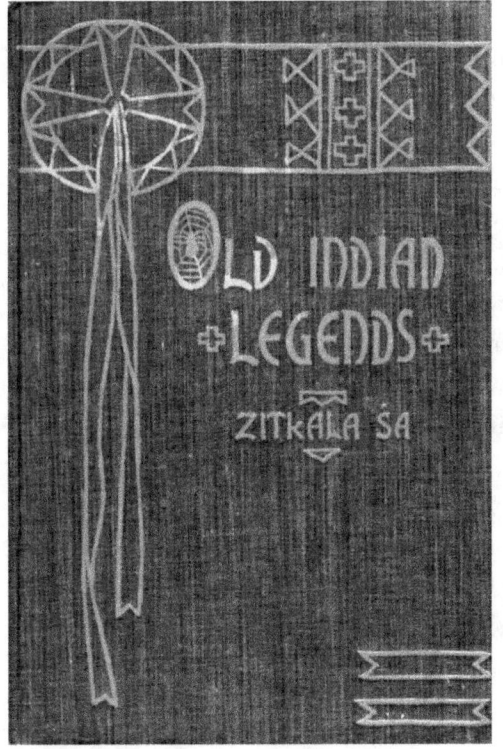

FIGURE 70 Angel DeCora, cover design for Zitkala-Sa, *Old Indian Legends* (Boston: Ginn, 1901).

tivism that might be used to argue for the preservation of lifeways under attack by assimilationist policies. Anticipating a strategy used by Alain Locke to elevate the status of African art in the 1920s, DeCora singled out the popularity of Japanese art as a justification for paying attention to her own racial artistic traditions.[67] She repeatedly claimed that Indian people like herself "want to find a place for [their] art even as the Japanese have found a place for theirs throughout the civilized world."[68] She offered this argument as much to Indian audiences as non-Indian, for she saw art not only as a place to communicate understanding of Indian experience but also to build a sense of pride and community.

INDIAN ARTS AND CRAFTS AND NATIVE INDIAN ART

At the same time that DeCora began exploring book decoration, she was invited to expand her exploration of applied art by designing furniture for the Bureau of Indian Affairs exhibition at the Buffalo Pan-American Exposition in 1901. The bureau's exhibitions had been DeCora's only consistent exhibition venue. She had contributed sketches and paintings to their displays at the Chicago and Omaha Expositions in 1893 and 1898. As a photograph of her paintings hanging in the background of the Bureau of Indian Affairs installation at the Louisiana Purchase Exposition in 1904 shows (figure 71), these exhibits were a jumble of artwork, documents, and models produced by people under the the bureau's care. For the 1901 exposition, however, the bureau attempted to create a more unified presentation by placing their objects in a "room" with furniture designed by DeCora and constructed by students at various boarding schools.

In 1900, the commissioner of Indian affairs, William A. Jones, asked DeCora to design a mantel, andirons, and a wooden settle with cushions and to supply a painting of her own to hang over the fireplace. Jones utilized the aesthetic language and implicit nationalism of the arts and crafts movement in his correspondence, telling DeCora to aim for a "harmonious" effect, and to limit herself to "native" materials.[69] The objects he chose were those being celebrated for their consonance with domestic comfort and old-fashioned values. Despite being quite busy with illustration and book cover commissions at the time and knowing little about furniture design, DeCora accepted without comment. Perhaps she was intrigued by the challenge. Certainly she, like Jones, was familiar with the vogue for Indian handicrafts

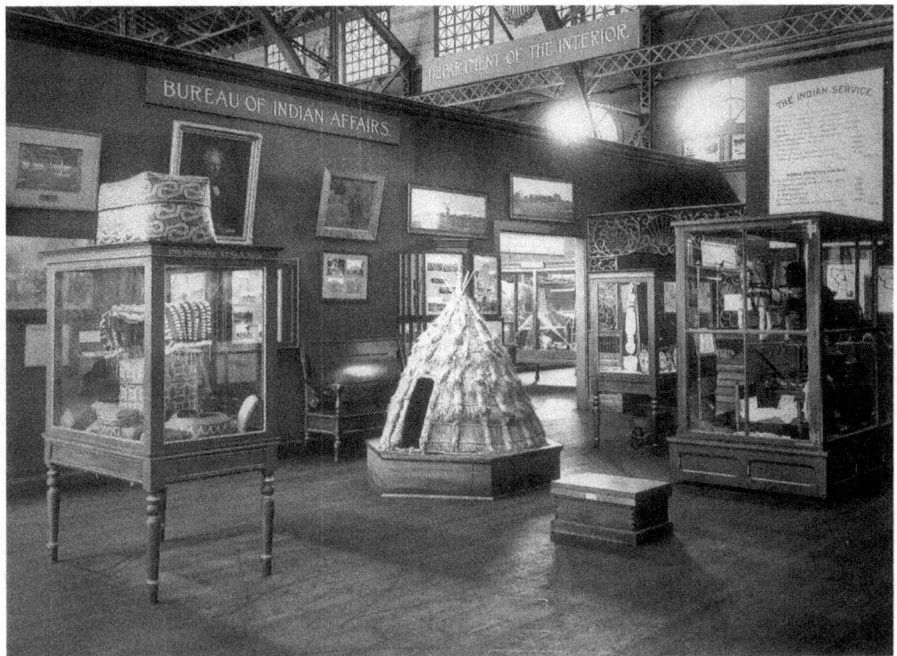

FIGURE 71 Bureau of Indian Affairs section, Interior Department exhibition, Louisiana Purchase Exposition, St. Louis, 1904. Record group 56, Records of World's Fairs, National Archives and Records Administration, Washington, D.C.

in contemporary house decoration. Both probably saw the potential for such an installation to focus the exhibition's visitors on the potential contributions Indians could make to modern American culture. The commentary on DeCora's installation illuminates how she used this opportunity to further explore making connections between European American and Native American artistic traditions: "Miss Decora [*sic*] has combined the native symbolism of fire with our own tradition of the fireside. Upon the space below the shelf, in low relief of red wood, is a conventionalized 'thunder bird,' the plumes of its wings flashing out into flames. On the side uprights, and in a band around the upper part of the mantel, making a frame for the central painting, are conventionalized forms of the sticks used in making the 'sacred fire' by friction."[70]

The commission for the Pan-American Exposition is another turning point in DeCora's career, for it allowed her to participate in an artistic culture that included other Indian craftspeople. While her mature work had always been aimed at communicating with Indian audiences, suddenly she was collaborating with Indian craftspeople, providing them with the opportunity to demonstrate their own talents. At the same time, she was seeking a way to use these talents in ways that would be understood by non-Indians. DeCora's correspondence from this period begins to suggest that she was developing a theory of a distinct Native American artistic sensibility. As she wrote to Jones, "I have tried to suggest something of the Indian art in my decorative designs and if it is to be done by Indian workmen they perhaps will have some sympathy with my efforts."[71] DeCora's foray into this language is tentative and somewhat condescending; indeed, it is somewhat reminiscent of the way non-Indian reformers celebrated the products of underprivileged urban and rural communities. She writes that the craftspeople will *perhaps* respond to her ideas, as if she is not sure if innate Indian aesthetics actually exist, or, if they do, if she has mastered them.

Over the rest of her career, DeCora tried to isolate the qualities of Indian art and use them as a basis for her own production and in her pedagogy. She was given a unique opportunity to devote herself to this task when she began teaching at the Carlisle Indian school in 1905. Though hired to fill the position of drawing instructor, DeCora and her superiors understood her job as teaching and preserving Indian art. DeCora developed a two-pronged approach to the subject. First, she used her classes as a place where students could learn to value their tribal and cultural traditions. Then she encouraged them to develop individual creativities that drew on tribal traditions but also reflected their experience with other Indian and non-Indian cultures. As she proudly put it, she quickly saw "the members of the different tribes influence each other in their style of designing" in her classes, producing art of a "composite Indian character."[72]

DeCora took the position at the invitation of the new commissioner of Indian affairs, Francis Leupp, who made it part of a concerted effort to increase the curricular focus on native culture. While Leupp did not envision Indian sovereignty, he was more accepting of tribal traditions than his predecessors, as his words demonstrate. He wrote, "The Indian is a natural warrior, a natural logician, a natural artist. We have room for all three in our highly organized social system. Let us not make the mistake, in the process of absorbing them, of washing out of them whatever is distinctly Indian. Our aboriginal brother brings, as his contribution to the common store of character, a great deal which is admirable, and which needs only to be developed along the right line. Our proper work with him is improvement, not transformation."[73]

Leupp's actions as commissioner support this view. One of his first efforts was to bulk up and expand Native industries projects.[74] Another was to hire DeCora. Leupp went to great efforts to place DeCora in the position, working against her reluctance to give up her illustration career and his superiors' lack of interest in hiring Indians as full-time teachers.[75] Although the position DeCora filled was that of a teacher of drawing, Leupp gave her free reign to invent a curriculum to encourage the development of Indian design. She replaced the casts that usually were the first object of study with native designs from objects and books.[76] Working with the most basic materials — colored pencils and paper — she developed a curriculum designed to cultivate her students' racial identities and provide them with skills they might later use to earn a livelihood. Self-esteem and self-sufficiency were what she perceived as being the greatest gifts she could give her students. As I will show, these goals did not demonstrate an abandonment of her aesthetic ideals, but a reformulation of them.

Almost as soon as she began teaching, DeCora was invited to give speeches about her work at various conferences of educators, ethnologists, and Indian reformers. These talks show her evolving pedagogical and aesthetic approach to Indian aesthetics. DeCora saw her first job as drawing out the racial and tribal qualities in her students that recent history had suppressed. Many of DeCora's students came from homes where cultural identity had broken down in the face of poverty and corrupt reservation administration. She was appalled upon her arrival at Carlisle to see how little sense her students had of their culture. As she wrote in her first end-of-the-year report, "When I first introduced the subject — Indian art — to the Carlisle Indian students, I experienced a discouraging sensation that I was addressing members of an alien race. I realized that I must have an Indian audience if the subject was to continue. For a week, when each new class came to me, I appealed to their race pride, calling on them in mass and individually for Indian history, not as the white historian has pictured it in words, but as some of us have heard it from the Indian story-tellers by the light of the camp fire."[77]

Sometimes DeCora's appeals to race pride were not enough and she had to, as she put it, "manufacture my Indians." But rather than give them the training they might have received at home, she gave them an understanding of "Indian" identity as a racial designation in a modern and culturally complex society that subsumed tribal differences. When a student from Alaska couldn't tell her the name of his people, they looked through a book on Northwest Coast tribes by ethnologist Franz Boas until he recognized pictures of Haida blankets. "When encouraged to be themselves," she wrote, "my pupils are only too glad to become Indians again, and with just a little further work along these lines, I feel that we shall be ready to adapt our Indian talents to the daily needs and uses of modern life."[78] Similarly, DeCora gave her students regular opportunities to share their work with one another at weekly exhibitions, a technique she had learned at Smith. DeCora suggests that these exhibitions gave the students interest in each other's work and also "a feeling of competition"—a quality essential to European art training and one of the qualities of European American culture that Indian pupils were still seen as needing.[79]

DeCora's formal approach to the teaching of Native American art stems in part from the materials she used, much of which came from anthropologists. Shortly after she accepted the job, William Henry Holmes of the Bureau of American Ethnology sent a letter to Leupp confirming that he had sent DeCora numerous volumes and offprints relevant to the study of Indian art from the bureau's *Annual Reports* and the *Report of the United States National Museum*.[80] While it is unclear from this letter whether or not the materials were requested by DeCora herself, her correspondence with Franz Boas indicates that she did use ethnological writings in her classroom.[81] We also see that she used Alfred L. Kroeber's 1902 study of the Arapaho, which included several charts of geometric symbols;[82] the designs on the blackboard shown in a photograph of her classroom printed in the 1909 *Carlisle Annual Report* are drawn directly from Kroeber's plates (see figure 72). The photograph also demonstrates the hybrid nature of her pedagogy. In stark contrast with the rank uniformity of students and artworks in photographs from art programs under Estelle Reel's control, the photograph seems designed to emphasize the individuality of each pupil. Neat rows of children seated in front of blackboards filled with diagrams of symbols focus intently on their diverse projects. While some students produce "traditional" Indian art—weaving on a Navajo loom—others are engaged in applying Indian aesthetics to new media. The seated girls appear to be engaged in making abstract designs in needlework—embroidery or needlepoint. The seated boys are using paintbrushes. DeCora's students applied their design skills to baskets, beadwork, and weaving and also to graphic design, upholstery, and pyrography.[83]

As soon as she was able, DeCora augmented the knowledge obtained from books by studying directly from craftspeople on reservations. She often used her speeches as an excuse to conduct primary research.[84] On her way home from the 1907 National Education Association annual meeting in Los Angeles, for example, she visited Albuquerque and the Omaha and Winnebago reservations in Nebraska.[85] DeCora also brought Native American artists into her classroom. In 1906, for example, she petitioned and received money to bring Navajo weavers to the school to help set up a rug-making project. But a close examination of her curriculum shows that, despite this interest in tribal artistic traditions, DeCora remained committed to developing a composite, aesthetically up-to-date, racial school of art. Significantly, as she moved from producing art that was the product of an *individual* who was an Indian to proposing a collective Indian aesthetic, she moved even farther away from the painting and drawing that had been her first love and closer to reformist aesthetics. By embracing an aesthetic position that had long validated Indian art, as well as publicly embracing the identity of a Native American artist, she helped shape this discourse to the advantage of her people.

DeCora capitalized on the increasing interest in Native American art within the art world by annexing its language for her own projects. The baldest example of this is her introduction of a magazine called *The Indian Craftsman* in 1909. The publication took its name from Stickley's *Craftsman*, the journal that outstripped all others in its interest in Indian art and Indian reform. The covers of the magazine showed celebratory images of potters, weavers, and basket makers while the initial letters, borders, and illustrations inside were made by the next generation of Indian artists. The covers featured mottoes drawn from Ruskin and Morris. DeCora's speeches similarly borrowed the therapeutic language from the arts and crafts movement to explain the value of Indian art. The strong colors in Indian art, she explained in one talk, come from the fact that the artists work outdoors in the

FIGURE 72 (PAGES 206–207) Native Indian art classroom. From Richard Henry Pratt, *The Indian Industrial School, Carlisle, Pa.: Its Origin, Purposes, Progress and the Difficulties Surmounted* (Carlisle, Pa.: Hamilton Library Association, 1908), 98.

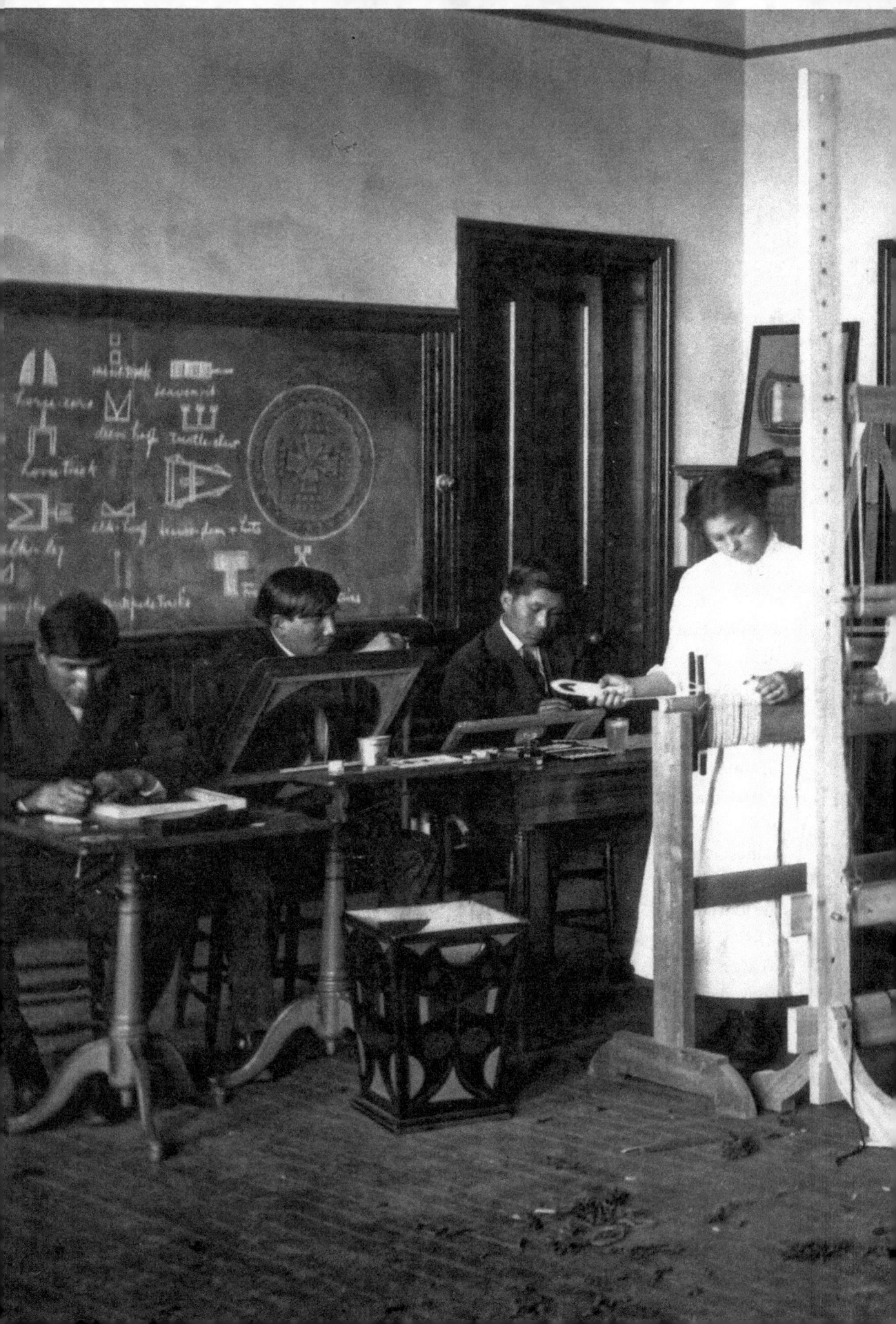

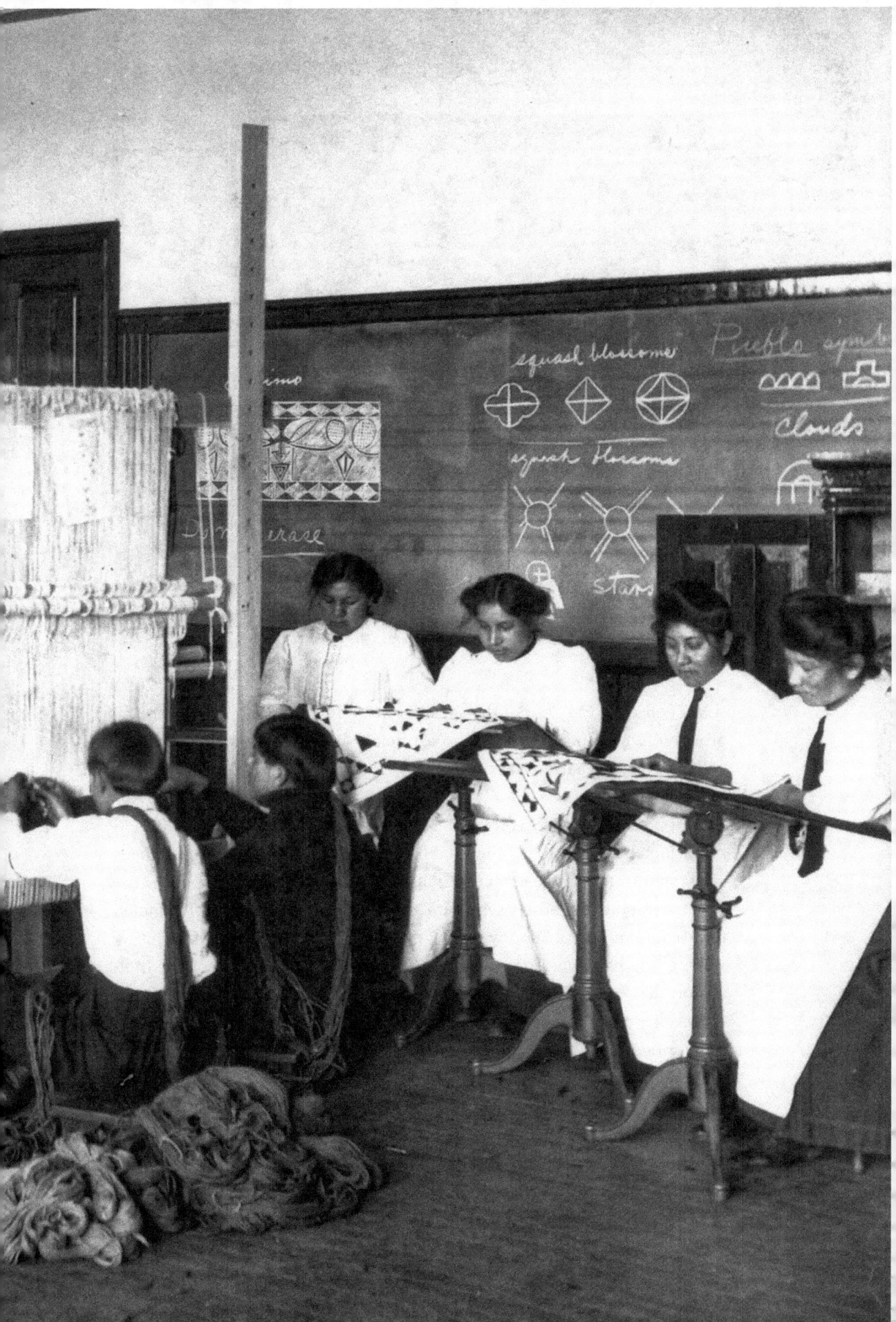

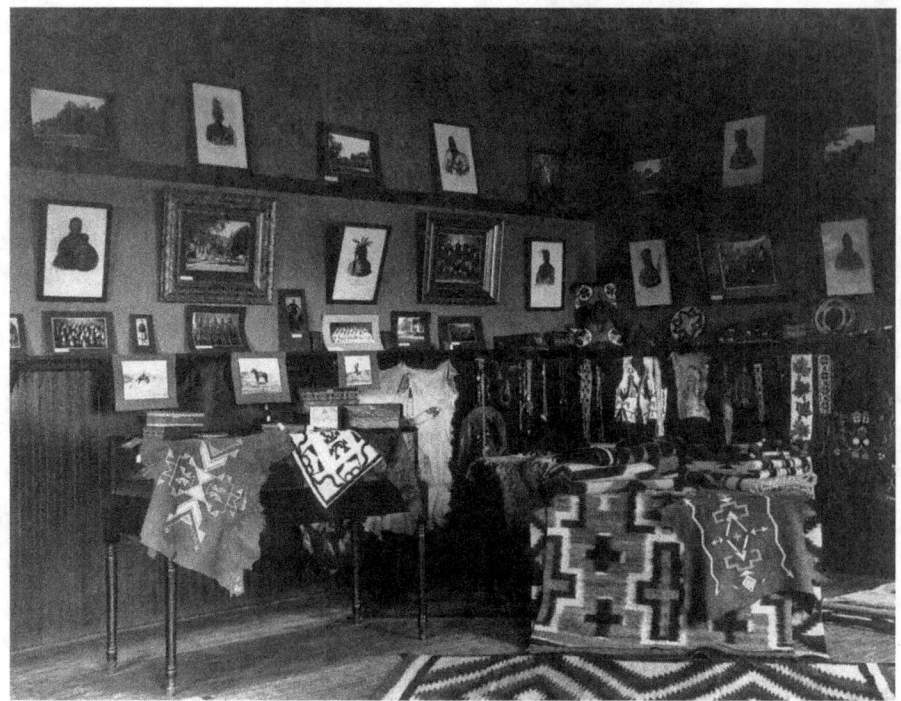

FIGURE 73 Leupp Art Studio, Carlisle Indian Industrial School, ca. 1909. Record group 75, Records of the Bureau of Indian Affairs, National Archives and Records Administration, Washington, D.C.

sun. Their artwork "shocks the sensitive whiteman, whose perception has grown softened and perverted thro' artificial living, and he calls the Indian's color scheme barbaric and crude."[86]

Another aspect of DeCora's contribution was her use of the market to garner support for her efforts toward education and self-support. In imitation of settlement house work, she established a Native Indian art department salesroom in 1909. The shop used mission-style furniture to appeal to the owner of an Indian corner (see figure 73). As an advertisement in *The Indian Craftsman* put it, the shop was designed to be "a medium for distributing some of the handwork of our students and the products of the older Indians on the reservation . . . at a price which will be a fair remuneration to the worker as well as a reasonable price to the buyer."[87] The advertisement drew connections between the readers' interest in art and their social goals, noting the trend I have discussed throughout this study: "People who are interested in the Indian usually have a liking for the Arts and Crafts — desire something which has been made by these people."

For DeCora, this strategy not only enhanced the marketability of her students' work; it linked the immediate cultural and economic goals of her courses with the system of aesthetic beliefs that she had been taught. By making connections with the mainstream art world, DeCora began to envision how Native American art could not merely participate in broader American artistic culture, but could make a unique contribution to it. But though she borrowed heavily from the racialized language of the arts and crafts movement, it is never clear whether DeCora actually believed in an essential racial sensibility. She usually described specific imagery and techniques as "Indian" by tradition and history rather than by inspiration. At the same time, she also suggested that Native creativity was somehow innate. Her writings and speeches identify all Indians as particularly talented artists. Similarly, her understanding of the importance of tribal identity is unclear. She told one audience, "For me no two Indian drawings are alike, and every one is original work."[88] But she also wrote, in 1906, that she thought that, if left alone to draw on the imagery in their own minds, Indian artists would stay "true to [their] tribal method of symbolic design."[89]

A group of rug designs from her class illustrate her pedagogy (figure 74). Students began their work by drawing designs on paper, which is not part of the Navajo tradition. The designs all conform to one basic layout, suggesting that they were made in response to a specific assignment. Moreover, this design problem was not necessarily posed as requiring a distinctly Navajo solution. Much of the imagery is Navajo, and is appropriate to rugs being made at the time, including swastikas, crosses, lozenge (diamond) shapes, and stepped triangles, but other motifs are of more ambiguous origin — the arrows, for example, or the shapes in the end triangles of the two rugs on the right. In fact, while the arrangement of the design in four quadrants divided by crossing bands that is seen in all five is not unheard-of in Navajo weaving, this layout is also typical of Plains parfleche decoration as it is illustrated in Kroeber's essay on the symbolism of the Arapaho Indians.[90]

DeCora may have also felt that she needed to downplay tribal aesthetics in order to maximize her students' opportunities. She didn't want to advance any idea that might limit the kinds of work Indians were allowed to do in

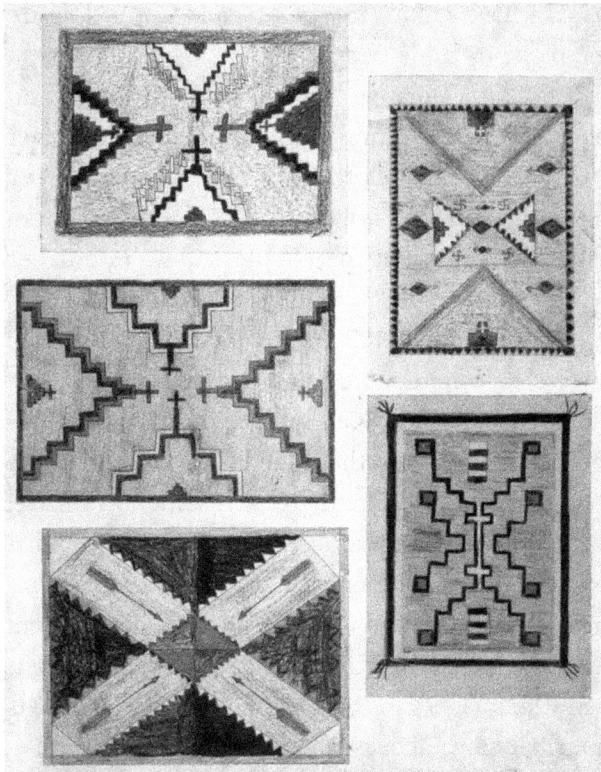

FIGURE 74 Rug designs produced in Angel DeCora's classes at Carlisle Indian Industrial School, ca. 1909. Record group 75, Records of the Bureau of Indian Affairs, National Archives and Records Administration, Washington, D.C.

terms of medium, style, or technique. Students were encouraged to draw on tribal and racial traditions, but they were not limited to them. DeCora's rug-making project demonstrates how she came to understand "Native Indian art" as a sensibility rather than any specific material practice. Following the contemporary vogue for both rugs in Indian and rural industrial reform projects, DeCora wrote to Leupp at the end of her first year asking for funds to purchase supplies and build looms for her students.[91] Significantly, her students learned both Navajo and Persian weaving techniques.[92] While DeCora understood the spiritual importance of weaving within Navajo culture, she saw no reason that all Indians should feel comfortable using that technique. Indeed, she found that the Persian style "allows more freedom to carry out the more intricate designs" than the Navajo.[93] Given that most of her students were not Navajo themselves, she may have reasoned, it seemed logical that they would explore a variety of means of bringing their racial artistic sensibilities to their rugs.

DeCora's teaching also disregarded tribal traditions dictating the gender of people using specific symbolism or materials. In the photograph of her classroom, it is clear that both boys and girls made rugs despite the fact that among the Navajo, weaving is an almost exclusively female activity. DeCora did not discuss gender as a significant factor in Indian art in her critical writings, either. Her silence on the issue of gender in Indian art is intriguing, given the clear impact that her own gender had on her educational and professional opportunities. It was only because of art's association with social goals defined as specifically female that her female mentors encouraged her to pursue her career. Art's relationship to social uplift made it a more acceptable female pursuit than many other fields. DeCora's artistic education occurred only because of the dramatic increase in training opportunities for women of her generation. Perhaps being part of the first generation of American women attending art school gave her an optimism about the eventual acceptance of women as male artists' equals. Perhaps her familiarity with the way the discourse of Indian art celebrated Indian women's creativity led her to see Indian women and men as equally capable of producing modern Indian art.[94] Such an outlook would not be inconsistent with her embrace of other progressive aspects of contemporary aesthetics.

Despite her commitment to Indian art as an expanding and evolving artistic category, DeCora was herself conflicted about the degradation of traditional forms. Occasionally she even claimed for herself the authority to decide what did and didn't count as Indian art. While she found Persian weaving techniques acceptable in her classroom, for example, she forbade her students to use floral designs that had been originally adapted from European folk art, even though they had been a vital part of Woodlands art for over a century: "I discourage any floral designs such as are seen in Ojibway beadwork. Indian art seldom made any use of the details of plant forms, but typified nature in its broader aspects, using also animal forms and symbols of human life."[95] Despite her interest in finding ways to apply Indian aesthetics to turn-of-the-century needs, her very definition of the qualities of Indian art reify an idea of "Indian art" as having an authentic history that was interrupted by contact with European Americans at the same time that she proposes Indian aesthetics as ongoing.

Like the theorists from whom she borrowed the idea of cultural aesthetics, DeCora was never able to describe the exact mechanism by which racial qualities were supposed to manifest themselves in art. DeCora's ideas seem designed to maximize opportunities for the economic and cultural validation of art made by Indian people. The belief in Indian aesthetics gave Indian artists a positive self-image and enhanced the marketability of their products.

PAN-INDIAN ICONOGRAPHY

When her Carlisle responsibilities allowed her the time, DeCora continued to explore the application of "Indian" aesthetics to modern art in her own work. This imagery shows her own pursuit of a pan-Indian iconography that would draw on America's diverse tribal traditions, providing an illustration of the "composite Indian character" she described to Leupp. A significant project during these years was providing the titles for *The Indians' Book*, an anthology of Native American history, story, and song compiled by Natalie Curtis and published in 1907. Curtis had gathered the contents from Indians of different regions, culture areas, and ages, attempting to alter their words as little as possible. At every stop, she asked one of her informants to provide a drawing that would head up each tribal section. DeCora was initially asked only for an image for the Winnebago title page (see figure 75). But her fanciful lettering so charmed the compiler and her publishers that they hired her to design the title page and cover and to add lettering to each of the drawings. DeCora matched the diverse tribal sensibilities in her letters without disavowing her artistic training. The lettering in *The Indians' Book* demonstrates not only her comfort with graphic media, but also a familiarity with the vogue for figurative letters—"allusive typography"—that dominated magazine covers and lithographed posters of the period.[96] Sometimes this has an unintended effect, when the artist's confident lines often overwhelm the accompanying illustrations, drawn in crayon by people used to using other tools. The drawings by a Zuni child, Ema-liya, for example, look coarse next to DeCora's elegant professional calligraphy (see figure 76).

On the title page, DeCora attempted to create a visual analog to this lingua franca by selecting symbols that she believed would be easily understood by all Native American readers (see figure 77). Using a geometric style that is sparer and more linear than her previous book designs, she presents a visual metaphor of the book itself. At the top and bottom of the border that frames the type are two large, stylized birds with stepped lines emanating

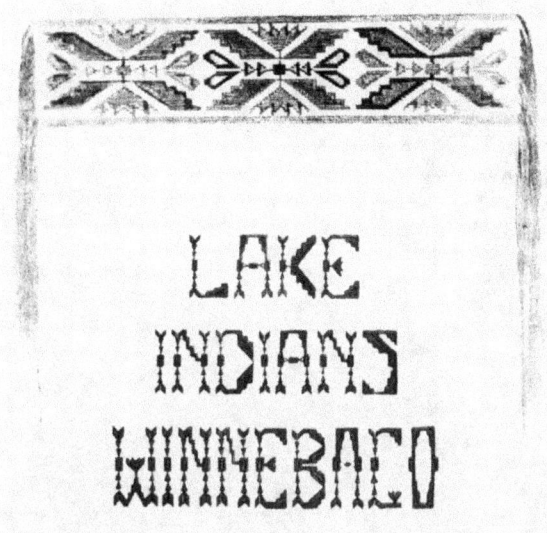

FIGURE 75 Angel DeCora, "Lake Indians Winnebago." Design for Natalie Curtis, *The Indians' Book* (New York: Harper and Brothers, 1907).

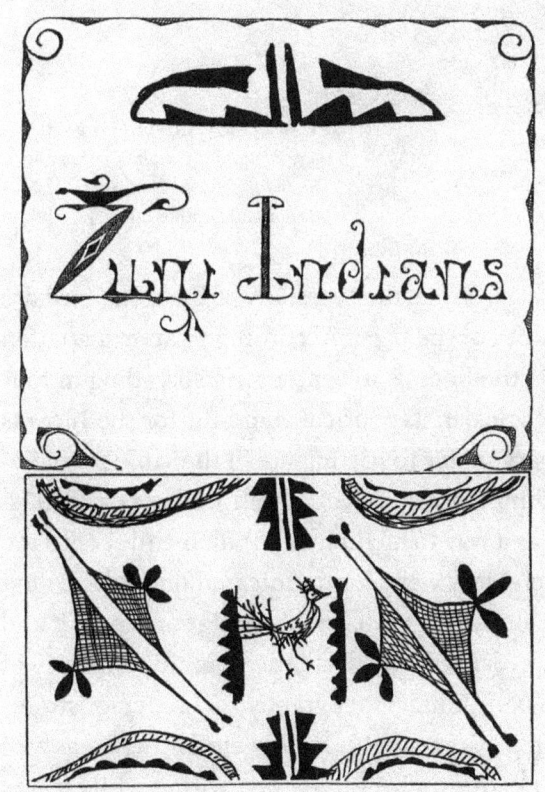

FIGURE 76 Angel DeCora and Ema-liya, "Zuni Indians." Design for Natalie Curtis, *The Indians' Book* (New York: Harper and Brothers, 1907).

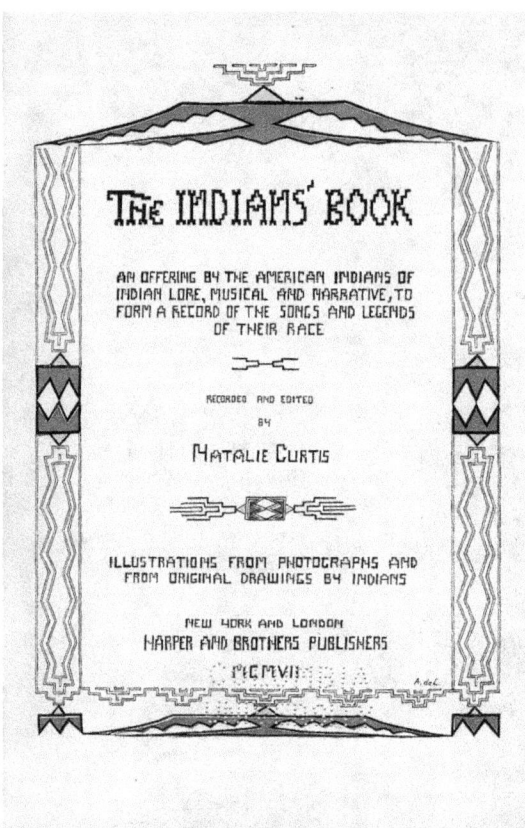

FIGURE 77 Angel DeCora, title page design for Natalie Curtis, *The Indians' Book* (New York: Harper and Brothers, 1907).

from their beaks. Along the sides, six smaller versions of the same bird are shown facing the top and bottom of the page. According to an explanation printed on the following page, the lines represent a song spreading in four directions from the beaks of eagles, metaphorical stand-ins for the Indians themselves.[97] While this imagery seems to participate in the same problematic relationship to traditional Indian culture that infiltrated her early illustrations, DeCora promoted it as a way to facilitate an Indian entrée into the *modern* world, a world in which ideas were communicated not only around the fire in a tipi at night, but on the pages of books written in English and shared over great geographic expanses. The dramatic graphic simplicity of this design and the interest in pan-Indian iconography that it demonstrates are reminiscent of the emblem DeCora would later create for the Society of American Indians. In this work, she appears to be saying that while it was good to value the cultural traditions of the Indian past, it was in the future that Indian people had their greatest contribution to make.

This project put DeCora's artistic training to work less in technique than in the formation of her understanding of the definition and role of art. Gone were the subtle tonalities of Tryon and the historical stage sets of Pyle. What remained was the importance of art as a site of individual and racial development. Much like the European American women who saw their involvement with Indian art as a way to simultaneously cultivate their own power and contribute to social welfare, DeCora was excited about what Indian art could offer both the artists and the American public. By stressing the application of racial talents, including her own, to everyday objects, she endorsed the idea of improving American society through the dissemination of good design. The identification of geometry and conventionality as the heart of Indian design helped her argue that Indian aesthetics were distinct from European American ones, and therefore had something unique to contribute.[98]

DeCora further honed her definition of this racial style and iconography in her work for the Society of American Indians. In 1911, she had served on a committee convened to design an emblem for the society. In collaboration with the Seneca archeologist Arthur C. Parker and John M. Oskinson, a part-Cherokee editor of *Colliers* magazine, she settled on an eagle copied from a sheet-copper ornament unearthed from a burial mound in southern Illinois (figure 78). Identified as an eagle produced by a pre-Columbian civilization, the object had the racial associations the committee desired without being linked to any specific tribe. Moreover, the age of the artifact supported the society's claims to a lengthy and sophisticated Indian cultural heritage. In addition, Parker believed that the eagle was universally revered by all American Indians.[99]

DeCora had already turned to the eagle as a unifying symbol in *The Indians' Book*, and she supported the choice of an ancient symbol over a hybrid of contemporary motifs for the Society of American Indians emblem, as she was familiar with the frustration Indian people felt with the way non-Indians frequently mixed up images from different tribal traditions. As her design shows, the image fit her definition of Indian formal aesthetics (see figure 79). It was graphically simple and bold, using conventionalized geo-

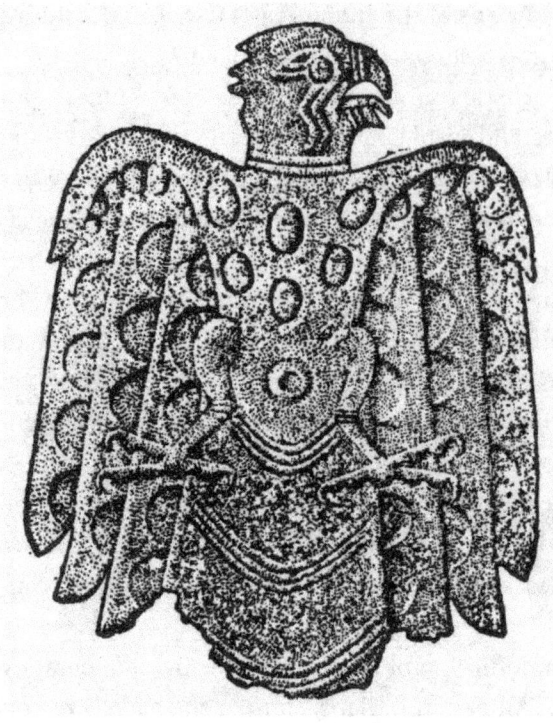

FIGURE 78 "Sheet-Copper Eagle," from Frederick Webb Hodge, "Handbook of The American Indians North of Mexico," *Bureau of American Ethnology Bulletin* 30.1 (1910): 346.

metric design.[100] As Parker put it, the ornament was "of good proportion and [a] good example of Indian conventional art."[101]

One of DeCora's most simple works of art *visually*, the emblem is *conceptually* very complex. In turning an ancient object into a modern graphic design, DeCora altered few details. She kept the rough edge at the bottom lefthand side of the eagle's tail as an index of the original object's age. But she has simplified the relief designs into crisp lines that give the symbol a boldness that looks very modern. Though little changed, the very transition of the symbol from a unique bronze sculpture to a mass-produced graphic design marks a dramatic reconfiguration of its visual significance. The simplification of the ancient eagle's lines helped it in its modern uses. From an elaborate three-dimensional object made of several different materials, it became a clean, eminently reproducible graphic design, one that would be easily legible on the pamphlets and magazines that were the primary means for building support for their movement among geographically dispersed educated Indians.

The definition of Indian aesthetics in DeCora's address at the Society of

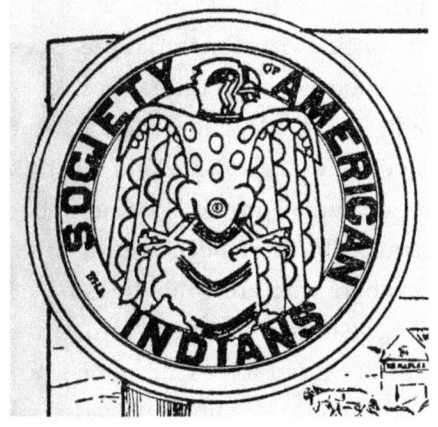

FIGURE 79 Angel DeCora, design for the emblem of the Society of American Indians. Detail of an illustration in *Quarterly Journal of the Society of American Indians* 1.1 (April 1913): 87.

American Indians conference helps bring out the importance of geometric simplicity and modernity of the logo. As DeCora presents it, Indian art followed racial aesthetic principles that could provide a model for American cultural development. For while the contemporary art world was only beginning to grope its way through abstraction, Indian art had been interested in geometric design from the beginning. Moreover, Native American art's symbolic content was derived from distinctly American subjects: its landscape and original inhabitants. She argued that Native Americans were consummate designers, ready to lead American design into the new century. This rhetoric not only enhanced the economic value of DeCora's students' work; it also linked the cultural and economic goals of her courses with the system of aesthetic beliefs in which she had been immersed—beliefs directed, ultimately, toward cultural pluralism. DeCora began to envision how Native American art could not merely participate in broader American artistic culture, but could make a unique contribution to it.

DeCora's assumption that integration into European American art systems and the advance of national artistic culture were the goal of Native American artists demonstrates the degree to which she had embraced a Western attitude toward art. Her attitude was unrealistic for artists working on reservations with no sense of the aesthetic goals to which she aspired; it was even unappealing to other educated Indians, including fellow members of the Society of American Indians, as the reception of her 1911 talk illustrates.

While DeCora oriented Native American aesthetics toward the future, the lively discussion that followed her talk showed that her peers were unable to shift their idea of Indian art from specific tribal material practices to a racial design sense. Some felt art should be a site of cultural preservation, that Indians should maintain the traditional media and uses of art and avoid the market for Indian handicrafts entirely. DeCora's friend Charles Eastman, who had written several articles on Indian art for *The Craftsman*, led the call for a conservative approach, saying, "We have been drifting away from our old distinctive art. . . . [O]ur teachers who are white people . . . have mixed the different characteristics of the different tribes, so that you cannot tell an Arapaho from a Sioux now, and cannot tell a Cheyenne from a Crow. I hope that in this gathering we will come to some realization of these things in the proper sense; that we may take a backward step, if you please, in art, not in the sense of lowering our standard, but returning to the old ideas that are really uplifting."[102] Eastman and his supporters confirmed DeCora's interest in exploring tribal traditions as a means of cultural affirmation, but were unwilling to follow her call for a progressive "pan-Indian" aesthetic.

Others were anxious about being able to maintain control over the economic potential of Indian art. Laura Cornelius, for example, suggested the formation of an organization designed to "place a censorship on that manufacture, to prevent the use of these deteriorated forms, and to insist upon the manufacture of the real article."[103] Her concern was echoed by Thomas Doxon, who worried that European American firms reaping economic gain by copying Indian designs.[104] Cornelius built on the desire to maintain control over the capital spent on Indian art by enforcing strict definitions over the people who could make it, and the forms it could take had been manifest in the non-Indian reform efforts of Estelle Reel and the Sequoya League.

Other commentators on DeCora's speech found Indian art incommensurate with modernization. Carlos Montezuma criticized the movement to teach "Indian basketry, Indian blanketry, Indian pottery, Indian art, Indian music and other general industries of a past generation. . . . Where does this help Indian children into the ways of civilization?'"[105] Horton Elm took a more moderate view. While he was not the wholesale assimilationist Montezuma was, he worried about feeding stereotypes that would characterize Indians as purely anything. "Nobody appreciates more than I do [that] this matter of Indian art is important, yet at the same time, we as a race cannot all be artists." Elm proposed Indian rights based on human rights, not on innate racial talents: "The Indian race is like any other race if they are subject to the same environments. There are good Indians and there are bad Indians; there are good white people and there are bad white people; there are good mechanics among the Indians and there are bad mechanics among the Indians; there are intelligent Indians and there are others who are not so intelligent, just as it is with other races. . . . We all belong to the human family and we are subject to the same natural laws; we are subject to the same civil laws; we are subject to the same government, and I want you to identify yourselves with every interest and phase of American life."[106]

DeCora was unprepared for the different agendas her audience brought to Indian art. She had made the assumption, not uncommon among artists of the time, that the values they placed on design and craftsmanship were natural and universal. She expanded the idea of art's value for individual expression and cultural affirmation to include commercial art, and her aesthetic approach assumed a level of participation in cosmopolitan American culture beyond what most Indian people could experience. Her attitude is similar to other ways in which some middle-class members of the Society of American Indians alienated Indian people who did not share their belief in the rewards of education, hard work, and the transcendent value of art, as was demonstrated, among other examples, in their condemnation of the peyotism of the Native American church.[107]

DeCora attempted to bridge the poles of purely traditional Indian art and culturally blind formalism by advancing the importance of racial aesthetic sensibilities as opposed to discrete and unchanging tribal practices. Her conception of Indian art belongs to the Progressive aesthetics of the time. The point of panracial imagery was to provide language to facilitate and recognize Indian contributions of her racialized culture to the larger national culture. In the twenty-first century we are accustomed to think of aestheticism as an elitist attitude toward art that reifies exclusionary cultural hierarchies. But DeCora saw in this position a potentially liberating relativism. For her, an emphasis on "the sensuous pleasure of form" provided an opportunity to sidestep an evolutionary mindset that would keep Indian people from participating in contemporary American culture until they had moved through the stages of civilization. Though she was blinded to the ways in which she reproduced many of the contradictions embedded in the progressive, middle-class values with which she'd been educated, her career allows us to examine the vexed interaction of cultural and economic concerns Native Americans confronted when they tried to participate in the discourse of Indian aesthetics.

While the Society of American Indians never explicitly rejected DeCora's political aesthetics, art did not remain an important part of their political platform. Though the organization lasted until 1919, DeCora's involvement waned. She spent the years leading up to her untimely death in the 1918 flu epidemic distancing herself from her public career, including resigning from Carlisle and not seeking any offices in the society after 1912. Meanwhile, after its first conference, the society increasingly focused its attention on specifically legislative issues, including Native American citizenship, the codification of Indian law, and access to the U.S. Court of Claims.[108] The growing lack of interest in the question of art reflects not only DeCora's limited authority, but also the waning centrality of aesthetics to political discussions of the years between 1910 and 1920. As Eileen Boris has observed, the progressive spirit of the aesthetic reform movement had largely dissipated by 1915; while handicrafts retained a therapeutic association, aesthetics became less associated with political struggle.[109]

At the same time, discussions of modernism within mainstream circles became increasingly dominated by an interest in the European avant-garde. Americans with connections to dealers and collectors such as Alfred Stieglitz and Gertrude Stein had already started to become familiar with post-impressionist movements during the height of the Indian craze, but the flood of European artists into America that attended World War I and the display of avant-garde works in major exhibitions of this time introduced fauvism, cubism, and futurism into popular discussion. In this context, Native American art came to stand for tradition rather than progress, as when Theodore Roosevelt famously said he appreciated the artistic merits of the Navajo rug in his bathroom to the pretensions of Marcel Duchamp's notorious cubist contribution to the 1913 Armory show, *Nude Descending the Staircase, No. 2*.[110] While Native American art *did* continue to figure in modern art exhibitions, for example at the 1920 Society of Independent Artists exhibition in New York City, it has not been seen as an essential factor in American modernism.[111] Nevertheless, the ideas and strategies of the Indian craze remain with us, as I will explore in the epilogue.

◇ ◇ ◇ *Epilogue*

The Society of American Indians conference in 1911 was not the only time Native artists and intellectuals gathered to discuss the proper place of Native American art in mainstream American society. In 1959 the Rockefeller Foundation convened a conference at the University of Arizona titled "Directions in Indian Art"; in March 1970, Princeton University hosted "The First Convocation of American Indian Scholars," which included a session titled "Native Arts in America" and was organized by the Luiseño painter Fritz Scholder. In 1980, Native artists, art historians, and others interested in indigenous art began gathering for biennial conferences in which they attempted to clarify and expand the understanding of both "traditional" and "contemporary" Indian art and its relationship to the mainstream art world. This group, which became known as the Native American Art Studies Association, has convened regularly ever since. The 1970 Princeton convocation is perhaps the least well-known of these events, but it is instructive, as the discussion between Scholder and his respondents—who included fellow painters Dick West (Cheyenne), Frank LaPena (Maidu/Wintu), the sculptor-jeweler Charles Loloma (Hopi), and other Native intellectuals and culture workers—reveals that many of the issues raised at the 1911 Society of American Indians conference had yet to be resolved. As with the earlier conference, the proceedings of the Princeton meeting were published in full, making it possible to trace the diversity of opinions Native intellectuals have had toward the visual arts.[1]

Like DeCora, Scholder argued that a "well-developed aesthetic sense" was an inherent Indian trait, and, like her, he rejected the idea that this sense required Indian people to work in specific media or styles and heralded the emergence of a "new Indian art."[2] Challenging the separation of Native and non-Native work into different artistic worlds, he argued that Indian art could take its place beside the most avant-garde products of mainstream modernism: "Today a Zuni War God would not look out of place at the Museum of Modern Art, and a shield design can certainly compete with the best non-objective painting. The universal power of these objects is undeniable" (193). Proclaiming the artist's freedom to engage both tribal and mainstream aesthetic traditions, he argued that the "new Indian art . . . will take many forms and . . . will be vital, not faddish" (196). As in Cleveland over half a century before, his audience responded in a variety of ways. While many supported the notion of artistic freedom, Jack Reynolds (Cheyenne) was concerned that artists weren't mindful of their responsibility to their tribes and their traditions (208). Some were concerned about the diversity of the kinds of objects presented as Native American art and whether all were equally capable of bearing aesthetic and cultural value. Several of those present were concerned about the limited access that Native artists had to venues for exhibition and sale, and about the Anglo control of those venues. Some called for institutional solutions to the problem of supporting and promoting Native artists, ranging from nonprofit galleries to a professional artists' association and government agencies who regulate the market.

Scholder and his colleagues were reacting to the historical developments in Native American art history in the interwar and cold war years, but their comments reveal that many of these developments were rooted in the ideas and problems of the beginning of the century. This epilogue will focus on the legacy of the Indian craze, tracing its influence on Native art in the 1930s, the 1970s, and the present. Making these connections allows us to see the persistent linkage between Native American art and Indian welfare, the difficulty both Indians and non-Indians face in defining Native American art as indigenous and modern at the same time, and the general ambivalence about the aesthetic status of handicrafts.

The history of Native American art related by Scholder was focused on Santa Fe, New Mexico, which had become the preeminent center for Indian art by the 1920s. This was in part because of the remarkable success of the local tourism industry, which emphasized indigenous culture as an important regional attraction. The Santa Fe Railroad and its retail partner, the Fred Harvey Company, had been promoting Native American art in its ads and through its depots since the early years of the twentieth century, but southwestern tourism expanded in the 1910s and 1920s, first because of the blossoming of domestic tourism during the years when World War I made European travel impossible and then with the expansion of automobile travel in the twenties. The latter prompted Harvey to develop packaged "Indian detours," which brought carloads of tourists into pueblos where they could buy handicrafts directly from the producers. While Native material culture was incorporated into the tourist industries of other regions, particularly the Pacific Northwest and the western National Parks, few regions had the same combination of factors that made the southwestern story so successful. The development of tourism in Santa Fe benefited not only from its proximity to a major transcontinental railroad, but also from the active support of the local government, a small and tightly networked community of Anglo-American civic leaders, and, to a certain extent, Native communities.[3]

Anglo-Americans who had relocated from the East to Santa Fe and, to a lesser extent, Taos, were particularly important in bringing the ideas of the Indian craze to the region. They included some individuals who had been involved in the earlier celebration of Native art and others who had developed their ideas about the relationship between art and society during the Progressive Era. Among the former were Edgar Lee Hewett, an archaeologist who had spoken about the Southwest at a lecture at the National Arts Club (see chapter 3) in 1905.[4] Within a few years, he became the director of the School of American Archaeology (in 1907) and the Museum of New Mexico (in 1909), positions from which he exerted a strong influence on the scholarship on Native American art. Hewett is known for his promotion of the careers of Native artists such as Maria Martinez and Alfonso Roybal

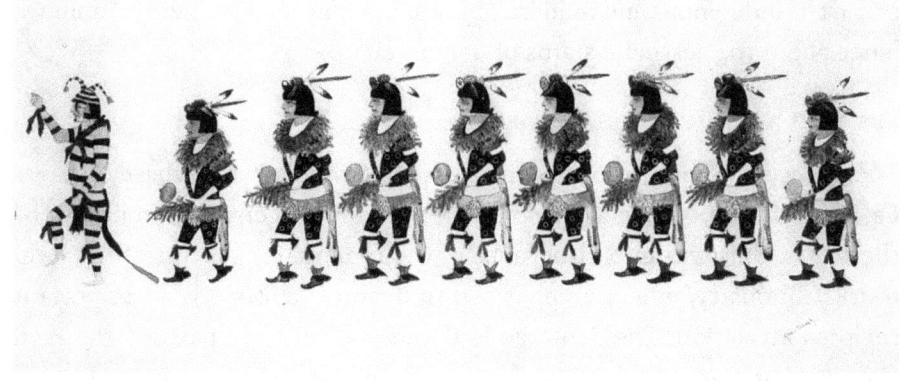

FIGURE 80 Alfonso Roybal (Awa Tsireh) (San Ildefonso Pueblo), *Thunder Dance Procession*, ca. 1922. Watercolor on paper. Inv. no. 35461/13, Museum of Indian Arts and Culture / Laboratory of Anthropology, Museum of New Mexico, Santa Fe. Photo by Blair Clark.

(Awa Tsireh) (see figure 80), both from San Ildefonso Pueblo, as well as for inviting modernist painters such as Robert Henri, John Sloan, and Marsden Hartley to visit the region. The artists and Anglo intellectuals in Hewett's circle shared his interest in southwestern Native art and supported projects to promote it, including organizing exhibitions in the East, such as Sloan and Oliver LaFarge's 1931 Exposition of Indian Tribal Arts at the Grand Central Galleries in New York City, and establishing local institutions focused on encouraging preserving and perpetuating local traditions, such as the Pueblo Pottery Fund (later renamed the Indian Arts Fund) and the annual Indian Fair at the Santa Fe Fiesta (both established in 1922).[5]

As Molly Mullin and Margaret Jacobs have demonstrated, these efforts were spearheaded by Anglo-American women who were grounded in the social ideas of the Progressive Era, including Elizabeth Sergeant, Martha and Elizabeth White, and Mabel Dodge Sterne (later Luhan).[6] Experienced in urban philanthropic work, they were familiar with the progressivist notion that art could be the site of economic and cultural revitalization for Indian people as well as a meaningful medium of cross-cultural contact, and they saw the patronage of art as a means of social activism. Indeed, Mabel Dodge Sterne's first trip to the Southwest was the result of her husband's invitation that she come "and save the Indians."[7] Similarly, John Collier was a follower of John Dewey who spent the 1910s working for the New York City People's Institute, a social center built on the settlement idea. Collier became an Indian rights activist as a result of a visit to Sterne in 1919, and went on to head the federal Bureau of Indian Affairs, where he oversaw the several projects geared toward promoting Native arts in the 1930s.[8]

In keeping with their community orientation, this generation married patronage with political activism. Santa Feans were involved in Indian rights organizations such as the Eastern Association on Indian Affairs and the New Mexico Association on Indian Affairs and were leaders of the effort to defeat the Bursum Bill, a piece of federal legislation aimed at resolving southwestern land disputes in favor of Anglos. They used this battle to publicize other issues they thought important, including the preservation of religious freedom and other cultural traditions. They saw the support of Native art as directly related to these efforts, not only because they defined Indian art as an expression of religion but also because they had witnessed the poverty faced by Native people firsthand and believed the support of art offered much-needed economic support.

AESTHETICS AND POLITICS

Like Estelle Reel and members of the Indian Industries League, many promoters of Native arts of this generation believed that the government had a role to play in the development of Indian art. In 1928, investigators from the Institute for Government Research (now the Brookings Institute) undertook a survey of Indian conditions for the secretary of the interior, Hubert Work. The IGA investigator Lewis Meriam directed the survey with the help of nine others, including the veterans of the Indian reform movement Fayette McKenzie and Henry Roe Cloud. The report, commonly called "The Meriam Report," recommended that the government get involved in what it called "Native Arts and Industries" through reservation-based projects and by developing an arts curriculum in the Indian schools. In the chapter on "Women and Handicrafts," we read that "Indians as a race, and particularly the Indian women, show a great fondness and aptitude for handicrafts."[9] This racial propensity, the commission argued, offered an important potential source of income as well as a means of strengthening tribal and community ties. Although none of the members of the survey team were part of the Santa Fe community, their ideas may have been influenced by the Indian craze and the subsequent work of Sterne, Hewett, the Whites, and Chapman to promote Native art in the 1920s. The report also encouraged the government to get involved in regulating the production and sale of

Native goods, creating standards of style, materials, and workmanship that could be used to demand fair compensation for Native craftspeople. It calls for the appointment of a person whose responsibilities would be "to arrange for increasing production and better marketing of native Indian products, a work which will interest the Indians, permit them to make a distinctive contribution, and materially increase their income."[10]

The federal government immediately began exploring how to implement these suggestions, soliciting input from Collier's Indian Defense Association. Around the time Collier became commissioner of Indian affairs, the Indian Defense Association director, James W. Young, was tapped to chair a federal "Committee on Indian Art and Crafts," which included several members of the Santa Fe scene, including Dodge and LaFarge and the Indian trader Lorenzo Hubbell. In 1935, the committee became the Indian Arts and Crafts Board; to this day the group works to promote the economic development of Native communities through the promotion and distribution of Native American art.[11] The new organization operated under Collier's direction and emphasized the industrial economic development of handicraft production over the cultural and aesthetic goals championed by the earlier group. The projects undertaken reveal the bureaucratic nature of the board. One was an attempt to create a trademark that would be affixed to Navajo wool products and Navajo, Pueblo, and Hopi silver products, offering an official guarantee of their authenticity. Another was adapting traditional products for modern uses, a project that was at the heart of an exhibition organized by the board's assistant general manager, Rene d'Harnoncourt, for the Golden Gate International Exposition in San Francisco in 1939. As explored in great detail elsewhere, this exhibition, and the 1941 Museum of Modern Art exhibition that grew out of it ("Indian Art of the United States"), used contemporary display techniques to draw attention to the utility of Native products for contemporary clothing and house decoration, a strategy with an obvious connection to the Indian craze.[12] As critics of the Indian Arts and Crafts Board have pointed out, the standards of quality developed by the board were dictated by the board representatives' tastes, biases, and expectations of what could be manufactured in a style and quantity that could sell.[13]

The Meriam Report also advocated a reintroduction of Native industries at the Indian schools. The authors called for vocational training "that will preserve the original craft values and yet give the Indians the full benefit of their skill and creative genius."[14] During the early 1930s, W. Carson Ryan, the director of education at the Bureau of Indian Affairs and a member of the Meriam Commission, addressed this issue by reinvigorating training programs in Native arts in various schools and creating a special arts and crafts program at the Santa Fe Indian School for graduates of Indian schools seen to have particular artistic talent. "The Studio," as this art school came to be called, included a program in handicrafts (weaving, embroidery, pottery, beadwork, basketry, carding, tanning, wool dying, silverwork, and wood-working) and a program in painting that built on the success of the earlier generation of Pueblo watercolorists.[15] The teaching methods of the Anglo-American women in charge of these two programs differed. Mabel Morrow, who ran the arts and crafts program, emphasized collaboration and sought to ground her students in distinct traditions by hiring indigenous master craftspeople as teachers. Dorothy Dunn, who taught painting, encouraged students to develop their work as individuals, in dialogue with their tribal traditions and what she identified as the key aesthetic qualities of Native American art, but not with one another. Nevertheless, each stressed the importance of skilled commercial artists for resolving the economic and cultural problems facing Indian people, including the problem of defining the positive value of Native culture for mainstream Americans. As one writer proclaimed upon describing the new program in 1932, the program would stress the "peculiar racial capacities and arts" of Native Americans, which would offer "a permanent contribution to our national life."[16]

Whether or not they were aware that their ideas and habits of thinking were informed by the Indian craze, the leaders of these programs perpetuated a turn-of-the-century habit of linking art and social and economic well-being. It is worth pointing out that this tendency was not at odds with discussions going on in the mainstream art world, particularly among the directors of federal relief projects directed toward artists (some of which employed Native artists).[17] As with those projects, we can see the 1930s as reviving Progressive ideas that once emerged from local or community organizations and now were coming under the increased institutional and bureaucratic control of the federal government. But while most New Deal art projects might be understood as being committed to the idea that art benefits the community, only those projects directed toward the Native

American community were thought to offer a solution to the economic and cultural problems of an entire race.[18]

Subsequent generations have come up with new ideas about the proper way for the U.S. government and supporters of Indian rights to foster the development and sale of Native American art. In so doing, they have continued to link Indian art with the broader place of Native Americans in American culture. In 1962, for example, the federal government replaced the Santa Fe Indian School's Studio with a new secondary and postsecondary art school called the Institute of American Indian Arts, which was designed to offer pupils more freedom in working in both mainstream and traditionally Indian mediums and styles.[19] Speaking in 1970, at the first convocation of American Indian Scholars in Princeton, Fritz Scholder, who had taught design, drawing, printmaking, and art history at the institute for five years, argued that Indian artists should pursue their training outside of government-run institutions. But this doesn't mean that he saw no role for the government to play in the Indian art world. He proposed, for example, that the government should maintain a directory of Indian artists.[20] Speaking at the same convocation, the Cree singer and activist Buffy Sainte-Marie felt the need for a "non-profit corporation of some sort to promote and protect authentic Indian art."[21] While she focused on the private sector, Sainte-Marie perpetuated the idea that "authentic Indian art" could be defined and that this definition should be policed, thus lending her voice to the cause of racialist aesthetics that was then almost a century old.

The task Sainte-Marie describes is one that has continually been undertaken by the Indian Arts and Crafts Board. At the end of the twentieth century, the board (now headed by Indian people) accelerated its legislative efforts, passing a series of bills that gave legal significance to the description of an object as a piece of "American Indian Art." The Indian Arts and Crafts Act of 1990 and the Indian Arts and Crafts Enforcement Act of 2000 made it a criminal act to sell a product as Indian if it was produced by someone other than an enrolled member of a federally recognized or state-recognized tribe or an artisan certified by such a tribe. The law was designed primarily to protect craftspeople from competition by foreign-made wares fraudulently presented as Native-made; this is a significant problem, especially for artisans producing for the souvenir and curio trade. But it has been received with ambivalence by some Native artists, who are concerned about its definition of Indian identity, which privileges government records made during the height of American control of Indian people as the authoritative determinant, leaving out members of Indian nations who have not achieved federal recognition as well as those who, due to the history of their tribal nation or for reasons of mixed heritage, might not be able to use these documents to prove a legal Indian identity.[22] As this book has argued, the very notion of authenticity that the board privileges is itself an artifact of American colonial control of Indian people.

Some Native artists have also pointed out the way the Indian Arts and Crafts Act uses authenticity primarily as a sales tool, reinforcing the association between Indian art and its market, and cutting creativity off from other associations. In response to the act, the photographer Hulleah Tshinhnahjinnie, whose mixed Navajo, Seminole, and Muscogee ancestry bespeaks the complex interactions of Indian people with each other as well as non-Indians in the twentieth century, produced the "Creative Native" series, which consists of self-portraits with her tribal enrollment number and sometimes also a bar code tattooed on her face, exposing how the act denies an artist's critical faculties to privilege her place within a bureaucratic, industrialized system.[23]

MODERN INDIAN ART

Tsinhnahjinnie is pointing to the way in which the Indian Arts and Crafts Act perpetuates a distinction between the Native creative process, which is beholden to a legally defined ethnic identity, and that allowed to a mainstream artist, which is valued for its freedom from socially bound constraints.[24] Native artists have recognized and reacted to this problem steadily since Angel DeCora gave her speeches and published her articles. Each mainstream campaign to recognize the aesthetic qualities of indigenous art has encouraged some Native artists to aspire to participate in the mainstream American art world. At times artists have argued that Indian people can conform to the aesthetic standards of a New York gallery system. At others, they have sought to broaden the art world to include diverse cultural expressions of aesthetic value and be open to art made using a variety of mediums and techniques.

As this book has shown, while the Indian craze facilitated the development of American modernism, it was ambivalent about the potential for

Native Americans to be modern artists. This problem continued for subsequent generations. This is most apparent in the course taken by Native American painting. While painting is understood by many to be an inherently modern medium, the rigorous control over the boundaries of Native American painting exercised by Dorothy Dunn and her successors at the Studio kept it in a separate category from mainstream modern painting. While the history of "modern" Indian painting begins before Dunn's project, the Santa Fe Indian School is where it became codified. As other scholars have related, Dunn's program, which trained a large number of painters from the Southwest and beyond, encouraged students to work in a distinctive "Indian" style, which centered on flat, decorative compositions depicting preservation or ceremonial subjects.[25] Receiving support from the local community, the federal government, and an emerging network of exhibition venues focused on Indian art, the Studio allowed several artists to achieve national prominence, but they did so only by working in Dunn's prescribed style. Studio graduates who began working outside these parameters, such as Oscar Howe, found themselves barred from Indian art world events, such as the annual exhibition of Indian painting at the Philbrook Museum in Tulsa, Oklahoma, and also not fully welcomed into a mainstream art world, which persisted in expecting work by indigenous artists to maintain recognizable Indian style and subject matter despite the increasing emphasis on formal abstraction within European American painting.[26]

Howe understood Dunn's desire to restrict the definition of Native art as a dimension of the colonial control to Indian people. He wrote, "Are we to be held back forever with one phase of Indian painting, with no right for individualism, dictated to as the Indian always has been, put on reservations and treated like a child, and only the White Man knows what is best for him?"[27]

Howe's opinion was not unique, and, beginning in the late 1950s, Native artists and their European American supporters began exploring ways to redirect current discussion of "modern Indian art." This effort was concentrated in the Southwest Indian Art Project, a two-year project based at the University of Arizona and funded by the Rockefeller Foundation, that resulted in the creation of the Institute of American Indian Arts. At the conference with which this project began, both Indians and non-Indians argued that Native artists should not be kept separate from developments in the mainstream art world. For example, the Anglo artist Andreas Andersen claimed that attempts to keep Indian art "within the tradition" had been a failure and called for a "transition between the Indian-artist and the artist."[28] As Joy Gritton has pointed out, the individualist rhetoric used by the Institute of American Indian Arts supported contemporary Indian policy, which had recoiled from the emphasis on tribal sovereignty during the Collier years to emphasize relocation and termination.[29] However, Native artists associated with the Institute of American Indian Arts, such as the late Lloyd Kiva New, have stressed the fact that Native artists did not have to give up their identities when they moved away from tradition. As he said, "Let's try to find challenging opportunities for the young Indian mind. Let's be more concerned with the evolution of artists rather than of art products. . . . Indian art of the future will be in new forms, produced in new media and with new technological methods. The end result will be as Indian as is the Indian."[30]

New had obtained his artistic training outside of the federal Indian school system, at the Art Institute of Chicago. Several other founding faculty members, such as Fritz Scholder, who had studied in California, and Charles Loloma (Hopi), also had mainstream art school training, but the Institute of American Indian Arts was eventually criticized for being too similar to previous government-funded efforts to cultivate indigenous art. Scholder decried it as "the same old story of bureaucracy and inefficiency in the government, resulting in disenchantment of the Indian people."[31] Yet artists continued to struggle to articulate how art could be modern and Native at the same time. For example, several of those involved in the Princeton conference were active members of their tribal communities who contributed to ceremonial life, yet they were ambivalent about allowing this to dictate their work. Charles Loloma suggested that Hopi people should retain control over the use and representation of their well-known Snake Dance, for example, but when he was asked about his own work, he claimed "I am not selling my work as Indian work, I am selling my work as Charles Loloma," leading Jack Reynolds to ask "if there is such a thing as an Indian artist."[32] Just over a decade later, in 1982, George Longfish and Joan Randall proclaimed the arrival of *another* "new Indian art," one grounded in "concepts which were clearly reflective of their perspectives as Native American in a modern setting."[33] In subsequent decades, Native artists have made great inroads into the mainstream art world. Native artists have increasingly been featured in exhibitions at major museums and involved in the art fairs and biennials that constitute the center of the contemporary art world. But there continues to be what one writer refers to as a "buckskin ceiling," a barrier that prevents indigenous artists from achieving the same fame and financial success as European American artists.[34]

ART AND CRAFT

One of the challenges involved in defining "modern" Native American art is the place of so-called traditional work. During the Indian craze, mainstream collectors and critics celebrated the aesthetic potential of handicrafts, in large part because they were part of a mainstream art world that was interested in the aesthetic qualities of applied and decorative arts. Though its openness to truly valuing the work of Native craftspeople was compromised by its racism, the Indian craze posed the theoretical possibility that modern Native American art could take both "traditional" and European American forms. Histories of modern Native American art of the rest of the century tend to isolate the histories of fine arts genres and those of other mediums, internalizing the mainstream hierarchy and separation of genres that fell more or less solidly into place with World War I. The twentieth century witnessed the emergence of celebrity craftspeople such as the Pueblo potters Maria Martinez and Lucy Lewis (Acoma), but their work has not usually been integrated into the narrative of "Native moderns." While they have been reluctant to dismiss the value of traditional work, Indian intellectuals have contributed to this problem of genre hierarchies. At the convocation of American Indian scholars at Princeton in 1970, Frank La Pena's question of the place of "the so-called traditional arts" in the "new Indian art" spurred a discussion revealing the panelists' anxiety about broaching the boundaries between painting and other mediums.[35] Yeffe Kimball, an artist who self-identified as Osage, suggested that there was a difference between objects that had historic value and those that were examples of "the highest expression" (212). When challenged by La Pena, she admitted that crafts *could* make an aesthetic statement but not that they always did. Pushed further, she resorted to the notion of taste to describe the distinction between what she categorized as "authentic" and inauthentic art, the latter including objects made for the curio trade. Fritz Scholder moved the conversation away from the question of authenticity toward an interrogation of the degraded conditions under which souvenir producers worked (213).

In his review of the 1991 exhibition "Our Land/Ourselves: American Indian Contemporary Artists," W. Jackson Rushing pointed out the flawed assumptions behind privileging painting and sculpture in discussions of modern Native American art: "The subliminal message being sent here, albeit unintentionally, is that weaving, pottery, basketry, woodcarving, embroidery, and other 'pre-Modern' forms are less able to speak meaningfully to a 'contemporary' art audience."[36] Fortunately, curators and artists are beginning to undermine this assumption. Institutions such as the National Museum of the American Indian's Gustav Heye Center in New York continually stage exhibitions that put innovative work in traditional mediums on view at the same time as cutting-edge works in more mainstream genres, and New York's Museum of Art and Design has organized a three-part exhibition devoted to contemporary Native work in clay, glass, fiber, jewelry, metal, and wood.[37] At the same time, Native artists operating within the mainstream gallery system are increasingly referencing traditional materials and techniques. Examples of artists working in this vein range from Nora Naranjo-Morse to Jolene Rickard and Brian Jungen. While each of these works in mediums and practices that are fully integrated into the contemporary art world (primarily installation and photography), their work draws viewers' attention to the complex historical frames needed to understand their work.

It may be that the current openness demonstrated by the mainstream art world in this moment of "postmedium" practice has helped these artists break a boundary that was vexing to their forebears a generation ago. But it would be wrong to assume that the desire to define Native American aesthetics across the art/craft divide is a recent development. Despite their flawed politics and problematic assumptions about the government's role in fostering indigenous art, both the Santa Fe Indian School and the Institute of American Indian Arts were established on the principle that Indian artists could pursue a range of practices. As I have argued in the case of the Indian craze, a full understanding of this framing of Native American aesthetics requires an exploration of how they fit into debates going on in the mainstream art world as well as those referring to Native art and politics. It is important to know, for example, how Lloyd Kiva New and Charles Loloma's ambitions for Native artists were influenced by their own studies in design-oriented mainstream art schools at a time when the American studio crafts movement was beginning to build up steam.

With the arrival of the National Museum of the American Indian on the Mall in Washington, D.C., in 2004, debates over the definition and value of modern Native American should continue for some time.[38] The fact that there is no single answer to this question does not render it unimportant, for any answer must address how Native identity has been constructed historically, often in ways that served the mainstream, and how contemporary Indian artists and curators create their own evolving definitions in dialogue with others at the individual, communal, tribal, and pan-Indian levels. Those participating in these discussions would do well to pay attention to earlier debates, not only to learn from the past but also to understand the ways in which the very terms that they use draw on the assumptions and struggles of their forebears. Though often overlooked, the Indian craze contributed a great deal to this history, providing an early link between Native American art and Indian welfare that continues to this day, suggesting the potential for a definition of Indian aesthetics that can embrace practices that cross the traditional/modern and high/low divides, and providing an early example of how Indian people themselves reflected on the relationship between art and identity. As Robert Warrior has pointed out, scholars of Native cultural history have frequently dismissed the cultural debates of the beginning of the twentieth century as tainted by a problematic assimilationism, but to do so distorts the historical record and blinds us to the serious questions raised in the period. As he writes, without "allow[ing] their sincerity to blind us to the perturbing implications of their work," a recovery of this history "provides a means of asking difficult ethical, cultural, and political questions in the context of complex, often dire, situations."[39]

Notes

INTRODUCTION

1. DeCora, "Native Indian Art," 87.
2. "Some Wall Decorations: Remarks on the Craze for Using Indian Orna-ments," *American Homes* 17.2 (March 1904): 34.
3. Lears, *No Place of Grace.*
4. Good introductions to modernist primitivism include Gill Perry, "Primi-tivism and the 'Modern," in *Primitivism, Cubism, Abstraction: The Early Twentieth Century*, ed. Charles Harrison, Francis Frascina, and Gill Perry (New Haven, Conn.: Yale University Press, 1993), 3–85; and Marianna Torgovnick, *Gone Primitive: Savage Intellects, Modern Lives* (Chicago: University of Chicago Press, 1990).
5. On connections between early modernist theory and progressivist so-cial thought, see Linda Dowling, *The Vulgarization of Art: The Victorians and Aesthetic Democracy* (Charlottesville: University Press of Virginia, 1996). I have also benefited from Suzanne Clark's *Sentimental Modern-ism: Women Writers and the Revolution of the Word* (Bloomington: Indiana University Press, 1991).
6. David Craven has argued that the term "modernism" was coined by Latin American critics to describe work that resisted imperialism even as it embraced aspects of contemporary European culture (Craven, "The Latin American Origins of 'Alternative Modernism,'" *Third Text* 36 [au-tumn 1996]: 29–44).
7. Ortiz, *Cuban Counterpoint*, 97–103.
8. Ibid., 98.
9. On this idea, see Cheryl Walker, *Indian Nation: Native American Literature and Nineteenth-Century Nationalisms* (Durham, N.C.: Duke University Press, 1997); and Phillips and Steiner, *Unpacking Culture*, 10.
10. This idea is articulated in David Scott, *Refashioning Futures: Criticism after Postcoloniality* (Princeton: Princeton University Press, 1999), 8–9.

11. See, for example, Tillyard, *The Impact of Modernism*; Burns, *Inventing the Modern Artist*; Corn, *The Real American Thing*; Mancini, *Pre-Modernism*; Kathleen Pyne, *Art and the Higher Life: Painting and Evolutionary Thought in Late Nineteenth-Century America* (Austin: University of Texas Press, 1996); and Helen Anne Molesworth, "At Home with Duchamp: The Readymade and Domesticity," Ph.D. diss., Cornell University, 1998. This history is discussed further in chapter 3.

12. See Brody, *Indian Painters and White Patrons*; Brody, *Pueblo Indian Painting*; Rushing, *Native American Art and the New York Avant-Garde*; and Anthes, *Native Moderns*.

13. This quotation comes from the Indian education pioneer Richard Henry Pratt. For more on Pratt, see chapter 2.

1. UNPACKING THE INDIAN CORNER

1. "Some Wall Decorations: Remarks on the Craze for Using Indian Ornaments," *American Homes* 17.2 (1904): 34.

2. Charles Francis Browne, "Elbridge Ayer Burbank: A Painter of Indian Portraits," *Brush and Pencil* 3.1 (1898): 16–35. For more on Burbank, see M. Melissa Wolfe, *American Indian Portraits: Elbridge Ayer Burbank in the West (1897–1910)* (Youngstown, Ohio: Butler Institute of American Art, 2000).

3. See, for example, *Brush and Pencil* 6.4 (1900): n.p. (advertisement pages).

4. *Brush and Pencil* 5.1 (1899): inside front cover. This issue also includes an advertisement for Rinehart's photographs.

5. Alvida Kelton Lee, "My Indian Portraits," *Brush and Pencil* 4.3 (1899): 144.

6. Lears, *No Place of Grace*, xv. For excellent articles that offer examples of this kind of reading, see Elizabeth Cromley, "Masculine/Indian," *Winterthur Portfolio* 31.4 (1996): 265–280; and Carolyn Kastner, "Collecting Mr. Ayer's Narrative," in *Acts of Possession: Collecting in America*, ed. Leah Dilworth (New Brunswick, N.J.: Rutgers University Press, 2003), 138–162.

7. Mary Louise Pratt, *Imperial Eyes: Travel Writing and Transculturation* (New York: Routledge, 1992), 6.

8. An early comprehensive study of traders is Frank McNitt, *The Indian Traders* (Norman: University of Oklahoma Press, 1962). More recent studies of curio sales include Jonathan Batkin, "Tourism Is Overrated: Pueblo Pottery and the Early Curio Trade, 1880–1910," in Phillips and Steiner, *Unpacking Cultures*, 282–297; Kathleen L. Howard, "Benham, Barnes, Brizard, and the Curio: A Study in Early Arizona Entrepreneurship, 1895–1908," *Journal of Arizona History* 42 (2001): 1–22; Kate C. Duncan, *1001 Curious Things: Ye Olde Curiosity Shop and Native American Art* (Seattle: University of Washington Press, 2000); and Weigle and Babcock, *The Great Southwest of the Fred Harvey Company and the Santa Fe Railway*.

9. Philip J. Deloria, *Indians in Unexpected Places* (Lawrence: University of Kansas Press, 2005), 6.

10. Ruth Phillips traces the history of collecting in the Northeast in *Trading Identities*. Jefferson's Indian Hall was recreated at Monticello in 2003 and can be accessed through the online exhibition "Framing the West at Monticello" (http://www.monticello.org/jefferson/lewisandclark/hall.html).

11. On this transition, see Karen Halttunen, "From Parlor to Living Room: Domestic Space, Interior Decoration, and the Culture of Personality," in Bronner, *Consuming Visions*, 157–189.

12. Boris, *Art and Labor*. An overview of the American arts and crafts movement can be found in

Wendy Kaplan, ed., *"The Art That Is Life": The Arts and Crafts Movement in America, 1875–1920* (Boston: Little, Brown for the Museum of Fine Arts, Boston, 1987).

13. John Ruskin, *Sesame and Lilies: Two lectures Delivered at Manchester in 1864* (London: Smith, Elder, 1865), 148.

14. On the use of medieval and folk traditions, see Nicola Gordon Bowe, "The Search for Vernacular Expression: The Arts and Crafts Movements in America and Ireland," in *Substance of Style: Perspectives on the American Arts and Crafts Movement*, ed. Bert Denker (Winterthur, Del.: Henry Francis du Pont Winterthur Museum, 1996), 5–24. On the use of Native American art, see Melanie Herzog, "Aesthetics and Meanings: The Arts and Crafts Movement and the Revival of American Indian Basketry," in Denker, *Substance of Style*, 69–91. See also Cheryl Robertson, "House and Home in the Arts and Crafts Era: Reforms for Simple Living," in Kaplan, *"The Art That Is Life*," 336–357. For a related argument, see Leah Dilworth, *Imagining Indians in the Southwest: Persistent Visions of a Primitive Past* (Washington, D.C.: Smithsonian Institution Press, 1996), ch. 3.

15. Helen Hunt Jackson, *Ramona* (1884; Boston: Roberts, 1888). For more on Jackson, see chapter 4.

16. For example, Jackson's collection is praised as an origin in Juan del Rio, "Relics of Old California," *Land of Sunshine* 14 (1901): 207. Sylvester Baxter describes Cushing's collection in "The Father of the Pueblos," *Harpers New Monthly Magazine*, 65.385 (1892): 79–80. See also Curtis Hinsley, "Boston Meets Southwest," in *The Southwest in the American Imagination: The Writings of Sylvester Baxter, 1881–1889*, ed. Curtis Hinsley and David R. Wilcox (Tucson: University of Arizona Press, 1996), 28.

17. Beverly Gordon, "The Niagara Falls Whimsey: The Object as a Symbol of Cultural Interface," Ph.D. diss., University of Wisconsin–Madison, 1984.

18. Doubleday, "Our Industrial Work: Portions of Report Read at Meeting of the National Indian Association, Dec., 1902," *The Indian's Friend* (March 1903): 10.

19. Mason, *Indian Basketry*, 504–511.

20. Keppler's correspondence can be found in the Joseph Keppler Jr. Iroquois Papers, 1882–1944, collection no. 9184, Native American Collection, Division of Rare and Manuscript Collections, Cornell University Library; provenance: Huntington Free Library (gift to Huntington Free Library from Joseph Keppler, 1943). Parker and the Cornplanters are noted for collecting and publishing Seneca lore and literature. Keppler and Parker shared many friends, and more about these and Keppler's other Seneca correspondents can be found in Joy Porter, *To Be Indian: The Life of Iroquois-Seneca Arthur Caswell Parker* (Norman: University of Oklahoma Press, 2001). For more on "culture brokers" see Margaret Connell Szasz, ed., *Between Indian and White Worlds: The Culture Broker* (Norman: University of Oklahoma Press, 1994).

21. Joseph Keppler, "Comments on Certain Iroquois Masks," special issue, *Contributions from the Museum of the American Indian* (Heye Foundation) 12.4 (1941): 3–40.

22. For more on Heye, see Clara Sue Kidwell, "Every Last Dishcloth: The Prodigious Collecting of George Gustav Heye," in *Collecting Native America*, ed. Shepard Krech III and Barbara A. Hail (Washington, D.C.: Smithsonian Institution Press, 1999), 232–257.

23. For the history of American museums in this period, see Steven Conn, *Museums and American Intellectual Life, 1876–1926* (Chicago: University of Chicago Press, 1998).

24. "Humboldt Indians," *Out West* 21 (1904): 510–511.

25. Molly Lee, "Tourism and Taste Cultures: Collecting Native Art in Alaska at the Turn of the Twentieth Century," in Phillips and Steiner, *Unpacking Culture*, 267–281.

26. In addition to the works already cited, see James Clifford, "On Collecting Art and Culture," in Clifford, *The Predicament of Culture* (Cambridge, Mass.: Harvard University Press, 1988), 215–251; and Berlo, ed., *The Early Years of Native American Art History.*

27. T. J. Jackson Lears, "From Salvation to Self-Realization: Advertising and the Therapeutic Roots of the Consumer Culture, 1880–1930," in *The Culture of Consumption: Critical Essays in American History, 1880–1980*, ed. Richard Wightman Fox and T. J. Jackson Lears (New York: Pantheon, 1983), 1–38. See also Lears, "Beyond Veblen: Rethinking Consumer Culture in America," in Bronner, *Consuming Visions*, 73–97.

28. Lears, *No Place of Grace*, 37. Similarly, Susan Stewart writes: "The function of belongings within the economy of the bourgeois is one of supplementarity, a supplementarity that in consumer culture replaces its generating subject as the interior milieu substitutes for, and takes the place of, an interior self" (Stewart, *On Longing*, xi).

29. Thorstein Veblen, *The Theory of the Leisure Class*, with an introduction by C. Wright Mills (New Brunswick, N.J.: Transaction Publishers, 1992), 60–80.

30. Pierre Bourdieu, *Distinction: A Social Critique of the Judgement of Taste*, trans. Richard Nice (Cambridge, Mass.: Harvard University Press, 1984), 6–7 and passim.

31. Walter Benjamin, "Unpacking My Library," in *Illuminations: Essays and Reflections*, ed. and intro. Hannah Arendt (New York: Schocken Books, 1968), 60.

32. Jean Baudrillard, "The System of Collecting," in *Cultures of Collecting*, ed. John Elsner and Roger Cardinal (London: Reaktion, 1994), 7–24.

33. "A Rare Collection," *The Papoose* (January 1903): 5.

34. For more on James, see Kathleen Whitaker, "George Wharton James: The Controversial Author of *Indian Blankets and Their Makers*," *American Indian Art Magazine* 25.1 (1999): 66–77.

35. George Wharton James, "Indian Basketry in House Decoration," *Chautauquan* 33 (1901): 620.

36. Alice M. Kellogg, *Home Furnishing, Practical and Artistic* (New York: Frederick A. Stokes, 1905), 51–52.

37. For an overview of the Japan craze, see Warren Cohen, *East Asian Art and American Culture* (Baltimore: Johns Hopkins University Press, 1992).

38. Olive M. Percival, "Indian Basketry: An Aboriginal Art," *House Beautiful* 2.5 (1897): 152.

39. Sargent, "Indian Basketry," 332.

40. Eunyoung Cho, "The Selling of Japan: Race, Gender, and Cultural Politics in the American Art World, 1876–1915," Ph.D. diss., University of Delaware, 1998; Neil Harris, "All the World a Melting Pot? Japan at American Fairs, 1876–1904," in Harris, *Cultural Excursions: Marketing Appetites and Cultural Tastes in Modern America* (Chicago: University of Chicago Press, 1990), 29–55.

41. Elaine Goodale Eastman, *Sister to the Sioux: The Memoirs of Elaine Goodale Eastman, 1895–91*, ed. Kay Graber (Lincoln: University of Nebraska Press, 1978), 34.

42. Doubleday, "Two Ways to Help the Indians," pt. 2, *The Indian's Friend* (February 1901): 6.

43. Julian Ralph, "My Indian Plunder," *Scribners* 20 (1896): 638.

44. Delos Kittle to Keppler, December 9, 1904, May 3, 1909, and another between November 20, 1913, and 1916, Joseph Keppler Jr. Iroquois papers.

45. For a native perspective, see George H. J Abrams, "The Case for Wampum: Repatriation from the Museum of the American Indian to the Six Nations Confederacy, Brantford, Ontario, Canada," in *Museums and the Making of "Ourselves,"* ed. Flora E. S. Kaplan (London: Leicester University Press, 1994), 351–384.

46. Edward Cornplanter to Joseph Keppler, July 19, 1901, in Joseph Keppler Jr. Iroquois Papers.

47. Kastner, "Collecting Mr. Ayer's Narrative," 142.

48. Gustav Stickley paraphrased in Boris, *Art and Labor*, 77.

49. Thomas F. Barnes, "The Washoe Baskets," *The Papoose* (March 1903): 15. For more on the desire for "complete" collections see Dorothy Washburn, "Dealers and Collectors of Indian Baskets at the Turn of the Century in California," *Empirical Studies of the Arts* 2.1 (1984): 61.

50. For more on Keyser, see Marvin Cohodas, *Degikup: Washoe Fancy Basketry, 1895–1935* (Vancouver: Fine Arts Gallery of the University of British Colombia, 1979).

51. Percival, "Indian Basketry," 152–156; Walter Channing Wyman, "The Navajo Blanket," *House Beautiful* 3.5 (1898): 153–156; Claudia Stuart Coles, "Aboriginal Basketry in the United States," *House Beautiful* 7.3 (1900): 142–151; Edith Cooley, "Navajo Blankets," *House Beautiful* 7.5 (1900): 302–307; Julia Mills Dunn, "Indian Pottery," *House Beautiful* 15.5 (1904): 306–307; Henry Horn, "The Story of the Chilcat Blanket," *House Beautiful* 18.5 (1905): 18–19.

52. As Susan Stewart points out, modern bourgeois collections demonstrate the commitment to objective knowledge in their very composition, which is dependent on principles of organization and classification (Stewart, *On Longing*, 153).

53. Boris argues convincingly that Stickley promoted a connection between his furniture and Roosevelt's ideology in *The Craftsman* (Boris, *Art and Labor*, 76).

54. John Higham, "The Reorientation of American Culture in the 1890s," in *The Origins of Modern Consciousness*, ed. John Weiss (Detroit: Wayne State University Press, 1965), 81.

55. "Nursery Wall Coverings in Indian Designs," *Craftsman* 5.1 (1903): 96.

56. For more on the woodcraft Indians, see Philip Deloria, *Playing Indian*, ch. 4.

57. Cromley, "Masculine/Indian," 277. See also Cheryl Robertson, "Male and Female Agendas for Domestic Reform: The Middle-Class Bungalow in Gendered Perspective," *Winterthur Portfolio* 26.2/3 (1991): 135, in which the author describes Native American objects as "evocative of warrior exploits and primitive simplicity."

58. Navajo aesthetic principles are described in Eulalie Bonar, ed., *Woven by the Grandmothers: Nineteenth-Century Navajo Textiles from the National Museum of the American Indian* (Washington, D.C.: Smithsonian Institution Press, 1996).

59. For an overview of the historical directory of Navajo weaving, see Kate Peck Kent, *Navajo Weaving* (Santa Fe, N.M.: School of American Research, 1985).

60. For more on Hubbell and his trading post, see Kathy M'Closkey, *Swept under the Rug: A Hidden History of Navajo Weaving* (Albuquerque: University of New Mexico Press, 2002).

61. George Wharton James, "Imitation—Artistic and Vicious," *Basket* 2.1 (1904): 35–36.

62. Ruth B. Phillips and Christopher B. Steiner, "Art, Authenticity, and the Baggage of Cultural Encounter," in Phillips and Steiner, *Unpacking Culture*, 9–13.

63. Mason, *Indian Basketry*.

64. This idea has been explored provocatively by Beverly Gordon and Ruth Phillips. See Gordon, "The Niagara Falls Whimsey," and Phillips, *Trading Identities*, especially ch. 5.

65. For more on Hudson, see Lucienne Lanson and Patricia L. Tetzlaff, *Grace Hudson: Artist of the Pomo Indians, a Biography* (Virginia Beach: Donning, 2006).

66. For articles by Doubleday and Coles, see Doubleday, "Our Industrial Work"; Doubleday, "Two Ways to Help the Indians," pts. 1 and 2, *The Indian's Friend* (January 1901): 7–8, and (February 1901): 2, 5–6; Coles, "Aboriginal Basketry in the United States."

67. See Mathes, *Helen Hunt Jackson and Her Indian Reform Legacy*.

68. Doubleday, "Our Industrial Work," 10.

69. Gail Bederman, *Manliness and Civilization: A Cultural History of Gender and Race in the United States, 1880–1917* (Chicago: University of Chicago Press, 1995), 21 and chs. 1 and 3 passim.

70. Jacobs, *Engendered Encounters*. Jacobs focuses on the Southwest, and the antimodernists she discusses are active after the Indian craze, but she draws many of the same conclusions about the motivations of non-Indian women drawn in this study.

71. Even Lears admits this, allowing for what he calls "modernist antimodernism" (Lears, *No Place of Grace*, 312). For more on cultural primitivism, see George Boas and Arthur Lovejoy, *A Documentary History of Primitivism and Related Ideas in Antiquity* (1935; Baltimore: Johns Hopkins University Press, 1997).

72. William Leach, *Land of Desire: Mechants, Power, and the Rise of a New American Culture* (New York: Pantheon Books, 1993); see particularly ch. 2.

73. See Michael Leja, *Looking Askance: Skepticism and American Art from Eakins to Duchamp* (Berkeley: University of California Press, 2004).

74. Tony Bennett, *The Birth of the Museum: History, Theory, Politics* (New York: Routledge, 1995), 59.

75. Simon J. Bronner, "Object Lessons: The Work of Ethnological Museums and Collections," in Bronner, *Consuming Visions*, 217–254.

76. Herbert Gibbons, *John Wanamaker* (New York: Harper and Brothers, 1926), 2:81, quoted in Neil Harris, "Museums, Merchandizing and Popular Taste: The Struggle for Influence," in Harris, *Cultural Excursions*, 65.

77. *The M.H. de Young Memorial Museum, Golden Gate Park, San Francisco, California; story of its foundation and the objects of its founder; description of its various galleries; brief sketches of the most notable exhibits, with accounts of their origin and of the periods of history and industries represented by them* (San Francisco: Park Commission, 1921), 13.

78. "Navajo Indian Blankets: The Remarkable Products of an Arizona Tribe," *New-York Tribune*, March 19, 1898, suppl., 2.

79. The Wanamaker family expressed its interest in Native Americans in diverse ways. Wanamaker's son Lewis Rodman sponsored several expeditions led by Joseph K. Dixon to learn about Native Americans. Photographs from these expeditions were exhibited and sold at Wanamaker's stores and formed a basis to the *Wanamaker Primer of the North American Indian* (Philadelphia: Wanamaker Stores, 1909). John Wanamaker also supported the erection of the National Indian Memorial, dedicated in 1913. See Joseph H. Appel, *Golden Book of the Wanamaker Stores* (Philadelphia: John Wanamaker, 1911), 241–242. On the memorial, see Wanamaker Stores, "A Tribute to the North American Indian" (1909), Wanamaker Archive, Pennsylvania Historical Society, box 260; and Alan Trachtenberg, *Shades of Hiawatha: Staging Indians, Making Americans* (New York: Hill and Wang, 2004), ch. 5.

80. "Navajo Indian Goods: Interesting Facts about the Wonderful Blanket," *New-York Tribune* June 12, 1897, 5.

81. *House Beautiful* 13.3 (1903): inside front cover.

82. Advertisement for the Wanamaker Store, *New York Times* April 5, 1897, 4.

83. For example, an advertisement in the *New York Times* on April 5, 1901, 5, describes Dutch furniture, French perfumes, oriental rugs, and Irish covert cloths.

84. Advertisement for the Wanamaker Store, *New York Times*, December 11, 1901, 4.

85. See Lloyd Wendt and Herman Kogan, *Give the Lady What She Wants! . . . The Story of Marshall Field & Company* (Chicago: Rand McNally, 1952), 281.

86. Advertisement for the Wanamaker Store, *New York Times*, April 14, 1903, 4.

87. The invoice, dated March 30, 1901, is in carton 4, folder 76, George Wharton James Collection, Braun Research Library, Southwest Museum, Pasadena, California.

88. See advertisement for the Wanamaker Store, *New York Times*, April 5, 1901, 4.

89. George Wharton James, "Indian Handicrafts," *Handicraft* 1.12 (1903): 272.

90. Advertisement for the Wanamaker Store, *New York Times*, March 28, 1901, 4.

91. For the Fred Harvey Company, see Kathleen L. Howard and Diana F. Pardue, eds., *Inventing the Southwest: The Fred Harvey Company and Native American Art* (Phoenix: Heard Museum, 1996); and Weigle and Babcock, *The Great Southwest of the Fred Harvey Company and the Santa Fe Railway*. For specific artists, see Barbara Kramer, *Nampeyo and Her Pottery* (Albuquerque: University of New Mexico Press, 1996); and Laura Jane Moore, "Elle Meets the President: Weaving Navajo Culture and Commerce in the Southwestern Tourist Industry," *Frontiers: A Journal of Women Studies* 22.1 (2001): 21–44.

92. Advertisement for the Fred Harvey Company's Chicago outlet, *Chicago Daily Tribune*, December 22, 1903, 4.

93. Advertisement for the Wanamaker Store, *The New York Times* December 11, 1904, 4.

94. On Indians "playing Indian," see Deloria, *Playing Indian*, 122–124, 147, 168, 187–189.

95. Luther Standing Bear, *My People the Sioux* (1928; Lincoln: University of Nebraska Press, 1975), 177–190.

96. "Up-to-Date Navajo Art: Remarkable Locomotive Blanket Owned by Mr. James," *New-York Tribune*, January 27, 1901, suppl., 13.

97. George Wharton James, *Indian Blankets and Their Makers* (Chicago: A. C. McClurg, 1914), 125. This story is likely a fabrication. Kathy Whitaker notes that there is no record of James's studying the Navajo language, and that, at this time, an elderly female such as he describes would not have been able to communicate with him (Whitaker, "George Wharton James," 73).

98. Phillips, *Trading Identities*, 10.

2. THE WHITE MAN'S INDIAN ART

1. Estelle Reel, *Annual Report of the Superintendent of Indian Schools* (Washington, D.C.: Government Printing Office, 1904), 22.

2. Reel, *Course of Study for the Indian Schools of the United States*.

3. On borders, see Kate Peck Kent, *Navajo Weaving: Three Centuries of Change* (Santa Fe, N.M.: School of American Research Press, 1985), 112.

4. See Dorothy W. Hewes, "The First Good Years of Indian Education: 1894 to 1898," *American Indian Culture and Research Journal* 5.2 (1981): 63–82; and Lomawaima, "Estelle Reel, Superintendent of Indian Schools, 1898–1910."

5. Vernon J. Williams, *Rethinking Race: Franz Boaz and His Contemporaries* (Lexington: University Press of Kentucky, 1996).

6. Robert F. Berkhofer Jr., *The White Man's Indian: Images of the American Indian from Columbus to the Present* (New York: Alfred A Knopf, 1978).

7. An overview of the history of American Indian education can be found in Margaret Connell

Szasz and Carmelita S. Ryan, "American Indian Education," in *Handbook of North American Indians*, vol. 4, *History of Indian-White Relations*, ed. Wilcomb E. Washburn (Washington, D.C.: Smithsonian Institution Press, 1988), 284–304. Pratt's own account of his work in Florida and Pennsylvania can be found in Richard Henry Pratt, *Battlefield and Classroom: Four Decades with the American Indian, 1867–1904*, ed. and with an introduction by Robert M. Utley (Lincoln: University of Nebraska Press, 1964).

8. William A. Jones, *Annual Report of the Commissioner of Indian Affairs to the Secretary of the Interior* (Washington, D.C.: Government Printing Office, 1900), 23.

9. Thomas J. Morgan, *Indian Education* (Washington, D.C.: Indian Rights Association, 1890), 7.

10. Ibid., 5.

11. Lomawaima, *They Called It Prairie Light*, 83, 87.

12. Luther Standing Bear, *My People the Sioux* (Lincoln: University of Nebraska Press, 1975), 147.

13. Richard H. Pratt, "The Advantages of Mingling Indians with Whites," in *Official Report of the Nineteenth Annual Conference of Charities and Correction* (1892), 46–59; reprinted in *Americanizing the American Indians: Writings by the "Friends of the Indian," 1880–1900*, ed. Francis Paul Prucha (Cambridge, Mass.: Harvard University Press, 1973), 260.

14. Lomawaima *They Called It Prairie Light*, xiv.

15. David Wallace Adams, *Education for Extinction: American Indians and the Boarding School Experience, 1875–1928* (Lawrence: University Press of Kansas, 1995), 316.

16. William N. Hailmann, *Annual Report of the Superintendent of Indian Schools* (Washington, D.C.: Government Printing Office, 1894), 341.

17. Francis Paul Prucha, *The Great Father: The United States Government and the American Indians* (Lincoln: University of Nebraska Press, 1984), 2:686–687, plate 5 caption.

18. See, for example, "Uniform Course of Study for Indians," *Denver Republican*, August 19, 1901, n.p. (item 11, clipping envelope 9, Estelle Reel Papers, Northwest Museum of Art and Culture, Spokane, Washington).

19. Prucha, *The Great Father*, 2:818.

20. See Dorothy Dunn, *American Indian Painting of the Southwest and Plains Areas* (Albuquerque: University of New Mexico Press, 1968), and the reassessments of her work in Brody, *Indian Painters and White Patrons*, and Bernstein and Rushing, *Modern by Tradition*.

21. Brody, *Pueblo Indian Painting*.

22. Drawing is listed as a subject in *The Hampton Normal and Agricultural Institute Session of 1887–1888* (Hampton, Va.: The Institute, 1888), and *Catalog of the Indian Industrial School, Carlisle, PA 1902* (Jamestown, N.Y.: The Journal, 1902).

23. Reel, *Course of Study for the Indian Schools of the United States*, 55.

24. Letters to Office of Indian Affairs, no. 1902–54276, record group 75, National Archives and Records Administration, Washington, D.C.

25. Report of the Superintendent of the Round Valley School, Letters to Office of Indian Affairs, no. 1902–53987, record group 75, National Archives and Records Administration.

26. Joseph C. Hart, "Report of the Superintendent of the Oneida Indian School," *Report of the Superintendent of Indian Schools for 1903* (Washington, D.C.: Government Printing Office, 1903), 33.

27. For more on Crow beadwork, see Joseph D. Horse Capture, *Beauty, Honor and Tradition: The Legacy of Plains Indian Shirts* (Washington, D.C.: National Museum of the American Indian,

Smithsonian Institution; Minneapolis: Minneapolis Institute of Arts, distributed by University of Minnesota Press, 2001), 88–89.

28. Sybil Carter, "Address on Lace-Making," in *Proceedings of the Eighth Annual Meeting of the Lake Mohonk Conference of Friends of the Indian* (Philadelphia: Lake Mohonk Conference, 1890), 46–48. For more on Carter's work, see Kate C. Duncan, "American Indian Lace Making," *American Indian Art Magazine* 5 (1980): 28–35; and Elizabeth Hutchinson, "Progressive Primitivism: Race, Gender and Turn-of-the-Century American Art," Ph.D. diss., Stanford University, 1999, ch. 2.

29. A history of the Indian Industries League can be found in Erik Krenzen Trump, "The Indian Industries League and Its Support of American Indian Arts, 1893–1922: A Study of Changing Attitudes toward Indian Women and Assimilationist Policy," Ph.D. diss., Boston University, 1996.

30. *Indian Industries League Annual Report for 1900*, 5, quoted in Trump, "The Indian Industries League and Its Support of American Indian Arts," 260.

31. Constitution of the Sequoya League, reprinted in *The Papoose*, April 1903, 18.

32. For more on urban handicraft reform projects, see Boris, *Art and Labor*, ch. 5.

33. Many of these projects are discussed in Eileen Boris, "Crossing Boundaries: The Gendered Meaning of Arts and Crafts," in *The Ideal Home: The History of Twentieth-Century American Craft*, ed. Janet Kardon (New York: American Craft Museum, 1993), 32–44.

34. Max West, "The Revival of Handicrafts in America," *U.S. Bureau of Labor Bulletin* 55 (1904): 1573–1622.

35. Ibid., 1622.

36. Boris, "Crossing Boundaries," 44.

37. Hart, "Native Industries in the Indian School," 446.

38. "Granville Stanley Hall," *American National Biography Online* (http://www.anb.org) accessed February 26, 2007.

39. Lears, *No Place of Grace*, 78.

40. Nicholas Murray Butler, "The Argument for Manual Training" (1888), in *The Social History of American Education*, ed. Rena L. Vassar (Chicago: Rand McNally, 1965), 2:158–167. See also Robert L. Church and Michael W. Sedlak, *Education in the United States: An Interpretive History* (New York: Free Press, 1976), 371.

41. Gustav Stickley, "Manual Training and Citizenship," *Craftsman* 5.4 (1904): 407–408.

42. Booker T. Washington, "Industrial Education for the Negro," from *The Negro Problem* (New York: James Pratt, 1903), reprinted in Vassar, *Social History of American Education*, 2:62–63.

43. Stickley, "Manual Training and Citizenship," 407.

44. Ella Flagg Young, quoted in Boris, *Art and Labor*, 97, n. 54.

45. Estelle Reel, *Teaching Indian Pupils to Speak English: Primary Methods and Outlines for the Use of Teachers in the Indian Schools* (Washington, D.C.: Government Printing Office, 1904).

46. See Otis Tufton Mason, *Indian Basketry*, 83, which includes four illustrations of basket starts credited as "after Mary White."

47. See, for example, W. T. Harris, "Art Education the True Industrial Education—A Cultivation of Aesthetic Taste of Universal Utility," *Journal of Proceedings and Addresses of the Annual Meeting of the National Educational Association for 1889* (Topeka, Kans.: The Association, 1889), 647–655; and Leslie W. Miller, "Craftsmanship in Education," *Journal of Proceedings*

and Addresses of the Annual Meeting of the National Educational Association for 1903 (Chicago: The Association, 1903), 627–633.

48. Ruby Hodge, "The Relation of Primitive Handicraft to Present-Day Educational Problems," *Journal of Proceedings and Addresses of the Annual Meeting of the National Educational Association for 1907* (Winona, Minn.: The Association, 1907), 815–820.

49. An abstract was printed in the *Journal of Proceedings and Addresses of the Annual Meeting of the National Educational Association for 1903* (Chicago: The Association, 1903), 644–645.

50. Reel, *Course of Study for the Indian Schools of the United States*, 54.

51. Ibid., 55.

52. "Report of the Superintendent of the Navajo Boarding School," *Annual Report of the Commissioner of Indian Affairs for the Year 1902* (Washington, D.C.: Government Printing Office, 1902), 157; Kathy M'Closkey notes that a significant number of Navajo weavers during this period were school-age girls, including some as young as ten: M'Closkey, *Swept under the Rug: A Hidden History of Navajo Weaving* (Albuquerque: University of New Mexico Press, 2002), 83.

53. Advertisement, inside front cover, *Indian School Journal*, January 1905.

54. Jonathan Batkin, "Tourism Is Overrated: Pueblo Pottery and the Early Curio Trade, 1880–1910," in Phillips and Steiner, *Unpacking Culture*, 297.

55. Report of the Superintendent of the Phoenix Agency, Letters to Office of Indian Affairs, no. 1904–77610, record group 75, National Archives and Records Administration.

56. "Uplifting of Poor Lo," *Washington Post*, December 12, 1902, 9.

57. "Indian Art Not Declining," *Indian School Journal* (October 1905), 37. In 1907, *Out West* magazine claimed that several successful O'Odham weavers were graduates of the Phoenix Indian School ("Indians of Arizona," *Out West* 26 [1907]: 497).

58. Karen Daniels Petersen, *Plains Indian Art from Fort Marion* (Norman: University of Oklahoma Press, 1971), 66–69 and 261. See also Pratt, *Battlefield and Classroom*, 157.

59. "Indian Educators," *The Papoose* 1.8 (July 1903): 17.

60. Reel's collection is mentioned in a clipping in her scrapbook ("Collection of Baskets on Display in Washington, D.C.," *Austin Statesman*, June 18, 1901, n.p., in clipping envelope 6, Estelle Reel Papers). The fate of the collection is discussed in Mary Dodds Schlick, *Columbia River Basketry: Gifts of the Ancestors, Gift of the Earth* (Seattle: University of Washington Press, 1994), 173–174.

61. Roderick Randum, "A Little Journey to Chilocco, Home of the Indian Roycrofters," *Indian School Journal* 5 (1905): 11–19.

62. "The Indians of Arizona," *Out West* 26 (1907): 471–497.

63. William A. Jones, *Annual Report of the Commissioner of Indian Affairs to the Secretary of the Interior* (Washington, D.C.: Government Printing Office, 1903), 11.

64. Circular dated March 10, 1901, circulars issued by the superintendent of Indian Schools, entry 719, record group 75, National Archives and Records Administration.

65. Untitled clipping from the *Boston Evening Transcript*, January 7, 1903, n.p., item 7, clipping envelope 16, Estelle Reel Papers.

66. Untitled clipping from *The Red Man and Helper*, September 19, 1902, n.p., item 4, folder 15, Estelle Reel Papers.

67. The photograph appeared in the superintendent's 1905 *Annual Report* and was frequently reproduced in the well-circulating monthly journal of the Chilocco Indian School, the *Indian School Journal*.

68. Boris, *Art and Labor*, 91.

69. Letters to Office of Indian Affairs, no. 1906–47861, record group 75, National Archives and Records Administration.

70. Lida Quimby, "Report of the Matron of the Puyallup Reservation," *Annual Report of the Commissioner of Indian Affairs for the Year 1904* (Washington, D.C.: Government Printing Office, 1904), 364.

71. Lomawaima, *They Called It Prairie Light*, xiv and passim.

72. "World's Fair Exhibit News," *Chilocco Farmer* (April 1904): 282.

73. Hart, "Native Industries in the Indian School," 445.

74. Hart, "Report of the Superintendent of the Oneida Indian School," 359.

75. Hart, "Native Industries in the Indian School," 445.

76. Lomawaima, "Estelle Reel, Superintendent of Indian Schools," 29.

77. Gerald Vizenor, *Manifest Manners: Postindian Warriors of Survivance* (Hanover, N.H.: University Press of New England, 1994).

78. J. K. Bloomfield, *The Oneidas* (New York: Alden Brothers, 1907), 344.

79. Benson L. Lanford, "Great Lakes Woven Beadwork: An Introduction," *American Indian Art Magazine* 11.3 (1986): 62–67, 75.

80. Phillips, *Trading Identities*, chs. 3 and 5.

81. See Laurence M. Hauptman and L. Gordon McLester III, eds., *The Oneida Indians in the Age of Allotment, 1860–1920* (Norman: University of Oklahoma Press, 2006).

82. Ibid., 92–95.

3. PLAYING INDIAN

1. Carl Purdy, "Pomo Indian Baskets," *Out West* 16 (1902): 157–158.

2. Sally McLendon, "Collecting Pomoan Baskets, 1889–1939," *Museum Anthropology* 17.1 (June 1993): 49–60.

3. Berlo, introduction to *The Early Years of Native American Art History*, 6.

4. S. A. Barrett, "Basket Designs of the Pomo Indians," *American Anthropologist* 7 (1905): 648–653; Roland Dixon, "Basketry Designs of the Indians of Northern California," *Bulletin of the American Museum of Natural History* 17 (1902): 1–32.

5. For more on Nicholson's role in promoting "named" artists, see Marvin Cohodas, *Basket Weavers for the California Curio Trade: Elizabeth and Louise Hickox* (Tucson: University of Arizona Press, 1998).

6. This history is traced in Berlo, *The Early Years of Native American Art History*.

7. James Clifford, "On Collecting Art and Culture," in *The Predicament of Culture* (Cambridge, Mass.: Harvard University Press, 1988), 215–251.

8. Exposition of Indian Tribal Arts, *Introduction to American Indian art: To accompany the first exhibition of American Indian art selected entirely with consideration of esthetic value* (New York: The Exposition, 1931).

9. See, for example, Rushing, *Native American Art and the New York Avant-Garde*.

10. For more on this history, see Brody, *Indian Painters and White*.

11. These are discussed in Rushing, *Native American Art and the New York Avant-Garde*, 15–16, 30, 32, and 34.

12. See, for example, Tillyard, *The Impact of Modernism*, and Aileen Dashi Tsui, "Nothing of Sub-

stance: Aestheticism, Modernism, and Strategic Duplicity in the Paintings of James McNeill Whistler," Ph.D. diss., Harvard University, 2001.

13. Rushing refers to it only in passing (Rushing, *Native American Art and the New York Avant-Garde*, 13); see also Mullin, *Culture in the Marketplace*, 190, n. 7.

14. William Morris, "Speech to the Arts and Crafts Exhibition Society," *Pall Mall Gazette*, November 2, 1886, quoted in Tillyard, *The Impact of Modernism*, 29. The ideas presented in this and the preceding paragraph come from ch. 1 of Tillyard's book.

15. Leila Mechlin, "Primitive Arts and Crafts Illustrated in the National Museum Collection," *International Studio* 35 (August 1908): suppl., 62–63, 64.

16. In 1908, *Brush and Pencil* had a circulation of 10,000; *The Craftsman* of 19,000; *International Studio* of 10,000 (Source: N. W. Ayer and Son, *American Newspaper Annual* (Philadelphia: N. W. Ayer and Son, 1909). In addition to the works discussed specifically below, see also H. M. Carpenter, "How Indian Baskets Are Made," *Cosmopolitan* (October 1900): 638–640; George Wharton James, "Indian Handicrafts," *Handicraft* 1.12 (1903): 269–287; "Indian Blankets, Baskets and Bowls: The Product of the Original Craftworkers on This Continent," *Craftsman* 17 (February 1910): 588–591; Natalie Curtis, "The People of the Totem-Poles: Their Art and Legends," *Craftsman* 16 (September 1909): 612–621; Charles A. Eastman, "Indian Handicrafts," *Craftsman* 8 (August 1905): 659–662; Eastman, "My People: The Indians' Contribution to the Art of America," *Craftsman* 27 (November 1914): 179–186; Constance Goddard Dubois, "The Indian Woman as a Craftsman," *Craftsman* 6 (1904): 391–393; George Wharton James, "Primitive Inventions," *Craftsman* 5 (November 1903): 125–137; George Wharton James, "Aboriginal American Homes: Brush, Mud and Willow Dwellings," *Craftsman* 8 (July 1905): 459–471 and (August 1905): 640–649.

17. "Ancient Peruvian Pottery," *Keramic Studio* 3.8 (1901): 170; "Indian Pottery," *Keramic Studio* 3.8 (1901): 168–169; "Indian Pottery," *Keramic Studio* 6.7 (1904): 147–148; Mertice MacCrea Buck, "Indian Basketry," *Keramic Studio* 9.7 (1907): 169–170.

18. Elbridge Ayer Burbank, "Studies of Art in American Life III: In Indian Teepees," *Brush and Pencil* 7 (November 1900): 75–91.

19. See Peter H. Hassrick, *The Frederic Remington Studio* (Cody, Wyo.: Buffalo Bill Historical Center in association with University of Washington Press, 1994).

20. In 1904, *The Craftsman* ran a "Special Holiday Offer" offering four prints with each subscription: *The Craftsman* 7 (1904): 359.

21. Sarah Burns, *Inventing the Modern Artist: Art and Culture in the Gilded Age* (New Haven, Conn.: Yale University Press, 1996), 5–16.

22. Linda Jones Docherty, "A Search for Identity: American Art Criticism and the Concept of the 'Native School,' 1876–1893," Ph.D. diss., University of North Carolina, 1985.

23. Mancini, *Pre-Modernism*, 9.

24. On symbolism, see Gloria Lynn Groom, *Beyond the Easel: Decorative Painting by Bonnard, Vuillard, Denis, and Roussel, 1890–1930* (Chicago: Art Institute of Chicago; New Haven, Conn.: Yale University Press, 2001); for secessionism, see Peter Vergo, *Art in Vienna, 1898–1918: Klimt, Kokoschka, Schiele and Their Contemporaries* (London: Phaidon, 1993). For Roger Fry, see Tillyard, *The Impact of Modernism*.

25. For more on the British arts and crafts movement, see Peter Stansky, *Redesigning the World: William Morris, the 1880s, and the Arts and Crafts* (Princeton: Princeton University Press, 1985).

26. See William Hosley, *The Japan Idea: Art and Life in Victorian America* (Hartford, Conn.: Wadsworth Atheneum, 1990).

27. On Whistler's design work, see Deanna Marohn Bendix, *Diabolical Designs: Paintings, Interiors, and Exhibitions of James McNeill Whistler* (Washington, D.C.: Smithsonian Institution Press, 1995).

28. For more on early folk revivals, see Wanda M. Corn, *The Great American Thing: Modern Art and National Identity, 1915–1935* (Berkeley: University of California Press, 1999), 319–334.

29. Mechlin, "Primitive Arts and Crafts Illustrated in the National Museum Collection," 64.

30. Mrs. Hugo Froelich, "A Coiled Basket—Lazy Squaw's Stitch," *Keramic Studio* 5.8 (1903): 189; G. Pomeroy, "Bead Work," *Keramic Studio* 6.9 (1905): 206–209. See also Henrietta Barclay Paist, "Treatment for Indian Plaque," *Keramic Studio* 3.4 (1901): suppl., 89; and Charles Babcock, "Indian Box," *Keramic Studio* 12.9 (1911): 202.

31. "Nursery Wall Coverings in Indian Designs," *Craftsman* 5 (1903): 95–99; "Table Scarfs with Indian Designs," *Craftsman* 5 (1904): 507; "Three 'Craftsman Canvas' Pillows [Derived from Pueblo Designs]," *Craftsman* 5 (1903): 94.

32. "Pueblo Architecture Adapted to Modern Needs in New Mexico," *Craftsman* 19 (1911): 404–406; Ethel Rose, "New Hopi Architecture on the Old Mesa Land," *Craftsman* 30 (1916): 374–382.

33. Charles F. Binns, "Building in Clay," *Craftsman* 4 (1903): 303–305.

34. Deloria, *Playing Indian*, chs. 1 and 4.

35. Sargent, "Indian Basketry," 321.

36. "Bead Work and Its Use," *The Papoose* (July 1903): 1–2.

37. Rayna Green, "A Tribe Called Wannabee: Playing Indian in America and Europe," *Folklore* 99 (1988): 31.

38. Sargent, "Indian Basketry," 321.

39. For an overview of Brush's career, see Berry-Hill Galleries, *George de Forest Brush, 1855–1941: Master of the American Renaissance*. With an essay by Joan B. Morgan (New York: Berry-Hill Galleries, 1985).

40. While both the textile and the concho belt worn by the weaver are Navajo, Brush may have confused the Navajo with their neighboring Pueblo Indians, for whom weaving was a male tradition. Ethnographic accuracy seems less important to this image than the opportunity to update the academic nude as an "American" subject. Brush's Indian paintings are the subject of a traveling exhibition organized by the National Gallery of Art with the Seattle Art Museum opening in late 2008.

41. George de Forest Brush, "Art in Its Relation to Life: A talk by Mr. Brush," *Art Interchange* (April 1901): 76.

42. "American Studio Talk," *International Studio* 11 (August 1900): ix.

43. Frederic W. Coburn, "The New Life at the League," *Art Education* (February 1900): 65.

44. Frederic W. Coburn, "George de Forest Brush and the Brush Guild," *Art Education* (February 1901): 257.

45. Ibid.

46. A brief description of the Brush Guild can be found in Paul Evans, *Art Pottery of the United States: An Encyclopedia of Producers and Their Marks: Together with a Directory of Studio Potters Working in the United States through 1960* (New York: Feingold and Lewis, 1897), 32–33. Evans was unaware of Coburn's articles and thus doesn't mention the group's early dedication to Native American models.

47. For an overview of women's involvement in the art pottery movement, see Nancy Elizabeth Owen, *Rookwood and the Industry of Art: Women, Culture, and Commerce, 1880–1913* (Athens: Ohio University Press, 2001).

48. "Chautauqua Crafts Village," *Keramic Studio* 5.6 (1903): 121.

49. "Primitive Arts Club," *Keramic Studio* 6.3 (1904): 118–119.

50. A biography of Binns can be found in Margaret Carney et al., *Charles Fergus Binns: The Father of American Studio Ceramics* (Manchester, Vt.: Hudson Hills Press, 1998).

51. Advertisement, *Keramic Studio* 5.1 (1903): v.

52. "The Summer School of Clay Working at Alfred, N.Y.," *Keramic Studio* 5.6 (1903): 125–126.

53. Charles F. Binns, "Building in Clay," *The Craftsman* 4 (1903): 304.

54. "Exhibition of the New York Society of the Keramic Arts," *Keramic Studio* 4.10 (1903): 216–217.

55. Charles F. Binns, "The Arts and Crafts in America: Prize Essay," *Craftsman* 14 (1908): 279.

56. Charles F. Binns, "Clay in the Potter's Hand," *Craftsman* 6 (1904): 164.

57. Charles F. Binns, "Clay in the Studio Number Seven," *Keramic Studio* 5.1 (1903): 13.

58. "Art of the American Indian," *Brush and Pencil* 15 (1905): 86.

59. Batchelder, *Design in Theory and Practice*. The chapters were published separately in *The Craftsman* between October 1907 and September 1908.

60. Dow's pedagogy is also discussed in Rushing, *Native American Art and the New York Avant-Garde*, 41–43.

61. Marilee Boyd Meyer, "Arthur Wesley Dow and His Influence on Arts and Crafts," in *Arthur Wesley Dow, 1857–1922: His Art and His Influence* (New York: Spanierman Gallery, 1999), 49.

62. Dow, *Composition*.

63. Brody, *Indian Painters and White Patrons*, 63.

64. Mason, "Mr. Arthur W. Dow's Summer School at Ipswich, Mass.," 123.

65. Sylvester Baxter, "Handicraft, and Its Extensions, at Ipswich," *Handicraft* 1 (1903): 253.

66. Mason, "Mr. Arthur W. Dow's Summer School at Ipswich, Mass.," 123.

67. Baxter, "Handicraft, and Its Extensions, at Ipswich," 255.

68. An introduction to Cushing and his ethnological method can be found in Curtis M. Hinsley and David R. Wilcox, eds., *The Lost Itinerary of Frank Hamilton Cushing: Frank Hamilton Cushing and the Hemenway Southwestern Archaeological Expedition, 1886–1889* (Tucson: University of Arizona Press, 2002). See also Edwin Wade and Lea McChesney, *America's Great Lost Expedition: The Thomas Keam Collection of Hopi Pottery from the Second Hemenway Expedition, 1890–1894; Featuring the Collections of the Peabody Museum of Archaeology and Ethnology, Harvard University, Cambridge, Massachusetts* (Phoenix: Heard Museum, 1980).

69. Nancy Parezo, "Now Is the Time to Collect," *Masterkey* 59.4 (1993): 15.

70. See Hinsley and Wilcox, *The Lost Itinerary of Frank Hamilton Cushing*; Sylvester Baxter, "An Aboriginal Pilgrimage," *Century Illustrated Monthly Magazine* 24 (1882): 526–536; and Sylvester Baxter, "Father of the Pueblos," *Harper's New Monthly Magazine* 65 (June 1882): 72–91.

71. Jesse Green, introduction to Frank Hamilton Cushing, *Zuñi: Selected Writings of Frank Hamilton Cushing* (Lincoln: University of Nebraska Press, 1979), 6.

72. Ernst Grosse, *The Beginnings of Art* (New York: D. Appleton, 1897).

73. George E. Marcus and Fred R. Myers, introduction to *The Traffic in Culture: Refiguring Art and Anthropology* (Berkeley: University of California Press, 1995). The important figure for

Boas was probably the Austrian art historian Alois Riegl, who applied his formalism to Western and non-Western objects alike.

74. Brad Evans, "Cushing's Zuni Sketchbooks: Literature, Anthropology, and American Notions of Culture," *American Quarterly* 49.4 (1997): 717–745.

75. Frederick C. Moffatt, *Arthur Wesley Dow (1857–1922)* (Washington, D.C.: Smithsonian Institution Press, 1977), 92.

76. Curtis M. Hinsley and David R. Wilcox, eds., *The Southwest in the American Imagination: The Writings of Sylvester Baxter, 1881–1899* (Tucson: University of Arizona Press, 1996), 253.

77. Mason, "Mr. Arthur W. Dow's Summer School at Ipswich, Mass.," 123.

78. Arthur Wesley Dow, "Designs from Primitive American Motifs," *Teachers College Record* 16 (March 1915): 34.

79. Batchelder, *Design in Theory and Practice*, 170–171.

80. Marsha Morton, "Missionaries of Culture," in *Pratt and Its Gallery, the Arts and Crafts Years* (New York: Pratt Institute, 1999), 52.

81. Erik Krenzen Trump, "The Indian Industries League and Its Support of American Indian Arts, 1893–1922: A Study of Changing Attitudes toward Indian Women and Assimilationist Policy," Ph.D. diss., Boston University, 1996: 250–252.

82. *Art of the First Americans: From the Collection of the Cincinnati Art Museum* (Cincinnati, Ohio: Cincinnati Art Museum, 1976), 8–9.

83. Richard Conn, *Native American Art in the Denver Art Museum* (Denver, Colo.: Denver Art Museum, distributed by the University of Washington Press, 1979), 81.

84. Charles P. Wilcomb, *Annual Report: Golden Gate Park Memorial Museum, 1900*, n.p., quoted in Melinda Young Frye, "Charles P. Wilcomb, Cultural Historian (1865–1915)," in *Natives and Settlers: Indian and Yankee Culture in Early California: The Collections of Charles P. Wilcomb* (Oakland, Calif.: Oakland Museum, 1979), 30. For more on Wilcomb, see the other essays in this catalogue, especially Bruce Bernstein, "A Native Heritage Returns: The Wilcomb-Hall-Sheedy Collection," 69–87; and Sherrie Smith-Ferri, "'Hidden at the Heard': The Harvey Company Pomo Collection," in Weigle and Babcock, *The Great Southwest of the Fred Harvey Company and the Santa Fe Railway*, 125–140.

85. Katherine Louise Smith, "An Arts and Crafts Exhibition in Minneapolis," *Craftsman* 3 (March 1903): 373–377; Irene Sargent, "A Recent Arts and Crafts Exhibition," *Craftsman* 4 (May 1903): 69–83; *Exhibition of the Society of Arts and Crafts, Together with a Loan Collection of Applied Art: Copley and Allston Halls, Boston, 4–15 April 1899* (Boston: George H. Ellis, 1899); *Exhibition of the Society of Arts and Crafts, Copley Hall* (Boston: Heintzemann Press, 1907).

86. Sally Price, *Primitive Art in Civilized Places* (Chicago: University of Chicago Press, 1989). See also James Clifford, "On Collecting Art and Culture," in *The Predicament of Culture* (Cambridge, Mass.: Harvard University Press, 1988), 215–251.

87. Mary Anne Staniszewski, *The Power of Display: A History of Exhibition Installations at the Museum of Modern Art* (Cambridge, Mass.: MIT Press, 1998), 4.

88. "National Arts Club" (brochure dated 1901), series 8.1, reel 4261, National Arts Club Records, Archives of American Art, Smithsonian Institution.

89. Ibid.

90. *1902 Yearbook of the National Arts Club*, series 8.1, reel 4260, National Arts Club Records, Archives of American Art, Smithsonian Institution.

91. Jacobs, *Engendered Encounters*, 153. The Indian Arts Fund is discussed at length in Jacob's sixth chapter, "Women and the Indian Arts and Crafts Movement."

92. Lee Glazer, "'A Modern Instance': Thomas Dewing and Aesthetic Vision at the Turn of the Century," Ph.D. diss., University of Pennsylvania, 1996, 181.

93. *Official Catalogue of Exhibitors*, Universal Exposition, St. Louis., 1904. Division of Exhibits Department B. Ar., rev. ed. (St. Louis: Official Catalogue Co., for the Committee on Press and Publicity, 1904).

94. S. Geijsbeek, "The Ceramics of the Louisiana Purchase Exposition," *Transactions of the American Ceramic Society* (1905), 349.

95. John William Troutman, "'The Overlord of the Savage World': Anthropology, the Media, and the American Indian Experience at the 1904 Louisiana Purchase Exposition," M.A. thesis, University of Arizona, 1997, 41.

4. THE INDIANS IN KÄSEBIER'S STUDIO

1. Tillyard, *The Impact of Modernism*, 3.

2. "Some Indian Portraits."

3. L. G. Moses calls the period 1900–1917 the "heyday" of the show and gives an account of one Buffalo Bill performer estimating daily attendance at New York shows at three to four thousand (Moses, *Wild West Shows and the Images of American Indians, 1883–1933* [Albuquerque: University of New Mexico Press, 1996], 180).

4. See Ulrich Keller, "The Myth of Art Photography: a Sociological Analysis," *History of Photography* 8.4 (1984): 249–275; and Geraldine Wojno Kiefer, "The Leitmotifs of *Camera Notes*," *History of Photography* 14.4 (1990): 349–360.

5. This relationship is explored extensively in Christian A. Peterson, "The Photograph Beautiful, 1895–1915," *History of Photography* 16.3 (1992): 189–232.

6. Michaels, *Gertrude Käsebier*, 25.

7. "Indians at a Studio Tea," *New York Times*, April 10, 1898, 14.

8. Burns, *Inventing the Modern Artist*, 58.

9. The 1899 telephone directory for Manhattan and the Bronx shows that commercial photographers were clustered on lower Broadway and 5th Avenue between 14th and 23rd streets; see the directory entry "Photographers," 984–986.

10. "Artistic Photography," *Brooklyn Daily Eagle*, February 13, 1897, 7; and the editorial "Attracting Customers to the Studio," *British Journal of Photography*, October 14, 1910, 777.

11. Sarah Burns, "The Price of Beauty: Art, Commerce, and the Late Nineteenth-Century American Studio Interior," in *American Iconology*, ed. David C, Miller (New Haven, Conn.: Yale University Press, 1993), 237–238.

12. Arthur Wesley Dow, "Mrs. Gertrude Käsebier's Portrait Photographs," *Camera Notes* 3 (July 1899): 22.

13. Joseph T. Keiley, "Mrs. Käsebier's Prints," *Camera Notes* 3 (July 1899): 34.

14. Alfred Stieglitz, "Modern Pictorial Photography," *Century Magazine* 64.6 (1902): 824–825.

15. Eva Watson-Schütze, "Signatures," *Camera Work* 1 (January 1903): 35–36.

16. Joseph T. Keiley, "Gertrude Käsebier," *Camera Work* 20 (October 1907): 27–31 (reprinted from *Photography*, March 19, 1904).

17. Edgerton, "Photography as an Emotional Art," 88.

18. For connections between antimodernist representations of peasants and the representation of racial others, see Gill Perry, "Primitivism and the 'Modern,'" *Primitivism, Cubism, Abstrac-*

tion: *The Early Twentieth Century*, ed. Charles Harrison, Francis Frascina, and Gill Perry (New Haven, Conn.: Yale University Press, 1993), 3–85.

19. Gertrude Käsebier, "Peasant Life in Normandy," *Monthly Illustrator* 3 (February 1895): 269.

20. Ibid., 271.

21. Käsebier, "An Art Village," *Monthly Illustrator* 4 (April 1895): 12.

22. Käsebier, "Peasant Life in Normandy," 272.

23. Edgerton, "Photography as an Emotional Art," 80.

24. Nancy E. Green, *Arthur Wesley Dow and His Influence* (Ithaca, N.Y.: Herbert F. Johnson Museum of Art, Cornell University, 1990), 14.

25. See, for example, Wanda M. Corn, *The Color of Mood: Tonalism in America* (San Francisco: M. H. de Young Museum, 1972).

26. Sandra Lee Underwood, *Charles H. Caffin: A Voice for Modernism, 1897–1918* (Ann Arbor, Mich.: UMI Research Press, 1983), 47.

27. "Our Illustrators," *Camera Notes* 1.2 (October 1897): 40.

28. Joseph T. Keiley, "Tonality," *Camera Notes* 2.4 (April 1899): 135.

29. Ibid., 136.

30. Ibid., 142.

31. Charles Caffin, "Gertrude Käsebier and the Artistic Commercial Portrait," in *Photography as a Fine Art* (New York: Doubleday, Page, 1901), 51–81. The book was originally published as a series of essays in *Everybody's Magazine*.

32. J. P. Mowbry, "The Making of a Country Home," *Everybody's s Magazine* 4.18 (1901): 99–115. Subsequent installations appeared throughout the volume.

33. Frances Benjamin Johnston, "The Foremost Women Photographers in America," *Ladies Home Journal* 18 (May 9, 1901): 1.

34. Boris, *Art and Labor*, 99.

35. Catherine Weed Barnes, "Woman's Work: A Woman to Women," *American Amateur Photographer* (May 1890): 186; Käsebier, "Studies in Photography," 272. On photography as a female activity in this period, see Jane Gover, *The Positive Image: Women Photographers in Turn of the Century America* (Albany: State University of New York Press, 1988); Judith Fryer, "Women's Camera Work: Seven Propositions in Search of a Theory," *Prospects* 16 (1991): 57–117.

36. Catherine Weed Barnes, "Photography as a Profession for Women," *American Amateur Photography* 3 (May 1891): 175.

37. Juan C. Abel, "Women Photographers and Their Work," *The Delineator* 58 (1901): 406.

38. "Sioux Chief's Party Calls," *New York Times*, April 24, 1898, 14.

39. Käsebier, "Studies in Photography," 271.

40. For circulation information, see N. W. Ayer, *American Newspaper Annual* (Philadelphia: N. W. Ayer and Sons, 1902).

41. John D'Emilio and Estelle B. Freedman, *Intimate Matters: A History of Sexuality in America* (New York: Harper and Row, 1988), 175.

42. From a manuscript annotated "Material Taken Down by a Woman who Once Wanted to Write Granny's Life—some quite incorrect," MS 149, box 1, folder 7, Gertrude Käsebier Papers, Special Collections, University of Delaware Library.

43. Käsebier, "Studies in Photography," 272.

44. "Indians at a Studio Tea," 14.

45. "The Indian as a Gentleman," *New York Times*, April 23, 1899, 20.

46. "Indians at a Studio Tea," 14.

47. Helen Hunt Jackson, *Ramona* (Boston: Roberts, 1888); E. Pauline Johnson, *The Moccasin Maker* (1913; Tucson: University of Arizona Press, 1987).

48. This information comes from the catalogue of the Library of Congress.

49. Kay Graber, introduction to Elaine Goodale Eastman, *Sister to the Sioux: The Memoirs of Elaine Goodale Eastman, 1895–91* (Lincoln: University of Nebraska Press, 1978).

50. Valerie Sherer Mathes, *Helen Hunt Jackson and Her Indian Reform Legacy* (Austin: University of Texas Press, 1990), 83.

51. Deborah Gordon, "Among Women: Gender and Ethnographic Authority of the Southwest, 1930–1980," in *Hidden Scholars: Women Anthropologists and the Native Southwest* (Albuquerque: University of New Mexico Press, 1993), 129.

52. Jacobs, *Engendered Encounters*, 78.

53. William Leach, "Transformations in a Culture of Consumption: Women and Department Stores, 1890–1925," *Journal of American History*, September 1984, 342.

54. New York Exchange for Women's Work, *Annual Report* (New York: New York Exchange for Women's Work, 1899), 8; New York Exchange for Women's Work, *Annual Report* (New York: New York Exchange for Women's Work, 1900), 31.

55. Käsebier's correspondence with Pratt is in the Pratt Papers, Western Americana Collection, Beinecke Rare Book and Manuscript Library, New Haven, Connecticut. Her correspondence with Carlos Montezuma is avauilable in a microform edition, *The Papers of Carlos Montezuma, M.D.: Including the Papers of Maria Keller Montezuma Moore and the Papers of Joseph W. Latimer*, ed. John William Larner Jr. (Wilmington, Del.: Scholarly Resources, 1983).

56. Edgerton, "Photography as an Emotional Art," 90.

57. Caffin, "Gertrude Käsebier and the Artistic Commercial Portrait," 80.

58. "The Pictures in This Number," *Camera Work* 1 (January 1903): 63.

59. Kristen Swinth, *Painting Professionals: Women Artists and the Development of Modern American Art, 1870–1930* (Chapel Hill: University of North Carolina Press, 2001), 154–155. This idea is carried through in the photographic community. Joseph T. Keiley told Stieglitz that his fellow-pictorialist Eva Watson-Schutze had "certain traits peculiar to the feminine mind from which no woman is free and which make it hard for the masculine mind to be in entire harmony with them on matters of policy and judgment. It is next to impossible for a woman to be entirely impersonal." Keiley to Alfred Stieglitz, August 20, 1902, Alfred Stieglitz Papers, Beinecke Rare Book and Manuscript Library.

60. Käsebier, "Studies in Photography," 269.

61. Spencer B. Hord, "Gertrude Käsebier, Maker of Photographs," *Bulletin of Photography*, June 8, 1910, 363–364, 367, quoted in Michaels, *Gertrude Käsebier*, 58.

62. A plan of the Camera Club is printed in *Camera Notes* 2 (October 1899): 64.

63. Carol Mavor, *Pleasures Taken: Performances of Sexuality and Loss in Victorian Photographs* (Durham, N.C.: Duke University Press, 1995), 25.

64. For more on Hartmann, see Hartmann, *Sadakichi Hartmann: Critical Modernist*, ed. Jane Calhoun Weaver (Berkeley: University of California Press, 1990).

65. Sadakichi Hartmann, "A Decorative Photographer: F. H. Day," *Photographic Times* 32 (March 1900): 102.

66. Sadakichi Hartmann, "Gertrude Käsebier," *Photographic Times* 32 (May 1900): 199.

67. Sadakichi Hartmann, "A Purist," *Photographic Times* 31 (October 1899): 451.

68. Käsebier, "Studies in Photography," 270.

69. Burns, *Inventing the Modern Artist*, passim.

70. The control of the growing commercial art world was also being consolidated in the hands of men at this time. See Michele H. Bogart, *Artists, Advertising, and the Borders of Art* (Chicago: University of Chicago Press, 1995).

71. See Swinth, *Painting Professionals*; Sarah Burns, "The 'Earnest, Untiring Worker' and the Magician of the Brush: Gender Politics in the Criticism of Cecilia Beaux and John Singer Sargent," *Oxford Art Journal* 15.1 (1992): 36–53.

72. Burns, *Inventing the Modern Artist*, 2.

73. Reina Lewis, *Gendering Orientalism* (New York: Routledge, 1996), 4.

74. See, for example, Michaels, *Gertrude Käsebier*, 29–44; Debora Jane Marshall, "The Indian Portraits," in *A Pictorial Heritage: The Photographs of Gertrude Käsebier*, ed. William Inness Homer, 31–32 (Newark, Del.: University of Delaware Press, 1979); Jennifer Sheffield Currie, "Gertrude Käsebier's Native American Portraits," *Dimensions of Native America: The Contact Zone*, ed. Jehanne Teilhet-Fisk and Robin Franklin Nigh (Tallahassee: Museum of Fine Arts and School of Visual Arts and Dance, Florida State University, 1998), 114–119. Michelle Delaney's *Buffalo Bill's Wild West Warriors: A Photographic History by Gertrude Käsebier* (New York: HarperCollins, 2007) came out too late to be incorporated into this discussion.

75. Michaels, *Gertrude Käsebier*, 38.

76. Currie, "Gertrude Käsebier's Native American Portraits," 115.

77. Luther Standing Bear's memoirs of his years traveling with Buffalo Bill poignantly describe the pressure he felt to represent his people with dignity while on the road and his efforts to ensure other performers gave the best impression of the beauty of a prereservation lifestyle they no longer led (Luther Standing Bear, *My People the Sioux* [Lincoln: University of Nebraska Press, 1975 (1928)], 245–273).

78. Ibid., 246 and 254.

79. Burns, *Inventing the Modern Artist*, 2.

5. ANGEL DECORA'S CULTURAL POLITICS

1. DeCora, "Native Indian Art," *Southern Workman* 36 (October 1907): 527–528.

2. For example, the Dakota writer Charles Eastman published several articles on Indian art in the arts and crafts magazine *The Craftsman*.

3. Some of DeCora's students, including her husband, Lone Star Dietz, and a few Native Americans working at other government schools, were beginning to develop a self-consciousness about Indian aesthetics in this period. However, she is unique until the 1920s in her access to the means of promoting her ideas about Native American art to a geographically and culturally diverse American audience.

4. The magazine illustrations that have been identified are: Hinook Mahiwi Kilinaka (DeCora), "Gray Wolf's Daughter"; Hinook Mahiwi Kilinaka (DeCora), "The Sick Child"; the cover illustration for *The Red Man* (Carlisle Indian School Magazine), September 1913; and illustrations for Charles A. Eastman, "On the Trail: The American Eagle and Indian Symbol," *American Indian Magazine* 7 (summer 1919): 89ff. There may be more. In addition, reproductions of her work appeared in Natalie Curtis, "The Perpetuating of Indian Art," *Outlook*, November 22, 1913, 625–626; and Curtis, "An American Indian Artist," *Outlook*, January 14, 1920, 64–66. DeCora provided illustrations and, where indicated, cover designs

for the following books: Francis La Flesche, *The Middle Five: Indian Boys at School* (Boston: Small, Maynard, 1900), frontispiece and cover design; Mary Catherine Judd, *Wigwam Stories as Told by the North American Indians* (Boston: Ginn, 1901), illustrations and cover design; Zitkala-Sa, *Old Indian Legends* (Boston: Ginn, 1901), illustrations and cover design; Natalie Curtis, ed., *The Indians' Book* (New York: Harper and Brothers, 1907), title pages and cover design; Elaine Goodale Eastman, *Yellow Star: A Story of East and West* (Boston: Little, Brown, 1911), illustrations (made in collaboration with her husband). The extant paintings include an undated watercolor sketch and several small sketches of heads in the collection of the Hampton University Museum. The original painting for the frontispiece *The Middle Five*, and a fragment of "Firelight" (made before 1913) are in private collections, as are the original sketches for illustrations for *The Indians Book* (personal communication with Anna Romero). The Hampton University Museum also owns a photographic copy of an oil sketch of a Mandan lodge interior that was acquired by the Office of Indian Affairs in 1903.

5. DeCora's correspondence can be found in her student file at the Hampton University Archives, Hampton, Virginia; and in record group 75.4, General Records of the Bureau of Indian Affairs Papers, 1801–1952, National Archives, Washington, D.C. NB: The archive divides letters received by the bureau and letters sent into two separate files.

6. Sarah McAnulty, "Angel DeCora," *Nebraska History* 57 (1976): 143–199; McAnulty, "Angel DeCora: American Indian Artist and Educator," M.A. thesis, University of New Mexico, 1976. A more recent article, which does not analyze DeCora's artworks but takes a more transcultural approach, is Anne Ruggles, "An Art of Survivance: Angel DeCora at Carlisle," *American Indian Quarterly* 28.3–4 (summer–fall 2004): 649–684. See also Margaret L. Archuleta, "The Indian Is an Artist," in *Away from Home: American Indian Boarding School Experiences, 1879–2000*, ed. Archuleta, Brenda J. Child, and K. Tsianina Lomawaima (Phoenix: Heard Museum, 2000), 84–97.

7. Angel DeCora, "Address," in *Proceedings of the Thirteenth Annual Meeting of the Lake Mohonk Conference of Friends of the Indian*, ed. Isabel C. Barrows (Philadelphia: Lake Mohonk Conference, 1895), 63–64.

8. Angel DeCora to Cora Mae Folsom, January 5, 1904, and January 2 and October 14, 1902, Hampton University Archives.

9. DeCora to Folsom, 18 January 1915, Hampton University Archives.

10. Zeynep Çelik and Leila Kinney, "Ethnography and Exhibitionism at the Exposition Universelles," *Assemblage* 13 (1991): 40.

11. Cora M. Folsom, "The Careers of Three Indian Women," *The Congregationalist and Christian World*, March 12, 1904, 375.

12. Richard Wayne Lykes, "Howard Pyle, Teacher of Illustration," *Pennsylvania Magazine of History and Biography* 80 (July 1956): 345.

13. Quoted in Henry C. White, *The Life and Art of Dwight W. Tryon* (Boston: Houghton Mifflin, 1930), 100, 102, 104; Merrill, *An Ideal Country*, 79.

14. Clipping from *Southern Workman*, July 1896, scrapbook in Hampton University Archives.

15. DeCora, "Address," 63.

16. DeCora's interest in this style, especially in the early years of her career, is demonstrated by the fact that she made a painting titled *A Nocturne* while at Smith and that she produced at least two other pictures of landscapes at sunset in the following years. Her firelit interior scenes also seem related to this style.

17. Merrill, *An Ideal Country*, 48.

18. Kathleen Pyne, "Resisting Modernism: American Painting in the Culture of Conflict," in *American Icons: Transatlantic Perspectives on Eighteenth- and Nineteenth Century American Art*, ed. Thomas W. Gaehtgens and Heinz Ickstadt (Chicago: University of Chicago for the Getty Institute, 1993), 301.

19. Dwight W. Tryon to George Alfred Williams, September 16, 1923, quoted in Merrill, *An Ideal Country*, 65.

20. Dwight W. Tryon to Charles Lang Freer, September 1889, quoted in Lee Glazer, "'A Modern Instance': Thomas Dewing and Aesthetic Vision at the Turn of the Century," Ph.D. diss., University of Pennsylvania, 1996, 20.

21. Linda Dowling, *The Vulgarization of Art: The Victorians and Aesthetic Democracy* (Charlottesville: University Press of Virginia, 1996), 15 and passim.

22. Renato Rosaldo, "Imperialist Nostalgia," *Representations* 26 (1989): 107–122.

23. Angel DeCora, "Angel DeCora—An Autobiography," *The Red Man* (March 1911): 279.

24. Deloria, *Playing Indian*, 144–145.

25. On the Indian princess, see Rayna Green, "The Pocahontas Perplex: The Image of Indian Women in American Culture," in *Unequal Sisters: A Multicultural Reader in U.S. Women's History*, ed. Ellen DuBois and Vicki Ruiz (New York: Routledge, 1990), 15–21.

26. Thorstein Veblen, *The Theory of the Leisure Class* (1899; New York: Mentor, 1953).

27. Homi Bhabha, "The Other Question—The Stereotype and Colonial Discourse," *Screen* (November–December 1983): 28.

28. Marsha Clift Bol, "Lakota Women's Artistic Strategies in Support of the Social System," *American Indian Culture and Research Journal* 9.1 (1985): 44.

29. See Joanna Cohen Scherer, "The Public Faces of Sarah Winnemucca," *Cultural Anthropology* 3.2 (1988): 178–204.

30. DeCora to Folsom, undated (spring 1908), Hampton University Archives.

31. Patricia Albers and William James have made an exhaustive study of this genre of visual culture. See, for example, Albers and James, "Illusion and Illumination: Visual Images of the American Indian Women in the West," in *The Women's West*, ed. Susan Armitage and Elizabeth Jameson (Norman: University of Oklahoma Press, 1987), 35–50.

32. MSS S-1174, box 31, folder 737, Richard Henry Pratt Papers, Western Americana Collection, Beinecke Rare Book and Manuscript Library, New Haven, Conn.

33. The *Harper's* press release is quoted in "A Native American Literature," *The Red Man* 15.10 (December 1899): 8.

34. DeCora to Folsom, February 18, 1904, Hampton University Archives.

35. Howard Pyle, "The Present Aspect of American Art from the Point of View of an Illustrator," *Handicraft* 1.6 (September 1902): 133.

36. Pyle, quoted in Curtis, "An American Indian Artist," 64.

37. DeCora to Folsom, November 27, 1892, Hampton University Archives.

38. DeCora, "Angel DeCora," 280.

39. DeCora to Folsom, September 27, 1899, Hampton University Archives.

40. Pyle, "The Present Aspect of American Art from the Point of View of an Illustrator," 126.

41. Michele H. Bogart, *Artists, Advertising, and the Borders of Art* (Chicago: University of Chicago Press, 1995), 315 n. 46.

42. See Trevor J. Fairbrother, *The Bostonians: Painters of an Elegant Age, 1870–1930; With contributions by Theodore E. Stebbins, Jr., William L. Vance, Erica E. Hirschler* (Boston: Museum of Fine Arts, 1986).

43. Laurene Buckley, "Joseph DeCamp," in *Ten American Painters* (New York: Spanierman Gallery, 1990), 93.

44. McAnulty, "Angel DeCora: American Indian Artist and Educator," 22.

45. Amy Helene Kirschke, "Reclaiming Our Own: Africa Comes to Harlem," paper presented at the 85th Annual Conference of the College Art Association, New York, February 1997. For more on Du Bois's relationship to Douglas, see Amy Helene Kirschke, *Aaron Douglas: Art, Race, and the Harlem Renaissance* (Jackson: University of Mississippi Press, 1995). Native American and African American civil rights leaders recognized their shared concerns and, on occasion, bonded together. Du Bois was particularly interested in indigenous political organization and was a member of the Society of American Indians. For more on this relationship, see Elizabeth Hutchinson *"Native Indian Art": Angel DeCora's Essentialist Aesthetics*, paper presented at the College Art Association Conference, Philadelphia, February 22, 2002.

46. The critical literature on DeCora's work is scant, but references to her can be found in "A Native American Literature," *The Red Man* 15.10 (December 1899): 8; Cora Mae Folsom, untitled review of *Wigwam Stories*, *Southern Workman* (July 1901): 411–412; untitled review of *Old Indian Legends*, *Southern Workman* 31 (1902): 35–37; untitled review of *The Indians' Book*, *Southern Workman* 36 (December 1907): 694–696; Charles A. Eastman, "My People: The Indians' Contribution to the Art of America," *The Craftsman* 27 (November 1914): 179–186; "News and Notes-Angel DeCora Dietz," *The Indian's Friend* (May 1919): 5; Elaine Goodale Eastman, "In Memoriam: Angel De Cora Dietz," *American Indian Magazine* 7 (spring 1919): 51–52.

47. Sally McBeth, *Ethnic Identity and the Boarding School Experience of West-Central Oklahoma Indians* (Washington, D.C.: University Press of America, 1983), 141.

48. DeCora to Francis LaFlesche, 14 April 1900, Francis LaFlesche Papers, Alice Cunningham Fletcher Collection, National Anthropological Archives, Smithsonian Institution, Washington, D.C.

49. As she does in the plate titled "The Indian of Today" in *Wigwam Stories*.

50. DeCora to Folsom, April 26, 1911 (Hampton University Archives), records difficulty in finding Algonquin models.

51. Lomawaima, *They Called It Prairie Light*, xiii.

52. See Charles Eastman, response to DeCora, "Native Indian Art," in *Report of the Executive on the Proceedings of the First Annual Conference of the Society of American Indians Held at the University of Ohio*, 1:89; Arthur C. Parker to Angel DeCora, November 25, 1911, *The Papers of the Society of American Indians* (microform), ed. John W. Larner (Wilmington, Del.: Scholarly Resources, 1987); Lone Star, "How Art Misrepresents the Indian," *Literary Digest* 44 (January 27, 1912): 160–161.

53. Her correspondence from the New York years is riddled with references to meeting old friends and colleagues.

54. The clippings in DeCora's student file at Hampton University come primarily from such publications.

55. Clipping from *The Red Man*, undated (1899), student file, Hampton University Archives.

56. Beverly K. Brandt, "'Mutually Helpful Relations': Architects, Craftsmen and the Society of Arts and Crafts, Boston, 1897–1917," Ph.D. diss., Boston University, 1985, 143.

57. See Day's correspondence with Chamberlin and Zitkala-Sa, F. Holland Day Papers, Archives of American Art, Washington, D.C.

58. Ida Chamberlin to Day, 5 September, 1899, F. Holland Day Papers. DeCora may have met Zitkala-Sa in 1897 through the Cowles Art School, which had merged with the Fine Arts Department of the New England Conservatory of Music, where Zitkala-Sa was studying. But it is equally likely that two young, educated Indian women would be brought together through Indian reformers like Alice Fletcher or Edward Everett Hale, whom both knew.

59. *Modern Bookbindings and Their Designers*, special winter number of *The Studio* (1899–1900): 3–73.

60. Briggs Brothers, *Twentieth-Century Cover Designs* (Plymouth, Mass.: V. H. and E. L. Briggs, 1902).

61. Esther Wood, "British Trade Bookbindings and Their Designers," *Modern Bookbindings and Their Designers*, special winter number of *The Studio* (1899–1900): 10.

62. See *Atlantic Monthly* 85 (January–June 1900): advertising section, 15; and 86 (June–December 1900): advertising section, 29.

63. Nancy Finlay, "A Millennium in Book-Making: The Book Arts in Boston," in *Inspiring Reform: Boston's Arts and Crafts Movement.* (Wellesley, Mass.: Davis Museum and Cultural Center, distributed by Harry N. Abrams, 1997), 129.

64. Wood, "British Trade Bookbindings and Their Designers," 28.

65. DeCora, "Angel DeCora," 285.

66. Smith College, *Official Circular* (1892), 28, Drexel Institute Papers, Archives of American Art. I am grateful to Margaret N. Sly, Smith College archivist, for this information.

67. Alain Locke, "The Legacy of the Ancestral Arts," from *The New Negro: An Interpretation*, ed. Locke (1925; reprint, New York: Johnson, 1968), 258.

68. DeCora, "An Effort to Encourage Indian Art," 209.

69. DeCora to Jones, September 27, 1900, Letters Received; William A. Jones to Angel DeCora, September 27, 1900, Letters Sent (both in record group 75.4, General Records of the General Records of the Bureau of Indian Affairs, 1801–1952, National Archives). I have been unable to find a photograph of this installation in either the Bureau of Indian Affairs records at the National Archives or any of the Buffalo archives.

70. Department of the Interior, *Annual Report of the Commissioner of Indian Affairs to the Secretary of the Interior* (Washington, D.C.: Government Printing Office, 1902), 49.

71. DeCora to Jones, November 26, 1900, Letters Received, record group 75, General Records of the Bureau of Indian Affairs Papers, 1801–1952, National Archives.

72. DeCora to Francis Leupp, June 7, 1906, Letters Received, record group 75, General Records of the Bureau of Indian Affairs Papers, 1801–1952, National Archives.

73. Department of the Interior, *Annual Report of the Commissioner of Indian Affairs to the Secretary of the Interior* (Washington, D.C.: Government Printing Office, 1905), 12.

74. Cf. Department of the Interior, *Annual Report of the Commissioner of Indian Affairs to the Secretary of the Interior* (Washington, D.C.: Government Printing Office, 1906), 65–66.

75. Leupp to Ethan Allen Hitchcock, December 6, 1905, Letters Received, record group 75, General Records of the Bureau of Indian Affairs Papers, 1801–1952, National Archives.

76. Josephine Foard to Leupp, February 20, 1906, Letters Received, record group 75, General Records of the Bureau of Indian Affairs Papers, 1801–1952, National Archives.

77. Department of the Interior, *Annual Report of the Commissioner of Indian Affairs* (1906), 66.

78. DeCora, "An Effort to Encourage Indian Art," 207–209.

79. U.S. Department of the Interior, *Annual Report of the Commissioner of Indian Affairs* (1906), 67.

80. William Henry Holmes to Leupp, 9 February 1906, Letters Received, record group 75, General Records of the Bureau of Indian Affairs Papers, 1801–1952, National Archives.

81. DeCora to Franz Boas, Boas Papers, American Philosophical Society.

82. Alfred L. Kroeber, "The Arapaho," pt. 2, "Decorative Art," *Bulletin of the American Museum of Natural History* 18 (1902): 36–138.

83. *Catalogue, United States Indian School, Carlisle, Pennsylvania, 1910* (Carlisle, Pa.: Carlisle Indian Press, 1910), 58.

84. DeCora mentions these trips in "Native Indian Art," in *Proceedings of the 16th Annual Meeting of the Lake Mohonk Conference of Friends of the Indian*, ed. Lillian D. Powers (Philadelphia: Lake Mohonk Conference, 1908), 16–18. See also her correspondence with Francis Leupp, 1908–1909, Letters Received, record group 75, General Records of the Bureau of Indian Affairs Papers, 1801–1952, National Archives.

85. *Carlisle Arrow* (September 6, 1907): n.p., clipping in Hampton University Archives.

86. DeCora, "An Effort to Encourage Indian Art," 207.

87. *Indian Craftsman* (February 1909): 36.

88. DeCora, "An Effort to Encourage Indian Art," 208.

89. Ibid, 206.

90. See, for example, "Arapaho Symbolism in Embroidered Designs," plate 27 in Alfred L. Kroeber, "The Arapaho," pt. 2, "Decorative Art." (Plates follow page 139.)

91. DeCora to Leupp, June 7, 1906, Letters Received, record group 75, General Records of the Bureau of Indian Affairs Papers, 1801–1952, National Archives.

92. DeCora to Leupp, September 14, 1906, Letters Received, record group 75, General Records of the Bureau of Indian Affairs Papers, 1801–1952, National Archives.

93. DeCora, "Native Indian Art," *Southern Workman* 36 (October 1907): 527–528.

94. DeCora's decision to keep her own last name after her marriage is interesting in this light. She gave her reason as being the recognition that name changing was not a tradition in her or her husband's culture, and that to do so would devalue the reputation of her maiden name in artistic circles.

95. DeCora, "Address," 82.

96. The term is defined in Finlay, "A Millennium in Book-Making," 129.

97. "Drawings," in Curtis, *The Indians' Book*, n.p. This unsigned note is presumably by Curtis.

98. DeCora, "Native Indian Art," in *Report of the Executive on the Proceedings of the First Annual Conference of the Society of American Indians Held at the University of Ohio*, 1:85.

99. Scholars now identify the image as a peregrine falcon—an image of intertribal warfare, not unity (Joyce Szabo, personal communication, August 19, 1999).

100. These qualities are described as distinctly "Indian" in DeCora's public lectures.

101. Arthur C. Parker to Angel DeCora, October 23 and November 23, 1911, *The Papers of the Society of American Indians* (microform), ed. John W. Larner (Wilmington, Del.: Scholarly Resources, 1987). It is worth noting that while this organization comprised members from the United States and that they identified themselves with pre-Columbian civilizations on both continents.

102. Charles Eastman, response to DeCora, "Native Indian Art," in *Report of the Executive on the Proceedings of the First Annual Conference of the Society of American Indians Held at the University of Ohio*, 1:88.

103. Laura Cornelius, response to DeCora, "Native Indian Art," in ibid.

104. Thomas Doxon, response to DeCora, "Native Indian Art," in ibid., 89.

105. Quoted in Hertzberg, *The Search for an American Indian Identity*, 119.

106. Horton Elm, response to DeCora, "Native Indian Art," in *Report of the Executive on the Proceedings of the First Annual Conference of the Society of American Indians Held at the University of Ohio*,1:91.

107. For an extensive discussion of the peyote controversy, see Hertzberg, *The Search for an American Indian Identity*, 239–286.

108. Ibid., sec. 1.

109. Boris, *Art and Labor*, 189–193.

110. Theodore Roosevelt, "A Layman's Views of an Art Exhibition," *Outlook*, March 29, 1913, 719. For more on the Armory Show, see Milton Brown, *The Story of the Armory Show* (Greenwich, Conn.: Joseph H. Hirshhorn Foundation; distributed by New York Graphic Society, 1963).

111. The Society of Independent Artists rejected the jury system that allowed academic exhibitions to censor the work of avant-garde artists. Officers included several participants in the Indian craze, notably Arthur Wesley Dow. The display of Native American art at the Society of Independent Exhibitions is discussed in Rushing, *Native American Art and the New York Avant-Garde*.

EPILOGUE

1. See *Directions in Indian Art* and *Indian Voices*.

2. Fritz Scholder, "Native Arts in America" (conference talk), in *Indian Voices*, 192, 195.

3. For more on this story, see Leah Dilworth, *Imagining Indians in the Southwest: Persistent Visions of a Primitive Past* (Washington, D.C.: Smithsonian Institution Press, 1996); Kathleen L. Howard and Diana F. Pardue, *Inventing the Southwest: The Fred Harvey Company and Native American Art* (Phoenix: Heard Museum, 1996); and Weigle and Babcock, *The Great Southwest of the Fred Harvey Company and the Santa Fe Railway*.

4. Hewett gave a talk on January 3, 1905, titled "Historic and Pre-Historic Ruins in the South West," in *National Arts Club Yearbook for 1906*, 16, available in microfilm, frame 214, reel 4260, Papers of the National Arts Club, Archives of American Art, Smithsonian Institution, Washington, D.C.

5. For more on this history, see Brody, *Pueblo Indian Painting*.

6. These women are discussed extensively in Mullin, *Culture in the Marketplace*, and Jacobs, *Engendered Encounters*.

7. Mabel Dodge Luhan, *Movers and Shakers* (New York: Harcourt Brace, 1936), 534, quoted in Brody, *Pueblo Indian Painting*, 93.

8. For more on Collier, see Lawrence C. Kelly, *The Assault on Assimilation: John Collier and the Origins of Indian Policy Reform* (Albuquerque: University of New Mexico Press, 1983).

9. Lewis Meriam et al., *The Problem of Indian Administration: Report of a Survey Made at the Request of Hubert Work, Secretary of the Interior, and Submitted to Him, February 21, 1928* (Baltimore: Johns Hopkins University Press for Institute for Government Research [Brookings Institution], Washington, D.C., 1928), 645.

10. Ibid., 25.

11. For more on the Indian Arts and Crafts Board, see Robert Fay Schrader, *The Indian Arts and Crafts Board: An Aspect of New Deal Indian Policy* (Albuquerque: University of New Mexico Press, 1983).

12. For this history, see W. Jackson Rushing, *Native American Art and the New York Avant-Garde:*

A *History of Cultural Primitivism* (Austin: University of Texas Press, 1995). It should be noted that Southwest-based reformers were not the only non-Indians celebrating the aesthetic potential of Native American art in the decades following World War I. The surrealists were quite interested in indigenous American material culture. They collected objects, particularly from Alaska and the Northwest Coast, reproduced them in their publications, and displayed them alongside their own work in exhibitions. As was the case when turn-of-the-century artists included indigenous artwork in the exhibitions, however, this effort did not include recognizing the individual efforts of living Native artists. Indian objects were displayed anonymously, as the product of primitive mythical drives. See Kirk Varnedoe, "Abstract Expressionism," in *"Primitivism" in 20th Century Art: Affinity of the Tribal and the Modern*, ed. William Rubin (New York: Museum of Modern Art, 1984), 2:615–659; Rushing, *Native American Art and the New York Avant-Garde*.

13. Ann McMullen, "More Than Curiosities," book review, *American Indian Culture and Research Journal* 26.3 (2002): 152–155.
14. Meriam et al., *The Problem of Indian Administration*, 391.
15. On the Santa Fe Indian School, see Bruce Bernstein and Jackson Rushing, *Modern by Tradition: American Indian Painting in the Studio Style* (Santa Fe: Museum of New Mexico Press, 1995); and Cary C. Collins, "Art Crafted in the Red Man's Image: Hazel Pete, The Indian New Deal, and the Indian Arts and Crafts Program at the Santa Fe Indian School, 1932–5," *New Mexico Historical Review* 78.4 (fall 2003): 437–470.
16. "Seek to Save Indian Arts Education," *Santa Fe New Mexican*, February 23, 1932, clipping, Mabel Morrow Collection, Museum of Indian Arts and Culture, Laboratory of Anthropology, Santa Fe, New Mexico. I am grateful to Mark Watson for this source.
17. On Native artists and the Works Project Administration, see Christine Nelson, "Indian Art in Washington: Native American Murals in the Department of the Interior Building," *American Indian Art Magazine* (spring 1995): 70–83.
18. It is worth noting that, while African American artists of this generation also operated within an art world whose market, exhibitions, and critical writing was essentialist, the production and consumption of art was never seen as a significant part of black economics or politics.
19. On the Institute of American Indian Arts, see Joy Gritton, *The Institute of American Indian Arts* (Albuquerque: University of New Mexico Press, 2000).
20. Fritz Scholder, discussion of "Directions in Indian Art," in *Indian Voices*, 205.
21. Buffy Sainte-Marie, ibid., 213–214.
22. For a discussion of these issues, see Richard Schiff, "The Necessity of Jimmie Durham's Jokes," *Art Journal* 51.3 (fall 1992): 74.
23. On Tsinhnahjinnie, see Elizabeth Archuleta, "Refiguring Indian Blood through Poetry, Photography, and Performance Art," *Studies in American Indian Literatures* 17.4 (winter 2005): 1.
24. For more on this notion of artistic freedom and its Kantian roots, see the introduction by Phillips and Steiner, *Unpacking Culture*, 6–8.
25. See Bernstein and Rushing, *Modern by Tradition*, and the report of the first convocation of American Indian Scholars, *Indian Voices*.
26. This issue is discussed in Ann Eden Gibson, *Abstract Expressionism: Other Politics* (New Haven, Conn.: Yale University Press, 1997), and Bill Anthes, *Native Moderns: American Indian Painting, 1940–1960* (Durham, N.C.: Duke University Press, 2006).

27. Oscar Howe to Jeanne Snodgrass (King), curator of Indian Art at the Philbrook Museum, April 18, 1958, quoted in Jeanne Snodgrass King, "The Preeminence of Oscar Howe," in *Oscar Howe: A Retrospective Exhibition*, ed. Frederick J. Dockstader, ed. (Tulsa, Okla.: Thomas Gilcrease Museum Association, 1982), 19.

28. *Directions in Indian Art*, 13.

29. See Gritton, *The Institute of American Indian Arts*.

30. Lloyd Kiva New, discussion of "Directions in Indian Art," in *Indian Voices*, 28.

31. Fritz Scholder, ibid., 196.

32. Jack Reynolds, ibid., 203–204.

33. George Longfish and Joan C. Randall, "New Ways of Old Visions: the Evolution of Contemporary Native American Art," *Artspace* 6 (summer 1982): 27. The text of this article was originally given as a talk at the third national conference of the Native American Art Historians (now Native American Art Studies Association) titled "Confluences of Tradition and Change," named after a traveling exhibition of contemporary Native art.

34. Ken Shulman, "The Buckskin Ceiling and Its Discontents," *New York Times*, December 24, 2000, AR37. The term is modeled on the well-known "glass ceiling," which was coined to describe the invisible barrier that prevents women from achieving the highest ranks in the business world.

35. *Indian Voices*, 212–214.

36. W. Jackson Rushing, "Contested Ground," *New Art Examiner*, November 19, 1991, 26.

37. At the Heye Center, "The Language of American Baskets," which included both old and innovative work, ran at the same time as "Continuum: 12 Artists." For the Museum of Art and Design exhibition, see David McFadden and Ellen N. Taubman, *Changing Hands: Art without Reservation*, vol. 1 (London: Merrell, 2002), and David McFadden and Ellen N. Taubman, *Changing Hands: Art without Reservation*, vol. 2 (New York: Museum of Art and Design, 2005). The third volume is forthcoming.

38. For an excellent discussion of this museum and the issues it raises, see Amanda J. Cobb, "The National Museum of the American Indian as Cultural Sovereignty," *American Quarterly* 57.2 (June 2005), 485–508.

39. Robert Warrior, *Tribal Secrets: Recovering American Indian Intellectual Traditions* (Minneapolis: University of Minnesota Press, 1995), 8 and ch. 1 passim.

Selected Bibliography

This bibliography includes only critical sources cited at numerous points in the text. All other sources are cited fully in the notes.

Anthes, Bill. *Native Moderns: American Indian Painting, 1940–1960.* Durham, N.C.: Duke University Press, 2006.

Batchelder, Ernest A. *Design in Theory and Practice.* New York: MacMillan, 1912.

Berlo, Janet C., ed. *The Early Years of Native American Art History: The Politics of Scholarship and Collecting.* Seattle: University of Washington Press, 1992.

Bernstein, Bruce, and W. Jackson Rushing. *Modern by Tradition: American Indian Painting in the Studio Style.* Santa Fe: Museum of New Mexico Press, 1995.

Boris, Eileen. *Art and Labor: Ruskin, Morris, and the Craftsman Ideal in America.* Philadelphia: Temple University Press, 1986.

Brody, J. J. *Indian Painters and White Patrons.* Albuquerque: University of New Mexico Press, 1971.

———. *Pueblo Indian Painting: Tradition and Modernism in New Mexico, 1900–1930.* Santa Fe, N.M.: School of American Research Press, 1997.

Bronner, Simon J., ed. *Consuming Visions: Accumulation and Display of Goods in America, 1880–1920.* New York: Norton, 1989.

Burns, Sarah. *Inventing the Modern Artist: Art and Culture in the Gilded Age.* New Haven, Conn.: Yale University Press, 1996.

Corn, Wanda M. *The Real American Thing: Modern Art and National Identity, 1915–1935.* Berkeley: University of California Press, 2000.

Curtis, Natalie, ed. *The Indians' Book.* New York: Harper and Brothers, 1907.

DeCora, Angel. "An Effort to Encourage Indian Art." *Congres International des Americanistes—XVe Session,* 2:205–209. Quebec: Dessault and Proulx, 1907.

————— (as Hinook Mahiwi Kilinaka). "Gray Wolf's Daughter." *Harper's New Monthly Magazine* 99 (November 1899): 860–862.

—————. "Native Indian Art." In *Report of the Executive on the Proceedings of the First Annual Conference of the Society of American Indians Held at the University of Ohio, Columbus, Ohio — October 12–17, 1911*, 1:82–87. Washington, D.C.: Society of American Indians, 1912.

—————. "The Sick Child." *Harper's New Monthly Magazine* 98 (February 1899): 446–448.

Deloria, Philip. *Playing Indian*. New Haven, Conn.: Yale University Press, 1998.

Directions in Indian Art: The Report of a Conference held at the University of Arizona on March Twentieth and Twenty First, Nineteen Hundred and Fifty Nine. Tucson: University of Arizona Press, 1959.

Dow, Arthur Wesley. *Composition: A Series of Exercises in Art Structure for the Use of Students and Teachers*. New York: Baker, 1899.

Edgerton, Giles. "Photography as an Emotional Art." *Craftsman* 12 (April 1907): 80–93.

Hart, Lucy P. "Native Industries in the Indian School." *Chilocco Farmer and Stock Grower* 3 (July 1903): 445–446.

Hertzberg, Hazel. *The Search for an American Indian Identity: Modern Pan-Indian Movements*. Syracuse, N.Y.: Syracuse University Press, 1971.

Indian Voices: The First Convocation of American Indian Scholars. San Francisco: The Indian Historian Press, 1970.

Jacobs, Margaret D. *Engendered Encounters: Feminism and Pueblo Cultures, 1879–1934*. Lincoln: University of Nebraska Press, 1999.

Käsebier, Gertrude. "Studies in Photography." *Photographic Times* 30.6 (1898): 269–272.

Lears, T. J. Jackson. *No Place of Grace: Antimodernism and the Transformation of American Culture, 1880–1920*. New York: Pantheon, 1981.

Lomawaima, K. Tsianina. "Estelle Reel, Superintendent of Indian Schools, 1898–1910: Politics, Curriculum, and Land." *Journal of American Indian Education* 35 (1996): 5–32.

—————. *They Called It Prairie Light: The Story of Chilocco Indian School*. Lincoln: University of Nebraska Press, 1994.

Mancini, JoAnne Marie. *Pre-Modernism: Art-World Change and American Culture from the Civil War to the Armory Show*. Princeton: Princeton University Press, 2005.

Mason, Elizabeth. "Mr. Arthur W. Dow's Summer School at Ipswich, Mass." *Keramic Studio* 4.6 (1902): 123.

Mason, Otis Tufton. *Indian Basketry: Studies in a Textile Art without Machinery*. New York: Doubleday, Page, 1904.

Merrill, Linda. *An Ideal Country: Paintings by Dwight Tryon in the Freer Gallery of Art*. Washington, D.C.: Freer Gallery, 1990.

Michaels, Barbara L. *Gertrude Käsebier: The Photographer and Her Photographs*. New York: Harry N. Abrams, 1993.

Mullin, Molly. *Culture in the Marketplace: Gender, Art, and Value in the American Southwest*. Durham, N.C.: Duke University Press, 2001.

Ortiz, Fernando. *Cuban Counterpoint: Tobacco and Sugar*. Translated by Harriet de Onís. Durham, N.C.: Duke University Press, 1995. Originally published in Spanish in 1940 and in English in 1947.

Phillips, Ruth B. *Trading Identities: The Souvenir in Native North American Art from the Northeast, 1700–1900*. Seattle: University of Washington Press, 1999.

Phillips, Ruth B., and Christopher Steiner, eds. *Unpacking Culture: Art and Commodity in Colonial and Postcolonial Worlds*. Berkeley: University of California Press, 1999.

Reel, Estelle. *Course of Study for the Indian Schools of the United States, Industrial and Literary*. Washington, D.C.: Government Printing Office, 1901.

Rushing, W. Jackson. *Native American Art and the New York Avant-Garde*. Austin: University of Texas Press, 1995.

Sargent, Irene. "Indian Basketry: Its Structure and Decoration." *Craftsman* 7 (1904): 321–334.

"Some Indian Portraits." *Everybody's Magazine* 4.17 (January 1901): 2–24.

Stewart, Susan. *On Longing: Narratives of the Miniature, the Gigantic, the Souvenir, the Collection*. Durham, N.C.: Duke University Press, 1993.

Tillyard, S. K. *The Impact of Modernism, 1900–1920: Early Modernism and the Arts and Crafts Movement in Edwardian England*. New York: Routledge, 1988.

Weigle, Marta, and Barbara Babcock, eds. *The Great Southwest of the Fred Harvey Company and the Santa Fe Railway*. Phoenix: Heard Museum, 1996.

Index

Note: Page numbers in italics refer to illustrations

ELIZABETH HUTCHINSON is an assistant professor of art history at Barnard College, Columbia University.

Library of Congress Cataloging-in-Publication Data
Hutchinson, Elizabeth.
The Indian craze : primitivism, modernism, and transculturation in American art, 1890–1915 / Elizabeth Hutchinson.
p. cm. — (Objects/histories : critical perspectives on art, material culture, and representation)
Includes bibliographical references and index.
ISBN 978-0-8223-4390-5 (cloth : alk. paper)
ISBN 978-0-8223-4408-7 (pbk. : alk. paper)
1. Indian art—Collectors and collecting—United States—History—19th century. 2. Indian art—Collectors and collecting—United States—History—20th century. 3. Indian art—United States—Influence. 4. Indian art—United States—History—19th century. 5. Indian art—United States—History—20th century. I. Title. II. Series: Objects/histories.
E98.A7H88 2009
709′.01′1—dc22   2008048037

www.ingramcontent.com/pod-product-compliance
Lightning Source LLC
Chambersburg PA
CBHW080954170526
45158CB00010B/2805